CREATING HEALTHY ORGANIZATIONS

How Vibrant Workplaces Inspire Employees to
Achieve Sustainable Success

The current global economic environment is characterized by unprecedented uncertainty, a premium placed on knowledge, and the threat of future talent scarcity. Key to an organization's success under these conditions is its ability to strengthen the links between people and performance. *Creating Healthy Organizations* provides executives, managers, human resource professionals, and employees an action-oriented approach to forging these connections by creating and sustaining vibrant and productive workplaces.

A healthy organization operates in ways that benefit all stakeholders, including employees, customers, shareholders, and communities. Using a wide range of examples from a variety of internationally based industries, Graham Lowe integrates leading practices with research on workplace health and wellness, quality work environments, employee engagement, organizational performance, and corporate social responsibility to make a compelling business case for creating healthy organizations.

Creating Healthy Organizations offers readers, whether CEOs or frontline workers, an innovative framework and practical tools for planning, implementing, and measuring healthy change in their workplaces.

GRAHAM LOWE is a leader in the field of workplace consulting and the author of numerous articles and books including *The Quality of Work: A People Centered Agenda*. His consulting firm, The Graham Lowe Group Inc., has helped numerous organizations in the private, public, and non-profit sectors create healthy and productive work environments. His evidence-based approach to consulting is based on a successful research career as a professor of sociology (now emeritus) at the University of Alberta. In recognition of his contribution to creating healthy organizations, he received the 2004 Canadian Workplace Wellness Pioneer Award.

GRAHAM LOWE

Creating Healthy Organizations

How Vibrant Workplaces Inspire Employees to Achieve Sustainable Success

UNIVERSITY OF TORONTO PRESS
Toronto Buffalo London

© Graham Lowe 2010
Rotman/UTP Publishing
Toronto Buffalo London
www.utppublishing.com
Printed in the U.S.A.

Reprinted in paperback 2012

ISBN 978-0-8020-9980-8 (cloth)
ISBN 978-1-4426-1429-1 (paper)

Printed on acid-free paper

Library and Archives Canada Cataloguing in Publication

Lowe, Graham S.
Creating healthy organizations : how vibrant workplaces inspire
employees to achieve sustainable success / Graham Lowe.

Includes bibliographical references and index.
ISBN 978-0-8020-9980-8 (bound). — ISBN 978-1-4426-1429-1 (pkb.)

1. Employee motivation. 2. Job satisfaction. 3. Employee health
promotion. 4. Quality of work life. 5. Leadership. 6. Corporate culture.
7. Organizational effectiveness. 8. Organizational change. I. Title.

HF5549.5.M63L69 2010   658.3'14   C2010-900545-7

University of Toronto Press acknowledges the financial assistance to its
publishing program of the Canada Council for the Arts and the Ontario
Arts Council.

 Canada Council   Conseil des Arts    ONTARIO ARTS COUNCIL
for the Arts   du Canada   CONSEIL DES ARTS DE L'ONTARIO

University of Toronto Press acknowledges the financial support for its
publishing activities of the Government of Canada through the Canada
Book Fund.

To Ella and Penny

Contents

Figures

Preface to the Paperback Edition, 2012

As I wrote *Creating Healthy Organizations*, the global financial crisis was tightening its grip on the economy. Fast-forward to 2012. While growth is sputtering back in North America, the recession lingers in parts of Europe. Yet with forty million unemployed people in advanced industrial economies, some companies can't meet their staffing needs.[1] This puts a brake on growth, stifles innovation, and slows recovery. A big part of the overall solution to our economic malaise is to foster a healthy, resilient, and productive workforce. For employers, this is today's most pressing people challenge. That's why the goal of creating healthier organizations is more important than ever.

Future prosperity will be powered by a healthy, energized, and capable workforce. In my workshops, managers and employees are expressing a greater sense of urgency to improve their culture, workplaces and leadership. Urgency can fuel action, but only if one seizes opportunities to nudge change forward. As I describe in this preface, there are five signs of progress, each of which opens up new possibilities for building healthier organizations:

1. There is a stronger business case for organizational health.
2. Employers are learning from each other how to achieve this goal.
3. Culture is playing a central role in supporting health and performance.
4. There is a growing emphasis on psychologically healthy workplaces.
5. Progressive employers are using innovative approaches to healthy work design.

A Stronger Business Case

A broader perspective on organizational health is beginning to reshape how business leaders think about the drivers of success. Scott Keller and Colin Price, two McKinsey & Company consultants, have devised a business argument for organizational health.[2] They conclude that the route to high performance is through better people management practices. An organization's health depends on its ability to align, execute, and renew itself – all of which can be managed and improved. These points echo key messages in *Creating Healthy Organizations*.

Employee wellness is also moving into the executive spotlight. The *Harvard Business Review* (HBR) recently reported the return on investment (ROI) from employee wellness programs.[3] While wellness ROI is well-documented, the evidence is buried in health promotion journals. What's significant about the HBR article is that the case for wellness is being made in a flagship management publication. Leading corporations such as SAS, Johnson & Johnson, and Chevron show how employer-sponsored wellness initiatives can reduce health risks and employer health care costs, improve employee quality of life, and enable people to be more effective on the job. The take-away for executives is that this sort of progress is most readily achieved when wellness goals are central to their business strategy.

Additional encouragement to do just that comes from new research showing how happy employees improve the bottom line. Successful companies such as Costco, Quik-Trips, and Trader Joe's understand that low costs, excellent customer satisfaction, and strong financial performance depend on positive employee work experiences which equate with happiness.[4] Researchers at the University of Michigan's Center for Positive Organizational Scholarship explain: 'We think of a thriving workforce as one in which employees are not just satisfied and productive but also engaged in creating the future – the company's and their own.'[5] Employees thrive in jobs that give them a sense of purpose and room to develop their potential – two attributes of a healthy organization.

Employers Learning from Each Other

Employers are actively sharing lessons on how to boost employee well-being and performance. This happens through networks such as the Innovative Employer Roundtable hosted by the University of Kentucky's

Institute for Workplace Innovation (IWIN). IWIN's studies document how local employers have integrated health and wellness into their culture and business processes, achieving greater pay-offs than those of traditional health promotion programs.[6] IWIN's healthy organization project developed the HealthIntegrated Model as a tool for change. The project is a unique partnership, bringing together employers, researchers, and sponsors, including the National Institute of Occupational Safety and Health, CVS Caremark, and UK (University of Kentucky) HealthCare.

The bar for organizational health is also being raised in health care, where more employers are linking the quality of work environments with the quality of patient care. To share effective practices and to recognize leaders in the field, in 2010 the Ontario Hospital Association (OHA) launched its Quality Healthcare Workplace Awards. The annual awards focus on how hospitals in Ontario are improving their performance by fostering workforce engagement in healthy and productive workplaces.[7]

Recipients of the Platinum Award (there are also gold, silver, and bronze award levels) are distinguished from other hospitals by a strategically integrated and comprehensive approach to staff health and wellness.[8] In these leading hospitals, corporate scorecards include healthy workplace and staff satisfaction measures. The board and executive use workplace and employee well-being metrics in planning and decision-making. Human resource and wellness goals are closely tied to the corporate mission, vision, and values. And all levels of management are engaged in setting targets and measuring progress on key human resource and wellness strategy goals.

IWIN and OHA illustrate how employers can collaborate with partners such as universities or industry associations to share effective practices for improving health and performance. These examples show a greater receptivity to viewing employee well-being as a performance driver rather than just a cost driver, which marks an important shift in management thinking toward healthy organizations.

Culture Plays a Central Role

Another positive development is how culture is becoming a bridge between wellness and performance. For example, a survey of Canadian employers discovered that 75 per cent want a healthy workplace culture as the outcome from their wellness programs.[9] But what exactly does a healthy workplace culture look like? Depending on how employers answer this question, they will choose one of two distinct paths to culture change.

On the first path are a growing number of companies in North America that reframe their employee health and productivity goals in terms of creating a culture of health. A culture of health encourages employees to take greater responsibility for their health and well-being, reducing their health risk factors and accessing appropriate health care services.[10] This approach emphasizes employees' responsibility to become aware of wellness program options and health plan costs, and to make better health-related decisions. While this can reduce the employer's health benefit costs, it overlooks how the workplace affects well-being.

Employers on the second path take a more organizational view, emphasizing how employee well-being goals are aligned with the corporate values, vision, and mission. Employee well-being is supported by a shared understanding that each individual must take responsibility for his or her overall mental and physical health. The values that define a healthy culture help everyone see how healthy employees in healthy workplaces are the key to business success. And a healthy culture requires a commitment from management to ensure that employees have the work environment, resources, and supports they need to be healthy and productive.

Together, these features of a healthy culture go beyond the popular wellness initiatives found in most large companies. Healthy culture thinking leads to actions by management that will give employees meaningful input on their work arrangements, job design, and career development – all vital elements for achieving organizational health.

Psychologically Healthy Workplaces

Increased attention to workplace mental health provides new ways to connect wellness and performance. A major focus is depression. By 2020, depression is expected to be the second leading cause of disability worldwide. Annual prevalence rates for depression in workplaces range between 4 per cent to 6.4 per cent.[11] Depression imposes significant costs on employers through absenteeism, presenteeism (reduced productivity while at work), long-term disability, and health benefits such as prescription drug utilization. While depression is seen as an illness influenced by many personal factors, it is also important to address how workplaces pose mental health risks.[12]

Stressful working conditions are a major risk to employees' well-being and the long-term success of a business. The evidence supporting this point is overwhelming. The experience of chronic stressors has been linked to heart disease, depression, diabetes, asthma, migraines, and ulcers.[13] Not surprisingly, stress is the leading health risk motivating employers to invest in employee wellness programs.[14]

A promising approach for improving employees' mental health is the psychological risk-reduction framework. The goal is a psychologically safe workplace.[15] Workplaces are psychologically unsafe when harassment, discrimination, verbal abuse, unfairness, and disrespect are permitted or when employees lack reasonable influence over their daily work. When employees feel psychologically unsafe, their commitment, satisfaction, and job performance are reduced. The Mental Health Commission of Canada is leading the collaborative development of a voluntary national standard for psychological health and safety in the workplace, to be released in 2012.[16]

It is too early to say if psychological risk-reduction will provide the tools employers need for action. For example, interventions often target bullying, defined as generalized workplace harassment.[17] Yet training sessions can only go so far. Furthermore, the recession may have led more companies to tolerate bullying from managers as long as they get results.[18] A truly healthy organization makes respect – the antidote to bullying – a foundation for all working relationships. Bullying and other forms of 'bad behaviour' aren't tolerated because they are inconsistent with deeply held corporate values.

Healthy Work Design

Some employers are creatively redesigning work, involving employees and managers in experimenting and learning as they create their future workplace. The result is a more humanly sustainable organization.

Capital One Financial Services Corporation, a Fortune 500 company, has a collaborative, values-based culture that encourages employees to be innovative and independent.[19] Consistent with their culture, Capital One's Future of Work (FOW) program redesigns how work gets done. FOW uses computers, the internet, and mobile communication technologies to enable employees to choose how, when, and where to work so they can be most effective. Facilities were redesigned to reflect preferred work-styles, work activities, and team interaction. These changes have led to improved employee satisfaction and teamwork, as well as reduced real estate costs.

Consumer electronics retailer Best Buy introduced a Results Only Work Environment (ROWE). Employees are empowered to decide the best way to deliver results – a culture shift that requires managers to trust employees to do their work.[20] ROWE was a major step beyond flexible work arrangements because employees at any level can decide to change their work times and locations without having to ask their manager's permission. Employees in ROWE teams, compared with other teams, reported less presenteeism, less work-life conflict, more energy, and better sleep and fitness. Best Buy benefited from higher employee commitment and job satisfaction.

Both Best Buy and Capital One have relatively young and tech-savvy workforces that embrace innovative work design. Yet employers also need to design workplaces to meet the needs of an older workforce, as BMW did when it designed a factory for workers age 50 and older.[21] BMW recognized that the average age of its production workers would increase to 47 by 2017. While its older workers are absent more and work harder physically just to keep up, their expertise is essential for productivity. 'Project 2017' recruited a team of production workers over the age of 50 (supported by engineers and health professionals) to redesign assembly line work to reduce physical strains and the chance of errors. Worker-suggested changes were mostly simple and inexpensive, such as wood flooring, orthopedic footwear, magnifying lenses, adjustable work tables, large-handled tools, larger fonts on computer screens, rest breaks, and ergonomically optimal job rotation.

BMW has built a new factory that is based on Project 2017 and employs only workers over age 50. BMW's comprehensive solution for its aging workforce follows basic principles for building healthier organizations: consult with workers, involve them directly in the design process, be open to a wide range of solutions, and evaluate and learn from changes. By following these principles, any employer can develop a successful long-range workforce plan.

Seizing Opportunities

Creating Healthy Organizations continues to offer a relevant guide for change agents looking for new opportunities to improve their workplace. In light of recent workforce and workplace trends, the ideas and suggestions in the book have become increasingly relevant. The pall of uncertainty cast by the recession pushed many businesses and governments into survival mode. Short-term thinking and cost-cutting were the order of the day. If anything, these reactions served to highlight the importance of long-term, integrative, and people-centred thinking about the sustainability of organizations. The five signs of progress I have just outlined show different ways that organizational leaders are putting in place a basic principle of healthy organizations: business sustainability depends on continually re-energizing and renewing employees' efforts to contribute to their fullest potential.

The building blocks of a healthy organization – a positive culture, an inclusive approach to leadership, a vibrant workplace that inspires the best in employees – are being strengthened in different industries, regions, and types of businesses. Perhaps the best tactical advice offered to me came from a mid-level manager at a recent workshop, who described how she achieved healthy organization goals by 'thinking big and acting small.' The accumulation of small steps can, over time, be transformative. That's why it is so vital for change agents to be constantly scanning the horizon as well as monitoring the shifting dynamics of their own organization. There just may be an emerging opportunity to be found in a new study by workplace experts, a change in corporate leadership, or an updated strategic plan. Any of these has the potential to open more doors for workplace improvement initiatives to take root.

I have sampled only briefly the signs of progress that I have seen by looking at research and practice, as well as those occurring inside the many organizations I encounter in my work. *Creating Healthy Organizations* is meant to be not only a stimulus for change, but also a lens for viewing and interpreting emerging workplace trends. Your version of a healthy organization should be both aspirational and evolving: the bar edges up the more you do and the more you learn from others. That's what creating healthy organizations is all about.

NOTES

1 See, for example: Bishop, M. (2011), The great mismatch, *The Economist*, September 11 (http://www.economist.com/node/21528433); Blackwell, R. (2012), From coast to coast, a skills crisis in the making, *The Globe and Mail*, March 5, B1; ManpowerGroup (2011), Talent Shortage 2011 Survey Results, http://us.manpower.com/us/en/multimedia/2011-Talent-Shortage-Survey.pdf.

2 Keller, S., and Price, C. (2011). Beyond Performance: How Great Organizations Build Ultimate Advantage. John Wiley & Sons.

3 Berry L., Mirabito, A., and Baun, W. (2010). What's the hard return on employee wellness programs? *Harvard Business Review*, December, 104–12.

4 Ton, Z. (2012). Some companies are investing in their workers and reaping healthy profits. *Harvard Business Review*, January–February, 125–31.

5 Spreitzer, G., and Porath, C. (2012). Creating sustainable performance. *Harvard Business Review*. January–February, 93–9.

6 http://www.uky.edu/Centers/iwin/index.html.

7 http://www.oha.com/SERVICES/HEALTHYWORKENVIRONMENTS/ QUALITYHEALTHCAREWORKPLACE AWARDS/Pages/Default.aspx.

8 The 2011 Platinum Award winners were Halton Healthcare Services, Mount Sinai Hospital, St. Thomas Elgin General Hospital, the Hospital for Sick Children, and the University Health Network.

9 Dobson, S. (2012). Time to move past initiatives around health awareness, education. *Canadian HR Reporter*. 27 February, 2.

10 Conference Board of Canada. (2010). Creating a Culture of Health and Wellness in Canadian Organizations; Kennedy M. (2012). How healthy is your wellness program? *Benefits Canada*, 8 February. http://www.benefitscanada.com/benefits/health-wellness/how-healthy-is-your-wellness-program-25363.

11 Dietrich, S., Deckert, S., Ceynowa, M., Hegerl, U., and Stengler, K. (2012). Depression in the workplace: A systematic review of evidence-based prevention strategies. *International Archives of Occupational and Environmental Health*, 85 (1), 2.

12 Smith, P., Bielecky, A., and Frank, J. (2011). Intervention research on working conditions and mental health: Persistent challenges, new directions and opportunities to integrate research agendas. *Healthcare Papers*, 11, special issue, 70.

13 Mustard, C.A., Lavis, J., and Ostry, A. (2006). New evidence and enhanced understandings: Labour market experiences and health. In Heymann, J., Hertzman, C., Barer, M., and Evans, R. (Eds.), *Creating Healthier Societies: From Analysis to Action*. NY: Oxford University Press. 421–95.

14 Stress cited as top global health risk. (2009). *Benefits Canada*, 16 November, http://www.benefitscanada.com/acrossborders/news-111909.jsp.

15 Mental Health Commission of Canada, http://www.mentalhealthcommission.ca/English/Pages/workforce_workplace_pathways.aspx.

16 http://www.mentalhealthcommission.ca/english/pages/default.aspx.

17 Hauge, L. J., et al. (2010), The relative impact of workplace bullying as a

social stressor at work, *Scandinavian Journal of Psychology*, 51, 426-33; Bond, S., Tuckey, M., and Dollard, M. (2010), Psychosocial safety climate, workplace bullying, and symptoms of posttraumatic stress, *Organization Development Journal*, 28, 37-56.

18 Immen, W. (2011). Duking it out with bad managers. *The Globe and Mail*, 21 January, B14.

19 Khanna, S., and New, J.R. (2008). Revolutionizing the workplace: A case study of the future of work program at Capital One. *Human Resource Management*, 47, 795–808.

20 Moen, P., Kelly, E., and Chermack, K. (2008). Learning from a natural experiment: Studying a corporate work-time policy nitiative. In Crouter, A.C., and Booth, A. (Eds.), *Work-life Policies that Make a Real Difference for Individuals, Families, and Organizations*. Washington, DC: Urban Institute Press. Also see: *Business Week*, http://www.businessweek.com/careers/managementiq/archives/2009/09/gap_to_employee.html.

21 Loch, C. H., Sting, F. J., Bauer, N., and Mauermann, H. (2010). How BMW is defusing the demographic time bomb. *Harvard Business Review*, 99-102. Also see: http://www.impactlab.net/2011/02/19/bmw-opens-new-car-plant-where-the-workforce-is-all-aged-over-50/.

Acknowledgments

Producing this book was a collaborative enterprise. Many individuals generously shared with me their ideas and experiences. Others provided me with opportunities to learn first hand about how they were creating healthy organizations.

The framing of quality of work life and organizational performance in health terms goes back to work I did between 1999 and 2001 at Canadian Policy Research Networks, especially projects with Grant Schellenberg and Harry Shannon, with encouragement from Judith Maxwell. My immersion in the research on workplace health promotion deepened when Health Canada contracted me to write two discussion papers, one on healthy workplace strategies and the other on healthy workplaces and productivity. Deborah Connors and organizers of the annual Health, Work and Wellness conference in Canada connected me over the years with a dedicated network of workplace change agents, from whom I learned much. Ongoing discussions and collaborations with Greg Banwell and Craig Thompson at Wilson Banwell Human Solutions also helped to shape my thinking about healthy organizations.

As a consultant, workshop leader, and conference speaker, I have had the privilege of hearing and seeing hundreds of examples of individuals and organizations moving down a healthy trajectory. Several organizations have agreed to share their stories here. In this regard, I would particularly like to thank Mike Martin at Teck Cominco's Trail Operations, Richard Gotfried at Trico Homes, Jeff MacPherson at the City of Edmonton, Leanne Bilodeau at University of British Columbia Okanagan, Jeff Fielding at the City of London, David Minns at the National Research Council's Institute for Fuel Cell Innovation, Marie

Sopko at Nexen, Karen Jackson at Trillium Health Centre, and Seow Ping at the Singapore Health Promotion Board.

Jennifer Dixon provided research assistance with chapter 7. Joanne McKechnie helped to analyse the data from Great Place to Work Institute Canada's 2007 '50 Best Workplaces in Canada' list that I use in various chapters. I gained an inside view of outstanding workplaces during the 2005 to 2008 period, when Joanne and I were co-principals in the Great Place to Work Institute's Canadian affiliate before selling to new owners. Continued access to the institute's data is appreciated. I also draw on survey data from 'Rethinking Work,' a joint venture with Ekos Research, where Susan Galley was a creative source of ideas on workplace issues.

I also want to acknowledge the input I have received from the numerous participants at my workshops and conference presentations. More than anything, these conversations confirmed to me the need for a practical guide to creating healthier organizations.

Jennifer DiDomenico at the University of Toronto Press offered the right balance of encouragement, advice, and patience needed for me to complete this project.

CREATING HEALTHY ORGANIZATIONS

How Vibrant Workplaces Inspire Employees to Achieve Sustainable Success

Introduction

As the corporate hub of Canada's boom-bust energy economy, Calgary experienced a white-hot real estate market for most of this decade. Home prices in the Alberta city of 1 million people skyrocketed as buyers lined up to outbid each other. Then, in 2008 the global financial crisis and plummeting oil prices knocked the bottom out of Calgary's housing market. Home sales that year dropped about 50 per cent, unsold property piled up, and prices fell. It is now a buyers' market, but fewer people are buying, fearful about an uncertain future. Construction is a cyclical industry, caught in the updrafts and downdrafts of the economy. Yet despite knowing the good times could not last, many companies were caught off guard in 2008. Some closed their doors completely; others cut their workforce by 30 to 40 per cent.

However, at least one company – Calgary-based Trico Homes – likely will emerge from the economic crisis even stronger. The reasons are both simple and complex: Trico Homes is a healthy organization. It has designed, marketed, and built over 4,000 homes in the Calgary area and the interior of British Columbia. The company has won numerous building industry accolades. It has been recognized as one of the '50 Best Managed Companies' and '50 Best Workplaces' in Canada. But these accomplishments are not what make Trico a healthy organization. What is important is *how* it achieved these results. To understand the how, we have to appreciate Trico's operating philosophy – in other words, its corporate character. The company's character is rooted in a culture that blends social responsibility, caring values, and a performance-oriented ethic of teamwork.

The Trico philosophy is expressed in its vision and grounded in its values. The company vision is to enhance its customers' lives while enriching the community. Wayne Chiu, founder and CEO of Trico Homes, believes that a company should leave a legacy by contributing to the communities in which it does business. For Trico, philanthropy involves more than writing a cheque – it's about building lasting partnerships that strengthen communities. Trico has earned a reputation as a community leader through its partnerships and employee volunteering with the Kids Cancer Care Foundation, Bow Valley College, GlobalFest, UNICEF Canada, Volunteer Calgary, and Immigrant Services Calgary. Recently, Trico Homes initiated a $1.5 million partnership with southeast Calgary's Family Leisure Centre in support of a significant expansion program and the establishment of the Trico Centre for Family Wellness.

The corporate values are T.R.I.C.O. – trust, respect, integrity, community, and opportunity. Trico cultivates trusting and respectful relationships among employees, trades, suppliers, and community partners. All feel part of the Trico extended family. Employee surveys found high positive scores on management integrity and credibility, fairness, respect, team spirit, and pride. During the boom years, staff turnover stayed well below the industry average. People's interests and passions are tapped through training and career development opportunities. At weekly team meetings, a 'no bad ideas' philosophy encourages creative input from employees. When Trico's employees speak for themselves, here is how they described, in an anonymous survey, why it is a great company to work for:

- Right from the beginning of my employment with Trico I was welcomed as 'one of the family'. Even though I am a receptionist, I am taken seriously and the work I do here is appreciated. I am told often how much I mean to the company.
- Trico Homes is dedicated to making a difference in the community and encourages employee involvement in this process … Trico Home's culture has a strong business ethic which encourages growth and development for the company.
- The people are willing to help you in any situation. Giving back to the community has a great deal of importance for management and the staff. The staff get recognized for their accomplishments, their extra effort, and good ideas that help the company save time and money.
- Management treats me as a member of this big family, not just as an employee. They care about my needs and give flexibility for my own family and personal life.

Trico managers believe there are opportunities for well-managed companies to gain market share if they position themselves now for the recovery. As Richard Gotfried, vice-president of Corporate Communications, puts it: 'We can shine if we do things right.' Richard explains that 'right' for Trico means true to its philosophy and culture. By drawing on the strength and resilience of relationships within its extended family of employees and partners, Trico has so far weathered the economic storm.

Actually, Trico saw the storm coming. Trico's managers and employees knew the housing boom was unsustainable and saw signs of this in 2007. Trico's ability to adapt to the economic downturn was embedded all along in its sustainable people practices and business processes. During growth years, the company hired new employees only after ensuring that everything had been done to gain efficiencies by adjusting processes and workloads. Consistent with its values, Trico wanted to honour its commitment to employees over the longer term. Regarding business processes, Trico is always on the lookout for new products and services that will benefit customers. As building activity slowed, it had the time to reassess all aspects of a home, from design and customer appeal to materials and products used, to how it is built. By collaborating, Trico employees and business partners found cost savings through new products and streamlined construction methods.

Trico quickly did three things to survive the declining market. It offered a price assurance program, which adjusts the presale price of a house to the market value at time of occupancy if the market goes down. Customers also have a guarantee program – a preset price for their existing home if it does not sell before they move into their new Trico home. Trico also negotiated attractive financing options with its mortgage partners and committed to becoming a leader in affordable home ownership. The company now targets average-income workers who were frozen out of the overheated Calgary market – such as the three firefighters who were recruited from another city, but had to return because they could not afford to buy a family home in Calgary.

So far, the new strategy is working. But there was a painful price: staff cuts. When the global recession hit full force in the fall of 2008, Trico managers were communicating regularly with employees, explaining changes in the market, how the company was affected, and how it was responding. The CEO made it clear he was prepared to keep as many of the team employed as possible. The key message was that the continued success of the company depends on its dedicated staff and strong culture. Fortunately, Trico had gradually brought staffing levels down through attrition. But after much thinking and planning, the executive team announced in December 2008 that seven positions would be cut. Focusing on the team that will be needed when the market stabilizes, managers used performance-related criteria to identify who would leave. The workforce declined from 106 at its peak to 80 after the job reductions.

When Wayne Chiu explained to employees why the layoffs were being made, he also committed to no further job cuts for the twelve months starting in January 2009 in order to ease employees' insecurity. Because Trico's culture is performance oriented, the criteria for the layoffs were understood by everyone. Remaining team members saw the integrity in this approach. Trico's caring culture ensured that the people who left were treated fairly and with dignity, in accord with the company's values. The executive team wanted the departing staff to be proud of time they spent with the company. If anything, employees were surprised that the layoffs were not deeper. Morale rose after the layoffs because employees now had a greater sense of stability and security.

Trico took two other steps that strengthened it for the future. One step was to approach its six major community partners and confirm the company's commitment to maintaining ongoing financial contributions and volunteer support. After all, these long-term community partnerships had helped to define the character of the company. The other step was to invite any interested employee to join a new home design team competition. Employees and managers formed four teams, each with a professional designer to translate people's ideas into plans. The design parameters were challenging: a compact, environmentally friendly house on a small city lot. The four designs were independently judged, and the company has already built the 26-foot-wide design competition winner – 'The Liberty' – as a model home in a new community. This collaborative approach to design would have been difficult to use during boom times. In addition, it was fun for everyone involved.

Trico's story is about how a successful business with a progressive philosophy is navigating its way through a recession. Like a healthy person, the company is adaptable and resilient when faced with adversity. At a deeper level, the Trico story also is about the evolution of a healthy and sustainable organization. Indeed, the word *healthy* accurately describes companies – or organizations in the public or nonprofit sectors – with qualities similar to those of Trico Homes.

The Healthy Organization Ideal

This book outlines how to create healthier organizations. Being healthy is an ideal that any organization can aspire to achieve. We talk about healthy people using words such as *vigorous, flourishing, robust, thriving, resilient,* and *fit.* The same words also can be used to describe healthy organizations. Healthy persons experience physical and mental well-being because all physical, mental, and emotional systems are in sync. They effectively perform their roles as workers, citizens, partners, and parents while further developing their potential. And they have a positive relationship with the environment in which they live, drawing from it while contributing to it. The same can be said for a healthy organization. Its systems are well integrated, it operates successfully today, develops new capacity to thrive tomorrow, and it has mutually beneficial relationships with customers and communities, and the environment.

My goal is to provide a fresh perspective on how organizations operate and how they can be made more enduring in human terms. A healthy organization is at once healthy, successful, and responsible. I incorporate in a healthy organization model three previously separate streams of management practice and research: workplace health promotion, organizational performance, and social responsibility. These areas recently have started to converge. My contribution is to push this cross-fertilization to a higher level. So, while the ideas I present are not new on their own, what is new is how I bring them together in an integrated, healthy organization framework.

Looking at Your Organization through a Health Lens

What is to be gained by looking at your organization through a health lens? The main advantage is that when you make the connections between people, performance, and community more visible, it will be easier to make your organization sustainable into the future. A health lens provides insights about how to improve people practices, performance and community relationships. It encourages holistic and long-term thinking about what drives an organization's success.

My model of a healthy organization, presented in chapter 1, shows how the organization's structures, systems, and culture influence both employee well-being and business performance. What I call the 'healthy organization value chain' expands the idea of an employee-customer value chain by linking future success to how the organization nurtures its employees' capabilities and quality of life over the long term. A health lens also highlights an organization's evolving relationships with its customers or clients, shareholders or citizens, and the communities in which it operates. Ultimately, a healthy organization succeeds by renewing and replenishing its human and social capital. That is what I mean by sustainable success.

Business experts have done surprisingly little to adapt health ideas to corporate performance. I say 'surprisingly,' because the analogies are potentially powerful. Consider two interesting exceptions. When McKinsey consultants wrote about 'healthy organizations,' they had in mind caring for the long-term well-being, resilience, and renewal of the company rather than short-term financial results.[1] Organizational researchers Michael Beer and Russell Eisenstat borrowed the 'silent killer' idea, likening barriers to strategy implementation and organizational learning to cholesterol.[2] Poor vertical communication, they concluded, is one of the biggest silent killers of both strategy and learning.

Workplace health promotion experts operate in a separate sphere, which is part of the problem. Workplace health experts lack convincing ways to talk to managers and executives about the performance impacts of healthy and unhealthy employees and workplaces. As a result, the ample research on healthy workplaces has not been communicated to managers and other practitioners in terms that make sense for business strategy. For instance, *Healthy Work: Stress, Productivity, and the Reconstruction of Working Life* is a pioneering book on job stress written by Robert Karasek and Töres Theorell almost twenty years ago.[3] The book marked a huge advance in the field of workplace health, but went largely unnoticed by managers or organizational researchers. The authors' performance-enhancing solutions to job stress involved reorganizing work to improve 'creativity, skill development, and quality.'[4] In short, a healthy workplace also could be a higher-performing workplace.

Above all, healthy organizations forge an enduring link between employee well-being and performance. This link must become central to the business's philosophy, long-term strategy, and the way it operates day to day. I believe that this people-performance link can be strengthened if we have the right tools for thinking and talking about how organizations can be healthy – tools that I provide throughout this book.

Helping Change Agents

A growing number of managers, human resource (HR) practitioners, health and wellness professionals, and front-line employees are committed to achieving their own versions of the healthy organization ideal. These are the people I call 'change agents,' and this book is written mainly for them, so that they can exert even more positive influence inside their workplace.

Before the recession hit in 2008, these change agents were seeking ways to make workplaces healthier in order to address the growing challenges of recruiting, retaining, developing, and engaging employees. The economic crisis has not deterred these change agents, even if their steps forward now may be smaller and slower. While some companies have been forced by economic conditions into survival mode, others are seizing the opportunity to engage employees in figuring out how to do things better for the longer term. As Trico Homes found, it is important is to tap into your already healthy roots to adapt in creative ways to the market downturn. Because, as the recovery gets traction, that resilience you foster today will be critical for addressing the same employee challenges that beset organizations earlier in this decade.

For any organization adopting this positive mindset, the good news is that our understanding of health and performance has come a long way in recent years. To illustrate the progress that has been made, here are three examples:

- Back then, workplace health practitioners talked a lot about making the 'business case' for investing in employee wellness and healthy work environments. I recall a keynote speaker at a major workplace health conference in 2002 arguing that workplace health and well-being are barely on the HR radar screen, never mind the business radar screen. The message for practitioners back then was 'make yourselves organizationally relevant.' Indeed, many change agents have done just that.
- An occupational physician pointed out to me that, despite data from health benefit providers that showed mental health problems imposing huge costs on employers, there was little interest in addressing root causes. That is because the root causes of stress, burnout, and work-life conflict require changing the work environment – a black box that managers avoided opening. But workplace health professionals persisted, using what this physician called a 'foot in

the door' approach with CEOs and executive teams to make the case that a healthy social and psychological work environment is a bottom-line issue.

• At a conference of senior health benefits managers, one participant summed up how people experience a healthy workplace: 'It is so nice to go to work in a good mood and leave that way.' A good mood is a sure sign of positive mental, physical, and emotional health. It also is a sure sign of an employee who enjoys their work and takes pride in their contributions to the organization's goals. The fact that employee engagement has become a top priority for managers underscores the need to create positive employee work experiences – which require a healthy work environment.

I encourage change agents to focus on their organization's existing potential, strengths, and opportunities. You need to look for ways to build on these attributes. Certainly, an accurate diagnosis of problems is a basis for designing solutions. I propose a solutions-oriented mind-set, given that we know a lot about the causes and consequences of un-healthy and unproductive workplaces. Viewing organizations through a 'health' lens helps us to imagine what is possible. This approach is gaining momentum through the growing field of positive organization-al studies. Researchers in this area apply concepts such as resilience, wellness, innovation, creativity, justice, engagement, and mindfulness as tools for understanding how to develop the human potential in any organization.[5]

Similarly, viewing organizations through a health lens reveals how employees at all levels can be resourceful in doing their jobs and im-proving their immediate work environments. Often, this involves em-ployees' taking initiative, alone or together, within their limited sphere of influence to create small but tangible improvements. It is at the level of micro-action that progress towards a healthy organization ideal can be best made.

I encourage readers to develop a personal vision of a healthy organi-zation, which describes what your organization has the potential to be-come. When this personal vision becomes part of a shared vision with co-workers, you will have a powerful catalyst for change. Using your own language, this vision can guide improvements in performance and the quality of work life. Charting that path to a healthy organization cannot be based on a simple formula or a CEO directive. Building a healthier organization is a shared responsibility: everyone, regardless of level or position in the organization, can and should participate. What I offer are examples, ideas, and tools that can help you to mobilize others in pursuit of that shared healthy organization vision.

Leveraging Where You Are Today

In order to move forward, we need to understand where we are today. In this regard, I use the word *creating* in the title of the book to refer to an evolving and continual process. I am not suggesting that you, or your organization, are starting from scratch. I realize that most organizations are already on a healthy organization trajectory, through initiatives such as an occupational health and safety program, a wellness committee, or employee surveys. So, from a change perspective, what is important is to build from where you are, leveraging workplace health promotion and performance improvement initiatives that are already under way.

A particular challenge for organizations that are recognized leaders is sustaining their healthy cultures, high levels of employee dedication, and excellent performance – especially during tough economic times. As the CEO of Wegmans, a U.S. grocery store chain that ranked first on *Fortune* magazine's 2005 list of '100 Best Companies to Work For In America,' commented, 'we'll never be there, we're always on a journey.'

A relatively small number of companies, such as Wegmans or Trico Homes, are award winners, making it onto best workplaces, most admired companies, or corporate social responsibility awards lists. However, companies on these lists are atypical. They belong to a top tier of organizations – probably no more than 10 per cent – that are outstanding by business, workplace, and social responsibility criteria. My experience as a workplace consultant has taught me that many organizations are somewhere in the middle of the pack, maybe a little behind or just ahead of their peers. This book's messages are aimed primarily at this audience – the large group of organizations that are making some progress, but aspire to more.

I believe that many organizations of all sizes in all sectors strive to be better than they are in terms of the quality of their workplaces, performance, and community relationships. And as progress is made on these fronts, the bar is constantly raised. In this sense, becoming a healthier organization refers to an ongoing journey rather than a destination. This book is intended to help change agents make that journey faster and further.

Learning from Your Peers

While there is much to learn from high-profile award winners, we can draw equally valuable lessons from typical organizations that in their own way are trying to be healthier. These organizations are your peers. Perhaps the most important lesson is that there is hidden potential in most organizations to move further down a healthy organization pathway and there are employees and managers who are ready, willing, and able to lead this change.

Three examples illustrate how fairly typical organizations have seized opportunities to become healthier:

- A manager of internal audits in a large professional service organization launched a 'healthy organization' assessment, with a mandate from the executive team to figure out 'how to energize the organization to bring it to the next step.' The impetus for the assessment came not from human resources or occupational health and safety, but from a less likely source of change – an audit team. Over a period of several years of team-building, and after much reflection by managers, the culture shifted and became more supportive of both employee health and performance.
- An organizational development manager at a forest products company led an initiative to foster a collaborative management style. The first question the management team had to answer was 'what do we mean by collaboration?' The answer, in short, was 'it's how we work together' – in other words, healthy relationships. As a start, the management team worked for nine months to get a vision and guiding principles, which were rolled out to all production sites and used to update management training. This process took several years and had unexpected setbacks, owing to a tough market for wood products, but the company did move to a more values-based style of management.
- At a management retreat for a large municipality, a new HR strategy (called the 'people plan') and refreshed values focused attention on healthy workplace issues. One discussion turned to this question: 'what can you do to make time for people issues?' Creative ideas for addressing the workload problem were discussed. Someone pointed out that in her area, 'nobody is beating down doors to be a general manager.' Another manager stood up and admitted: 'I used to be proud of what I do. Now I just struggle to get through the day.' This

retreat accelerated actions already under way in various parts of the organization to create healthier work environments.

These examples involve mid-level and senior managers. Yet in each organization there also were employees taking active roles in healthy change. The managers realized they had to tap the energy of these front-line change agents. Furthermore, the kind of conversations taking place among managers already had occurred in some work units or teams. So there were pockets of innovation within each organization that exemplified the healthy ideal, yet had not been recognized or shared internally. The main point is that in most organizations there are ripe opportunities to harness and mobilize healthy organizational change.

Chapter Overview

The chapters that follow address three core questions:

1. What are the building blocks of a healthy organization?
2. How can you move down your own healthy organization path?
3. How can you measure and sustain progress?

Chapter 1 outlines a healthy organization model. The model combines elements from workplace health promotion, human resources, organizational performance, and corporate social responsibility. Convergent trends will help you to identify new opportunities to improve both the quality of work life and organizational results. Four building blocks support sustainable success. These building blocks are positive cultures, inclusive leadership, vibrant workplaces, and inspired employees. The model provides you with a guide for planning and action by encouraging integrative thinking about the underlying drivers of well-being, performance, and responsible business practices.

Chapter 2 lays out the limits – and promise – of practice and research on workplace health promotion. There is untapped potential to extend the benefits of your current healthy workplace practices beyond reduced employee health risks, health benefit savings, and lower levels of absenteeism. Workplace health promotion can be a springboard for a more holistic, organizational perspective, tightening the links between employee well-being and performance. Providing this springboard requires improvements in the psychological and social aspects of work that define a vibrant workplace. Employee health and wellness then become assets that contribute to a capable and inspired workforce.

Chapter 3 shows how your organization can achieve higher levels of employee wellness and performance by putting in place the ingredients of vibrant workplaces that truly inspire employees in their jobs. A vibrant workplace is grounded on the quality of relationships, jobs, teamwork, and human resource support systems. A vibrant workplace is more than healthy: it supports employees in learning, collaborating, and innovating in the interests of customers and society. By cultivating these conditions, you will do more than just engage your employees. You can inspire them to contribute their best and to feel part of a workplace community with a bigger purpose.

Chapter 4 explores the culture building block of a healthy organization. The chapter suggests steps you can take to nurture a positive culture. Strong, people-centred values are the foundation, shaping day-to-day interactions among co-workers; between managers and employees; and between employees and their customers or clients, suppliers, business partners, and the larger community. There is growing awareness among executives that a company's culture contributes in many ways to its business success. Indeed, your organization's culture can become a strategic advantage.

Chapter 5 outlines the way that leadership in healthy organizations must be widely shared. The chapter describes six elements of inclusive leadership. Employees are actively involved in shaping the organization's healthy trajectory; they do not need permission to do so because such behaviour is collectively valued. Certainly, executive support is a key enabler of healthy change, but an inclusive approach to leadership mobilizes everyone. Healthy organizations, then, are co-created through ongoing and coordinated actions across the entire workplace community, and change agents play a pivotal role.

Chapter 6 looks inside the change process, focusing on the dynamics of how healthy organizations actually evolve. The chapter offers practical insights for navigating change so that the experience for those affected is healthy. Examples are offered from a wide range of organizations that are improving the work environment, involving employees in the process, and achieving performance improvements. Five broad principles for healthy change are outlined: understand the readiness for change in your organization; align structure and culture; link changes to the business strategy; widen the circle of involvement; and learn and innovate along the way.

Chapter 7 discusses what sustainable success could mean for your organization and its implications for your human resources, environmental, and community practices. Practical ways your organization can thrive so that all stakeholders benefit are examined. The focus is on two significant drivers of sustainable success: the quality of relationships with stakeholders and the future workforce capabilities required for the organization to thrive. The chapter's theme is renewal, specifically how you can renew your relationships with customers and your community stakeholders and how you can renew your workforce.

Chapter 8 provides practical advice and resources for measuring progress along your healthy organization trajectory. Having the relevant metrics available contributes to healthy change and a positive culture. The chapter focuses on how to make better use of your own evidence to plan, implement, and monitor organizational improvements. There is no handy one-size-fits-all tool for evaluating whether an organization is becoming more, or less, healthy. Organizations therefore have no choice but to come to grips with why they need healthy organization measures, what measures are needed, and how to make the fullest use of them to learn and improve.

Chapter 9 is an action-oriented summary of the insights, arguments, and evidence provided throughout the book. I distil each chapter into a checklist of points for discussion, planning, and implementation. Readers are encouraged to use this guide to design your own strategies. Your focus can be a team, work unit, department, or your entire organization. Whether you sit at the executive table or are a front-line worker, there is a role you can play in helping your organization to achieve a better quality of work life for employees and improved performance.

1 The Healthy Organization

A subtle but profound shift is under way in workplaces. Human resources and workplace health experts are focusing increasingly on how employees' work environment influences their health and job performance. Managers are searching for ways to fully engage employees and unleash hidden talents. More companies are seeking to follow through on their social responsibility commitments in an era when public expectations for ethical business practices are rising. These trends are converging, opening up new opportunities to improve the quality of work life, organizational performance, and communities – all at the same time. It is not unrealistic to imagine a future in which boundaries have dissolved between employee wellness, performance, and corporate social responsibility and where these goals are central to every manager's job.

While this projection sounds promising, we have some distance yet to go. Even the most comprehensive health promotion initiatives have at best modest impacts on the overall well-being and performance of an organization's workforce. Employee engagement still is viewed as an HR issue, and limited efforts have been made to uncover its underlying 'drivers' in the work environment. While social responsibility codes surely apply to how an organization treats its own employees, these implications are only now being explored.

To help to close these gaps between thinking and practice, this chapter lays out a model of a healthy organization. The healthy organization model is intended to help executives, managers, practitioners in human resources and workplace wellness, and a host of change agents scattered throughout workplaces find better ways to connect work environments, quality of life on and off the job, business results, and community benefits.

Five key points are made:

1. Employee well-being is an organizational performance issue, not simply a matter of personal health.
2. There are good reasons to move beyond employers' current focus on employee engagement and healthy workplaces.
3. The model of a healthy organization helps us to think in holistic, long-term ways about the underlying drivers of well-being and performance.
4. A healthy organization rests on four pillars: vibrant workplaces, inspired employees, positive cultures, and shared leadership.
5. Healthy organizations put in place conditions for sustainable success, renewing their workforce capabilities and relationships with customers and communities.

Integrating Well-Being and Performance

By presenting a healthy organization model, I am challenging you to take a big step beyond what you may now think of as a 'healthy workplace.' My concept of a healthy organization combines ideas about what contributes to employee well-being and organizational performance from different areas of expertise. Economists want to know how firms can achieve more output for the same units of input. Managers and organizational experts are concerned about how organizations achieve higher levels of performance in ethical and socially responsible ways. Health promotion practitioners need to know how to involve managers and employees in creating genuinely health-promoting work environments. And those in the growing field of business ethics want social responsibility to apply to everything a company does.

These sound like separate agendas, but the healthy organization concept unifies them into a change tool that is far more useful than workplace health promotion will ever be on its own. That is because, in the twenty-first century knowledge economy, national prosperity and the performance of individual companies depend more than ever on human skills and abilities. Indeed, decades of research on the determinants of population health show that for people to thrive, they must live in environments that enable them to realize their human potential. In short, wellness and work performance go hand in hand.

Leading thinkers in the fields of occupational health and safety, workplace health promotion, and epidemiology agree that the most successful interventions target underlying workplace and organizational factors. Over the past decade this perception has led to calls for a holistic or systemic view of the determinants of employee health and well-being. Health then becomes a defining feature of the entire organization.

A holistic approach also emphasizes the importance of a healthy change process. This is achieved when workers and managers actively collaborate to identify and design improvements to their own work environments. Having employees at all levels co-create healthy and productive work environments builds on the World Health Organization's definition of health promotion as 'the process of enabling individuals and communities to increase control over the determinants of health and thereby improve their health.'[1] The two key words in this definition are 'control' and 'determinants.' In a healthy organization, employees at all levels are able to influence key aspects of the environments in which they work, including the culture of the organization.

An organizational perspective on employee health slowly has taken hold over the past decade. However, it has yet to get full traction. In the 1990s the U.S. National Institute for Occupational Safety and Health (NIOSH) stated that a healthy work organization is 'one whose culture, climate and practices create an environment that promotes employee health and safety as well as organizational effectiveness.'[2] More specifically, NIOSH identifies the importance of an organizational climate in which employees feel valued and are able to resolve group conflicts. Equally important are management practices that support workers to learn, collaborate, and grow.

In summary, employers and employees stand to reap substantial benefits by integrating work environments with individual health outcomes and organizational performance. Practically speaking, an integrated approach to workplace health requires leadership by senior management, active involvement of employees, and cooperation among diverse stakeholders. They include practitioners in occupational health and safety, human resources, health promotion, line managers, and employees' representatives in professional associations and unions. Individuals and groups in any of these positions can be agents of change – as can front-line employees who take initiative to improve their immediate work environment. Ideally, wellness goals must be embedded in the organization's strategy and employees need to feel a sense of shared responsibility for reaching them. The healthy organization model moves us in this direction.

Healthy Organizations in Action

Leading employers in Europe, North America, and elsewhere have developed their own approaches to health and performance. The European Network for Workplace Health Promotion (ENWHP) has been operating since 1996, providing a forum for employers, policy-makers, and occupational health and safety and health promotion practitioners to develop standardized criteria for workplace health promotion and to disseminate effective practices. I participated in one of the ENWHP meetings and was impressed with network members' integrative thinking about healthy work environments, employee wellness, business success, and social responsibility. This approach came from some global brand-name employers: Shell, Stora Enso, Volkswagen, GSK, Hilti, to name a few. The network's vision is 'healthy employees in healthy organizations.' Achieving this vision is seen as a key to social and economic prosperity.

Exemplifying a healthy organization is Stora Enso, an integrated forest-products company headquartered in Finland. Its major challenge is creating a performance culture among 45,000 employees in forty countries. Developing a highly skilled, motivated, and healthy workforce is a strategic priority. Regular Web-based surveys monitor workplace culture, employee satisfaction and well-being, and management practices to ensure they support these goals. This scrutiny complements rigorous safety practices. Survey results are reported to all work units, and accountability is through action plans, targeted improvements, and a performance-based reward system for managers. Environmental sustainability also is integral to the company's operating philosophy. Dr Paavo Jäppinen, a Stora Enso vice-president, explains: 'For customers and the general public it is becoming increasingly important that economic success is based on social responsibility. At Stora Enso, workplace health management and corporate culture based on partnership are essential elements of our human resource development, helping us to achieve our corporate goals.'[3] This cannot be dismissed as simply a corporate version of Nordic social democracy. Indeed, Stora Enso operates according to this philosophy in dozens of countries around the world.

In the United States, an outstanding example of a healthy organization is the SAS Institute, a leader in business intelligence software. At SAS, innovation and business growth are built on long-term relationships with employees and customers. As SAS president and CEO Jim

Goodnight explains: 'We've worked hard to create a corporate culture that is based on trust between our employees and the company, a culture that rewards innovation, encourages employees to try new things and yet doesn't penalize them for taking chances, and a culture that cares about employees' personal and professional growth.' SAS has been on *Fortune* magazine's 100 Best Companies to Work For In America list for ten consecutive years. SAS also has created a robust accountability framework using metrics and ongoing employee feedback. SAS's caring culture places importance on work/life balance and, by doing so, enables employees not only to have time for personal and family needs, but also to actively participate in their communities.

A Canadian example is Trillium Health Centre. As one of the largest tertiary care hospitals in Canada, Trillium offers advanced cardiac, neurosurgery, stroke, and orthopaedic services. Trillium's two sites provide emergency, inpatient, ambulatory and community-based care to over 1 million people in Mississauga, Ontario, and the surrounding area. With over 4,000 employees and 1,100 volunteers, one of Trillium's strategic directions was to 'engage people fully.'

The concept of an 'organic organization' was used by founding CEO, Ken White, to describe a non-bureaucratic environment that encourages innovation and individual leadership by fully engaging all employees, physicians, and volunteers to make decisions and take ownership for them. For people to be fully engaged, they must be supported by a healthy environment. That is why Trillium has set the explicit goal of creating and maintaining healthy workplaces. Trillium annually surveys staff, physicians, and volunteers to assess health, wellness, and work experiences. Managers are accountable for acting on the survey results and employees also are involved in this process. Healthy workplace changes support other major human resource goals, including recruitment, flexible work options, talent management, and professional development. The current strategic theme, 'outstanding people,' reflects how the present CEO, Janet Davidson, has build on this strong foundation with a dual focus on developing people and creating a working and volunteering environment that attracts outstanding new talent.

While Stora Enso, SAS, and Trillium follow different paths and use different language, each has a deeply rooted culture based on a virtuous connection between how employees are treated and business success. Each supports people in a healthy and productive environment, recognizing this as the best way to excel in meeting the needs of all major stakeholders: managers, employees, employees' families, shareholders or owners, partners and suppliers, and communities. These organizations also have adopted what experts identify as best practices for people management and organizational performance. Leading-edge HR management places a high value on treating employees as core business assets and 'bundles' practices such as teamwork, extensive training, employment security, reduced hierarchy, performance-based pay, employee involvement in decision making, and employee wellness into a comprehensive strategy directly tied to business goals.[4]

A Healthy Organization Model

As a guide for assessing the health of your company, worksite, or department, I offer a basic model of a healthy organization. This model generalizes from the examples just described, drawing widely on research evidence that shows the importance of work environments, employee experiences, culture, and leadership. The model also has been confirmed in practice, through my consulting work with numerous organizations wanting to move in this direction and through conversations with hundreds of managers and employees across Canada and internationally.

I present the model in two steps. First, I identify in figure 1.1 the four building blocks of a healthy organization: a positive culture, an inclusive approach to leadership, and vibrant workplaces that inspire employees. Taking action to make your organization healthier requires a clear understanding of how the main components of the healthy organization model are connected. So my second step, in figure 1.2, is to describe the logic of a healthy organization. I do this by adapting the concept of a value chain, which will be familiar to managers who track the relationship between employee and customer experiences.

A vibrant workplace is really the centrepiece of the model, because this is the environment in which people work day in and day out. Vibrant workplaces do more than engage employees. They actually cultivate a sense of personal inspiration about the work in hand. An engaged employee is satisfied and loyal. An inspired employee is more than this, actively seeking out ways to develop and use skills, knowledge, and abilities to further corporate goals. In today's knowledge-based economy, it is not enough for individuals to be skilled and well educated. In order for employees to apply their capabilities, they need relationships, resources, and systems that enable them to collaborate. When workers collaborate, the sum becomes greater than the parts: teams and organi-

Figure 1.1 Building blocks of a healthy organization

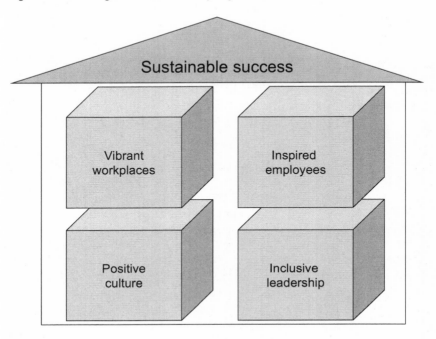

zation develop capabilities for performance, innovation, and creativity that far surpass what each individual member brings to their job – and to the organization, its customers, and society.

Two critical enablers of a vibrant workplace are culture and leadership. A positive culture based on strong people values will resonate with employees and managers, providing guidelines for healthy and productive work behaviours. While leadership from the top for a healthy organization vision and goals is important, this alone will not mobilize the workforce to move down the healthy organization path. What is needed is an inclusive approach to leadership that empowers all members of an organization to take responsibility for healthy changes.

Success is multidimensional. A healthy organization meets or exceeds its business goals in terms of customers' needs and financial results. It also does more than promote personal health and wellness, providing an overall high quality of work life for employees based on their to-

Figure 1.2 The healthy organization value chain

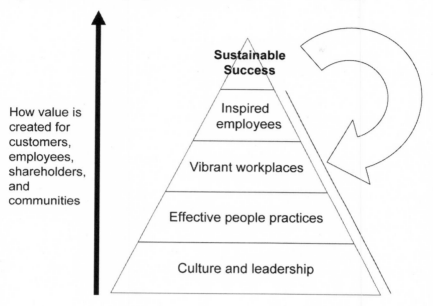

tal experience of their job and work environment. It also provides net benefits for communities by operating in socially responsible ways. In both business and human terms, these are the conditions for sustainable success. In every sector of the economy, we can find employers that have developed in their own way a healthy organization. While these journeys have not been guided by a pre-existing model, the approaches follow the same basic logic.

Here is the underlying logic. The stage is set for high quality of work life *and* high performance by having a strong culture grounded on people values, a commitment from top managers to improve the workplace as a way of achieving business results, and active encouragement for all employees to demonstrate leadership in their roles. These components of a healthy organization are foundational, which is why I devote entire chapters to the topics of culture and leadership. Living the values is a hallmark of a healthy organization. One of its clearest expressions can be found in an organization's people policies, programs, and practices – how it approaches all human resource management issues. As you will see, many of my examples illustrate the healthy organization building blocks by featuring specific people practices. At the core of a healthy organization are vibrant workplaces that inspire employees – goals that are within reach if all people policies, programs, and management actions reinforce and support them.

In the late 1990s Anthony Rucci, Steven Kirn, and Richard Quinn published their path-breaking *Harvard Business Review* article on the employee-customer-profit chain at Sears.[5] While Sears has since faltered, their theory that satisfied employees lead to satisfied customers who drive up profits has entered mainstream management thinking. This idea has strong intuitive appeal to managers, and it certainly has been used by HR professionals to make a case for their contribution to the bottom line. But it also is evident that senior managers have paid more attention to the customer-profit part of the chain, to the neglect of the first and perhaps most crucial link: employees. And when employees have been part of the value chain, managers have focused on the attitudes – usually satisfaction or engagement – that are correlated with customer service, and have paid less attention to their determinants.

Since this *HBR* article, new evidence has confirmed the importance of the employee link in the value chain. When the employee link is applied to a healthy organization, we see that other links also are important, because they put in place the preconditions for a vibrant workplace that will inspire employees. Anchor points in the value chain are culture and leadership, which give shape to effective and supportive people practices. By expanding the seminal work of Rucci and his co-authors, I describe what may be called a healthy organization value chain, where 'value' is defined as what matters most to customers, employees, shareholders, and communities.

The components of a healthy organization are mutually reinforcing, and success produces an upward spiral that further strengthens the culture, validates the importance of shared leadership, maintains vibrant workplace conditions, and continues to inspire employees. The more employees feel they are able to contribute to the organization's success, the more they feel empowered to further expand their capabilities in innovative ways. This process of innovation also encompasses refinements to the work environment, continually adapting jobs, processes, structures, and systems in ways that maximize people's contributions. Again, wellness is not an end goal but a natural result of healthy processes for involving individuals in improving all aspects of the organization's operations.

The rest of this chapter overviews the four building blocks of a healthy organization – vibrant workplaces, inspired employees, positive culture, and inspired leadership – and their interconnections. I illustrate how these building blocks contribute to higher levels of well-being and performance. This leads to sustainable success, which is how organizations can continue to benefit all stakeholders in future.

Vibrant Workplaces

To emphasize, a vibrant workplace is at the core of a healthy organization. Most successful organizations today have policies and programs in place designed to keep their employees safe and healthy. Increasingly, safety and health are viewed from the perspective of total physical, mental, and emotional wellness. This is my starting point for defining a vibrant workplace. The next plateau of wellness is attainable only by addressing the job characteristics, relationship qualities, work environments, and organizational supports known to shape positive employee experiences and develop performance capabilities. At the end of the work day or week, employees' well-being is enriched by their knowing they have made a meaningful contribution to a larger purpose.

Let us look more closely at the specific features of relationships, jobs, work environments, and organizational supports that constitute a vibrant workplace:

- *Jobs*: Employees have the autonomy to direct their own work, which they find both challenging and meaningful. Employees have ample opportunity to learn and to develop and apply their skills and abilities on the job. They know how their role fits in and makes a difference. Compensation and other rewards are fair and at a decent level.
- *Relationships*: Mutual respect characterizes working relationships among co-workers and between employees and managers. People trust each other and are committed to a shared vision and mission. Employees experience a sense of belonging because the workplace is a true community.
- *Environments*: The work environment is open, collaborative, and participatory. There is a premium on two-way communication throughout the organization. Employees have meaningful input into decisions affecting them. All employees' contributions are valued and recognized. Work is team based and cooperative.
- *Supports*: Supervisors support employees to succeed in their jobs,

develop their talents, and have a balanced life. Employees have adequate facilities, equipment, tools, and other resources needed to do their job well. There are appropriate policies and programs in place to promote health, safety, and effective human resource management practices.

Notice that few of these key ingredients specifically refer to health. Thus, a vibrant workplace is more than a healthy or safe workplace. It is all about the drivers of well-being and performance. For example, two major workplace challenges today are work/life imbalance and job stress. These issues are highlighted in media reports of employees not taking their vacations, working unpaid overtime because of job insecurity, younger workers' reluctance to become managers because of burnout fears, and the blurring of boundaries between personal and work time by 'smart' phones such as the BlackBerry.

Job stress and work/life imbalance are catch-all labels for a range of unhealthy and unproductive workplace conditions that undermine quality of work life, performance, and socially responsible business practices. Solutions to stress and imbalance require action aimed at the ingredients of a vibrant workplace – which essentially is the mirror image of an unhealthy, dysfunctional, and unproductive workplace. The most effective solutions to stress and imbalance involve finding the right mix of job autonomy, decision input, support, resources, and flexibility to offset job demands. Thus, by taking actions that address the root causes of stress and work/life imbalance, managers and human resources professionals will not only reduce workplace risks to both employee well-being and performance, but will be creating a more vibrant workplace.

Inspired Employees

Vibrant workplaces are the contexts in which employees in any position or corporate level are able to thrive at work. A vibrant workplace inspires employees to continually develop and apply their capabilities to deliver excellent results. Employees not only achieve their personal health and wellness goals – most of all, being highly satisfied with their jobs and employer – but they also learn and collaborate, two activities essential for an organization to fully tap into its human capabilities.

Workers who feel inspired actively learn, share their knowledge, and apply their skills. They collaborate effectively with co-workers, customers, and partners to ensure the highest quality of services or products. And they are able to adapt to changes in the business environment, customers' needs and preferences, and within the organization. They look forward to coming to work each day because they know they can make a difference, grow personally, and feel the pride of meaningful accomplishments. They do so within a web of supportive relationships, composed of co-workers, their immediate supervisor and the management group to whom they or their team reports, informal networks of colleagues, and their clients or customers. Experiencing work in this way, an employee moves beyond simply being engaged in her or his job.

Beyond Engagement

Engagement now sits alongside strategy as one of the most overused and fuzzy terms in the management vocabulary. Let us consider a definition of engagement that reflects what managers really want employees to experience in their work: 'Engagement is above and beyond simple satisfaction with the employment arrangement or basic loyalty to the employer – characteristics that most companies have measured for many years. Engagement, in contrast, is about passion and commitment – the willingness to invest oneself and expend one's discretionary effort to help the employer succeed.'[6]

What does it mean to invest oneself and give discretionary effort? Today, organizations need more than extra effort. Rather, they need employees who can be creative, innovative, think and act proactively, and find ways to exceed customers' expectations. Inspired employees do more than give extra effort. They channel their passion for their work and their commitment to the organization and its customers into how they work with others, how they acquire skills and knowledge and apply these in new ways for the benefit of the organization and its stakeholders, how they set high standards for themselves and their team, and how they anticipate and respond to internal and external change. This is a virtuous circle. The positive experiences of learning, teamwork, achieving job and career goals, and contributing to organizational success deepen that psychological state of feeling inspired.

The healthy organization model calls for a rethinking of employers' current fixation with workforce engagement. In its *2007 Global Workforce Study*, consulting firm Towers Perrin discovered that a mere 21 per cent of the 88,600 workers it surveyed in eighteen countries were engaged in their jobs. This hampers firm performance, Towers Perrin explains, by creating an 'engagement gap' between what employees are prepared to commit to and invest in their job and their employer's ability to tap into this potential. As Julie Gebauer, a Towers Perrin workforce effectiveness consultant puts it: 'Organizations ... are not getting the discretionary effort they need from their people to drive their performance and growth agendas, and it's hurting both their top and bottom lines.'[7] According to the report, the best way for senior managers to get higher levels of employee engagement is to inspire employees in their work, provide ample opportunities for skill development, build a solid reputation as a responsible corporation, and generally show an interest in their well-being.

But how do managers inspire the entire workforce of an organization? How do employees inspire each other? Answering these questions requires a clearer understanding of *how* employees' work experiences matter for business performance.

There are two reasons why employers do not achieve the engagement goals they seek. First is the confusion between engagement as an outcome and the actions, processes, and conditions that lead to this outcome. Second is the lack of a clear distinction between the behavioural and attitudinal aspects of engagement. Certainly, it is useful to know from surveys to what extent employees feel proud and passionate about their work. However, what really matters for performance is how these feelings are converted into productive workplace behaviours. What is more, these behaviours matter more than attitudes to an employee's well-being. Employee engagement surveys typically measure working conditions that lead employees to contribute to the performance of their work unit. The actual state of being engaged remains opaque. So I encourage HR and workplace wellness professionals to actively employ the concept of 'engagement.' Doing so will focus senior management's attention on healthy processes for involving (i.e., 'engaging') employees in decisions, initiatives, and changes that build more vibrant workplaces – thereby inspiring employees in their work.

The Capabilities of an Inspired Workforce

Inspiration describes how an individual experiences their work. But it exists only because an employee is in a supportive and enabling work setting. Think of the musician who practises on her own for many hours each day. This private activity provides a sense of accomplishment – getting it right, achieving higher personal standards – but what really matters for an inspired performance is the actual or virtual relationship the solo musician has with her audience, either as concert goers or listeners to her CDs or MP3 tracks. And if she performs with an ensemble, then critical to the inspirational process is her chemistry with the conductor and other musicians who together create the performance. Simply put, inspired performances depend on a web of positive relationships.

Inspired employees work collaboratively. By collaborating, individual employees and teams collectively generate and apply new knowledge and skills – leading to innovation. Management guru Peter Drucker observed that knowledge workers teach each other and learn together. Innovation flows from this collaborative teaching and learning, keeping an organization ahead of the competition or able to provide even higher levels of public service at lower costs. Richard Lyons, the chief learning officer at investment bank Goldman Sachs, defines innovation as 'fresh thinking that creates value.'[8] Innovation depends on employees taking practical insights from their knowledge and creatively applying their skills. Useable information is transmitted through interpersonal communication, a basic point that has given new relevance to what social scientists call 'social capital' and 'social networks.'

Two examples show the importance of workplace relationships to innovation. The first example takes us to a pulp and paper mill, where a paper-making machine operator retired after thirty years of service and was generously feted by his co-workers at a dinner. Within weeks of his departure, the paper-making machine malfunctioned. Facing lost production costs of about $400,000 daily, the company brought in engineers from the machine's maker to investigate the causes of the problem. Then someone thought to call the retired worker, whose first question was, 'has anyone been cleaning the paper dust from behind the machine?' This procedure is not in the operating manual, but the operator had figured it out as he mastered the machine's idiosyncrasies. He had come up with a simple innovation for keeping the machine running, but because plant communications traditionally were on a 'need to know' basis, this critical piece of knowledge remained in his head. The retired operator was passionate about keeping 'his' machine running, but a supportive context for making this private information organizational knowledge was lacking.

Another example is a telecommunications company's call centre, where hundreds of customer services representatives scramble to stay on top of a steady stream of new products and services. The company's knowledge management system, which customer service reps access online, was unable to keep up with all these changes. So the workers in this call centre invented informal ways to share their knowledge and to support each other. Recognizing that nobody could know everything about each of the new products and services, employees regularly shared their solutions and helped each other during customer calls (we hope that is happening when we are put on hold). This innovation in teamwork may seem small, but in a business where customer satisfaction drives revenues, every improvement in service counts. For the employees in this call centre, being able to devise and share their own solutions to customer problems boosted morale and instilled pride. What is more, these employees also had less stress and achieved higher call quality ratings than the company's other call centres.

Learning

Vibrant workplaces also encourage individual and group learning. Active learning is therefore a mark of the inspired employee. Leading thinkers on learning organizations agree that people learn in workplaces through a process that extends over time, is collaborative, and is based on continual knowledge acquisition and dissemination. Learning helps workers to avoid repeating mistakes, to reproduce successes, and to discover new work methods, services, or products. Harvard University's David Garvin describes 'learning facilitators' as those features of an organization and its people that support continual, widespread learning. In learning organizations, according to Garvin, employees at all levels and in all positions are able to actively acquire, interpret, and apply new knowledge or ideas. Learning facilitators include what I identify as attributes of vibrant workplaces: openly sharing and debating different perspectives, timely and accurate feedback, time and space for learning, and a 'sense of psychological safety.'[9]

There are parallels here with what often is labelled a 'learning organization.' In a learning organization, individuals and teams generate and share new knowledge, engage in critical thinking that is system focused, and are supported by a culture that values experimentation.[10] Organizational learning generates the capacity to continually improve performance. However, the learning organization concept is concerned with the connection between learning activities and work performance. While it is obviously important for companies to adapt and prosper, learning is only one feature of a healthy organization. Rather than treating learning as a defining characteristic of an organization, I see it as what inspired employees do when they are in vibrant work environments with positive cultures. In this way, learning is part of the internal dynamic of a healthy organization, contributing to employees' well-being and job satisfaction as well as their capacity to perform better.

As Peter Senge argues in *The Fifth Discipline*, his influential book on learning organizations, most organizations learn poorly because they are designed and managed in ways that actually create 'learning disabilities.'[11] These barriers to learning are visible in the failure of many large-scale organizational change initiatives, from the implementation of new IT systems to total quality management or business process reengineering. Projects like these fail to deliver desired productivity improvements because the people involved have neither the time nor the support to apply lessons from earlier systems to the new system. Learning also requires a longer-term perspective on people development, which calls for a marked departure from the short-term focus of most current workplace training programs.

Common people practices associated with learning include a long-term focus on people, supporting and developing employees, and an abiding belief that when these practices are followed, customers and shareholders benefit. For example, Graniterock is a California-based quarrying, concrete supply, and construction company with over 700 employees.[12] The company's quality goals and business plans are based on its customers' needs, efforts that have won it the National Baldridge Award for Quality. The company also places a high priority on employee development, health and welfare, and safety. Graniterock has performance measures on people development, financial performance, supplier performance, and customer needs. Work is team based, involving task forces, functional teams, and quality teams. Team members use individual development plans to track their own skill and knowledge development and to set long-term training and development goals. The company's future human resource needs and its quality objectives are linked with individual employees' aspirations and abilities. To support this approach, all managers are extensively trained in coaching and people skills. Employee development and performance are seen not as 'HR' issues, but as a shared responsibility for everyone in the organization.

Collaboration

Learning and collaboration go hand in hand. The twenty-first-century version of the learning organization can be called the collaborative organization. The twinning of learning and collaboration better reflects the realities of an emerging global economy that places a premium on creatively applying knowledge.

The project teams, business networks, and global supply chains of today's successful corporations require new ways for workers to create solutions. The emerging form of work organization in this century is post-bureaucratic. It is fluid, flexible, and ceaselessly recombining knowledge into business solutions. Some experts refer to the knowledge-based, flexible organization as a collaborative community, grounded in a shared ethic of interdependent contributions.[13] This makes trust in working relationships critical for the level of collaboration that successful businesses require. The twenty-first-century flexible organization takes many forms, such as short-term projects, supply chains, business alliances and partnerships, and outsourcing arrangements. It also can be virtual, such as communities of software developers that come together to expand open-source operating systems, such as Linux, or to create free online resources such as Wikipedia. Indeed, behind what is called Web 2.0 is any internet-based technology that enables higher levels of interaction and collaboration among users.

Being careful not to over-extrapolate from the IT world, there is still no denying the growing importance of collaboration in all businesses. Consider two cases from very different sectors: construction and health care. The industrial construction sector makes airports, pipelines, tunnels, refineries, and large facilities. Stakeholder relationships more often than not have been adversarial and the industry lags behind others in its HR practices. The sector is engineering dominated. Project management has been viewed as a way to limit project costs and marshal resources. But there is growing recognition that more cooperation, communication, and trust are needed as a basis for project success. A construction project is a complex web of short-term relationships involving different members with diverse skills. Project success depends on the strength and quality of these relationships. According to construction project management experts: 'a cooperative approach between construction organizations would bring about trust and commitment-induced efficiency, and better resource allocation and utilization which leads to increased industry performance.'[14] In short, the ability of project stakeholders to collaborate is what leads to projects being completed on time and on budget and to high technical standards.

The Mayo Clinic is an outstanding example of health care teamwork developed to a fine art. Len Berry, a Texas A&M University professor who spent months observing how the Mayo's teams serve patients, calls it simply 'a collaborative organization.'[15] While the clinic enjoys an enviable global brand and can attract leading talent, it is the Mayo's philosophy – pursuing the ideal of service ahead of profits, sincere concern for the welfare of each patient, and continuing interest among staff in each other's professional development – in which collaboration is grounded. At the Mayo, it takes a team to care for a patient. Collaborative patient care is supported through recruitment, leadership development and training, and infrastructure (from IT systems to physical work space). And it infuses the culture. When the Mayo conducted focus groups with patients, their families, staff, and volunteers to document the common elements in their experience, the dominant image that emerged was of people holding hands.

Whether it is online creation of wikis or open-source software, learning organizations like Graniterock, or the team-based health care practised by the Mayo Clinic, such examples point to a common feature in healthy organizations: people are inspired by opportunities to learn, collaborate, and contribute. Through these activities, people in a healthy organization also are resilient in the face of change. Indeed, they will be better able to anticipate and adapt to change. The Mayo Clinic trains for the future by focusing on the needs of tomorrow's patients. This orientation towards the future is also part and parcel of innovation, which demands thinking ahead to anticipate needs.

Culture and Leadership

Two other building blocks of healthy organizations – culture and leadership – are intertwined. A positive culture exudes the high value placed on employees, customers, and society. Inclusive leadership practises these values. It is a mindset that everyone in the organization has a responsibility to improve the workplace as the route to better business results – and a better society.

Culture and Leadership in Action

Baptist Health Care is a good illustration of how a positive culture and shared leadership for making improvements support employees to achieve excellent results. Baptist Health Care employs 5,500 workers in five acute-care hospitals, nursing homes, mental health facilities, and outpatient centres in Pensacola, Florida. Baptist Health Care attributes its current high levels of service excellence to the transformation of its culture and work environment, guided by three principles: employee satisfaction, patient satisfaction, and leadership development. It began this transformation in 1996 with the goal of improving the poor quality of its health services. Patient satisfaction was in the 18th percentile, positive employee morale was at 44 per cent, and turnover was 27 per cent annually. The five directions of transformation were creating and maintaining a great culture, selecting and retaining great employees, committing to service excellence, continually developing great leaders, and hardwiring success through systems of accountability. As a result of succeeding in all these areas, by 2003 Baptist Health Care was in the 99th percentile in patient satisfaction, positive employee morale was 83 per cent, and turnover had dropped to 14 per cent.

Baptist Health Care defines the key characteristics of a healthy culture as open communication, no secrets, a sense of employee ownership, and no excuses.[16] Responsibility for renewing the culture was handed over to employee-led committees. There are teams on culture, communication, customer loyalty, employee loyalty, and physician loyalty. Teams use a variety of measures to create transparency and accountability for key goals. Regular surveys of employees, physicians, and patients inform continual communication and action planning. People practices are consistent with the values, meeting employees' work/life needs.

CEO Al Stubblefield sums up the Baptist Health Care approach, emphasizing the importance of reinventing the organization's culture: 'At Baptist Health Care, we recognize the strong correlation between employee commitment and customer satisfaction. We know that happy, committed employees work more productively and provide better service. By valuing and recognizing our staff, we harness the power of motivation and generate sustained levels of achievement.'[17] Baptist Health Care mapped its own route to a vibrant workplace that inspires its staff to deliver excellent health care services. This, in brief, is the healthy organization value chain in action.

Better Workplaces

Baptist Health Care is on *Fortune* magazine's annual list of 100 Best Companies to Work For In America and has won awards for the quality of its patient care. Some of my other examples also are on the *Fortune* list, namely, Graniterock, Mayo Clinic, and SAS. The list is based on research by Great Place to Work Institute, a global workplace consulting firm that compiles annual 'best workplaces' lists in North and South America, Europe, Australia, and Asia. Because the *Fortune* list has been published annually since 1998 and features some of the most successful and widely admired publicly traded companies in the United States, we can gain useful lessons about what makes these companies inspiring to work for. The main insight from research on the *Fortune* list is that positive workplace cultures drive superior performance.

Great workplaces have high-trust cultures with strong core values, such as respect, fairness, and integrity. Great Place to Work Institute's research shows that employees trust managers who are concerned about their well-being, listen and respond to their input, are open and honest about change, and consistently reflect the organization's values. Trust is a fragile property of all employee-management relationships. The level of trust in workplace makes the difference between mediocre and exceptional performance. Employees who trust the people they work for also have pride in their work and feel a true sense of camaraderie with co-workers. The synergy between trust, pride, and camaraderie inspires employees to be creative and innovative. They are more likely to take the kind of risks expected of entrepreneurial business owners. More than three-quarters of the employees in companies on the *Fortune* list of 100 Best Companies to Work for in America look forward to coming to work every day. Most other organizations are lucky to achieve half that level of enthusiasm.

Evidence for the culture-performance link comes from independent financial analysts and academic researchers who have combed through the financial results for companies on the *Fortune* list.[18] The Russell Investment Group has calculated the annualized returns for the '100 Best' and the stock market (the S&P 500 and the Russell 3000 stock indexes). Between 1998 and 2007 a portfolio that had equal dollar amounts of stock in the companies on the 1998 list would have had 10.65 per cent annual returns if held until 2006, compared with rates of return of about 6 per cent for the two market indices. If the portfolio of '100 Best' companies was reset each year to reflect changes on the *Fortune* list, the annualized rate of return jumped to 14.16 per cent, or 2.3 times the market average.

Academics also have put the *Fortune* list through rigorous tests to see if the positive employee relationships – what financial experts call 'intangible assets' – influence market performance. One study compared the stock returns, return on assets, and ratio of market to book value of equity for fifty companies on the 100 Best list and fifty market peers (based on size, industry, operating revenues) not on the list.[19] On all measures, the 100 Best firms outperformed their peers. This better performance enables firms on the 100 Best list to provide the working conditions and perks that attract and retain talented and inspired workers. Amplifying these findings, research by Alex Edmans at the University of Pennsylvania's Wharton School shows that a portfolio of stocks from the 1998 list of 100 Best earned more than double the market return over an eight-year period.[20] In short, investing in people pays off over the long term.

Sustainable Success

An organization's future will be bleak indeed if it burns out employees, exhausts credit lines, alienates customers, acts unethically, and is irresponsible towards the environment. Quite simply, these practices deplete key resources, from operating capital and people to reputation. Failure is likely. By contrast, organizations that thrive constantly regenerate their resources. This requires long-term and holistic thinking, exactly as we have come to view the challenges facing the natural environment. Organizations, too, are fragile ecosystems. Continued success depends on renewing the fine balance needed between culture, people practices, systems, and structures.

I use the term 'sustainable success' to link financial, people, and ethical goals. This revises the triple bottom-line view of 'people, planet, profits' by highlighting how organizations can renew themselves. In this regard, organizations need to renew the capabilities of their workforce and they need to renew their relationships with customers and communities. At the top of the healthy organization value chain, the links between people and performance also benefit communities. Employees' pride comes from contributing to excellent products or services, as well as from being part of an organization that 'gives back' to the community by supporting public initiatives. I elaborate these points in chapter 7. For now, I encourage you to take a look at how local and national community-based non-profit organizations and charities are forming closer partnerships with businesses. A selling point for such partnerships is that they provide a way to realize corporate commitments to social responsibility and create employee volunteering opportunities. But none of this is possible, of course, without success in basic business terms. That is precisely why the vibrant workplace is at the heart of my healthy organization model. These kinds of workplaces are the generators of both economic and social performance.

Stronger People-Performance Links

There is a plain truth about organizational performance: enabling people to contribute their best work translates into better organizational results. This point is confirmed in studies involving many different organizations. Research shows that a cluster of working conditions and management practices, similar to what I call a vibrant workplace, encourages employees to achieve higher levels of job performance. In short, people-performance links can be made stronger, providing the basis for continued success.

An article in the *Journal of Applied Psychology* used Gallup organization data from 198,514 employees in 7,939 business units in thirty-six companies to test the relationship between employees' overall job satisfaction and their level of engagement in the performance of the business unit.[21] Business performance was measured by customer satisfaction, profitability, revenues, turnover, and safety (lost-time work injuries). Business units performed better when employees were satisfied and had managers and working conditions that engaged them. A book by two Gallup consultants, *12: The Elements of Great Managing*,[22] outlines the twelve key engagement drivers. These include clear job expectations, the resources needed to do the job, recognition, supportive supervisors and co-workers who care, doing what you do best, opportunities to learn and develop, connection to the company's mission, and having decision input.

Similar conclusions were reached by David Sirota, Louis Mischkind, and Michael Irwin Meltzer in their book, *The Enthusiastic Employee*.[23] Sirota and his colleagues view high employee morale as the key to a firm's performance. They extensively surveyed employees' attitudes as a way to help organizations improve their effectiveness. Employees' experiences of equity (being treated justly), achievement (doing challenging and skilled work, being recognized for and taking pride in one's contributions, and being proud to work for the company), and camaraderie (positive and cooperative relationships with co-workers) are strongly associated with both morale and performance. Companies with high morale, measured by overall employee satisfaction, performed about 20 per cent better than their industry peers. Enthusiastic workers also improve quality, reduce defects, and boost customer satisfaction and sales. The management practices that have the biggest positive impact on morale are actions addressing employees' needs for equity, achievement, and camaraderie.

For additional evidence of how vibrant workplaces produce healthy outcomes, we can turn to studies of high-performance workplaces (HPW).[24] These are productive and innovative firms that place human resources at the centre of their business strategy. As Jeffrey Pfeffer, a Stanford University organizational expert, explains: 'The fundamental premise of high performance management systems is that organizations perform at a higher level when they are able to tap the ideas, skill and effort of all their people.'[25] HPWs have flexible work systems that provide workers with considerable support and scope to make decisions and provide input. Thus, another label for a HPW is a high-involvement or high-trust workplace.

Indeed, there are parallels between a vibrant workplace and Gallup's data on employee engagement, Sirota et al.'s emphasis on employee morale, and high-performance workplace studies. But these approaches lack two main ingredients of sustainable success. First, they do not address whether the workplace conditions leading to higher job performance contribute to employees' overall health and wellness. Second, there is no community connection. The advantage of the healthy organization model, and the value chain described earlier, is that performance, wellness, and community benefits are interwoven.

Healthier Employees and Communities

Let us briefly consider these other links in the healthy organization value chain. The dynamics of a healthy organization generate benefits for the communities in which it operates. For example, healthier employees are less likely to use health care services. This has important implications for publicly funded health services and for employer-provided health benefit costs. The supportive work environment of a healthy organization helps employees to enjoy a fulfilling personal and family life. Employees have more time and energy to contribute to raising their children, assisting their aging parents, and volunteering in community activities that matter to them. The philosophy of a healthy organization is, above all, people focused, so there is consistency between treating employees and customers well and being a responsible corporate citizen. In short, a healthy organization's relationships with its external stakeholders will generate mutually beneficial outcomes.

The people-based values of a healthy organization also are evident externally in socially and environmentally responsible business practices. These values and ethics require longer-term, holistic thinking that balances profits (or in the public sector, 'value for money'), with what is good for community stakeholders. By doing good in this way, corporations can shore up public trust that has been eroded over this decade by a string of Enron-like corporate scandals up to the 2008 Wall Street-induced global financial crisis. They also are addressing a long list of consumer and investor concerns, from human rights and fair trade to a reduced carbon footprint, which were barely on the radar ten years ago.

As companies sort out how to strengthen their ethical standards and take actions that make meaningful contributions to good causes, employees, too, are holding employers to higher standards. While corporate responsibility comes in many forms, what is pivotal to 'walking the talk' is having a strong connection with human resource goals and practices. Branding a company as a responsible corporate citizen signals to prospective employees – especially young recruits – that the company cares, treats others well, and reflects their personal values. It also sets the bar higher for how employers actually support employees to personally contribute to the community, on company time and on their own time. In high-pressure workplaces that demand long hours, there is an obvious disconnect with corporate ethics of supporting local charities through volunteering.

Healthy organizations have figured out ways to integrate corporate social responsibility with their people practices. As critics have noted, CSR without HR is PR. This is a trap into which I have seen a number of organizations fall. For example, it is fine for senior executives to make time in their schedules to be on the board of the local United Way or other prominent community charities. Yet front-line employees are expected not only to make personal donations, but beyond that, to get personally involved in fund-raising campaigns, which their workloads and the emphasis the company places on achieving operational goals, not on community service, make extremely difficult. The World Bank's definition of CSR places employees at the centre: 'Corporate social responsibility is the commitment of businesses to contribute to sustainable economic development by working with employees, their families, the local community and society at large to improve their lives in ways that are good for business and for development.'[26] New research indeed confirms that companies with comprehensive CSR practices do have stronger employee relations.[27]

Clearly we need an expanded value chain for organizational performance, one that includes employees, customers, shareholders, and the community. Essentially, the issue comes down to integrity. If an organization claims to be a good corporate citizen committed to improving the quality of life, then how can it not apply the same principle internally? And if a company emphasizes to its employees the importance of open, respectful communication, how can it not apply this principle to employees' dealings with community stakeholders? Readers may well answer, 'it's not that simple.' But as I show in later chapters, by consistently and thoroughly living their values, healthy organizations expand their value chain to include employees and communities.

Making Well-Being a Priority

To recap, a healthy organization cultivates vibrant workplaces in which employees feel inspired. This process builds capabilities for ongoing success. The criteria for success will vary, or course, depending on the size, sector, and location of the organization. But generally speaking, benefits will flow to employees, customers, and owners and to the larger community in which the business operates. In short, the healthy organization can achieve a triple win.

For employees, benefits can be measured in terms of overall health and wellness, work/life balance, professional development and personal growth, and a generally high quality of work life. For the organization, success would include financial performance, operating efficiency, reduced human capital risks and costs, and future sustainability. There also are community benefits. The people-focused values of a healthy organization are expressed in a range of socially and environmentally responsible actions, from charitable contributions, to support for employee volunteering, to reduction of the organization's carbon footprint. And by contributing to a healthy and skilled workforce, the organization is reducing the burden on publicly funded health care and building capabilities that individual employees can carry into their personal, family, and community activities.

I also have emphasized that the healthy organization model invites us to take an integrative, future-oriented view of workplaces. The model provides an opportunity to connect internal people practices and values with how the organization operates within its communities. The concept of a value chain is a useful tool for thinking about how multiple internal and external stakeholders can be part of and benefit from the activities of the organization. A healthy organization is responsive to the needs of its employees, its social and physical environment, and most important, the needs of its customers or clients. Above all, it strives to improve the well-being of all these stakeholders. As chapter 2 will show, the very idea of a healthy organization has its roots in workplace health promotion. Indeed, the limits of the workplace health promotion paradigm are what led me to the expanded view of well-being and performance captured in the vision of a healthy organization.

2 Beyond Workplace Health Promotion

Visitors to Singapore are impressed by the city-state's economic dynamism, high living standards, and cosmopolitanism – not to mention its clean sidewalks and efficient public transit system. The Singapore government and business community have done many innovative things to build a knowledge-based commercial, financial, and manufacturing powerhouse. One of the country's success factors is the active promotion of healthy employees in healthy workplaces.

The 2008 biennial Singapore HEALTH awards, which I attended as a speaker and workshop leader, offer a window on the potential of workplace health promotion to take a more organizational focus.[1] The award, which stands for 'Helping Employees Achieve Life-Time Health,' is sponsored by the government's Health Promotion Board. The goal is a healthier workforce and ultimately higher economic productivity and living standards. In 2008 there were 358 public and private sector employers receiving awards in four categories: bronze, silver, gold, and platinum. To start the ball rolling, the Singapore government provides matching grants to employers to fund health promotion programs and it supports internal 'health facilitators' to be change agents. Beyond the government funding, what really seems to motivate employers and employees to participate in the HEALTH awards process is the useful feedback they receive, the public recognition from being an award winner, and recruitment and retention benefits. Also, for those in the gold and platinum levels, there are performance dividends.

Listening to the stories of the companies and public sector organizations at the awards event, I was struck by how many have progressed from basic health promotion towards their own vision of a 'healthy organization.' Bronze award recipients typically are newcomers to the idea of health promotion. These companies and government agencies have a mix of programs that encourage healthy eating, physical activity, mental well-being, chronic disease management, prevention of communicable disease, and smoking cessation – the basics in a comprehensive health promotion approach to workplace wellness. But this year's bronze award winners aspire to win a silver, gold, or even platinum award next time. As organizations move to higher levels, the distinction between health and organizational performance dissolves. At the platinum level, one sees organizations with healthy cultures. Business strategies incorporate employee health and well-being, providing a clear competitive advantage. And managers intuitively understand that a healthy and a high-performing workforce are one and the same.

Typical of platinum award winners are Nanyang Polytechnic and NatSteel Holdings. The chair of the workplace health promotion committee at Nanyang Polytechnic talked about the importance of core values and policies that supported a nurturing and caring culture and 'borderless' teamwork – factors that enabled successful workplace health promotion as well as innovation. The vice-president of human resources at NatSteel Holdings, which manufactures steel products for residential, commercial and infrastructure projects, described the sophisticated tools the company uses to assess needs and track and report progress on a wide range of workforce health and well-being issues. The goal is to create a 'happy, motivated and challenged' workforce and to galvanize the company's reputation as 'a great place to work.' These examples show that by challenging employers and employees to step forward and be evaluated and recognized for their workplace health promotion efforts, the Singapore government has put in place enabling conditions for truly healthy organizations. The more significant lesson is that employers and employees have taken up this challenge. As a result, workplace health promotion is a springboard for moving to a higher level of well-being and performance.

This chapter makes the case for a healthy organization by exploring the benefits and limitations of workplace health promotion. As in Singapore, workplace health promotion has taken root in many countries and businesses in the past decade, generating pent-up demand for an organizational approach to employee well-being. Workplace health promotion initiatives are, in my view, a launching pad for achieving better employee well-being and organizational performance. Workplace health promotion can put in place the building blocks for healthy organizations, contributing to more vibrant workplaces that actively involve employees in shaping a positive, supportive, and wellness-oriented corporate culture. As we saw in the Singapore HEALTH Awards, the next step for employers that have implemented wellness programs is to leverage them to uncover the organizational factors influencing success. This chapter offers change agents who are seeking to build on current health promotion approaches in their own workplace the following guideposts:

1. There is a solid business case for comprehensive workplace health promotion and prevention programs.
2. There is good potential to expand workplace health promotion by addressing the underlying causes of presenteeism, stress, and work/life imbalance.
3. Current health promotion initiatives can be a stepping stone to a more holistic organizational perspective that links employee well-being with performance.
4. For companies to move in this direction, employee health and wellness must be viewed as an organizational asset that contributes to a skilled and motivated workforce.
5. Also critical is understanding the root causes of health and performance, especially the psychological and social aspects of work.

The Wellness Paradox

Champions of workplace wellness must resolve a basic paradox in order to make progress: despite rising investments by growing numbers of employers in employee health and wellness, the performance benefits are limited mainly to savings related to lower absenteeism and benefit costs. Other innovations that have transformed workplaces – from information technology and improved knowledge management systems to business process redesign – have more visible performance payoffs, enabling people to create more value by working better. So why can similar performance benefits not flow from investments in healthier workplaces? The answer is that we have run up against the limits of health promotion.

I believe that the wellness paradox can be resolved by thinking in terms of organizational health. This approach helps us to see the value chain I laid out in chapter 1 – and shows us ways to move up that value chain.

Increasingly, managers, workplace wellness practitioners, and researchers recognize the need to examine the underlying workplace determinants of health and productivity. Actions are guided by the World Health Organization's (WHO) definition of health as complete physical, mental, and social well-being, not simply absence of disease or ill health. Job and organizational factors should, ideally, support positive mental and physical health outcomes for employees. It is widely assumed that healthy employees are more productive. It is now common, especially in the United States, to use the term 'health and productivity management' to integrate health promotion into all corporate functions from human resources, benefits, employee assistance programs, occupational health and safety, workers' compensation, organizational development, and business operations.

However, major stumbling blocks remain. Canada is typical of many countries in this regard. According to Buffett & Company Worksite Wellness Inc., the proportion of Canadian employers participating in its National Wellness Surveys that offered at least one wellness initiative to employees rose from 44 per cent in 1997 to 91 per cent by 2009.[2] Echoing international experts, Buffett & Company considers that comprehensive wellness includes multiple wellness initiatives, data analysis, employee follow-up and counselling, continual evaluation, and the calculation of return on investment. Yet relatively few employers make health and wellness a core component of their business strategy.

Employers' search for solutions to rising health and disability benefits costs has generated much rhetoric about the need to create healthier workplaces. However, action has been slower in coming. It is not that the current approach to workplace health is not paying off. Comprehensive workplace health promotion programs can reduce employee health risk factors, reduce employers' health care costs, and improve productivity. Yet most of the productivity gain is realized through reduced absenteeism.

This narrow focus fails to capture the many other sources of productivity affected by healthy or unhealthy work environment. So change agents must embrace a larger vision of a work environment in which employees thrive. Such visions are cast in terms of organizational effectiveness, performance, and social responsibility. Achieving individual well-being is a by-product of work systems, management practices, and organizational cultures that inspire employees to collaborate in the interests of customers or clients, shareholders, and the larger community.

Healthy Workplace Pay-Offs and Potential

I often am asked by managers and employees who are trying to improve their work environment: 'How do we make changes based on evidence?' 'How will we know the value of a healthier workplace?' Answers to both questions can be found in workplace health promotion research. As a brief review of these studies shows, we actually know a great deal about the kinds of changes that best contribute to healthy outcomes for individuals and organizations and the expected returns from healthy workplace investments.

Wellness Returns on Investment

A growing number of worksite health promotion programs have been subjected to rigorous cost-benefit analysis that calculates the employer's return on investment (ROI). Some studies also look at improvements in employees' health status, but it is notable from a healthy organization perspective that workplace health promotion ROI is all about employer costs. ROI is the most clear-cut 'business case' one can make for a workplace health and wellness program. And, as I show below, the business case for health promotion is compelling: reductions in employer health care costs, productivity gains, and better health outcomes for employees. The big result is improved quality of life.

We can identify three evidence-based insights about the strengths, limitations, and potential of workplace health promotion. These insights underscore the momentum that has been building for a broader organizational focus on health and performance:[3]

1. Focused worksite health promotion programs aimed at modifying an employee's diet, physical activity, and other lifestyle factors have limited results in terms of reducing health risk factors.
2. Comprehensive worksite health promotion and disease management programs generally have positive clinical and cost outcomes, showing the best results for employees who have the highest risk of heart disease and have other chronic conditions.
3. There is a growing consensus among experts that further improvements in employee well-being and organizational performance will require changes in work environments. In other words, an organizational approach is needed.

Much research exists showing the positive impact of worksite health promotion programs. We know that workplace health promotion interventions that are comprehensive, well designed, and successfully implemented will have a net positive ROI. Many studies also show that, in addition to cost savings, programs aimed at high-risk groups – such as smokers and obese individuals – contribute to improved health outcomes. So for employers, the issue is not whether to introduce such programs to reduce health risks and increase productivity, but how to design, implement and evaluate programs to achieve the best outcomes for employees and the organization.

Part of the motivation for employers to promote wellness is the potential to reduce or contain the rising costs of health benefits, thereby avoiding the alternative of cutting back benefits coverage. If anything, the recent recession prompted a line-by-line review of health benefits budgets. Employers taking the long view, as Trico Homes did, were seeking savings without reducing the benefits that are so important to retaining staff, maintaining a performance culture during tough times, and staying competitive for future recruitment.

Healthy Lifestyle Programs

Anyone working in an office, shopping mall, government facility, or large industrial site in the late 1980s and early 1990s in most parts of Canada and the United States witnessed one of the most remarkable single-issue public health initiatives ever. I remember the first winter the Canadian federal government banned smoking in all its offices in the late 1980s. As groups of smokers huddled around doorways in the frigid cold, the dark humour among bureaucrats was that pneumonia was now smokers' greatest health risk.

In fact, worksite smoking cessation policies and programs are the most widespread and successful initiatives by employers and governments to address pre-existing employee health risks. Results have been impressive: a steady decline in smoking rates in countries adopting such measures. Indeed, the elimination of smoking from most North America workplaces marks a significant public health milestone.

There is overwhelming evidence that smoking increases annual health care costs.[4] Medical costs of smoking in the United States range from 6 per cent to 14 per cent of annual personal health care costs. A study of telephone customer service workers estimated that smokers lost an average of 4.1 hours per week due to illness-related absences, short-term disability, and lost productivity (the latter is the largest component, at 3.5 hours). The Canadian Cancer Society suggests that the annual cost savings to employers when an employee quits smoking can be as high as $3,396 when absenteeism, decreased productivity from smoke breaks, and the costs of smoking facilities are included.[5]

Yet it would be a stretch to claim that companies and government departments have become high performing just because they introduced a smoking cessation campaign or set up an on-site gym. In short, beyond the health benefits to those employees who participate in these programs – and their non-smoking colleagues in the case of worksite smoking bans – there is little evidence of sustained performance benefits to organizations. However, the performance payoffs increase when single-focus programs are combined with a wider range of supports and resources that promote employee well-being.

Today, obesity has replaced smoking as the number one public health issue in the advanced industrial countries. According to the WHO, 'obesity has reached epidemic proportions globally.'[6] Some areas of North America, the United Kingdom, and Australia have seen a threefold increase in obesity rates since 1980. Obesity increases a person's risk of preventable chronic diseases, such as cardiovascular disease, hypertension, type-2 diabetes, arthritis, and some types of cancer. Direct costs of weight-related major chronic diseases to Canada's health system were estimated at nearly $1.6 billion in 2001, rising to $4.3 billion when indirect costs were included.[7] From the perspective of the healthy organization model presented in chapter 1, obesity can be seen as a societal issue that responsible employers can help to address through workplace actions. Success would be measured in terms of healthier employees, improvements in quality of life, and a more sustainable health care system.

Unlike smoking in workplaces, obesity does not impair the health of co-workers or impose fire and safety risks or added cleaning costs on employers. Consequently, employers are more reticent to directly take on what is a personal health issue. Even so, some employers are taking action to support healthy eating and exercise. Yet contributions to a more vibrant workplace will be minimal if actions to reduce obesity are just that – solving the obesity problem by targeting individuals' lifestyles. However, if such initiatives take the shape of employee-led activity challenges – such as using the stairs instead of the elevator, counting daily steps on pedometers, or seeing which group can 'walk around the world' – then we are into a whole other realm of fun, team-building, and generating a healthy culture.

Yet this approach may be expecting a great deal, because studies of the benefits of fitness programs find mixed results. Potential net financial benefits for employers who introduce fitness programs include reduced health care costs, absenteeism, injury rates, and turn-over and improved job performance, productivity, and morale.[8] Reviews of the financial impact show cost/benefit ratios ranging from $0.76 to $3.43 and from $1.15 to $5.52 when fitness programs are part of a comprehensive health promotion strategy. The major limitation of fitness programs, however, is overall low participation, mainly by those who are already reasonably healthy and active. What is not measured are the less visible organizational benefits, such as increased satisfaction, a sense of camaraderie, and the feeling that this is a fun place to work.

A final lifestyle program we will consider is stress management. Seminars on coping with job demands or work/family tension may offer useful personal tips. However, there is no evidence of real health and productivity pay-offs. Despite their popularity, stress management and other programs aimed at increasing an individual's coping skills generally are ineffective over the long run if they address superficial issues, not root causes. There are few, if any, lasting benefits for the organization and limited benefits for the individuals involved.[9] I am not suggesting that these types of programs be scrapped. After all, they do address employees' information needs, and they may signal to employees that the company cares about their well-being. But unless such stress-reduction sessions launch further discussions about more systemic solutions, such as changes in workload or job redesign, any benefits will be transitory.

Addressing Chronic Health Conditions

A goal of some workplace wellness programs is to help employees better manage pre-existing health conditions. Increasingly, employers see these health management programs as one way to contain rising health-related costs and meet the needs of an older and more diverse workforce, which includes more individuals with disabilities and chronic health conditions. Depending on the size and demographic profile of the workforce, there could be substantial benefits to employees and the bottom line from introducing a chronic-disease management program.

Allergies are a common chronic condition that affects people's health and work performance. One study of telephone customer service operators at a large U.S. financial services corporation examined the relationship between allergies and productivity using data from a computerized productivity measurement system.[10] The productivity of workers with allergies decreased as much as 10 per cent during peak pollen season. Based on average daily compensation at the time, this represented a loss of $52 per affected employee per week. Employees using antihistamines were more productive than were those not using medication. The researchers calculated the return on investment of providing drugs to allergy sufferers (average cost of $18 per week) to be 2:1.

If a program focusing on chronic health conditions is an employer's main healthy workplace initiative, it will have little impact beyond the productivity and cost benefits just noted. The same goes for fitness facilities or smoking cessation. As I explain below, a single-issue approach using a stand-alone initiative is less effective than when it is integrated within a comprehensive set of measures to promote wellness as part of a company's broader commitment to a healthy and productive workforce. When positioned within a comprehensive health promotion strategy, each specific component reinforces the message that the company cares about the well-being of its employees.

Targeting High-Risk Employees

Professor Vic Strecher, a health behaviour expert at the University of Michigan, described to a workplace health promotion conference audience a U.S. manufacturer 88 per cent of whose health care costs went to a small group of seriously unhealthy employees who comprised only 8 per cent of the company's total workforce. Another 40 per cent of employees were considered 'at risk' of developing a range of serious health problems, such as heart disease or diabetes. Numbers like these make the case for designing workplace health promotion programs that target high-risk employees.

Indeed, there is solid evidence for targeting high-risk employees.[11] For example, one study used a randomized control trial method (considered the 'gold standard' design among medical researchers) to assess the impact of a comprehensive worksite health promotion program on full-time, blue-collar workers in a large, multi-location industrial firm.[12] Workers in the program received support and resources on healthy lifestyles, fitness, nutrition, stress management, smoking cessation, health risk surveys, safety, and counselling. Workers in the two-year program had 11,726 fewer disability days, compared with similar workers at non-program sites. This amounts to a return on investment of $2.05 for every dollar invested, just in terms of reduced absenteeism. Other studies tracking high-risk employees over several years find similar benefits from comprehensive programs aimed at health-risk reduction:[13]

- A University of Michigan study at Steelcase Corporation found that for every employee who had excessive alcohol consumption, the firm spent $597 more annually in health costs. For every employee who was sedentary, the cost was $488 and hypertension cost $327.
- The Employee Benefit Research Institute determined that Citibank reduced health risks and saved between $4.56 and $4.73 for every dollar spent on its health education and awareness program.
- Dow Chemical's workplace disease management programs, targeting mainly individual employees who have chronic conditions, resulted in median benefits over time of over $8 for every dollar invested.
- Eight organizations in Halifax, Canada, calculated an ROI of $1.64 for every dollar invested in a comprehensive wellness program designed to reduce the risk of heart disease and even more for higher-risk employees such as smokers.

These ROI levels may be the best we can expect. For one thing, employees are becoming sensitive to how much meddling by their employers in personal health matters they will tolerate.[14] While the latest programs offer more powerful tools, they also lead to heightened concerns about privacy and individual choice. Sophisticated health-risk assessment (HRA) tools help high-risk employees to develop the motivation to change their behaviour and remove barriers, such as thinking they are unable to change. This requires 'smart' HRAs that personalize the information, resources, and approach depending on an individual's attitudes, strengths, and readiness for change. Because these tools require larger investments, employers expect more employees to 'voluntarily' participate. Some U.S. employers, such as courier service UPS, pay employees to complete the HRA. Others require it.

An Organizational View of Health and Wellness

We've seen that individual wellness – optimal physical, psychological,

Figure 2.1 Strategic impact of health and wellness

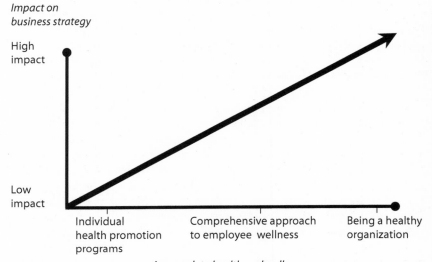

Impact on
business strategy

High
impact

Low
impact

Individual
health promotion
programs

Comprehensive approach
to employee wellness

Being a healthy
organization

Approach to health and wellness

and emotional well-being – is the goal of a comprehensive approach to health promotion. Wellness is promoted, whereas illness and injury are prevented. Wellness focuses on positive states of being, not simply the absence of illness, disease, or injury – although this, too, is a goal, as we saw in studies reviewed earlier. Individuals' overall quality of life depends in large part on whether they experience wellness.

A simple question can move us beyond this individual focus: what are the organizational benefits of wellness? To help in answering this question, figure 2.1 shows that as organizations expand their focus from stand-alone programs (occupational health and safety being the most common example) to a comprehensive health promotion approach, they can expect a modest impact on performance. Most of the managers and employees who have participated in my workshops locate their organization at or near the middle of the continuum in figure 2.1, because they take a comprehensive workplace health promotion approach. This would include, for example, a wellness committee, a wellness coordinator, and a range of programs and policies aimed at promoting healthy diets, weights, nutrition, lifestyles, and, increasingly, an emphasis on mental health promotion within the worksite.

Many of my workshop participants also aspire to a healthy organization ideal, recognizing that getting there may be a long and winding road. These managers and employees are looking for opportunities to realize deeper organizational benefits – such as more inspired employees and a reputation as an excellent workplace – from healthy workplace investments. Comprehensive wellness programs target underlying attitudes and behaviours that influence an individual's lifestyle: smoking, being sedentary, eating too much junk food, or not getting adequate sleep. Fewer, however, look at work environment influences on individual health and wellness. That is why workplace health experts have concluded that further progress is possible only through expanding the individual health promotion model to include workplace cultures, relationships, systems, and structures. As one workplace fitness expert stated: 'Positively influencing behaviour in the workplace requires a shift in focus from individual/personal behaviour change to more strategic, comprehensive approaches ... This will require a shift in thinking, so that "interventions" are not seen as short-term programs, but as part of the culture of the workplace.'[15] Adopting this expansive approach is a natural next step beyond a health-promotion focus. If you are looking for opportunities in your health-promotion programs to energize a healthy organization strategy, you must be clear about how they reflect the organization's values. And you also must show how a healthier work environment will support employees to implement the corporate strategy.

In this regard, consider using health promotion programs to strengthen culture and leadership, two of the building blocks of a healthy organization. Look for ways to maximize the non-health spin-offs from any workplace health initiative. Meeting employees' health and wellness needs becomes easier if they are active participants in the entire process, not merely end-users of health resources. In this way, employees take ownership – in other words, leadership – for the means and the ends. And as managers and employees work together to make the work environment healthier (and safer, too), the trust this establishes will result in more cooperative workplace relationships. Over time, higher levels of trust will foster a wider range of workplace improvements. For example, in unionized settings, the joint design and implementation of comprehensive health promotion programs has yielded more than reduced employee health risks and benefit costs. Positive results also flow from how the program is developed. Both the United Auto Workers in the United States and their Canadian counterpart, the

Canadian Auto Workers (CAW), have addressed workforce wellness issues through union-management cooperation, collaborative problem solving, and front-line employee 'ownership.'[16] Programs had active employee involvement through worksite committees and consultations to identify areas of need. What is especially innovative about the CAW-Chrysler wellness program is how it reaches out to the community. In fact, the local public health unit was a partner in a program called 'Tune Up Your Heart,' aimed at individuals at high risk of heart disease. While at first glance, these health-risk reduction programs resemble others in large worksites, this observation is based only on the 'what' of the program. An organizational health perspective provides useful lessons on the 'how,' highlighting the importance of shared leadership and a culture of cooperation.

Limitations of Workplace Health Promotion

In more general terms, putting in place the building blocks for a healthy organization requires that you recognize the limitations of workplace health promotion initiatives. With this recognition comes a shift in thinking, from an individual to an organizational focus. There are four basic limitations:

- Workplace wellness often is stand-alone, not fully integrated with other human resource management policies and practices to enhance the work environment.
- A narrow focus on individuals' health-related attitudes and behaviours often excludes workplace factors that affect employee health and well-being.
- Productivity benefits come mainly from reduced absenteeism and lower employee health care costs – and we know there is more to productivity.
- There is an accounting focus on ROI, rather than on attempts to broaden corporate thinking in ways that place wellness at the core of an organization's strategy.

For thinking to shift, senior managers must come to view employee wellness as a strategic goal. Currently, employee health promotion typically is viewed by management as just that – a health issue. Yet many experts propose what amounts to a seamless integration of health into a company's business strategy. As the editor-in-chief of the *American Journal of Health Promotion* explains: 'human performance is higher when people are physically and emotionally able to work and have the desire to work. Higher levels of human performance lead to higher levels of productivity, which in turn can lead to higher profits.'[17] The healthy organization of the future will infuse health promotion into all corporate functions, from human resources, benefits, employee assistance programs, occupational health and safety, workers' compensation, organizational development, and business operations.

Comparing Health Promotion and Organizational Perspectives

Let us look in detail at the differences between the workplace health promotion and healthy organization perspectives. I compare these approaches side by side in figure 2.2. Try using figure 2.2 as an assessment tool for identifying where your organization lies on the dimensions listed down the left side of the table. On each of the dimensions, assess whether your workplace is closer to one column than to the other, noting how this position may vary for each of the dimensions.

In short, workplace health promotion programs can be transformational. Change agents can use these programs to cultivate the holistic thinking, longer time horizon, and wider employee involvement that characterize a healthy organization. Most workplace health promotion initiatives can provide the momentum for an organizational approach. So the comparison between the two perspectives in figure 2.2 is not as cut and dried as it first may appear. You may lean more to one side than the other on specific dimensions. Knowing where your workplace has moved to on the organization side of the continuum is an important piece of information for planning change.

Studies have tested the healthy organization framework, with encouraging results. For example, a study at a large manufacturing firm in the United States identified a cluster of management practices – a commitment to continual improvement, having a well developed HR strategy, and fair pay and rewards – that predicted both organizational effectiveness and employee stress outcomes.[18] In addition, organizations whose cultures are characterized by innovation, cooperation, and a sense of belonging are higher on both effectiveness and wellness measures. Indeed, many of the job and work environment factors directly related to health and well-being reflect an organization's entire approach to human resource management. These include physical working conditions, ergonomics, work schedules, work content, work group relations, supervision, training and development, economic rewards, and organizational culture.

Figure 2.2. Comparing key dimensions of workplace health promotion and healthy organization perspectives

Dimension	Workplace health promotion	Healthy organization
	———————————————————▶	
• Target	• Individual	• Organizational
• Change model	• Health promotion	• Organization development
• Scope and focus	• Program based	• Systemic and holistic
• Time frame	• Short and medium term	• Ongoing and long term
• Individual benefits	• Reduced health risks	• Improved quality of work life and capabilities
• Organizational benefits	• Lower health benefit costs and absenteeism, improved morale	• Higher performance, effectiveness, and sustainability
• Community benefits	• Enhanced reputation and employer brand	• Tangible and sustainable benefits
• Links to strategy	• Part of people strategy or HR plan	• How the business operates
• Links to culture	• Reflects organizational values	• Embedded in corporate philosophy and values
• Responsibility	• Formal roles (e.g., Wellness Committee, Workplace Health Coordinator)	• Shared responsibility and accountability
• Leadership	• Usually top down	• Distributed throughout organization

Beyond this evidence, the idea of a healthy organization has strong intuitive appeal and this is sparking innovation in workplaces. The health care sector is adopting healthy organization thinking. In the United States, NIOSH's healthy organization model (introduced in chapter 1) has guided changes in health care work environments as a way to improve the quality of patient care.[19] This plan requires expanding continual quality improvement to include the quality of the work environment. In Canada, a coalition of professional and employer groups formed the Quality Worklife – Quality Healthcare Collaborative (QWQHC). It defines a healthy health care workplace as 'a work setting that takes a strategic and comprehensive approach to providing the physical, cultural, psychosocial and work/job design conditions that maximize health and well-being of health care providers, quality of patient outcomes and organizational performance.'[20] Making an explicit connection between working conditions and quality health care marks a significant shift in thinking, given that health care providers traditionally have put patients' needs ahead of their own health and wellness.

Leveraging Workplace Health Promotion

Husky Injection Molding Systems is a global leader in high-speed moulding injection systems that produce plastic bottles as well as products for the packaging, automotive, and telecommunications industries. Husky's comprehensive approach to wellness provides employees with incentives to participate in nutrition and fitness programs. Husky has documented cost savings such as reduced absenteeism, low injury rates, reduced drug costs, low turnover, and higher productivity.[21] Its corporate headquarters, located in Canada, has a Wellness Centre staffed by professionals, its manufacturing centres around the world have fitness facilities, and company cafeterias offer healthy foods.

Robert Schad, the company's founder, personally believes in a holistic approach to health. Employee wellness grew beyond a health focus, however, becoming a corporate goal associated with innovation, competitiveness, and profits. Husky belongs in that small but growing group of organizations that give new meaning to a 'comprehensive' approach to healthy workplaces. The company's guiding principles provide a road map for its employees around the world to innovate and act in customers' best interests. Specifically, employees strive for honesty and integrity, open communication, environmental responsibility, and improved quality of community life where the company operates. Not that every CEO needs to embrace personal wellness as the founder of Husky does. But a corporate commitment from the top goes a long way towards realizing this part of the strategy and culture.

One of the guiding principles is 'people are most productive in a safe, high-quality work environment.' This principle is put into practice not only via wellness, but also in open-concept environmentally friendly building designs and people development practices. Health and wellness are part of a culture that values and nurtures many connections between people, performance, and community. As a result, Husky has been on the *Globe and Mail Report on Business* and Hewitt Associates' 50 Best Employers in Canada lists and on other '50 best' lists in Canada for corporate citizenship and environmental responsibility.

Companies like Husky view health as a long-term business priority. Practically, this attitude makes sense, because improvements take time and persistence. Workplace health promotion evaluations that track the two big pay-offs – absenteeism and employee health care costs – will require several years to show any results from a new program or policy change. Tracking a wider range of results, as companies like Husky do, requires equal patience. For example, the University of Michigan's Health Management Research Center has worked with various companies to gain a broader understanding of workplace health promotion costs and benefits.[22] To do this, the Center calculates an 'overall wellness score' that includes measures of job satisfaction, life satisfaction, and stress.

These examples show the potential for leveraging strategic, company-wide, long-term benefits from workplace health promotion. There is a positive upward spiral created as soon as a company moves from an individual to an organizational approach. Health promotion initiatives can have collateral benefits, such as improving employee satisfaction and loyalty and reducing turnover. Workforce performance can only improve.

Organizational Solutions for Wellness

It is useful, therefore, to apply an organizational health perspective to several major workplace wellness concerns: absenteeism, presenteeism, stress, and work/life imbalance. What becomes clear is that these issues have as much to do with organizational performance – or the capacity to successfully implement strategy – as they do with wellness. Furthermore, solutions depend on placing the four healthy workplace building blocks firmly in position.

Rethinking Absenteeism

Lower absenteeism accounts for the largest component of the workplace health promotion program ROI. Not surprisingly, absenteeism has caught the attention of many employers. It is on the rise, costly, and a widely used indicator of employee health and productivity. But a closer look at absenteeism shows that to uncover its root causes, the ingredients of a vibrant workplace need to be addressed. This puts workplace relationships, organizational processes, job designs, and total work rewards squarely on the change agenda.

High absenteeism imposes huge costs on employers and the economy. According to the Health and Safety Executive, work absences cost U.K. private and public sector employers £12 billion annually.[23] Estimates for Australia suggest that 3 per cent of the workforce takes unscheduled leave each day, costing $800 (Australian) per worker annually.[24] U.S. employers face estimated absenteeism-related expenses of $74 billion (U.S.) annually, including overtime and overstaffing to cover these costs.[25] In Canada, the monthly Labour Force Survey shows that absenteeism has been rising since the 1990s. Actual work time lost for personal reasons increased from the equivalent of 7.4 days per worker in 1997 to 9.7 worker days in 2006 – an estimated 102 million work days for all full-time employees.[26] This trend contrasts with a steady decline in lost-time work injuries, which no doubt helps to explain why more employers are moving beyond workplace safety to address a wider range of health and wellness issues.

Ironically, health care workplaces are among the least healthy of any industry, so employers have increasingly sought healthy workplace solutions to bring down absenteeism costs. The U.S. Veterans' Health Administration calculated the costs of absenteeism and concluded that a modest reduction in nurse absenteeism would save $17.8 million annually across all of its facilities.[27] In the Canadian province of British Columbia, absenteeism rates in health care are 73 per cent higher than the provincial average. Reducing absenteeism in British Columbia's health care workforce to the provincial average would save enough to pay for the equivalent of more than 500 full-time positions – which would benefit the public.

However, solutions to high absenteeism require more than absentee-ism management policies. Such tactics focus on symptoms and are often viewed by employees as rigid and punitive. Cost savings can be best realized by addressing the root causes within the work environment. In health care, absenteeism among nurses and physicians is related to high levels of job stress and burnout.[28] A cluster of organizational factors drives up absenteeism and erodes the quality of work life. These include workplace relationships (especially teamwork), organizational culture, the quality of supervision, workloads, scope for autonomy and decision making, and professional development opportunities. Essentially, when employees have positive experiences of these features they have a vibrant workplace – one of the cornerstones of a healthy organization.

A holistic, organizational perspective on absenteeism also is guided by corporate values. A CEO of a financial services company described how moving from a traditional sick-day model to 'care days' improved employee wellness. Time off work declined under the new approach and contributed to employee perceptions of what the CEO called a 'thriving workplace.' Through discussions with employees the company realized that the old policy forced them to call in sick for an entire day when all they needed was a few hours to attend their child's school play or take their elderly parent to a doctor's appointment. Under the care days policy, employees took only the hours they needed to care for themselves or their family members. For the company, the goal was less about reduced absenteeism costs than it was about living up to its values, which included employees' wellness and family needs.

A truly comprehensive workplace wellness strategy needs to be grounded in an understanding of the complexities of absenteeism, including its organizational causes and costs. This sets the stage for solutions based on the kind of organizational culture and support systems employees need to experience mental well-being. As such, addressing absenteeism provides an opportunity to build a healthier organization.

Present but Not Productive

Focusing on absenteeism gives an incomplete picture of employee health and productivity. Most discussions of absenteeism use binary thinking: employees are either present or absent. But this assumption is flawed. In studies at Steelcase and Xerox, University of Michigan researchers discovered that 'not all absent employees are automatically nonproductive and not all employees present are automatically 100 per cent productive.'[29] Let us explore this last point, a phenomenon known as 'presenteeism.' Professor Deb Lerner, a work disability expert at the Tufts Medical Center in Boston, describes presenteeism as 'when you appear not to be absent.' In the past few years, presenteeism has caught the attention of senior managers. Paul Hemp, writing in the *Harvard Business Review*, describes presenteeism as a $150 billion hidden cost in the United States that reflects the health problems people bring to work, such as migraines, arthritis, and back pain.[30] Hemp makes the case for employer action, arguing that presenteeism reduces corporate performance.

Presenteeism takes several forms. It can occur when a worker who has been injured or is recovering from a medical condition returns to work after disability leave. The return-to-work process monitors the individual's work limitations, supporting recovery as close to full functioning in the job as possible.[31] Presenteeism also occurs among individuals with prior health conditions, such as allergies and migraines. According to a U.S. study, presenteeism costs (based on the level of self-reported work productivity) account for 61 per cent of total costs associated with ten common health conditions: allergies, arthritis, asthma, cancer, depression, diabetes, heart disease, hypertension, migraines and headaches, and respiratory disorders.[32] This type of lost productivity exceeds absenteeism, reinforcing the need for comprehensive wellness programs that include a chronic disease management component.

Presenteeism also occurs when employees experience work/life conflicts and heavy workloads. The causes are organizational. For example, one major study found that going to work when unwell was a consequence of high work/life conflict. More than four out of five employees with high work/family conflicts reported this behaviour, significantly more than other employees in the study. This form of presenteeism also results from employees with heavy workloads feeling compelled to put in long hours. It also reflects a sense of commitment to clients and co-workers. This is why nurses and other health care professionals show up for work even when they are sick.

In short, there are basically two perspectives on presenteeism, one focusing on working while sick or injured and the other focusing on work pressures. Actually, these perspectives are connected. That is because constant workplace change, increasing workloads, and growing job pressures have become standard features of working life and therefore health risks in their own right. To illustrate these links between worker health, work pressures, and absenteeism and presenteeism behaviour, I turn to a study I conducted in a government social services department. A survey asked employees to report absenteeism during the prior twelve months. Then it asked about presenteeism: 'during the past 12 months, how many days did you work despite an illness or injury because you felt you had to?' Those reporting presenteeism were asked to describe their main reasons for doing so.

Absenteeism in the department was double the regional workforce average. Employees attributed 43 per cent of all absenteeism to job stress. However, the typical employee also went to work 6.7 days when ill or injured in the twelve months prior to the survey because they felt they had to. Underlying this behaviour were a feeling of not wanting to fall behind in their work, heavy workloads or caseloads, and a feeling of responsibility to their clients. This was a stressed-out, overworked group of employees who exhibited multiple signs of poor physical and mental health. Most of these problems could be attributed to the cumulative impact of their working conditions. So it is not surprising that presenteeism was high, with roughly one day of presenteeism for every two days of absenteeism.

There are steps you can take to address the sources of presenteeism. First, it is important to diagnose the problem in your organization by adding questions to your employee survey on self-reported absenteeism and presenteeism. Second, ask employees to give their reasons for presenteeism. Third, designing proactive return-to-work processes can deal with this type of presenteeism, helping employees, their supervisors, and health professionals track functional improvements. And fourth, health experts are advising larger employers to provide on-site medical support for individuals suffering from the most common chronic health problems.

These are good initiatives, but equally important in the repertoire of solutions for presenteeism is improving the psychosocial work environment. That is the only way to address job stress, work/life imbalance, and other psychological pressures that have become all too common in twenty-first-century workplaces. Doing so is a precondition for a vibrant workplace.

Healthy Psychosocial Work Environments

This discussion of absenteeism and presenteeism highlights another weakness of workplace health promotion. Most employers are doing an adequate job of complying with occupational health and safety regulations and legislation. In North America, Europe, Australia, and other advanced industrial countries, lost-time injury rates have slowly and steadily declined over the past several decades. Yet despite the spread of workplace health promotion programs, the problems of stress, burnout, and work/life imbalance persist. The main reason is that most comprehensive workplace health promotion initiatives are not comprehensive enough. They do not adequately address the psychological and social dimensions of jobs and workplaces – what experts call the psychosocial work environment.

A healthy psychosocial environment enables well-being and performance. It also reduces employer costs. Employer-sponsored health care plans face double-digit rate increases over the next five to ten years, with prescription drugs the largest cost component.[33] Mental health-related pharmaceuticals are the biggest of these and a growing category of drug prescriptions. Much of the illness being treated is stress related.

Several decades of research pinpoint the causes of stress or, on the flip side, what is needed for a vibrant workplace.[34] People feel under stress when their job demands exceed their resources to respond to these demands. High psychological job demands – urgent deadlines, too much work, competing or conflicting goals – and a low level of control over these demands increase a person's exposure to 'job strain.' For example, a factory worker whose workday is controlled every minute by the unrelenting pace of an assembly line has a high-tension job. Over time, this strain can increase the risk of serious health problems, ranging from depression to heart disease. Among knowledge workers, persistently heavy job demands can result in 'burnout,' a psychological state where people feel mentally exhausted, cynical about their work, and professionally ineffective.

However, someone facing high psychological demands but who has the autonomy, job resources, and team support to manage these demands will have more positive mental health outcomes. This person has a healthy job, which enhances their quality of work life and contributes to organizational performance through increased initiative, learning, and collaboration. For instance, medical researchers who are expected by their employers and their colleagues to produce breakthrough treatments manage this pressure with the help of a great team, ample funding, a well-equipped lab, and the autonomy to set priorities and schedules. In such active jobs, employees can keep stress at tolerable levels. At the same time, they learn ways to do their job better and how to be resilient in the face of change.

Also important is whether a worker's job rewards – pay, job security, career opportunities, and satisfaction – match their mental and physical effort in the job. A lack of reciprocity in this regard is associated with increased risks of cardiovascular disease, depression, alcohol dependence, and poor self-rated overall health. Finally, social scientists have known for years that the support we get from the people around us – family, friends, and neighbours – influences our quality of life. So, too, in the workplace: supportive co-workers and supervisors are an important resource a worker can draw on to cope with pressure.

Work/life imbalance and job stress are close cousins. Balancing work

Figure 2.3 Relationship between work/life balance and job stress

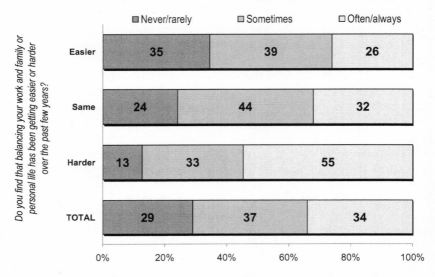

In the past 12 months, how often did you experience stress in your job?

Note: Differences between work/life balance groups are statistically significant. Chi-square test, $p < .001$
Source: *Rethinking Work*, EKOS Research Associates – Graham Lowe Group national worker survey, fall 2004

and non-work has become somewhat more difficult to achieve, according to Rethinking Work, a nationally representative study of Canadian workers.[35] The impact can be seen in an individual's health and well-being, job performance, and ability to be a good parent or spouse.[36] This is how work spills over into families and communities – either positively or negatively. For example, 55 per cent of Rethinking Work survey respondents who found it harder to achieve work/life balance reported often or always being under stress in their job. This compares with the 26 per cent who found work/life balance easier to achieve (see figure 2.3).

Solutions to stress and imbalance require a positive perspective, emphasizing the benefits of active jobs and work/life balance for achieving employee and organizational health. For the organization, these benefits are indeed significant. Employees who experience low job stress or who have work/life balance will contribute more and cost

Figure 2.4 Organizational impacts of job stress

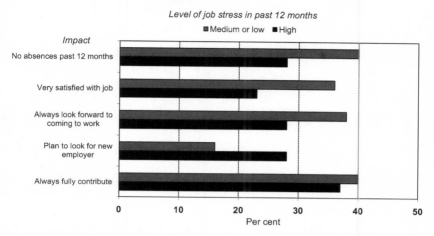

Level of job stress in past 12 months

■ Medium or low   ■ High

Note: All differences between the hgih and the medium-low stress groups are statistically significant. Chi-square test, $p < .05$
Source: *Rethinking Work,* EKOS Research Associates – Graham Lowe Group national worker survey, fall 2004

employers less than workers who lack these positive psychosocial job conditions. Key indicators of these benefits are lower absenteeism; higher job satisfaction; stronger commitment; lower turnover; and fully contributing skills, knowledge, and abilities. Many studies confirm this finding; figures 2.4 and 2.5 offer supporting evidence from the Rethinking Work study.

Stress and work/life imbalance are organizational problems that require organizational – not individual – solutions. When the Rethinking Work survey asked employees who experienced stress to suggest solutions, a reduced workload and better people management practices were at the top of the list. Additional suggestions covered economic rewards, hours, and schedules; relationships with co-workers; and more input and job resources. Furthermore, among those employees whose work interfered with their personal life, reduced workload also was a sought-after change, followed closely by more flexible work arrangements.

Employees know what makes a workplace vibrant. Their suggestions for improvement push beyond health promotion programs into this broader terrain – which I explore in chapter 3. A vibrant workplace

Figure 2.5 Organizational impacts of work/life balance

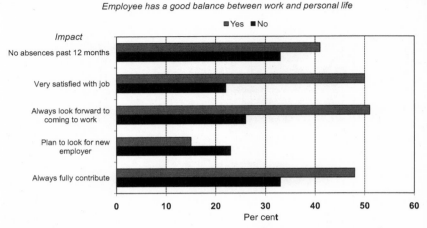

Employee has a good balance between work and personal life

Note: All differences between the yes and no groups are statistically significant. Chi-square test, $p < .05$
Source: *Rethinking Work*, EKOS Research Associates – Graham Lowe Group national worker survey, fall 2004

does not dwell on the negatives of stress, burnout, or work/life conflict. Rather, it sets positive goals. Work design, workplace relationships, and management practices are aligned around the twin goals of wellness and performance.

Talking about Health and Performance

To summarize, I've argued that when it comes to employee health and well-being, there is much more to productivity than reduced employee costs. Managers who understand this are more likely to introduce organizational systems, policies, and practices that support employees to flourish in their jobs and lives outside work. For these people innovations to take root in an organization, you will need to find a common language for talking about health and performance. This language must resonate internally. Eventually, it will be reflected in your operating philosophy about what contributes to responsible, long-term business success.

Actually, you may not use words such as *health* or *wellness*. Change agents must therefore take every opportunity to link employee health and safety to the organization's performance and its business goals.

When discussing employee health and wellness, try to expand the conversation beyond employees' health-related attitudes and behaviours to include their capacity to contribute to team and organizational success. And encourage others to think of healthy work environments as the enabling contexts for developing employees' capabilities. This can be achieved by talking about learning, collaboration, and innovation as by-products of a healthy workplace.

Conversations about performance often raise awareness of the importance of having vibrant workplaces. Describing the health/performance connection in terms that make sense to senior managers and business owners will, I believe, reposition employee health and wellness as effective and responsible business practice. Here are three brief examples:

- A senior manager in Xerox Global Services used the image of 'islands of floating knowledge' to describe the knowledge management challenges large organizations face. In a climate of mistrust and disrespect, nobody will want to share their good ideas. From an organizational health perspective, we are talking about basic requirements for a vibrant workplace.
- A growing number of industrial employers are now championing a safety culture as a way to reduce lost time injuries to zero. A safety culture focuses on the workplace fundamentals of a healthy organization, such as open communication, trust, collaboration, and shared responsibility for workplace improvements.
- An insurance company executive told a conference that long-term disability often is caused by stress resulting from interpersonal conflict with a boss or an overwhelming dissatisfaction with the job. In other words, what looks like a personal health issue is symptomatic of how the organization is managed and the quality of relationships between individual employees and their supervisors.

I'm encouraging you to view all parts of your organization through the wide lens of health. By doing so, you will be able to see the multiple advantages that flow from work environments that nurture employee well-being. You also will be better able to use what your organization has been doing to promote employee health to launch deeper improvements in the work environment. As a senior manager put it during a conference discussion about how to achieve healthy outcomes, 'we need to build great workplaces, not talk about health.' Subtle shifts in thinking and language can move you forward. That is why I have chosen to discuss vibrant workplaces that inspire employees. You need to find your own way to describe what lies beyond health and engagement in tomorrow's workplace. The next chapter challenges you to do just that.

3 How Vibrant Workplaces Inspire Employees

What does a healthy organization look and feel like? The most accurate way to answer this question is to ask your co-workers or employees. Most employees and managers I have posed this question to have their own shortlist of what defines a healthy workplace and why achieving this vision is important for them, their employer, customers – and society as a whole. Usually, the discussion also revolves around what makes people look forward to coming to work each day. What I have learned from these conversations about work experiences is that there is no difference between what really inspires them about their jobs and what makes the office, hospital, factory, store, or other setting in which they spend their day a fulfilling work environment.

This chapter looks at a healthy organization through the eyes of employees. I focus on individuals' personal work experiences, needs, and values to describe what makes a workplace more than just healthy and how these factors do more than just engage employees. I believe that the aspirations people carry into workplaces provide a larger common vision of a vibrant workplace. The big difference between a vibrant and a healthy workplace is that the former seamlessly connects well-being and performance, with the potential for greater benefits than are possible using stand-alone health promotion or HR programs.

While meeting the aspirations that workers carry into a workplace may be a desirable end in itself, it falls short of a business case for investing in an organization's human resources. So we also need a longer answer to the question about what a healthy organization looks and feels like. By taking action to address employees' aspirations for vibrant work environments, managers and other change agents are putting in place the cornerstones of a healthy organization. A vibrant workplace energizes the entire organization by inspiring employees to continually find better ways to meet customers' or clients' needs. The result is a talented, motivated, and healthy workforce able to sustain higher levels of performance. The healthy organization idea, used in this way, is an integrating framework that helps to 'connect the dots' of health, workforce capabilities, and performance.

My main objective in this chapter is to encourage readers to think about using employees' experiences in their workplace as a basis for change and improvement. Here, then, is a summary of the main action insights the chapter offers:

1. Just as companies focus on enhancing the 'customer experience,' they also must find ways to improve the employee experience, because these goals are connected.
2. By understanding what truly inspires employees, you can identify how a vibrant workplace develops employees' capabilities and promotes well-being.
3. Involving employees in crafting a vision of the kind of workplace they want provides a blueprint for improving the drivers of well-being and performance.
4. A vibrant workplace vision also can help you find solutions to human resource challenges, particularly retention, recruitment, engagement, and development.
5. Employees' assessment of whether they have a healthy workplace also gauges how well an organization is developing capabilities for future success.

I invite you to use the ideas in this chapter to stimulate discussions in your team, unit, department, or organization about a shared vision of a vibrant workplace. Once this conversation begins, you soon will be talking about what really inspires people to do their best work. That is how you can forge strong links in the healthy organization value chain.

How Employees Experience Healthy Organizations

At the Gaylord Palms Hotel and Convention Center in Orlando, Florida, the senior manager who opened the facility in 2002 implemented a culture-based strategy to achieve service excellence.[1] The manager expected that a customer-driven culture would have a competitive advantage over other hotels in attracting customers and employees. What is more, the culture would be a substitute for traditional management controls such as rules, procedures, and direct supervision. The first step was to define the hotel's mission, goals, and seven corporate values (service, citizenship, integrity, respect, excellence, creativity, and passion). The acronym STARS (smiles, teamwork, attitude, reliability, and service with a passion) defined how employees would perform their jobs. Then the mission, goals, and values were used to hire, train, and motivate employees who would be 'the STARS.' This sounds corny, but by common hospitality industry performance measures, it succeeded. The cultural dynamic operates at the emotional level of how employees experience and live the culture: 'positive emotional content is infused and mirrored in the behaviours of employees to themselves, to each other and to guests, customers and owners.'[2] Among all employee groups, even those who did not have direct customer contact, positive work experiences contributed to high job satisfaction and high customer satisfaction.

Like Gaylord Palms, many companies are striving to create the ultimate customer experience. They want every detail of how the customer receives services or buys products to be as genuinely positive as possible, providing what customers value most. Designing the right experience for the customer has become the ultimate goal in managing customer relationships. Outstanding experiences breed customer loyalty – and higher future revenues and profits.[3]

The public sector has picked up these ideas, developing client-first strategies of their own. In 2009 the state of Queensland, Australia, launched the Queensland Health Awards for Excellence to showcase high performance in the state's health system and recognize staff contributions to patient-centred care.[4] Among the award winners were projects to improve indigenous people's access to health care, a mobile women's health service, and initiatives to break down language barriers – all of which improved the overall health care experience of clients. Queensland Health also awards excellence in supporting and developing staff. The state includes workplace culture measures in its annual quality report on health care organizations, using measures obtained from its state-wide Better Workplaces Staff Opinion Survey. The survey measures the climate of the workplace – including what I have called vibrant workplace ingredients.

In examples as diverse as a Florida luxury resort and an Australian public health system, we see current efforts to link employee and customer or client experiences. I further explore this theme below, showing how employees' experiences of their job and work environment have an enormous impact on performance-related work attitudes and behaviours, as well as on their overall sense of well-being. That is why it is so important that these experiences are as positive as possible as often as possible.

Employers ignore at their peril employees' perceptions, just as it is a mistake for businesses to ignore their customers' opinions about their products or services. Hence the need for an employee-centred view of a healthy organization. Indeed, an accurate way to gauge what makes employees feel satisfied and committed – or, even better, to be inspired – is to ask them to describe the ideal workplace. Taking this positive approach, rather than starting with workplace problem-solving, mobilizes employees and managers around a shared vision of a vibrant workplace. The result is a collective aspiration that can be a powerful energizer for change and improvement.

My emphasis on employees' experiences may sound too subjective, particularly for managers who like numbers and measureable outcomes. These sceptics need to be reminded, however, that decades of employee research by academics and consultants – and some large employers – have been able to accurately quantify the impact of attitudes and values on well-being. It is well established that at the top of the hierarchy of human needs are two that can be met in large part through people's work. One is self-esteem, which flows from a combination of respectful relationships, recognition and feedback for contributions, and the sense of accomplishment from a job well done. Another basic need is to develop potential by having opportunities to learn, grow, and apply innate abilities. Both needs are essential for personal well-being and job performance, and both needs depend in large part on the work environment.

Research on psychological needs now focuses on the sources and benefits of happiness. Happiness is a positive state of psychological and emotional well-being. Martin Seligman, a University of Pennsylvania psychologist who launched the positive psychology movement, believes that finding authentic happiness instils meaning and purpose in life. He has developed an Authentic Happiness website with tools and resources to help people to make themselves and the world happier.[5] Work is central to happiness. Two University of British Columbia researchers discovered that 'happiness' (overall satisfaction with life) is strongly influenced by non-financial aspects of a job. Especially important is the level of trust in workplace relations, which depends on the quality of workplace communication.[6]

Employees' experiences are based on their assessments of many aspects of their work situation, including choices, trade-offs, and preferences. Such personal calculations are not like a mathematical formula. Rather, they are filtered through what each individual, or group, considers most important. In this way, values and perceptions shape our individual and collective definitions of a healthy organization.

Envisioning Vibrant Workplaces

I like to begin a workshop on creating healthy workplaces by inviting participants to think about what the 'ideal' healthy workplace looks and feels like for them. I ask participants to spend a few minutes writing down their personal vision of a healthy workplace, one in which they can imagine experiencing an excellent quality of work life. Sitting in small groups at round tables, they are then asked to share their personal visions with others at the table. It takes about fifteen or twenty minutes for people at each table to agree on the ingredients of a healthy workplace. And when the table visions are presented to others, it is remarkable how much convergence there is around what people consider most important in the ideal workplace – and how far beyond 'healthy' these visions move the discussion.

Indeed, absent from how employees and managers envision the ideal healthy workplace is an emphasis on individual health promotion or wellness programs. That is because in the minds of employees the fundamentals of a healthy workplace transcend personal health and wellness activities. This insight is important for managers and workplace health and wellness professionals, many of whom still operate within the health promotion mindset described in chapter 2.

This is a recurring theme in the examples I provide below of how front-line employees, professionals, and managers from a variety of organizations envision a vibrant workplace. A group of employees in an industrial facility stated that a healthy workplace means much more than 'management giving us gym passes or fitness programs.' It wasn't that they opposed what they called 'lifestyle programs.' They wanted more fundamental changes in the workplace. These workers went on to talk about the things that needed fixing, such as cleaning up dirty and cluttered workspaces, supervisors using respectful language when talking to their employees, and a variety of small changes that would give production workers a greater sense of dignity in their jobs. Later discussions with managers and workplace health and wellness staff in the same company acknowledged that launching a wellness program that did not address working conditions considered to be unhealthy would be a waste of time and money.

The examples below show how employees' visions of healthy workplaces go directly to the levers that managers are trying to pull to improve retention, engagement, and performance. These actions build an organization's reputation as an exemplary employer, fostering employee loyalty and sought out by talented job seekers. The following visions are about achieving these goals.

The five examples below of healthy workplace visions, like those from numerous other workshops, form a composite picture of the essential ingredients of a healthy organization that supports overall employee well-being. As noted in chapter 2, good mental health contributes to positive physical health, as well as to job performance and a sense of belonging to the organization. People's perceptions of the quality of their job and workplace put a premium on basics, such as self-worth, positive relationships with others, making a contribution, and developing personal potential. In a healthy organization, these conditions are continually encouraged and reinforced.

- *Municipal managers and professionals.* At a workshop for about 200 managers and professionals in a large municipality, the participants liked to imagine a 'healthy, high-quality' workplace. For them, this vision was broader than a healthy workplace. The use of 'quality' raised all sorts of issues about people being able to do their jobs well and make the city a better place to live in. It did not take long for this large group to zero in on the top two ingredients of a healthy, high-quality workplace: excellent working relationships within and between departments and excellent two-way communication. Discussion of these features identified a close connection: people cannot have good working relationships without honest and constructive communication.
- *Industrial managers.* Senior managers at an industrial processing facility reflected on what they had learned through consultations with managers and employees about a healthy and safe work environment. These leaders decided to state in their own words a more encompassing 'people vision.' This vision described a workplace resting on four pillars: clean, safe, and healthy; enables employee involvement and input; supports skill development and career growth; and values trust, cooperation, and open communication. The managers went on to say that achieving this vision has to be a shared responsibility requiring constant effort.

- *Health care managers and professionals.* At another workshop a large group of middle managers and front-line supervisors at a health care organization created a shared vision based on three primary goals. The first goal was teamwork. These health care managers and professionals imagined teamwork that cut across the existing silos created by departments and disciplines. Positive and respectful working relationships were seen as the basis for cooperation. The second goal concerned employees' connection with the organization. Making this stronger depended on recognizing everyone's contributions to patient care and cultivating staff involvement in and ownership of this mission. The third goal was the pay-off: staff would be healthier physically, mentally, and emotionally; they would be happy, satisfied, and excited about their work; and over time the organization would gain a reputation as an excellent place to work.
- *Laboratory scientists.* A group of forensic scientists working in several lab facilities configured their vision of a healthy workplace, beginning with how they wanted to feel each day at work. Above all was a sense of excitement and enthusiasm, so that they could not wait to go to work and would arrive with positive attitudes. They would be able to contribute to the goals of organization. Everyone could be a leader, having a balance of autonomy and responsibility in their job and being able to seek out opportunities to deal with change and to be innovative. Perhaps as a comment on perceived current gaps in the organization, the scientists viewed key enablers as 'managers who lead by example' and who would trust them to be innovative in their jobs. Labs as healthy workplaces also would have friendly co-workers and respectful working relationships. Excellence would be promoted through continual learning and time for reflection. Finally, there would be support for healthy lifestyles.
- *Community social service workers.* The following vision was created by several not-for-profit agencies providing similar services to persons with disabilities in dozens of communities. The group described healthy workplaces in two ways: 'Heard, happy, healthy, and here (i.e., present and eager to work)'; 'Appreciated, connected, dedicated, and satisfied.' Respectful relationships were considered foundational, as were trusting and caring relationships – which also extended to clients and their families. Other healthy workplace elements included valuing, recognizing, and celebrating people's contributions. One important way that healthy workplaces would value employees would be through fairness, especially in pay and

benefits, which were below average in the sector, owing to funding not keeping up with rising service needs in communities. In addition, a healthy workplace also meant open communication, a strong collective voice for staff in planning change, and flexibility in work arrangements.

Envisioning an Inspired Workforce

At this point, managers with a bottom-line focus may be asking, 'so what?' Scepticism about how employees (including managers, unless they also are business owners) envision a healthy workplace should evaporate once the connection with improving employee engagement is clear. In my experience, employees and managers see an engaging work environment and a healthy one as part of the same organizational fabric. Indeed, when asked to envision the ideal future workplace, what most often comes up sets the bar for employee well-being, performance, and passion about work much higher than it is today. All the more reason to think in terms of vibrant workplaces that inspire employees.

Let us consider what workshop participants in two different organizations had to say when asked for their vision of engaged employees or an engaging workplace. As above, I am providing the actual words used by these groups to express what this abstract concept of 'engagement' means to them. I encourage you to compare these descriptions with the words used in visions of a healthy workplace. You will see the similarities with engaging workplaces; in fact, they are the same thing.

- *Natural resources professionals.* A natural resources organization I worked with wanted to create a culture of engagement. To senior management, this meant a workplace that personally involved each and every employee in providing excellent service. A team of professional employees was brought together from across the organization and asked by senior management to create a vision and an action plan for increasing engagement. At a workshop, the team came up with an 'engagement vision.' By creating its own vision of engagement, the team realized where shifts in the corporate culture were required. Higher levels of engagement depended on a work environment with the following eight attributes:
  - Everyone feels as if they belong to one big team with common objectives and understands how their job contributes to these objectives.

- o All interactions are meaningful and positive.
- o Communication is open and based on trust.
- o Knowledge is gained and shared effectively.
- o Employees feel empowered to be innovative and take risks.
- o Managers support employees, bring out the best in them, and recognize their contributions.
- o Employees are motivated to do better and to embrace change.
- o Employees achieve a sense of accomplishment, work/life balance, and well-being.
- *Health care senior managers*: A world-class, research-intensive health care organization also developed a vision of engagement. At a workshop I conducted with its senior management team, discussions explored what an engaged employee actually looks like. The hospital had set as a goal increased employee engagement and now had to define what that meant in operational terms. The result was an 'engaged employee vision,' which the executive team used to guide its decisions and actions on a wide range of human resource issues. Ideally, the qualities of an engaged employee are as follows:
  - o Collaborative.
  - o Respectful.
  - o Communicates openly and listens well.
  - o Knowledgeable and open minded.
  - o Sees the 'big picture.'
  - o Solution-focused and problem-solving.
  - o Caring and compassionate.
  - o Dedicated, reliable, and accountable.
  - o Flexible and adaptable.
  - o Excited by results.

Notice how this vision describes personal attributes. The other visions I use as examples focus on workplaces, presenting the same factors in terms of what workplaces should support and encourage. In the end, they amount to the attitudes and behaviours of individual employees and teams.

These visions provide important practical lessons. First, the visions underscore the need for change agents in any position to focus on fundamentals, such as workplace relationships and supporting employees to grow and to do a good job. Second, the visions reinforce the need for individual managers to practise the most frequently mentioned features of healthy and engaging workplaces: open communication with employees and showing respect for them as individuals. Third, one of the most effective ways for senior managers to fine-tune the organization's strategies for engagement, wellness, and talent development is to take seriously employees' experiences.

One sign that some companies are moving in this direction is that exit interviews with employees who quit have given way to 'stay' interviews. Stay interviews are proactive consultations with existing employees, asking about the most positive feature of their experiences as an employee that keeps them with the company and feeling engaged. Yes, this is ground-up people strategy development. But it is no different from asking customers what they want and improving products or services to meet these evolving needs.

How Vibrant Workplaces Inspire Employees

The visions above describe the main ingredients of a vibrant workplace and how employees are expected to experience this sort of work environment. Now we can pull them together into composite visions that offer a ground-up perspective on the workplace conditions and employee experiences that describe the healthy organization of the future.

The vision summarized in figure 3.1 captures what many people want in their work environment. These factors combine personal and group visions of a healthy workplace. Similarly, figure 3.2 describes what people working in this kind of environment will experience – which is nothing short of inspired. The inspired employee vision describes work experiences that generate well-being and performance. Terms such as 'excited,' 'passionate,' 'happy,' 'enthusiastic,' and 'dedicated' describe the possible goals for a healthy organization.

Interestingly, 'promotes a healthy lifestyle' is the only specific reference to employee health promotion in figure 3.1. All the other ingredients describe characteristics of people's jobs, relationships, and organizational processes and systems. While not mentioning health, these ingredients have everything to do with it, providing the conditions for people to thrive at work. That is clear from figure 3.2. Again, mental and physical well-being, or health, is but one of many outcomes. Yet all the other results contribute to high levels of physical, social, psychological, and emotional well-being.

You can use these summary visions as checklists of potential improvements needed in your work environment and the expected benefits to co-workers or your employees of making these improvements.

Figure 3.1 Vibrant workplace vision

Relationships	• Respectful relationships • Friendly co-workers • Caring and compassionate
	• Open, honest two-way communication based on trust
Job	• Understand how your job fits into strategy • Employees are empowered to be innovative and take risks • Involvement and ownership
Team	• Cooperation and collaboration • Feel part of a team with common objectives • Gain and share knowledge effectively, learn from each other
Supports	• Supportive managers who bring out the best in staff • Value, recognize, and celebrate people's contributions • Fairness, including in pay and benefits • Promotes a healthy lifestyle

Figure 3.2 Inspired employee vision

- Experience mental and physical well-being
- Experience a sense of accomplishment
- Passionate, involved, enthusiastic and happy
- Positive attitude about work, co-workers and management
- Can't wait to go to work
- Flexible and adaptable in dealing with change
- Innovative, inquisitive, proactive and creative
- Self-driven and directed – a leader
- Excited by results
- Solution-focused and problem-solving
- Dedicated, reliable and accountable

In practical terms, addressing the workplace vision elements requires an assessment of your organization's component parts. That is where healthy workplace advocates must focus their energies if they want to move beyond the limits of individual health promotion.

Focusing on Work Experiences

What I am proposing is an employee-centred perspective on organizational success. The best route to excellent customer or client experiences is through excellent employee experiences. Or, according to the healthy organization value chain: vibrant workplaces = inspired employees = sustainable success.

Improving organizational performance by putting employee well-being first may sound counter-intuitive. But it works. This point is emphasized by Isadore Sharp, the founder and CEO of the Four Seasons luxury hotel chain.[7] Sharp describes how every employee focuses on one priority – pleasing customers – because every manager focuses on pleasing employees. Four Seasons' management trusts and empowers staff to do what is best for customers. As a result, employees are passionate about providing a quality of guest experience far superior to what is available in other hotels. Four Seasons' success comes down to a strong but simple corporate philosophy based on the Golden Rule – treat others as you want to be treated yourself.

Other companies express the same idea in their own terms. For example, FedEx's Purple Promise – people, service, profits – is grounded in the same thinking found at Four Seasons. Vancity, Canada's largest credit union, located on the west coast, makes a corporate commitment to creating a great workplace, which reflects the corporate philosophy that excellent customer experiences begin with excellent employee experiences. Clive Beddoe, former CEO of Canada-based WestJet Airlines states the people-performance connection in another way: 'Many years ago, I heard a story that said the people who suffer the most stress in life are front-line personnel who are charged with responsibilities but not given any authority. That, to me, is almost like an abuse of people. How can you ask someone to be responsible for something and yet not give them the authority to make decisions when confronted with an issue? Recognizing that, we empower our people and trust them to make decisions on the front line. And for them, a job that would otherwise not be particularly satisfying becomes very satisfying. When you empower people and trust them, you'll be amazed what they can do.'[8]

Good examples also can be found in the public sector. Britain's National Health Service (NHS) looked at its performance through the eyes of employees. Despite much effort, building quality into health care organizations has been an elusive goal, especially high-quality work experiences. Yet the NHS took an innovative approach to measuring and improving health care work environments.

In 2008 the Department of Health dug deeper into the drivers of NHS performance in a research project called *What Matters to Staff*.[9] This study took a ground-up approach to identifying the determinants of satisfaction and performance. Employee interviews and focus groups identified what makes NHS staff feel motivated and fulfilled at work. The language used by staff became the descriptors for the qualities and the management actions that staff considered most important for delivering each of the factors. A subsequent survey validated the factors identified in the staff consultations. Staff experiences of ten factors contributed the most to four key outcomes: staff motivation to provide high-quality patient care; staff advocacy of the NHS; patient satisfaction; and public satisfaction. Here are the ten factors that matter most to staff, grouped into four themes:

- Theme 1: The resources to deliver quality care for patients:
  - I've got the knowledge, skills and equipment to do a good job.
  - I feel fairly treated with pay, benefits and staff facilities.
- Theme 2: The support I need to do a good job:
  - I feel trusted, listened to and valued at work.
  - My manager (or supervisor) supports me when I need it.
  - Senior managers are involved with our work.
- Theme 3: A worthwhile job with the chance to develop:
  - I've got a worthwhile job that makes a difference to patients.
  - I help provide high-quality patient care.
  - I have the opportunity to develop my potential.
  - I understand my role and where it fits in.
- Theme 4: The opportunity to improve the way we work:
  - I am able to improve the way we work in my team.

The NHS staff survey was revised to reflect the factors identified in the *What Matters to Staff* research. These are now part of annual performance reporting and management accountability for improvements. The parallels with the vibrant workplace vision, above, is indeed striking. It is fair to say that in the highest-performing NHS organizations, staff are more than motivated and satisfied – they are inspired.

Defining Good Jobs

While these examples are useful, I also want to put the vibrant workplace-inspired employee link into an even broader context, so we are able to widely apply the visions outlined earlier. Based on input from hundreds of participants in my workshops, we now have a fine-grained picture of what a healthy and engaging workplace looks and feels like. I now will use survey data representative of a national workforce (Canada) to explore more precisely how peoples' experiences of high-quality jobs and healthy work environments are shaped by the vision elements in figure 3.1.

Some years ago, I conducted a study with Canadian Policy Research Networks (CPRN), a social and economic policy think tank, designed to answer a basic question: 'What's a good job?' The answer to that question is relevant today for the building blocks of healthy organizations. The study's goal was to provide decision-makers in government, business, unions and professional associations, and non-government organizations dealing with workplace and labour market issues with new insights about how the workforce downsizing and restructuring of the 1990s had transformed employment relationships. Several national roundtables convened by CPRN sparked heated debate about the end of loyalty – and job security – as employee-employer relationships weakened. Employers were worried that it would become more difficult to find and keep talent as the wave of baby boomer retirements gathered momentum.

This focus on employment relationships displays a panorama of positive workplace features, confirming the relevance of the factors listed in figure 3.1. Researchers had shown that workers' perceptions of the quality of their work environment are critical for outcomes such as job satisfaction, organizational commitment, absenteeism, and job performance. A growing number of human resource practitioners wanted to act on this evidence. But it was difficult for HR managers to convince their executive team that performance pay-offs logically flowed from higher-quality work environments. The study's report, *What's a Good Job? The Importance of Employment Relationships*, addressed this gap. It provided solid evidence that the strength of employee-employer relationships mattered for employees' quality of work life and for their employers' human resource goals and organizational performance.[10]

We knew more could be done to make an evidence-based case for workplace improvements. Also important, therefore, was clearly showing the connection between the defining features of 'good jobs' and the growing field of workplace health promotion. In short, the work-health connection provided a new avenue for convincing decision makers that investing in people and their work environments was the best recipe for organizational success.

During the 1990s occupational health researchers made progress unravelling the connections between work and health. The storyline they developed went as follows: workers who have autonomy, adequate job resources, appropriate levels of economic and psychological rewards, supportive managers with good people skills, are consulted on organizational changes, and have a sense of economic security will be healthier than workers who lack these conditions. And the same conditions benefit employers, because healthy workers are ready, willing, and able to do a good job.

The new information-based, global economy of the late twentieth century was not particularly healthy, even though fewer people did strenuous manual labour in factories, mines, forests, and other industries historically associated with occupational risks and hazards. New-economy jobs had their own musculoskeletal risks, such as repetitive strain of retail cashiers, back and shoulder pain caused by poorly designed desk chairs, and overuse problems from keyboarding. But the emerging health risks seemed mostly to be in the psychosocial domain – which, as we saw in chapter 2, lies beyond most workplace health promotion programs.

Healthy Workplaces through Employees' Eyes

Against this backdrop, two colleagues and I used the CPRN survey on changing employment relationships to answer a question that was foremost in minds of workplace health practitioners and researchers: 'What do employees perceive to be the ingredients of a healthy workplace?'[11] The answer, we hoped, would guide the design of healthier and more productive workplaces, as well as provide a bigger window for viewing healthy workplaces.

The *Harvard Business Review*, the leading publication for managers, has published dozens of articles on strategy, leadership, and innovation. In contrast, there are only a handful of articles on health and wellness topics, such as emotional intelligence, presenteeism, and 'extreme' work hours. Health remains at the margins of business strategy. Yet most executives consider employee capabilities a key business success factor. Capabilities are best developed and applied in the context of optimal quality of work life. So clearly there is an opportunity here to address what matters for managers through an exchange of ideas that bridges well-being, human resources, and performance.

Everyone stands to gain from eliminating silos of organizational practice and knowledge. Researchers and practitioners still live in separate worlds. And there is a lack of interchange between practitioners in occupational health, human resources, organizational development, training, and learning – not to mention line managers. Workplace health promotion practitioners could benefit from a broader understanding of work contexts and organizational systems. Human resource professionals could benefit from a broader understanding of how HR goals intersect with health and wellness. Managers could benefit from a 'health' lens that would help them to see the impact of decision options on individual and organizational health.

Social scientists have confirmed that ultimately it is the worker who judges job quality. Using this approach, we set out to understand a critical dimension of job quality: experiencing the work environment as healthy. We explored the links between workers' perceptions of a healthy work environment and outcomes that matter for employees and employers alike. In this regard, job satisfaction is the most widely used indicator by organizational researchers of a person's quality of work life. Moreover, HR professionals use job satisfaction measures in employee surveys to gauge employees' work experiences. From an employer's perspective, we also considered outcomes related to employee performance and costs: organizational commitment, morale, absenteeism, and intent to quit.

Why Some Workplaces Are Healthier Than Others

To summarize why some work environments are considered healthier than others, I draw on the Changing Employment Relationships Survey, described earlier. Perceptions of a healthy workplace were documented by asking: *To what extent do you agree or disagree that this describes your job*: 'The work environment is healthy.' In addition, respondents were asked how strongly they agreed or disagreed with a similar statement: 'The work environment is safe.'

Both measures are consistent with epidemiological research on health status among adults. Population health surveys in many countries use global self-reports of overall health as accurate indicators of health status. For example, Statistics Canada's Canadian Community Health Survey uses this type of measure, which correlates consistently with other, more specific, self-reported and clinical measures of health status. It does not mean we can do away with detail, but rather that such single self-reports are efficient and accurate key indicators of work experiences.

We first looked at the relationship between employees' perceptions of their work environment as being healthy and safe. Workplace health promotion practitioners do not focus on safety, assuming that the organization has safety systems and practices in place. However, we discovered that in employees' experience of their workplace, healthy does not necessarily mean safe, and vice versa. Just over two-thirds of employees surveyed reported that their workplace is both healthy and safe, based on the proportions of respondents who agreed or strongly agreed with each statement. Another 17 per cent reported that their workplace is safe but not healthy, and 4 per cent reported it to be healthy but unsafe. This means that only 15 per cent did not perceive their workplace to be safe, while 28 per cent did not perceive it to be healthy.

These findings resonate with the high priority many employers now place on removing safety hazards and preventing injury. This safety emphasis has grown over the decades, as employers responded to occupational health and safety regulations, financial incentives created by workers' compensation rates, and the professionalization of safety. Clearly, safety belongs within a broader set of health and well-being goals. Safety goals are best achieved within the context of a healthy work environment. Managers and professionals in health and safety, HR, and workplace wellness need to join forces for an integrated approach to supporting overall employee well-being.

Viewed even more broadly, the survey results corroborate the vibrant workplace vision outlined above. After considering many possible factors that could shape perceptions of a healthy workplace, including employees' demographic characteristics and their industry and occupation, we discovered that five distinct clusters of working conditions were most influential in this regard. Figure 3.3 summarizes this analysis (which isolated the 'net' effects of each factor, after taking into account the influence of all the other factors). I have provided the wording of the survey questions, so anyone designing or updating an employee survey can see if their measurement tool includes these indicators of healthy work experiences.

Communication and social support are central to one's work experiences. In practical terms, this tells us that good horizontal and vertical communication in a workplace, friendly and helpful co-workers, a positive relationship with one's supervisor, and receiving recognition are key enablers of a healthy work environment. Thus, perceptions of healthy workplaces reflect the relationships in which workers participate daily and that facilitate their job effectiveness. This certainly is one of the key messages coming out of the workplace visions presented ear-

Figure 3.3 The most positive and negative influences on employees' perceptions of a healthy work environment

---

Most positive influences

Communication and support
• Communication is good among the people you work with.
• The people you work with are helpful and friendly.
• You have a good relationship with your supervisor.
• You receive recognition for work well done.

Job resources
• How frequently have you lacked the necessary tools needed to do your job?
• You get the training needed to do your job effectively.
• You have access to the information you need to do your job well.

Job rewards
• The benefits are good
• The pay is good.
• Your job security is good.
• Your chances for career advancement are good.

Job autonomy
• You can choose your own schedule within established limits.
• Your job allows you freedom to decide how to do your work.
• You can influence decisions that affect your job or work life.

Most negative influences

Job demands
• Your job is very stressful.
• Your job is hectic.
• How often have you had difficulty keeping up with the workload?
• Are you free from conflicting demands that other people make?

Notes: This table summarizes the results of statistical analysis. Actual wording of survey questions are provided.
Source: Lowe, G.S., Schellenberg, G., and Shannon, H.S. (2003). Correlates of employees' perceptions of a healthy work environment. *American Journal of Health Promotion*, 17, 390–9.

lier. And it provides convincing evidence of the importance of a high-quality psychosocial work environment for employees' well-being.

This emphasis on communication and social relationships was echoed in a series of employee focus groups we conducted in four cities across Canada. Focus group participants described the quality of workplace relations and communications as indispensable for a 'good job.' Furthermore, the importance of communication also stood out in responses to an open-ended survey question, which asked people to state in their own words the single most important change they would like to see in their relationship with their employer. Of those seeking improvements in their employment relationship, the single most important change they wanted was improved communication, broadly defined. Typical suggestions included the following:

- Better communication; there's a lack of communication between the senior people and their employees.
- Better communication in the organization as a whole with everyone involved.
- I would like to see more clarity in the direction the company is headed.
- More personal evaluation.

The factors defining a healthy workplace transcend demographics. Characteristics such as age, gender, ethnicity, and education do not help to explain whether an employee experiences their workplace as healthy. Thus, employers need not waste time trying to devise specific workplace improvement strategies for young, or older, workers, for example. Three other sets of working conditions, while not as influential as communication and support, also are associated with positive perceptions of the work environment: having adequate resources, extrinsic job rewards, and job autonomy or 'having a say.' Job demands have a negative impact on healthy work environment experiences. Having job autonomy helps in addressing job demands. But none of the other factors offsets the negative impact on employees of having a stressful and overloaded job – a finding that resonates with our discussion in chapter 2 about the causes of stress, burnout, and work/life conflict.

Why Employees' Perceptions Matter

One additional piece of information from this study should encourage managers to pay careful attention to employee's work experiences. We also discovered that perceptions of a healthy work environment impact performance and costs. The more that employees viewed their work environment was healthy, the higher their level of job satisfaction and their commitment to their employer. Employees in the healthiest environments also had the lowest rates of absenteeism and were planning to stay, rather than quit. The positive effects of healthy work environments can be seen at the team or group level, too. Employees who believed they had really healthy workplaces also reported the best morale among co-workers.

These findings confirm that the summary visions in figures 3.1 and 3.2 of vibrant workplaces and inspired employees indeed are connected. Given managers' ongoing concerns about employee engagement, the commitment measure we used is worth examining more closely. It actually goes to the heart of what many managers define as engagement. Specifically, we measured commitment by a scale comprising four questions on personal identification with the organization's values, loyalty to the organization, willingness to work hard to help the organization succeed, and pride in working for the organization. These are attitudes and behaviours that almost every senior management team today wants to cultivate in its workforce.

What I've just presented are correlations, so they may not fully describe cause and effect. However, the strength and consistency of the links between perceived healthy environments and organizational performance certainly suggests that when management teams rethink their employee engagement strategy, or try to be more proactive in retaining employees, the goal of a healthy work environment should be high on the agenda.

Closing the Inspiration Gap

There are basic steps you can take to improve the work environment and provide more inspiring work experiences. I am speaking directly to managers, who have considerable power to ensure that vibrant workplace ingredients are in place. Actually, one of the most effective steps in this regard is relatively inexpensive in financial terms, but may require a major psychic investment.

To venture in this direction, a manager would have to make a determined effort to understand the filters employees use for assessing their jobs and work environment. These filters are peoples' work values – what is fundamentally important to them in a job, workplace, and career. That manager also would need the will to address major gaps between employees' work values and what they actually experience on a daily basis. I call this discrepancy between what employees want and what they have the 'inspiration gap.' Closing the gap will move an employer much further down the path to a truly healthy organization.

Specifically, closing the inspiration gap requires three pieces of information:

1. What workers value most in a job, an employer, and a career.
2. How they assess the specific features of their current job.
3. Where the biggest gaps are between what they value and what they have.

Most employee surveys conducted by employers provide only one of these pieces of information: assessments of various working conditions. So I would encourage HR professionals and others who manage internal employee surveys also to find out what really matters to their workforce by tapping into basic work values. It then will be possible to calculate the third piece of information: the inspiration gaps you need to close.

Earlier, I identified positive influences on employees' perceptions of whether their work environment is healthy. As for the negative influences – stressful and hectic jobs, heavy workloads, and conflicting demands – they obviously require remedial action. You can readily diagnose these problems in your workplace using an appropriately designed employee survey, or through focus groups, employee forums, or other consultation techniques. Doing so will address some of the biggest concerns employees – and employers – have voiced about unhealthy psychosocial work environments.

However, removing these toxic factors from a work environment does not make it healthy, never mind vibrant. But certainly it is a first step. There also must be a range of positive factors put in place, such as those listed in figure 3.3 or in the vibrant workplace vision in figure 3.1. Employee input on where to start is critical. A useful source of information in this regard can be gleaned from a basic gap analysis of employee survey results – assuming you have asked parallel questions about work values and work experiences.

Here is how to do this sort of gap analysis and what you might expect to find. Using the list of positive influences on perceptions of a healthy work environment in figure 3.3 as an illustration of this procedure, imagine that you also have employee survey data on the importance or 'value' your employees place on each factor. By comparing their assessments of these factors with how important each one is, you can calculate an inspiration gap score.[12] Most employee surveys use rating scales on a negative to positive continuum. The most common would be a five-category rating scale that goes from 'strongly disagree' to 'strongly agree.' The same statements used to assess jobs and the work environment also can be used to ask employees what they consider most important. A similar five-category rating scale is employed, but ranging from 'not at all important' to 'very important.'

When you have the survey results, compare the answers with the assessment and importance questions for each job or workplace dimension. Put them side by side in an Excel spreadsheet, and simply subtract the percentage who answered 'strongly agree' on the assessment from the percentage who answered 'very important' on the values version of the same question. This procedure will give you the gap score.[13] Look closely at the relative size of the gaps and then create a ranked list of priority issues you can address by discussing solutions directly with employees.

The Changing Employment Relationships Survey (used in figure 3.3) also asked about work values. This work value question included most of the positive factors identified in figure 3.3. I summarize the findings here to prompt you to think about what you might find if a similar assessment tool were used in your workplace. We discovered that the greatest room for improvement is in the following features of jobs and the work environment:

1. Career advancement opportunities.
2. Being able to choose your own schedule.
3. Freedom to decide how to do your work.
4. Receiving the training needed to do your job effectively.
5. Receiving recognition for work well done.
6. Good communication among the people you work with.

The gaps are rank-ordered above and range from 32 to 14 percentage points.[14] To revisit a prominent theme in this chapter, note that none of these workplace characteristics refers directly to health and wellness. Furthermore, all of them are already in the strategies and annual work plans of many HR departments. The implication, then, is that employers can make considerable progress in closing the inspiration gap by doing better what they already are doing.

Also important to point out is that there were gaps of about 20 percentage points for benefits, pay, and job security. HR professionals know that it is critical to have the right mix of economic rewards and, equally important, the perception that these rewards are 'fair.' However, decades of job satisfaction research tells us that extrinsic rewards are a source of dissatisfaction if perceived by employees to be deficient. Rarely are they a major source of satisfaction. So the six factors listed earlier are more important for the overall quality of one's work experience.

The Dynamics of a Healthy Organization

Managers and human resources professionals often make decisions based on assumptions about how higher-quality job and workplace conditions contribute to positive employee experiences and improved productivity. This is exactly what the healthy organization value chain proposes: talented and motivated employees in a supportive, well-resourced work environment will contribute to better results for customers and communities that can be sustained over time. Numerous studies show this to be sound thinking. Indeed, the quality of an employee's job and work environment has an influence on her or his overall quality of work life and job performance.

To fully appreciate the dynamics of a healthy organization we need to further unravel its inner logic. In this regard, it is useful to know how the defining characteristics of quality jobs and healthy work environments are related – and how they are shaped by other parts of the organization's systems, culture, and operating environment. Many practitioners assume a logical sequence, whereby quality jobs in healthy and safe work environments enhance an employee's quality of work life and well-being and, as a result, contribute to the organization's success. It is the ideal triple-win, because employees and their families, the company and its shareholders, and customers or clients stand to benefit. At least, that is the common assumption and what is implied in the summary visions I provided earlier.

However, organizational life is more complicated, because this neat chain of cause and effect can be influenced by many factors. Growing concerns over this decade about recruitment and retention, employee engagement, productivity and innovation, and controlling rising employee benefit costs has given new urgency to sorting out how all these job and workplace factors influence employees' work experiences and behaviours. The late-decade recession highlighted just how fragile are the gains in morale, well-being, and performance made by companies committed to becoming exemplary employers.

I would encourage you to examine these issues in your workplace, using your data and with the benefit of input from your employees or co-workers. Test out some of the ideas presented in this chapter. For example, are your most satisfied workers also highly motivated to innovate and collaborate – and if not, why? For your workforce, what are the vibrant workplace conditions that are most likely to stimulate employee and customer satisfaction? What would excite your employees or team members so they feel passionate about their work and how it contributes to making others' lives better? The point is, you need to explore ways to put in place two building blocks of a healthy organization – vibrant workplaces and inspired employees – in your unique context.

Now is the time to consider the role that the two other building blocks of a healthy organization play. The healthy organization value chain in chapter 2 depicted culture and leadership as foundational, because of their enabling role. The centre of the value chain is a vibrant workplace, and its most immediate result is cultivation of an inspired workforce. But change agents – whether senior managers, HR professionals, or an employee wellness committee – have to step forward to raise the issues, initiate a conversation about the potential for improvement, and find opportunities to implement solutions. Perhaps even more critical as an enabler of improvements to work environments is culture. This point has been illustrated in organizations as diverse as Gaylord Hotels, the Four Seasons, health care organizations in Australia and England, and airlines such as WestJet. Chapter 4 examines how a positive culture builds healthy organizations by the strength of its people values.

4 Positive Cultures

In 1995 Canadian National Railway (CN) was privatized after many decades of government ownership. To survive in the private sector and return shareholder value, CN had no choice but to shake off a low-productivity, bureaucratic culture. Typical of the old culture was the widespread practice of 'early quits' – workers going home early on a full day's pay. Under the leadership of CEO Hunter Harrison, CN adopted a high-performance business model. Called Precision Railroading, this model focused on customers' needs and delivery goals. Precision Railroading is more than a management or operating system; it is a way of thinking and behaving that became embedded in a customer-focused culture. Intensive effort to shift the culture included rebuilding the corporate strategy around Five Guiding Principles – service, cost control, asset utilization, safety, and people – against which every decision was tested.[1] Culture change brought behaviours in line with these principles. Front-line employees were empowered to meet customers' needs and were recognized for these efforts. The practice of 'early quits' disappeared, and CN became the best-performing, most profitable railroad in North America.

Toyota is famous for its relentless pursuit of product quality and customer satisfaction. The company's success is rooted in The Toyota Production System (TPS), an integrated model of 'lean' manufacturing that touches on all aspects of corporate strategy, systems, structures, and culture. TPS is a way of thinking – the fabled Toyota Way: it emphasizes long-term thinking over short-term financial goals. Customer value is added at every step of the production process through continual improvement and learning. The same approach eliminates waste and reduces costs in the production process. And the organizational culture respects, develops, and challenges employees and external suppliers. Most important, the cultural foundations of the TPS support all workers to continually improve production processes and product quality through skill development, learning, teamwork, and individual initiative.[2] (Toyota's massive safety recall in 2010 to fix gas pedals in its vehicles is putting the TPS under intense public scrutiny, creating an unprecedented test of the resilience of the company's culture.) A model of operational and product excellence, Toyota has influenced the global diffusion of lean production methods in manufacturing in the past two decades; however, few other companies have been able to replicate the unique cultural features of the Toyota Way.

In the early 1990s New York was one of the most crime-ridden cities in America. To bring down the crime rate, Mayor Rudy Giuliani appointed William Bratton police commissioner in 1994.[3] Bratton recognized that because police policies rewarded effort rather than results, crimes went unsolved. Consequently, morale was low, absenteeism rates were high, and public perceptions of the NYPD were negative. Change required a shift in the culture, so that police officers would view citizens as customers whose needs came first. A 'cultural diagnosis' identified what police officers believed were major impediments to solving and preventing crime. The policing process was re-engineered to remove these impediments. Information reporting and sharing was improved with new technology. The biggest change, however, was sending officers out into the community. As more officers were assigned from administrative tasks to district precincts and from patrol cars to neighbourhood foot patrols, they responded better to community needs and anticipated the potential causes of crimes. Within two years, crime rates dropped and started a steady decline that continues today.

The cases of CN, Toyota, and the NYPD illustrate the critical role culture plays in supporting employees to succeed in their jobs. Relative to their peers, these organizations have become healthy and sustainable, in large part because of the strength of a positive culture. What makes these cultures positive is the way they support employees to benefit customers and communities and experience the sense of accomplishment and pride that flow from this process. Positive cultures cultivate the human capabilities required for the organization to thrive in the long term. For example, CN managers and employees became more 'passionate' – the company's word for an engaged workforce – about excellent customer service because they wanted to, not because they had to. Toyota nurtures a highly committed workforce because it trusts and respects its employees, challenging and enabling them to further develop their talents. As NYPD decentralized decision-making to local precincts, patrol officers took more leadership, were recognized for doing so, and found their work more meaningful.

This chapter focuses on the makings of a positive culture. I offer examples, insights, and suggestions that will help you to nurture and strengthen your organization's culture so that it can become a solid building block of a healthy organization. To summarize the action implications:

1. Positive cultures have widely shared, people-centred values that guide managers and employees to act with stakeholders' best interests foremost in mind.
2. Negative cultures are unhealthy, unethical, toxic, and potentially disastrous for employees, customers, and society.
3. Successful organizations view their culture as a strategic advantage, giving them a competitive edge and a rallying point for a talented and motivated workforce.
4. The sense of community in healthy organizations reflects a culture of trust and ethical responsibility, benefiting the organization's relations with stakeholders.
5. Cultures can be changed by energizing and evolving the best of the organization's existing values and including employees in the process.

What Is Culture?

I am frequently asked some variation of this question: 'why are some organizations better places in which to work *and* better performing for customers than others?' A big part of the answer is culture. Culture is the organization personified. It tells the company's story: who it is; how the actions of employees, managers, and external partners overcame challenges to bring it to where it is today; and the qualities that will take it where it wants to go. An organization's culture expresses its unique personality, character, and philosophy. If the culture is negative, employees will be disgruntled – as in an episode of *The Office* TV series or a *Dilbert* cartoon – and words such as indifferent, self-serving, and uncaring will be fitting descriptions of customers' experiences. In contrast, a positive culture is based on strong and authentic people values. It instils employee pride and loyalty, giving their work a greater sense of purpose and meaning. Top management set the tone and direction for a positive culture, but they will not be its keepers. Everyone in the organization 'owns' the culture and feels a responsibility for contributing to its ongoing vitality.

Organizations are like mini-societies. Anthropologists' insights about how societies operate highlight the fact that cooperation – necessary to survive and flourish – requires groups to have shared beliefs, customs, rituals, language, and myths. Organizations also have their own cultural systems, reflected in what managers and employees collectively believe, say, and do in their jobs. Essentially, culture is a set of shared assumptions and beliefs about how organizational life ought to be conducted. Culture is visible in how things get done by managers and employees inside and outside the organization. To understand the culture of an organization, we need to see through employees' eyes how they interpret their work activities and, most important of all, the values that guide them to behave as they do.

Organizations can have multiple and sometimes conflicting cultures, which results from groups holding dissonant values. A 'them–us' mentality found in some unionized workplaces essentially is a conflict of two internal cultures. In organizations that have undergone years of budget cuts, layoffs, and restructuring, negativity can pervade the culture. One professional in a human service agency described this to me as 'a culture of embittered entitlement.'

Not all strong cultures have positive consequences. Just think of the individualistic values – what critics call 'raw greed' – that dominated Wall Street investment banks and hedge funds leading up to the 2008 global financial crisis, blinding otherwise clever financial professionals to the inherent risks in mortgage-backed derivatives. The sub-prime mortgage fiasco was in large part a product of a culture that left no room for questioning and provided no moral incentive for thinking through the consequences of complex derivatives for investors or mortgage holders.

Perhaps more common is the sense of being socially disconnected that comes from working in an organization with a weak culture. Employees in such an environment lack clear guidelines for how to do their jobs. Left to their own devices, workers in weak cultures fall back on their own informal work rules. This becomes the default culture. Sometimes, a default culture taps into an employee's personal or professional sense of responsibility.

At other times, the default culture may breed indifferent service at a restaurant, unhelpful 'help line' employees, or more dire consequences. Early in this decade, 2,500 residents of Walkerton, a small town in

Ontario, Canada, became seriously ill, and some died, from drinking contaminated water, because the local water utility had tolerated years of incompetence and indifference over testing water quality. The provincial government launched an inquiry into the Walkerton tragedy, which later concluded: 'For years, the Walkerton Public Utilities Commission operators engaged in a host of improper operating practices, including failing to use adequate doses of chlorine, failing to monitor chlorine residuals daily, making false entries about residuals in daily operating records, and misstating the locations at which microbiological samples were taken. The operators knew that these practices were unacceptable and contrary to Ministry of Environment guidelines and directives.' [4] While these lax work practices are contemptible, they are symptomatic of a more widespread indifference about regulating and enforcing water standards. Without a strong ethic of competent public service – which would emphasize public safety and service quality – disasters like Walkerton are bound to occur.

To avoid such fiascos, senior managers must give high priority to shaping a durable culture that connects every employee with the goals of the organization, particularly the needs of customers, clients, and other stakeholders. As sociologists have shown, the more deeply ingrained and widely shared the values of an organization, the less that management has to impose formal rules and regulations to ensure that employees pursue common goals. In organizations where strong and positive values are widely shared, people can trust each other to do the right thing. In other words, values-based organizations can be far less bureaucratic. This no doubt is a change that employees and customers alike will welcome.

Edgar Schein, the MIT professor credited with coining the term 'corporate culture,' separates culture into three levels. The first and most visible level is the organization's artefacts, including the physical workspace and its furnishings, corporate branding, employee dress, how employee contributions are recognized, and styles of personal interaction. Travellers on WestJet airlines cannot miss the flight crew's casual uniforms, friendly banter, and folksy jokes, all intended to make customers feel like guests in someone's home and generate a team spirit among employees. The second level consists of the ways that the culture gets expressed in mission and vision statements, values, codes of conduct, corporate annual reports, and the like. GE's 'Imagination at work' tag line brands the company as an innovator on the frontiers of green technology as well as in its other longer-standing business arenas.

The third and least visible level includes the unwritten assumptions about how organizational life should be conducted. In one professional service firm, my conversations with managers and employees revealed a tacit rule: be polite to each other. This politeness resulted in pleasant, if superficial, interactions. But the unintended side-effect was an inability to honestly challenge each other's ideas in planning sessions, which was a problem in a knowledge-based organization that needed a flow of fresh ideas. As the organization reflected on what it needed to do to become healthier, managers and professionals eventually brought this aspect of its culture into plain view and talked about the need for open and respectful debate as a way to make better decisions.

Organization experts also distinguish between corporate culture and organizational culture. The former is imposed from the top by senior management and may or may not be carried around in the heads of employees. The latter is a more genuine expression of the shared beliefs that bring managers and employees together around common goals and how best to achieve them, especially through positive relationships with each other, with customers, and with outside stakeholders. While this distinction may seem like splitting hairs, the difference is subtle but useful for anyone wanting to strengthen the culture in their workplace. The foundation of a healthy organization is a culture that has been and continues to be co-created by the members of the organization, rather than imposed from the top.

Culture as Competitive Advantage

Today, more and more executives understand how culture affects business success. The once fuzzy notion of corporate culture has honed a sharper strategic edge. Furthermore, in the wake of the 2008 global financial crisis, the need for corporate ethical standards of honesty and accountability have taken on a new urgency. But an organization's culture must provide more than an ethical compass steering employees away from corrupt or criminal acts. A positive culture – defined broadly by its strong people-centred values – can help to address a range of common challenges any organization faces.

Figure 4.1 summarizes how an organization's culture strengthens the link between people and performance. The beliefs and values embedded in the culture guide the organization's approach to leadership, help to shape its HR policies and practices, and make the quality of the work environment a priority. Employees know that they are genuinely

Figure 4.1 The culture connection

valued. In turn, they value what they have in their workplace, feeling it is 'theirs.' When employees and managers learn from and celebrate what they have achieved, the culture is further strengthened. This is how culture can energize a positive upward spiral of quality of work life and performance. This is how a robust culture becomes a powerful competitive advantage.

Increasingly, business leaders articulate how their organization's culture helps them to outdistance competitors and cultivate a talented workforce. We can see this effect in 'best companies to work for' lists created by Great Place to Work Institute and published in *Fortune* magazine and *HR Magazine*. Here are some examples:

- Al Stubblefield, CEO of Baptist Health Care, in Florida, asserts that 'culture will drive strategy or culture will drag strategy.' He attributes the organization's turn-around success to a rebuilt culture that equally values patients and staff.
- Wim Roelandts, CEO of XILINX, a California-based maker of programmable silicon chips, observes that while competitors can offer the same benefits and pay, they cannot replicate a culture.

- As Isadore Sharp, the founder and CEO of the luxury hotel chain Four Seasons explains: 'A culture cannot be copied, it cannot be imitated. It has to grow from within over a very long time, based upon the consistent action of senior management. *That* is the barrier to entry for other hotels trying to compete against us. It isn't just having a fine building.'[5]
- The CEO of software firm Analytical Graphics believes that having fun at work is a catalyst for innovation. Chief Culture Officer Susan Schor's role at women's clothing retailer Eileen Fisher is to nurture 'a joyful atmosphere' that inspires people's best work, individually and collectively.
- Lee Lee James, COO and vice-chair of Synovus, a Georgia-based financial services firm, attributes continued growth and profitability to a strong focus over the past decade on creating a 'culture of the heart,' which puts people as the first link in the firm's value chain and guides decisions.
- Jeff Chambers, who headed human resources at software maker SAS, talks about three principles that inform the SAS culture: flexibility, trust and values. Above all, these principles guide the daily behaviour of managers because, as Chambers notes, 'managers are the hinge that swing the door between employer and employee.'

These examples highlight the benefits of positive cultures for business success. Al Stubblefield's comment that 'culture drives strategy' aptly summarizes complex organizational dynamics. Expanded, it means that a positive culture supports employees to implement the organization's strategy with a sense of pride and ownership in the results.

Some employers express this culture-people-strategy link using the language of health. Take, for example, ArcelorMittal Dofasco (formerly Dofasco), a steel producer in Hamilton, Ontario. Founded in 1912 and one of the corporate pillars of the local economy, Dofasco developed its own style of employee relations, called 'The Dofasco Way.' The Dofasco Way defines a corporate culture supported by programs such as profit-sharing, extensive training, and employee well-being. Senior management attributes a low voluntary turnover rate and productivity increases double the Canadian manufacturing sector average to a culture that has as its centrepiece health, safety, and wellness. When Dofasco received the National Quality Institute's Healthy Workplace Award for excellence in these areas, Don Pether, the president and CEO at the time, stated: 'From the top down and the bottom up, the health, safety and well-being of people is a deeply ingrained aspect of our corporate culture ... In addition to our shared responsibility for health, safety and well-being, it is a business advantage to have employees healthy and at work. Our responsibility as an employer is to create conditions where all Dofasco people can achieve and contribute to their full potential, work safely and remain in good physical and mental health.'[6]

Unhealthy and Healthy Cultures

ArcelorMittal Dofasco's success in a turbulent global industry attests to the strategic value of a healthy culture. But most organizations are not there yet. In fact, cultures range from healthy and robust to unhealthy and downright toxic. So the ongoing challenge that managers, employees, and HR professionals face is how to minimize the negatives and maximize the positives in their particular culture. To understand this, and also to appreciate the vital role of culture in an organization's effectiveness, a comparison of cultures in healthy and unhealthy organizations is instructive.

Unhealthy Cultures

Robert Sutton's refreshingly frank book, *The No Asshole Rule*, provides guidelines for creating a civilized workplace.[7] Sutton describes the 'culture of fear' that engulfs workplaces when managers and employees get away with bad behaviour, demeaning others, and generally acting like jerks. The repercussions can immobilize an organization. People retreat and/or quit, usually in that order, often at considerable personal and organizational costs. Sutton describes how a new CEO at a Fortune 500 company fixed a broken culture. The CEO purged about two dozen toxic senior managers by applying the performance management system the way it should have been used, to prevent bullying and harassment. The moves by this new CEO restored a large measure of humanity to the organization, benefiting both customers and employees. Sutton's candour about how jerks rob workplaces of civility and co-workers of their dignity strikes a chord for many of us. He spotlights jerks' behaviour: a repertoire of insults, threats, public humiliation, rude interruptions, dirty looks, passive aggression, and more. But workplaces do not have to be populated with jerks for their cultures to be negative.

At the extreme, an unhealthy culture can be disastrous, like the Walkerton contaminated water tragedy. Take the fatal end in February

2003 of the Space Shuttle Columbia, which was torn apart over Texas at a speed of Mach 19.5 just minutes from landing, killing the seven astronauts aboard. The world's attention focused on a chunk of foam dislodged from the shuttle's left wing seconds after take-off. However, the Columbia Accident Investigation Board concluded that there were deeper organizational causes – specifically NASA's 'failed safety culture.'[8] Three critical goals for successful space missions – safety, system reliability, and quality assurance – were jeopardized by communication breakdowns. Contrary to NASA's official line that employees were empowered to stop an operation if they detected even the hint of a problem, the margin for risk tolerance and error had grown perilously wide in the space program.

As a result, foam problems were accepted when there was no engineering rationale for doing so. Budget cuts, staff shortages, thick bureaucracy, and intense pressures to meet deadlines contributed to this complacent attitude about safety. Professionals who were supposed to be operating the best safety and quality engineering programs in the world over the years had become unable or unwilling to communicate openly about potential hazards that space missions faced. Communication breakdowns also were a failure of professional responsibility. While the inquiry report does not address working conditions or employee experiences, we can only imagine how it must have felt to be an engineer or manager connected to the Space Shuttle Columbia, knowing that corners were being cut and things could go wrong.

A less extreme but more common example of a negative workplace culture is one that encourages overwork. A culture that tolerates and even rewards overwork is counterproductive, eroding employees' quality of work life and their ability and commitment to perform their jobs well.

I saw such a culture at the head office of a large energy company, described by one of the HR managers as 'a hard-driving place.' One division alone had accumulated millions of dollars in unused vacation time liability. With sixty-hour work weeks being common, turnover was a revolving door and morale was sagging. Employee cynicism increased when the company was named one of the city's top employers. The company also had gained a public profile for social and environmental responsibility. While charitable contributions showed generous corporate philanthropy, employees saw a huge disconnect: few of them had any time to do community volunteer work, given their demanding work schedules. When asked for explanations, professional employees described an 'engineering and accounting culture' that focused on operational results, a lack of people skills among senior managers, and a leadership team that believed hard work was a virtue. Some senior managers paid lip service to employee concerns about workload and how it interfered with their personal lives, but these issues did not make it onto the executive team's agenda. Meanwhile, talented employees – especially up-and-coming female professionals – left in search of a better quality of work life.

Even more extreme was what I witnessed at a non-profit professional organization that provides a wide range of services to members. Many employees of this organization saw their work as more than a job. For them it was a personal calling, because they believed in the service mission of the organization – improving the lives of members, their families, and communities. Over the years, the organization developed work norms and values that put member service ahead of employees' needs, even if their health and well-being was at risk. For professional member-service staff, fifty-hour work weeks were usual, plus extra time spent travelling and working out of the office. These employees attributed a chronic culture of overwork – a fact of organizational life that had been documented in employee surveys over many years – to increased service levels expected by members, more complex work, and rising management expectations for job performance.

In this unhealthy culture, work pressures and job dedication resulted in relatively low absenteeism but very high presenteeism, as workers felt they could not afford to take time off even when sick. This practice had become institutionalized as a cultural norm, but with significant costs. Feeling demoralized, employees had little trust that management would take their interests into account. Employees' personal health suffered, and surveys revealed above-average rates of major health risks, such as smoking, high blood pressure, diabetes, and obesity. Even though the organization was saddled with escalating long-term disability costs as more employees burned out, remedial action was slow to come. Employees told tragic stories about the human toll, recounting how co-workers had died on the job from complications arising from chronic health problems because they did not have time to care for themselves.

An unhealthy culture triggers a downward negative spiral. While this may not spell the end of an organization, it likely results in chronic underperformance, avoidable employee costs, and reduced quality of work life for employees, unless, of course, executives, line managers,

HR, and rank-and-file employees take decisive steps to expose these negative consequences and, at the same time, present a positive alternative.

Healthy Cultures

The biggest difference between healthy and unhealthy cultures is their values. Healthy organizations value respect, responsibility, honesty, fairness, and integrity. Indeed, these are the qualities most people want in any relationship. The power of these values lies in how they influence day-to-day interactions among co-workers; between managers and employees; between employees and their customers or clients, suppliers, and business partners; and between the organization and the larger community. The result is a positive upward spiral of improved quality of work life and performance.

Strong core values generate trust, which is a good barometer of the overall health of an organization. People need to trust each other in order for their work environment to be healthy and productive. Trusting someone means being comfortable taking risks in the relationship. One is more likely to open up and share ideas, reveal confidential information, ask for advice, offer help, willingly cooperate, and in other ways be vulnerable. Being vulnerable is safe only if there is confidence that the other person will behave in expected ways and that their actions will take others' interests into account. It is at the micro-level of personal interaction that trust is built. As philosopher Robert Solomon and business consultant Fernando Flores comment in their book, *Building Trust in Business, Politics, Relationships and Life*: 'Without trust, the corporate community is reduced to a group of resentful wage slaves and defensive, if not ambitious, managers. People will do their jobs, but they will not offer their ideas, or their enthusiasm, or their souls.'[9] The picture presented is poles apart from a healthy organization.

It is telling that some of my examples of healthy organizations are on the best workplaces lists produced by the Great Place to Work Institute in different countries. The assessment for these lists uses the institute's Trust Index employee survey, which measures what the institute identifies as three drivers of trust: management credibility, respect and fairness. As noted earlier, high-trust organizations have superior performance. Employees benefit, too. An analysis of Trust Index results for organizations on the 2007 list of 50 Best Workplaces in Canada, compared with those of organizations that applied for the list but did not make it, shows that employees in the 50 best workplaces are far more likely to experience their workplace as psychologically and emotionally healthy. This no doubt reflects the fair and respectful treatment they receive from managers and co-workers.

Researchers also have documented the personal and organizational benefits of trust. A research team at the University of Florida compared results from 132 studies of the relationship between trust and two big outcomes: risk-taking and job performance.[10] This research, published in the *Journal of Applied Psychology*, makes a useful distinction between trust and trustworthiness. Trust in a relationship between two people depends on the trustworthiness of each person in the eyes of the other. Trustworthiness refers to the qualities that must be present for someone to trust you. These qualities include loyalty, openness, caring, fairness, availability, receptivity, consistency, reliability, and discreetness – all of which can be learned. So trustworthiness can be incorporated into leadership training and development as part of efforts to build a healthier organization.

There is good reason for employers to do so. The more that managers are trustworthy, the more that employees feel committed to the organization, perform their jobs well, take risks in their work, and are 'good citizens' by helping others and contributing to a positive work environment. When trustworthiness is widespread among managers, employees are less likely to partake in counterproductive behaviours. These include disregarding safety procedures, making threats, tardiness, absenteeism, and other actions subject to discipline. From the employees' perspective, these examples of trustworthiness add up to a more vibrant workplace.

To be meaningful, corporate values and ethics must extend from the inside out. Internal relationships based on trust will foster stakeholder trust in the organization. Unfortunately, public confidence in corporations, governments, and other large institutions has steadily declined over the past several decades, reflecting an erosion of trust. It has not helped, of course, that the opening decade of the twenty-first century is book-ended by corporate scandals, from the likes of Enron to the entire global financial system teetering on the brink. Unsurprisingly, the average person feels that whoever makes decisions in these organizations does not care about their interests. Corporate ethics, ideally, should ensure that an organization and its employees can be trusted by external stakeholders to consistently 'do the right things.' That is, dealings will be honest, transparent, accountable, fair, and respectful of others' rights and interests. The almost total absence of these qualities explains the public outrage over the implosion of Northern Rock and Lehman Brothers and government bail-outs of other huge financial institutions.

In a healthy organization, the culture naturally encourages mutually beneficial relationships with stakeholders. The idea of 'community' aptly describes a healthy organization's internal and external worlds. For example, I recently facilitated workshops with professionals who provide health services to Aboriginal communities in Canada. The shared vision of a vibrant workplace crafted by the group ranked 'a sense of community' as the key ingredient. For them, community meant two things: a feeling of collegial support and common values within each worksite and the organization as a whole; and a strong connection with the individuals in the Aboriginal communities with whom they worked. When discussing what constitutes a vibrant workplace, these workers believed that the bonds they had cultivated within their teams enabled them to contribute to healthier Aboriginal communities. Or, in more general terms: healthy workplaces support healthy communities.

These connections between internal and external communities can be described in terms of citizenship. Organizational citizenship refers to the altruistic behaviours that workers engage in to support each other. This goes beyond being a team player, requiring employees to proactively think of ways to help co-workers succeed in their tasks and personal lives. These are the good citizens noted in the University of Florida study, described above. For example, corporate citizenship could be displayed as helping a colleague deal with a family medical emergency, sending a co-worker relevant articles or websites for a new project, offering to pitch in and help others who are overloaded, or volunteering to organize work group social events. In some organizations, employees contribute their unused paid sick days to an employee who is off work for several weeks or months recovering from an operation or illness. These are the small ways that individuals rise above their own immediate needs and interests, putting co-workers first.

Similarly, corporate citizenship describes the stance of a healthy organization towards society (see chapter 7, below, for more on this topic). Responsible corporate citizens provide financial support for arts, culture, community services, and a host of charitable causes from operas and art galleries to food banks and cures for cancer. But they also go beyond philanthropy. For example, each year TD Financial makes generous donations to community causes. What is more, the bank's employees select charities and community events to fund and in which to volunteer. As a result, less mainstream and more diverse charities receive support, such as local gay/lesbian/bi-sexual/transgendered pride events and help for people with HIV-AIDS. This community involvement supports TD's commitment to diversity and inclusiveness within its workforce, 25 per cent of whom are visible minorities. According to the bank's manager of diversity, all of its actions on diversity align with the corporate value of respect. Ed Clark, TD's CEO, states that 'diversity is how we do business,' and therefore it is central to the bank's long-term business strategy. For the bank, the goals of supporting diversity among both customers and employees are mutually reinforcing.

Culture Change

My point is that a positive culture enables all the organization's relationships to be rewarding. That is how culture helps to build healthy organizations. The attributes of a positive culture transcend values and beliefs about employee well-being. Indeed, positive cultures have values that run broad and deep – such as trust, which as we have seen is fundamental to business performance and responsible dealings with customers and communities. Even if the ideal culture is labelled healthy or positive, it is necessary to minimize some things on the negative side of the cultural ledger and maximize other things on the positive side. In other words, the culture may need to change.

Cultures Can Be Revitalized and Can Evolve

How do you change a culture to make it more positive and values based? The answer to this question depends on how you approach organizational change. One approach advocates transformational change: reinventing the organization, shaking it up, ushering in a new era, and radically altering how people work together and how the business operates. A contrasting approach claims that culture change happens incrementally. Based on my interpretation of the research on change and my consulting experience, I find myself in the latter camp. In reality, successful cultural change is more evolutionary than revolutionary. Over time and with persistent effort, it is possible to incrementally strengthen a culture in ways that look and feel transformational.

The operative word here is 'evolve.' As management expert Henry Mintzberg explains: 'You don't change cultures – you revitalize existing cultures. You can't take a company that has existed for years and just throw out its culture and drop a new one in place. What you do is bring back the energy that is still there.'[11] Change agents can take some comfort from this view. Surely, moving into place the culture building block of a healthy organization becomes a less daunting task if approached as step-by-step improvements, rather than having to orchestrate a radical make-over.

As you consider options for revitalizing your culture, here are some points to keep in mind. The examples I used of organizations at their cultural worst point to four cultural features that are incompatible with a healthy organization:

- Not meeting employees' human need for dignity and respect.
- Pursuing operational goals in ways that sacrifice the health, safety, and well-being of employees.
- Not understanding, or reflecting upon, the unintended consequences of your organization's culture for the businesses' long-term sustainability and success.
- Weak accountability for the consequences of actions.

At the other end of the continuum, positive organizational cultures meet all the following criteria, setting the standard for culture as a healthy organization building block:

- There are deeply held core values that define the basic operating philosophy of the organization, particularly how all individuals will be treated and are expected to treat each other.
- Employees see their personal values reflected in company values.
- There is wide recognition, continually reinforced by senior management, that the organization's culture is a foundation for its success.
- From the top of the organization down to the front lines, everyone actively is involved in living the core values daily.

The Culture-Strengthening Process

Let us examine how cultures can be strengthened. As you undertake this important task, bear in mind the systemic nature of culture. You cannot isolate culture as a target for change. Nor can you afford to ignore it when trying to change other parts of your organization. As such, culture can be elusive. Its features cannot be grasped in a concrete way, as, for instance, putting your hands on a marketing plan, an employee benefits handbook, or an organization chart. The practical implication, then, is that it is not always easy to pinpoint what needs changing in a culture. A few examples follow that will help you to identify culture's connections throughout your organization.

Positive cultures are modelled by the actions of senior management. This observation is based on a recurring theme in my conversations with HR and OD practitioners: their diagnosis of a need to 'transform' the organization's culture. Transformation is the solution, they explain, because the existing culture blocks the path to becoming a healthier and more highly performing workplace. Yet further discussion reveals that the changes sought have more to do with aligning senior managers' actions to existing organizational values, such as respect, integrity, and learning and innovation. For example, senior managers at a public agency participated in a values assessment, which showed that they believed operational efficiency and cost control were most important for the success of the organization. In contrast, all the organization's espoused values were about people. To address this disconnect in values, HR facilitated discussions with the senior management team about how they could better achieve operational goals through the application of corporate values.

Culture cannot be taken for granted. Doing so creates a blind spot when management implements a new organizational system, structure or process. To illustrate, a large telecommunications company wanted to notch up its customer service levels. New service standards and incentives focused on customer service quality, rather than on the volume of calls handled. In preparation, supervisors and managers were trained to coach call centre customer service agents to be more responsive to customers' needs. But the existing culture placed more value on supervisor behaviours that boosted call quantity rather than on customer service quality. A values shift was required to support the new customer service objectives and coaching. By not putting this issue on the table for discussion during training sessions, elements of the existing culture actually held back progress.

Organizational restructuring requires careful attention to culture. This is especially evident in mergers and acquisitions. For example, a health care organization providing rehabilitation services was created through the merger of two successful and well-established institutions, each with distinctive cultures. Little time was invested in creating a blended culture, other than developing statements of the new entity's

mission, vision and values. Senior managers and HR-OD professionals who led a new strategic planning initiative recognized that a unified culture would make it easier to successfully implement the plan.
These change agents did not want to signal to staff that the existing
culture was broken. Rather, they wanted to build on the best of the old
culture, while at the same time focusing everyone on the future. Timing was good, given a recent move from two separate facilities into a
new, state-of-the-art building, and senior managers initiated an organization-wide conversation on the organization's future that included
revitalized values.

Progress on culture change may be uneven. A large regional health
service organization had clearly committed to becoming a healthy
organization. The organization combines several facilities, each with
a distinctive history and culture. The overall vision is healthy people
in healthy communities, and a healthy workplace is a priority in the
strategic plan. A Healthy Workplace Council was established to coordinate actions on healthy workplace goals. People volunteer to be on the
council so membership is diverse, from front-line employees to senior
executives and union officials. As a member of the council put it, their
work injected 'more humanity' into how staff are treated. As the council
became a catalyst for regenerating the culture, it accepted that progress
would be uneven across departments and sites – a reality that fit its
community development approach to change. From this perspective,
the council cultivated work-unit leadership and empowered teams to
act on issues they consider important.

Strengthening Values

I recently gave a talk on how vibrant workplaces inspire employees at a
corporate educational forum. Forum organizers had chosen quality as
the theme – quality improvement, quality client services, and quality
workplaces. I asked the employees attending the forum how well they
knew their organization's values. Someone in the front row admitted
that, while she could not recite the values, she 'knew where to find
them.' This was a good opener for what turned out to be a frank discussion about how the values support the organization's quality goals.
What became clearer to these employees during a seventy-five- minute
interactive session is that they personally need to see their own values
reflected in the organization's values. This point was driven home by
a number of participants, who explained how they feel most inspired

about their job when, at the end of the workday, their personal values are reaffirmed because they and their team have done something they truly believe makes a difference for clients and society.

The Importance of Values

Values act as cultural glue, holding together the people and groups in an organization. The *Oxford English Dictionary* defines values as 'the principles or standards of a person or social group; the generally accepted or personally held judgement of what is valuable and important in life.' Sociologists refer to values as the beliefs that guide the behaviour of individuals and groups. Or, more simply, values act like social glue. In organizations, values often appear alongside the corporate mission (its purpose) and vision (its aspirations). The mission expresses 'what are we in business to do' and the vision articulates 'where we want to go,' while its values express 'how we will run the business and go about achieving our goals and aspirations.' More specifically, an organization's values should do these six things:

- Influence relationships with all stakeholders.
- Guide decision-making and priority-setting.
- Link employees to the mission and vision.
- Inspire and empower employees in their jobs.
- Provide the foundations of the organization's culture.
- Stand the test of time.

Rosabeth Moss Kanter, a Harvard Business School professor, studied some of the world's largest organizations to discover how they were able to quickly develop creative solutions to major social and environmental challenges.[12] The agility of these huge multinational companies – IBM, Procter & Gamble, Omron, CEMEX, Cisco, and Banco Real – defied conventional thinking about lumbering bureaucracies. As Kanter explains: 'In the most influential corporations today, a foundation of values and standards provides a well-understood, widely-communicated guidance system that ensures effective operations while enabling people to make decisions appropriate to local situations.' This echoes the conclusion that Jim Collins and James Porras reached in their best-selling book, *Built to Last: Successful Habits of Visionary Companies*.[13] Companies featured in this study had strong core values, which guided their adaptation to massive economic, political, and social changes in the twentieth century. Collins and Porras refer to core values as enduring principles that keep everyone focused on long-term viability as opposed to short-term financial expediency.

I will present three cases that illustrate the importance of values to an organization's success. The first, the Vancouver Organizing Committee for the 2010 Olympic and Paralympic Games (VANOC), is a new organization with a short lifespan. The second is IBM, which recently adapted its early twentieth-century founder's values to the twenty-first century. The third is mining company Teck Cominco's smelter operations, where senior managers launched a values exercise that led to guiding principles with clear behavioural expectations.

New Values

Achieving a successful Olympic and Paralympic Games presents huge organizational challenges in full public view. People from very different backgrounds – administrators, lawyers and accountants, engineers, former elite athletes, media experts – have to be forged into a high-performing team, knowing that the team will disband soon after the last athletes leave the games venue. The Vancouver Organizing Committee for the 2010 Olympic and Paralympic Games rose to this challenge by crafting a clear vision, mission, and set of values.[14] The vision and mission are appropriately lofty for the games but realistic, given the potential spin-offs:

- VANOC's vision is: A stronger Canada whose spirit is raised by its passion for sport, culture and sustainability.
- VANOC's mission is: To touch the soul of the nation and inspire the world by creating and delivering an extraordinary Olympic and Paralympic experience with lasting legacies.

However, it is the following explicit values that unify a diverse and expanding group of employees at VANOC:

- *Team* – We recognize that success and excellence can only be achieved and sustained by a deep commitment to working as a team and the practice of focusing on collective rather than individual effort and rewards.
- *Trust* – We act consciously to inspire the trust of everyone whose lives we touch by modeling the highest standards of honesty, integrity and ethical behaviour at all times.

- *Excellence* – We model individual and collective performance by working as a team with our partners to promote social cultural, health and sport excellence. Improve the sport performance of Team Canada and deliver on our vision.
- *Sustainability* – We proactively consider the long-term interests of all stakeholders in the Games, both here in Canada and throughout the World, to ensure that our impact is positive and our legacy sustainable for all.
- *Creativity* – We embrace new ideas, encourage input to foster breakthrough thinking and solutions that will allow us to amaze even ourselves in our ability to exceed expectations and deliver on our vision.

By following each single-word value with a description of how it plays out in practice, VANOC provides existing and prospective employees with a clear set of behavioural expectations. Because the organization has been in a steady recruitment mode, the values have provided a useful tool for screening applicants and orienting new recruits. Indicative of the importance VANOC places on values fit, its website provides a Values Assessment that prospective applicants are encouraged to use to determine if they share VANOC's values. The message: do not apply if you do not already believe in our values. As the website states: 'At VANOC, we have a vision, mission, and a set of values to which we are 100% committed. As a potential member of our team, you would need to fully ascribe to these values as well.' Overall, VANOC has created a simple checklist for a healthy culture:

Team
1. Do you enjoy working as part of a team, or are you a person that likes to work on your own?
2. Do you believe there are benefits to working as part of a team? If yes, what are the benefits?
3. What would you do if a member of your team was falling behind and needed your help?

Trust
1. Do you trust others easily?
2. Do you value honesty in others and in yourself?

Excellence
1. Do you aspire to excellence in all that you do?
2. Do you expect to be held accountable for all that you do?

Sustainability
1. Do you link your personal interests and values for creating healthy natural environments and social well-being with some of your work activities?
2. Are there ways you link your purchasing choices with your values?

Creativity
1. Do you enjoy thinking 'outside of the box'?
2. Do you enjoy working in a continually changing and fast-paced environment?

Renewed Values

IBM provides a good illustration of a well-established organization with a distinctive brand and culture that stood it in good stead for decades. Thomas Watson, the company's founder, laid down what he called Basic Beliefs in 1914: respect for the individual, the best customer service, and the pursuit of excellence. These proved enduring, but when the digital information revolution took off in the late 1980s, the company faltered. It struggled to find a new footing in a global information technology market, where its dominant role as a manufacturer of mainframe and then desktop computers had been eclipsed by low-cost newcomers. IBM had to reinvent its business model, moving out of manufacturing and into information technology, business consulting, and outsourcing services.

In 2003 IBM's newly appointed CEO, Samuel J. Palmisano, sought to re-energize employees. He launched an ambitious project to redefine the company's values using a high-tech, high-involvement process. IBM had developed an intranet-based tool that facilitates and summarizes discussions across all IBM's operations on key business issues. Palmisano presented four concepts – respect, customer, excellence, innovation – to a meeting of 300 executives to test the idea of values renewal. 'Respect' was jettisoned because of negative connotations (IBM had gone through a painful period of layoffs). The result was three draft values – commitment to the customer, excellence through innovation, and integrity that earns trust – that were proposed to employees in the 'Values Jam' online forum. There was lively debate and reflection on issues like internal silos, trust, integrity, and respect. After the Jam, Palmisano told an executive committee meeting: 'You guys ought to read every one of these comments, because if you think we've got this place plumbed correctly, think again.' An employee team sifted through the voluminous transcripts and results from pre- and post-Jam surveys. The result was three new values:

- Dedication to every client's success.
- Innovation that matters, for our company and for the world.
- Trust and personal responsibility in all relationships.

In 2004 another Jam was conducted in which more than 52,000 employees exchanged best practices for seventy-two hours. This event was focused on finding actionable ideas to support implementation of the values identified previously. A new post-Jam ratings event was developed to allow IBMers to select key ideas that supported the values. This values renewal at IBM is significant for its process. The new values were not imposed from the top but were the creation of employees from across the sprawling company. IBM has since adapted this grassroots approach for business development. In 2006 it launched 'Innovation Jam' to bring together employees, their family members, and IBM customers to discuss future products. IBM's use of executive blogs and its active encouragement of its staff to discuss in open forums the future direction of IBM products show how it lives the corporate values – and stays ahead of its main competitors.

From Values to Behaviours

Canadian mining giant Teck Cominco's operations in Trail, British Columbia, is one of the world's largest fully integrated zinc and lead smelting and refining complexes. The sprawling facility also produces other specialty metals, chemicals, and fertilizer products and generates its own hydro power. Mining and smelting have a long history in the mountainous Kootenay region of British Columbia. The Trail operations have become a global leader in smelting and refining technology. Several years ago, senior management developed and implemented a comprehensive 'People Strategy' to ensure that the facility maintained its competitive positions in global commodities markets. The strategy responded to its human resource challenges, which included sustaining the highest standards of workplace safety and health, unprecedented retirements due to an aging workforce, and recruitment and retention pressures created by a very competitive labour market especially for skilled trades.

Like IBM and other companies with long histories, the Trail Operations had a values statement, but it no longer resonated with managers or employees. So, as part of developing the People Strategy, senior managers also revisited the old values and came up with a draft of new values, with the idea of consulting with line managers, supervisors, and employees to consolidate them. The People Strategy's specific action items were implemented. They included improvements in new employee orientation, strengthening a safety culture, a wellness initiative, service recognition, enhanced leadership development, and profit sharing. But the discussion of values was put aside for more than a year.

The senior management team returned to the draft values that the People Strategy had successfully launched. A candid discussion identified concerns that are often voiced when executives scrutinize the meaning of specific values: they are too vague, they do not get close enough to explicit behaviours, they need to reflect what managers will actually do, and they are not really values but operational goals. For example, references to 'excellent results' were seen not as values, but rather as operational goals. This realization led the Trail Operations' top management to think in terms of guiding behavioural principles rather than values. They agreed that, first and foremost, any values statement had to be a meaningful guide to how they worked together and showed leadership. Here is what they developed and subsequently rolled out to managers, supervisors, and non-union professional and administrative staff:

> These guiding principles define what we value, how we behave, and what we expect of others. Living by these guiding principles will ensure Trail Operations' future success.
>
> - We act with *integrity*, treating all with *dignity, fairness,* and *respect.*
> - We commit to everyone going home *safe* and *healthy* every day.
> - We take *personal responsibility* for our actions and results.
> - We *support* each other to achieve our fullest potential.
> - We *act responsibly* to support a sustainable future for the *communities* and *environment* in which we operate.

An important step in developing the guiding principles was for the senior management team to agree upon specific behaviours that reflected how the principles translated into effective leadership. They went one step further. In order to communicate the importance of the guiding principles, not as abstract concepts but as explicit criteria for good management practice, they also illustrated each value with examples of how a member of the senior management team had followed one of the principles when making a decision or taking an action. As I show in chapter 5, these guiding principles became the basis for strengthening leadership skills across the Trail facility.

Revitalizing Your Organization's Culture

To summarize: healthy organizations consistently treat employees as *the* core business asset and the key to long-term success. Managers in these organizations are guided in their decisions and actions by strongly felt, people-oriented values. A positive culture requires more than just high ethical standards. Culture comes alive in the relationships that bind employees with each other, with managers and with customers. In this way, culture reinforces ethical imperatives, reaching deeper into the foundations of performance excellence. Positive cultures will help to address an organization's people challenges, especially by finding better ways to encourage employees to excel in their jobs and supporting them to meet their personal needs and professional goals. In short, an organization's cultural qualities may be decisive in shaping its future.

Senior managers must face the fact that their organization's culture is critical to attaining the high quality of work life employees want and the high performance shareholders and customers want. So it is important that culture be openly discussed and reflected upon, starting with top management. These conversations may not come easily, but you must look for opportunities to raise the issues we have just discussed. For some senior managers, talking about culture is far outside their comfort zone – the organizational equivalent to personal counselling. I have been inside organizations where the senior HR manager specifically asks that the word *culture* not be used in discussions with the executive team about developing a healthy workplace strategy. I also have been asked by managers to remove slides from presentations for leadership development workshops that list the corporate values, because the values are 'dormant' and showing them could provoke questions about why this is the case.

This chapter has provided various examples of organizations at different stages of cultural evolution. My intent is to help change agents to plan next steps that can contribute to a healthier culture in their workplace. Some organizations already are cultivating a positive culture. Indeed, on numerous occasions, I have heard employees and managers enthusiastically describe a culture of mutual respect, in which people trust one another and everyone's contributions are valued and recognized. Conversations about culture in these workplaces have a different objective: how to keep the culture fresh, alive, and 'owned' by everyone in the organization.

When you are considering how to revitalize your culture, it helps to recap key points about culture change. It is more useful to talk about revitalizing positive aspects of an existing culture that are critical for the organization's future direction rather than about creating a different culture. As one newly appointed CEO of a financial services firm put it reassuringly at an all-staff conference, 'I'm not here to change your culture but to help you to harness its strengths.' Harnessing the strengths of your culture requires collective reflection on the values that are going to guide you into the future. A way to kick-start the process of revitalizing your organization's culture is to find ways to breathe new life into its values – which may be relevant but dormant. This revitalization takes time and commitment from the top. View cultural change not as an end in itself, but as an evolving process that connects with any type of change in the organization. And strive to involve, consult, and empower employees to strengthen the culture so that it becomes theirs. The last point underscores why inclusive leadership also is a healthy organization building block – and it is the subject of chapter 5.

5 Inclusive Leadership

Emile is a health and safety coordinator at a large manufacturer. Several years ago, he was asked by the company's HR manager to look into wellness programs. The human resource plan for the year included a wellness program feasibility study. Emile had fixed parameters in which to work. A thorough needs assessment of thousands of employees was out of the question. And any plans would need the blessing of several unions. So his approach was to convene a series of focus groups representative of professional, administrative, and production staff and also invite key union reps. Focus groups identified current strengths in occupational health and safety that could be expanded to address wellness and agreed that a wellness initiative was needed. In the following year, a union-management wellness committee was launched. Emile was a member of the committee, but not the chair. Off to a slow start, the committee moved into action after making site visits to other unionized worksites that had comprehensive wellness programs. These visits showed what union and management cooperation could achieve. The committee's work opened the door to address a wide range of people issues as vital to the future of the business.

Lin is the vice-president of human resources in a large health care organization. The organization offered a long menu of programs in safety, workplace health and wellness, learning, and career development. Some showed success, such as reduction in lost-time injury rates and improvement in the return to work process for injured staff. Yet employees faced a bewildering array of support services, often not well understood and therefore underutilized. Lin and her team saw the need to consolidate and streamline these people initiatives, so the team developed a healthy workplace framework that tied them together. The framework grew out of a vision of what a healthy workplace looks like, developed by the HR-OD team at a retreat. The executive did not accept the need for what it saw as yet another HR initiative. Undeterred, Lin and her team adopted the framework as their internal guide, never losing an opportunity to communicate to the executive the strategic value of taking a holistic and integrated approach to workplace and workforce issues. After several years and a new CEO, a revised corporate strategy recognized that fostering healthy employees in healthy work environments is a key to health care excellence.

These real cases illustrate that the actions required to create healthier organizations can be led from many places and positions. In this chapter, I suggest that positive cultures and vibrant workplaces – two basic healthy organization building blocks – are products of combined efforts by many people. Healthy organizations do not result when a few lead and others follow. Certainly, it helps when senior managers make a commitment to improving the workplace and strengthening the culture – and to 'walking the talk.' But top-down leadership is not sufficient. In quite different ways Emile, Lin, and their co-workers show that even without executive-level commitment, progress still is possible with adequate time, determination, and patience. In fact, the greater the number of healthy organization champions there are in a workplace, the more likely it is that these changes will put down roots and become sustainable.

Whether your goals focus on elements of a vibrant workplace, supporting employees to be more inspired in their jobs, or refreshing your corporate values – the change agenda has to be 'owned' by everyone. In this way, healthy organizations are co-created through the ongoing and coordinated actions of all members of the workplace community. Impetus for a healthy organization can come from the bottom, middle, and top of the organization. Even if the full support of senior management is lacking, others in the organization have considerable scope to make improvements, often more than they might think. Any employee should feel motivated and enabled to make the organization healthier.

The key action implications flowing from my discussion in this chapter of the leadership required to build healthy organizations can be summarized as follows:

1. Achieving healthy organization goals requires an inclusive approach to leadership. Improvements have to be a shared responsibility.

2. Everyone in your organization has the potential to play a leadership role in achieving healthy organization goals. They need to be enabled to do so.
3. Each employee can show leadership in day-to-day relationships through values-based behaviours that contribute to a vibrant and inspiring workplace.
4. Inclusive leaders motivate by inspiration, are caring and connected, are trustworthy and trusting, are action-oriented, involve others, and are self-aware.
5. The tone, direction, and support for widespread leadership on healthy organization goals depends on the behaviours of supervisors and managers.

Leading the Way to Healthier Organizations

Adopting an inclusive approach to leadership invites others to participate actively in shaping their work environments. This point will resonate for anyone with a health promotion background. It enshrines the proven principle that people thrive in environments that they have intentionally created to be health promoting. This also is sound organizational development practice. The impetus and ideas for improving the organization's systems, structures, and culture spring organically from within. Each member of an organization has the potential to positively influence its healthy trajectory and should not have to wait for permission from top management to take initiative.

Leading at the Micro Level

Inclusive leadership extends our earlier discussion of vibrant workplaces. Recall that vibrant workplaces depend on the quality of relationships among co-workers and with managers. So we need to think about leadership at this micro level. It is through daily working relationships that you contribute, collaborate, support, and learn with others. Every time you pitch a new customer service idea to your team, acknowledge a co-worker's contributions, step forward to help others deal with a crisis or solve a new problem, or take initiative to improve the way you do your job, you are contributing to a vibrant workplace. When multiplied across an organization day after day, these small actions and values-based behaviours add up to a more vibrant and inspiring workplace.

Micro-level leadership also energizes the culture. This happens every time you consciously strive to live the organization's core values in your dealings with co-workers, staff who report to you, customers, and community stakeholders. These are small acts of leadership, simply because you are setting a positive example for others. As we saw in chapter 4, what distinguishes healthy cultures from unhealthy ones is the extent to which employees' behaviour is guided by strongly held common values. In positive cultures, behaviours are responsive, supportive, and constructive because people are highly valued. These behaviours are evident in how people plan and implement decisions, go about their tasks, and relate to each other, customers, and other stakeholders. It is through values-based behaviours that an organization realizes its vision. Some would argue that living the organization's core values should be like a habit – you do it simply as a matter of routine. But I believe it also requires intentional leadership. You must be proactive, anticipate others' needs, take initiative, be a role model, and more.

Micro-level leadership actions will become more frequent if the constraints of positions are loosened up. People will collaborate across functional boundaries and think beyond their job description. As the organization becomes more fluid, it is better able to tap into the skills, ideas, and knowledge of all employees. Employees feel more empowered to learn and contribute. Work experiences move to the positive end of the scale in terms of improved levels of satisfaction, commitment, and inspiration. This does not mean dispensing with defined roles and responsibilities or layers of management. These remain basic requirements: people need to know what is expected of them and how their efforts will be coordinated with others. But there is untapped potential for employees to take more leadership within their own roles and working relationships. Senior managers therefore must actively encourage others to do so.

Previous chapters described how senior managers enabled others to help move the organization towards a healthier ideal. The personal convictions of the executives at IBM, Teck Cominco's Trail Operations, and Trillium Health Centre set in motion what would become much wider discussions about the organization's values, vision and goals. These examples illustrate an inclusive approach to leadership, one that challenges others to be actively involved in shaping a better collective future. Inclusive leadership breaks through bureaucratic rigidities and the tendency these structures impose for employees to passively follow or react to edicts sent down from the executive suite. In the spirit of shared responsibility, employees, too, must seek out new ways to contribute, leverage the knowledge of others, and improve the way work gets done.

Who Are the Leaders?

I am challenging the conventional view of leadership that it is a few people at the apex of an organization who lead and employees who dutifully follow. This outmoded view reflects a twentieth-century model of bureaucracy – a top-down chain of command and boxed-in job descriptions. The successful twenty-first-century workplace has to move beyond bureaucracy to become flexible and flatter, agile and collaborative. Surely, this calls for a different approach to leadership. As a start, we should clarify where to draw the line between leaders and managers – or if there even needs to be a line. Reflect on your personal views in this regard. Do you view leadership as exclusive or inclusive? Do you assume that the CEO and other executive team members are the organization's leaders? Or do you believe that all employees can and should be encouraged to take leadership? In your organization, are the words *leader* and *leadership* used mainly to refer to the CEO and the entire executive team, or does it extend to middle managers? How and when do front-line supervisors show leadership? Are the leadership attributes required in that role clearly defined and well understood?

As you attempt to answer these questions, you may run into a basic dilemma. Business writing on leadership leaves the impression that all leaders are managers, but not all managers are leaders – a gap that needs closing. I frequently see this disconnect when middle managers are expected to participate in 'leadership development' sessions. But, in practice, decision-making that sets the organization's future direction – and impacts their roles – is done by the executive.

Growing emphasis by businesses on employee engagement has raised the expectation that all managers and supervisors need to be good at leading people. In twenty-first- century organizations, functional management positions require 'soft' people skills to inspire, develop, and retain staff. Increasingly, these activities are no longer something HR does through programs and policies, but rather are being built into the roles of managers. One sign of the diffusion of responsibility for people goals is the popular idea that managers should be coaches and mentors. And managers indeed are taking on these supportive roles. I hear more managers today than five years ago talking about wanting to inspire their staff, which is another way of saying they want to be great people leaders. Inspired front-line employees almost certainly will display leadership in their jobs and teams, which, of course, is a necessity in any organization aspiring to high performance.

The answer to the question 'Who are the leaders?' is 'everyone in your organization.' A good number of leadership experts would agree. For example, management thinker Henry Mintzberg challenges the exclusive view of leadership – the cult of the lone executive whose personal vision and determination guide the company to greatness. As Mintzberg argues: 'let's stop the dysfunctional separation of leadership from management. We all know that managers who don't lead are boring, dispiriting. Well, leaders who don't manage are distant, disconnected. Instead of isolating leadership, we need to diffuse it throughout the organization, into the ranks of managers and beyond. Anyone with an idea and some initiative can be a leader.'[1] I am not proposing a new model of leadership. Rather, I am reinforcing the importance of prominent themes in existing leadership models for building healthy organizations. Combing through the leadership literature, we can find nuggets of advice for anyone, regardless of their position in the organization, who wants to take initiative to shape a healthier and more productive work environment. This advice is summarized below into six attributes of inclusive leadership.

Widely Distributing Leadership Responsibility

The approach to leadership I am advocating also is referred to as 'distributed leadership.' In practice, distributed leadership involves a large number of employees in setting the direction of the organization. This is accomplished by breaking down hierarchical barriers and enabling people at the front lines of an organization to influence decisions that affect their clients, their work environment, and their jobs. Distributed leadership fosters collaboration to solve complex organizational problems, going beyond the traditional roles and lines of authority. If collaboration is a hallmark of a healthy organization, distributed leadership is the approach to direction setting, planning, and problem-solving that best fits.

Distributed leadership has been applied in schools. Its use has been prompted by dissatisfaction with the traditional principal-as-leader approach, where a single administrator is responsible for 'running' a school. A distributed approach focuses on how staff can take leadership for achieving learning and teaching goals. It recognizes that the problems of providing quality education have become so complex that the best solutions will be collectively generated from a holistic perspective. Another advantage of distributed leadership is succession, because it builds a broader base of leadership capabilities and interest among junior teachers in moving into administrative roles. This is achieved partly by creating recognition that the stresses of being a school principal can be reduced if leadership is shared.

For example, a study of thirty-eight government-funded secondary schools in New South Wales, Australia, found that schools using distributed leadership achieved exceptional educational outcomes, compared with those that used a traditional principal-leader approach.[2] Schools that distributed leadership to all teaching staff encouraged innovation in teaching and supported a school culture based on trust, mutual respect, sharing of authority, and collegiality. This study shows that responsibility does not rest on the shoulders of one person to drive a school's performance and its students' academic success. The solution is not simply adding more leaders, but a holistic and collaborative approach to thinking about learning and teaching.

Similar ideas have been tried in other industries. In health care, Trillium Health Centre adopted distributed leadership with considerable success. Trillium has been recognized by its peers as a leading example in Canada of a healthy, high-performing health care organization.[3] In the late 1990s the board and senior management team moved away from a command-and-control model of management and set out to fully engage all staff. Reaching this goal required encouraging all employees, physicians, and volunteers to make decisions and take ownership for them. Trillium strives to achieve healthy outcomes for its people in a work environment that nurtures innovation and health service excellence. To communicate this thinking, the organization adopted the concept of '1001 leaders,' which identified and publicly recognized people who showed leadership in their own area. Over the past decade Trillium has evolved. It continues to find effective ways to develop leadership in everyone, recognizing that the ability to positively impact the lives of patients lies solely in the hands of the people who work and volunteer in the organization.

Qualities of Inclusive Leaders

Leadership means taking action to achieve a shared vision of a vibrant workplace, knowing that this will benefit you and your co-workers, customers, and the larger community. The features of a vibrant workplace depend on both personal and organizational leadership. Leadership is not something separate or special, reserved for specific times and places. To emphasize an earlier point, we all can show leadership by how we go about our daily work and in our relationships with co-workers, direct reports, customers, and external stakeholders.

Inclusive leadership happens at the personal and organizational levels. As I have emphasized, there are many micro-level actions you personally can initiate, regardless of your position. Individuals in any position need to make a commitment to be guided by personal and organizational values, develop relationships based on mutual trust and respect, take initiative in their jobs, be responsible for learning and for teaching others, offer suggestions and ideas for now to do things better, engage in open and honest communication, support their co-workers or direct-reports, and recognize others' contributions.

At the organizational level, managers and professionals can ensure that the right support systems are in place. These are the effective people practices referred to in the healthy organization value chain in chapter 1. Professionals in HR, organization development, learning, health and safety, and related areas become change agents by crafting the policies, programs, resources, and systems that support employees to succeed in their jobs. To help to determine the potential effectiveness of people practices, you can use this question as a filter for assessing the merits of plans and decisions: how will it contribute to making the workplace more vibrant, strengthen the culture, and inspire the workforce?

Some people may read this and conclude that it is 'not them' to be this kind of leader. The good news is that leadership skills can be learned. Leaders are made not born. The qualities of leadership are not innate characteristics that individuals bring into the workplace as part of their personality or character. Leadership skills are 'soft' people and personal skills, not 'hard' technical skills. Leadership experts James Kouzes and Barry Posner observe that leaders motivate others to act on values and make visions a reality.[4] They also argue that 'leadership is everyone's business.' Everyone, regardless of their position or level of formal authority in an organization, must take personal responsibility for showing leadership within their sphere.

According to Kouzes and Posner, 'Leadership is about relationships, about credibility, and about what you do.'[5] The action verbs Kouzes and Posner use to describe the practices of exemplary leaders in all walks of life are 'model,' 'inspire,' 'challenge,' 'enable,' and 'encourage.' Leading by example is showing others the way forward. Inspiring

employees with a compelling vision and clear collective goals is what
motivates teams. Challenging old ways of thinking and doing is what
leads to innovative solutions that propel organizations into the future.
Actions that enable collaboration, knowledge-sharing learning, trust-
building, and higher performance are, in fact, showing leadership. In
more personal terms, leadership also means showing you care about
co-workers in heartfelt ways, recognizing their work, and celebrating
their successes.

Now let us apply these ideas directly to healthy organizations, following the inclusive approach I outlined above. Six qualities define the
kind of leadership that anyone can bring to their roles and relationships:
inspire yourself and others; be caring and connected; be trustworthy
and trusting; be action-oriented; empower others; and be self-aware.
By cultivating these qualities, you will become a healthy organization
change agent.

1. *Inspirational.* Inspire yourself and encourage and support others to
   set and achieve higher goals for quality of work life and performance. Employees who are not in management should focus on what
   they can bring to their own role and to their team or work unit.
   Simple things – such as a positive attitude towards one's job and clients or customers, seeking out opportunities to improve teamwork,
   and strengthening the workplace community by volunteering in
   the local community – all contribute to the bigger goals of a healthy
   organization. Managers have more scope in this regard. Studies
   show that managers who use genuine inspiration to motivate their
   employees achieve significant change.

   Some call this 'transformational leadership.' Transformational
   leaders rally others around a higher purpose, a big vision, and
   higher moral and ethical goals. And they show they care about
   others' well-being. Barack Obama in his 2008 presidential election
   campaign passionately communicated a vision of a united America.
   His great success was the way he used that personal conviction to
   reach out to diverse audiences and make his 'Yes We Can' message
   about them, not about him. This style of leadership contrasts with a
   more instrumental, traditional style of leadership that emphasizes
   the effective management of employees so they get their jobs done,
   telling them what to do and motivating them with rewards and incentives.
2. *Caring and connected.* Whether as a manager or a co-worker, you

need to care about and be connected to those with whom you work. This attitude extends to appreciating others' contributions and viewpoints, providing honest and constructive feedback, and validating the capabilities they bring to the organization. Creating a sense of connection among employees fosters a workplace community. It also helps individuals to feel connected to the organization's mission.

Part of fostering connection is helping others to keep the bigger picture in view, so they see how they fit into it. People need to execute tasks, meet deadlines, and achieve operational goals. But when these nuts and bolts are the sole focus of your workday, the potential for meaningful and connected work experiences diminishes. Leaders keep the big picture in view and understand how their actions contribute to the workplace community and the organization's mission. They look beyond these basics, connecting people to the bigger purpose and encouraging learning and reflection as part of the process of task execution and goal achievement.

3. *Trustworthy and trusting.* Effective leadership requires a high level of trust. In high-trust relationships, managers rely on employees to do whatever is needed to meet customers' needs and to act ethically and honestly at all times. And employees trust managers. Knowing their views are respected, employees are going to offer new ideas, even if they are not well developed, and point out mistakes and errors as ways to learn and improve. Everyone is more willing to take risks that can lead to innovation in internal processes, services, or products.

This leadership quality is healthy because performance, pride, and satisfaction are internally generated as part of work processes. Such a work environment is diametrically opposite to that of old-style bureaucracies, where everyone was risk averse and everything was done by the rules. We know that these traditional environments stifled initiative and creativity and sucked the meaning and humanity out of work for many people. Stephen M.R. Covey, in his book *The Speed of Trust*, asserts that 'Leadership is getting results in a way that inspires trust.'[6] This comment applies to managers and non-managers alike. The corollary is that leadership is about inspiring others to pursue with you outstanding results because they trust you and everyone else in the organization.

4. *Action-oriented.* Talking about visions, values, and commitment is a starting point. The result is a common language that enables

a shared direction and change objectives. But this talk must lead quickly to action, or it becomes a waste of time. As leadership expert Michael Fullan puts it: 'The litmus test of all leadership is whether it mobilizes people's commitment to putting their energy into actions designed to improve things. It is individual commitment, but it is above all collective mobilization.'[7] Fullan warns that collective action will not have sustained results unless the actors pursue external goals with an internal, or personal, sense of moral purpose. The leadership mindset required in an environment of constant change, according to Fullan, is really an ongoing process of organizational development and performance enhancement. In his view, leading involves understanding the change process, fostering in others a moral purpose, making sense of the whole, creating and sharing knowledge, and, above all, building relationships. Again, it is not the goal that matters as much as the process for taking action to reach that goal together.

5. *Empowering.* Employee empowerment and autonomy have been promoted by management experts for decades and have taken on a tired ring. Yet people do want a say in their jobs and workplaces – regardless of the label placed on it. So a key ingredient of effective leadership is enabling others, especially your direct reports if you are a manager, to be actively involved in decision-making and, as Trillium advocates, taking ownership for their implementation.

Margaret Wheatley, a respected authority on leadership, offers a view of leadership that taps into our deep-seated personal need to shape our own life and not be controlled.[8] For managers, this way of thinking opens up opportunities to harness people's capacity to figure out ways to do things better. As Wheatley puts it, this is not optional for today's leaders: 'We ignore people's need to participate at our own peril. If they're involved, they will create a future that has them in it, that they'll work to make happen. We won't have to engage in the impossible and exhausting tasks of "selling" them on the solution, getting them to "enroll," or figuring out the incentives that might bribe them into compliant behaviors.'[9] The guiding principle here is that if people create something, they will support it. That neatly expresses what a healthy organization is all about.

6. *Self-aware.* At a personal level, leadership also requires you to apply to yourself the values and principles of a healthy work environment and behaviours– and to be conscious of how and when you do so. It is important to take the time, which usually is not long, to

reflect on how your intended actions will affect others and contribute to larger goals, beyond getting the task at hand done. Strong leaders are self-aware. This is a major step towards being aware of others' needs, interests, and emotional experiences in the workplace. And it is why some workplace health promotion experts define a healthy workplace as encompassing physical, mental, and emotional dimensions of well-being.

As Daniel Goleman points out in his influential book, *Emotional Intelligence*: 'imagine the benefits for work of being skilled in the basic emotional competences – being attuned to the feelings of those we deal with, being able to handle disagreements so they do not escalate, having the ability to get into flow states [being totally absorbed in the task at hand] while doing our work.'[10] If managers are expected to model healthy behaviours, they need to have an adequate level of self-awareness about those behaviours in the first place. So managers need to hold a mirror up to themselves and ask: do I personally make myself accountable for the behaviours I expect from others?

Let these six qualities guide your roles and relationships in the workplace. After all, leadership comes down to behaviour and the conviction and skills needed to put it into practice. Learning to lead the way to a healthier organization involves cultivating behaviours consistent with these six leadership qualities. It also means practising the values of the organization and showing others how its vision for its customers, employees, and society is being achieved – even if by small steps. The next section provides examples of leadership behaviours that can be the basis for training programs aimed at developing broadly based leadership capabilities across an organization.

Leading with People Skills

Many workplaces suffer negative consequences when managers regularly say one thing and do another – or do nothing at all to follow up on a commitment. The wider the gap between what managers say and do, the more dysfunctional a workplace can become. Employees retreat into the narrowest confines of their jobs and grow cynical when senior managers fail to meet the behavioural standards set for all employees through corporate values, codes of ethical conduct, and vision statements. The workplace will lack a sense of common purpose if managers do not put words into action, and employees' sense of personal meaning in work will be diminished, along with their energy to do an excellent job.

Most managers know these facts – at least intuitively. In discussions with middle managers, the point often is made that employees interact not with organizations, but with their immediate supervisor and unit or department managers. As one manager put it, 'we are the face of the organization for the employee.' How individual managers and supervisors behave in their relationships with employees is the most concrete expression of an organization's character. For this reason, people skills are the critical ingredients of effective leadership in a healthy organization.

Gaps in People Skills

The importance of managers' people skills cannot be underestimated for establishing vibrant work environments and inspiring employees. For example, lots of employers now talk about the total rewards offered employees as defining the company's employee 'value proposition.' An employee value proposition describes the organization's unique appeal to talented employees. It includes tangible rewards, such as pay, benefits, and perks. Equally important are the intangible rewards. These include a sense of personal accomplishment, being challenged to develop abilities and having opportunities to advance in a career, feeling connected with the team, and knowing that contributions are truly valued.

Employees' experiences of these intangible rewards are central to the vibrant workplace vision summarized in chapter 3. Supervisors play an important role in this regard. For example, supervisors can help employees to see their job in the bigger picture of the department's and organization's goals, enable the pursuit of career development goals, foster team spirit, provide constructive feedback, and recognize work well done. I often hear employees and executives complain that if only supervisors and middle managers had these people skills, the organization would be a better place to work. Evidence from employers, employees, and supervisors themselves backs up this observation.[11]

Part of the problem is that supervisors are recruited more often on the basis of technical proficiencies than on people skills. Not enough is being done to rectify this deficiency. As evidence of this, the Rethinking Work survey found that only 44 per cent of a representative sample of Canadian employers said they emphasized people skills when hiring or promoting individuals to front-line supervisor positions. Close to 40 per cent of employers had given no training in people skills to their managers and supervisors in the year prior to the survey. Only about one in four had provided such training to more than three-quarters of managers and supervisors.

From an employee's perspective, investments in people skills training for managers is high priority. For example, the Rethinking Work survey of Canadian employees asked respondents 'what type of training do you feel that managers in your organization need most, in order for them to be the best leaders they can be?' In response, employees emphasized interpersonal relations and communication, including listening skills. In the same survey, supervisors were asked to list what support, resources, or training they needed to be effective in their role. In addition to more training in people skills and leadership, time to be a people leader also was high on the list of needs. A good number of supervisors said they do not have enough time to communicate with their staff or to coach and mentor them. As they also pointed out, the job of 'managing people' is a low priority in their organization.

This evidence actually provides grounds for optimism. Yes, there are gaps in supervisors' people skills. But it also seems there is recognition of this lack among supervisors themselves and a readiness to do something about it. However, supervisors often face too many demands and a shortage of time, or an organizational culture that does not value good people leadership. But important as supervisors are in fostering a vibrant workplace, senior managers set the tone and expectations for people practices. Without positive role models at the top, even the most committed supervisor will have limited potential to rally her or his team around healthy organization goals.

Follow-Through on People Commitments

The test for employees is senior management's consistent and real follow-through on its commitments. This adds substance to corporate rhetoric about being an employer of choice, socially responsible, and environmentally friendly. On paper, many large and medium-sized organizations have perfectly adequate human resource policies, ethics, and environmental and community codes of conduct. An organization's policies are only as good as its practices, so that is what we need to look at. That is where the will of senior managers to ensure effective implementation values, ethics, and HR policies becomes critical. For example:

- Learning and development programs are common now, so we need clear evidence that the learning process is incorporated into people's jobs. This is the hallmark of a learning culture. Google has spectacular benefits, such as free gourmet cafeterias, at its headquarters. But the company's efforts to nurture employees extend far beyond such perks. All Google engineers spend 20 per cent of their time thinking up new ideas that will benefit the company, which takes them outside their job and into other areas of the business. In addition to the satisfaction that comes from developing new marketable ideas, this presents a huge opportunity for personal and career growth.

- Ethical standards and codes of conduct are displayed on most corporate websites these days. You need to find out how rooted these standards are in everyday practices, by asking questions such as: What are the guideposts that the executive team uses in a difficult situation? What is a recent difficult situation that tested these values? Environics Communications illustrates this point. The Toronto-based marketing and communications firm has turned down new business that is inconsistent with its strong ethical standards – no matter how much the opportunity may have been worth.

- Industry leader Genentech is a San Francisco-based biotechnology firm. The company is renowned for its commitment to innovative drugs that benefit patients. One executive also described it as having a 'culture of caring for employees.' Senior managers understand that a non-hierarchical, caring culture with a strong spirit of team work is a huge ingredient in the company's success. It is continually seeking employee input, listening to their suggestions, and understanding their needs. One of the sure signs that employees are truly valued is that the company has no vice-president of human resources. Instead, each of the seven members of its executive team has responsibility for people leadership.

- Respect is a cornerstone of a healthy, high-performing workplace. Many healthy organizations have a corporate philosophy built around respect for employees' contributions as a driver of performance. For example, Coastal Pacific Xpress (CPX) distinguishes itself in the trucking industry by its employee-first philosophy, which rests on the basic principle of treating its drivers with respect. Evidence of this philosophy can be found in stories about customers the western Canadian company 'fired' (as CPX puts it) because they were disrespectful and abusive towards staff.

These companies, which have been recognized by the Great Place to Work Institute in its annual lists of outstanding workplaces, demonstrate how senior managers show the kind of leadership that puts people first. The results are concrete practices that signal to employees – as well as to shareholders, customers, and society – that a strong culture is critical for business success. But these examples do not reveal how such decisions and actions were taken. Clearly, the decisions and practices outlined above would depend on open communication during the development, implementation, and evaluation phases. They also benefited from the input of employees. Once the decisions to act were made, they had to be applied in an even-handed manner. It is at this more basic level of connecting with employees that good leadership by managers, especially executives, is either strengthened or weakened.

Setting the Tone

How, then, can senior management set the tone for an inclusive approach to leadership? Realistically, senior managers cannot expect line managers, supervisors, and employees to be inspired by a vision that does not include them. It falls to senior managers to signal to others in the organization that it is through their dedicated efforts that the mission will be achieved. Senior managers must regularly and consistently communicate the importance of the organization's people to its success, using language that resonates down to the front lines.

Organizations that do better than their peers have created values-based cultures in which managers at all levels connect to employees' sense of purpose. That purpose has to be expressed in the quality of services or products today and the potential for even higher quality in future. Employees are valued and supported because they are the key to service excellence. So these high-performing organizations have a clear vision of the kind of workforce and workplace they are striving to create and maintain.

Consider an example from the public sector. In my work with governments across Canada, I have come across subtle but quite different ways of expressing public service values and visions. Most adequately describe how the public service will strive to meet the needs of citizens. Just as private sector companies talk about putting customers first, governments increasingly have tried over the past decade or more to improve the delivery of public services – in other words, putting citizens first. But it is rare to see the employees providing those services mentioned in the visions or values.

The province of Alberta stands apart from other governments in this regard, speaking directly to its public servants. The Alberta vision for public service is 'Alberta's Public Service ... Proudly working together to build a stronger province for current and future generations.' What speaks to employees is the sense of collective pride. And the Alberta definition of the public service value of respect (a common value within public services) is 'We foster an environment in which each individual is valued and heard.' Again, for employees the emphasis that matters is knowing their contributions are valued and that they have a voice in this large organization.

My point is that Alberta's public service vision and values speak directly to the individual employee, certainly more so than general statements about providing more innovative, cost-effective services and being responsive to citizens' needs. The lesson is that these statements need to reach out to employees. The language used must not only set the tone for people leadership across the organization, but also put in motion accountability. In the case of Alberta, regular employee surveys track progress on these and other ingredients of an engaged public service. Senior managers are held accountable for ensuring that there is progress by tying some of their annual performance bonuses to progress on these people goals. And supervisory training includes the soft skills required to foster the pride, teamwork, respect, and input espoused in the vision and values.

Focusing on Leadership Behaviours

The six qualities of inclusive leadership described above offer an effective approach to workplace roles and relationships. Theses guidelines need to be fleshed out with specific behaviours relevant to your organization's situation. Once you have identified behaviours, training and development programs can be adapted to equip managers, supervisors, and employees with the skills needed to put the behaviours into practice.

I will provide two examples of how organizations used their values or guiding principles to develop specific behaviours relevant to managers and employees, then used these behaviours as the basis for skill development, a process that also reinforced the values as collective guideposts of behaviour. The first example is Teck Cominco's Trail Operations in western Canada. Senior managers there took their guiding principles, described in chapter 4, and created specific behaviours for each principle. The second example is the City of London, a municipality of some 350,000 inhabitants located in southwestern Ontario, Canada. The city used a managers' leadership development program and an employee appreciation week to collect input on what these groups saw as the behaviours required to live the organization's values. My intent is not to recommend the specific behaviours developed by these two organizations. Rather, I want to illustrate different ways that any organization can involve managers and employees in discussions about how to lead by example.

Living the Guiding Principles

In chapter 4, I described how the senior management team at Teck Cominco's Trail Operations created a set of guiding principles. The goal was to develop clear behavioural guides that the management team would commit to following and that would lead the rest of the organization to foster a more positive and productive work environment. This initiative was not a defensive reaction to problems. In fact, the Trail smelter had achieved record productivity, profits and safety levels. But the leadership team, under the guidance of a new general manager and including several new members from outside the organization, felt it could achieve even higher levels of performance and at the same time improve working conditions – as long as everyone was part of the process.

Through a facilitated discussion of revised values, the senior managers crafted five guiding principles that expressed what they individually and collectively believed could help to guide the organization into the future. Each manager then had the opportunity to reflect on the principles. They provided descriptions of the behaviours they felt were essential to actually 'live' by the principle every day in the workplace. In a follow-up facilitated discussion, the behaviours for each guiding principle were reviewed and consolidated into the statement presented in figure 5.1.

Reading through these behaviours, note that the descriptions are simply stated. For example: no hidden agendas; listen first, then speak; honestly give and accept praise; and set up others to succeed. Because the goal was to make the guidelines useable throughout the facility, all workers must be able to relate to these behaviours. The company has a lengthy involvement in the community as the area's largest employer and has a commitment to environmental sustainability. Community and environmental dimensions of the guiding principles link internal and external behaviours. Such is not always the case, as many compa-

Figure 5.1 Teck Cominco's Trail Operations: examples of behaviours showing how we live by the guiding principles

---

We act with *integrity*, treating all with *dignity*, *fairness*, and *respect*.
- Always respect others' opinions and viewpoints.
- Avoid negative, behind-the-back comments or gossip about others.
- Speak to a person directly if you have concerns about his or her behaviour.
- Have courageous conversations about performance (others and your own).
- No hidden agendas.
- Listen first, and then speak.
- Don't jump to conclusions.
- Be courteous. Use language you would use at home with your family.
- Be forthright and honest with everyone, regardless of their position.
- Show respect for others by showing up for meetings on time and prepared.
- Try to make tough decisions so they are 'win-win.'
- Be honest about mistakes, learn from them, and improve.
- Expect honest feedback from others.
- Act ethically and honestly with business partners, even if you don't think they are doing the same.

We commit to everyone going home *safe* and *healthy* every day.
- Always take time to do your work safely.
- Intervene immediately if you witness an unsafe act or situation.
- Continually look for ways to reduce risks in your job.
- Consciously include safety and health leadership and management in evaluation of direct reports.
- Directly communicate care and concern when witnessing potentially harmful acts or situations.
- Reinforce learning from each other's errors.
- Positively recognize successes.
- Reinforce the idea that every incident is preventable.
- Make safety part of as many discussions as possible.
- Remind people about this principle if they are not following it.
- Follow up on incidents directly with the people involved.
- Talk about safety with each employee at least twice a year.

We take *personal responsibility* for our actions and results.
- Avoid rationalizing, explaining away, or accepting poor results.

- Deliver on what you say you are going to do. Live up to your commitments.
- Stay focused and use available resources to overcome barriers.
- Don't give up … find creative solutions to problems.
- Honestly give and accept praise.
- Pursue excellence where it really matters.
- Don't be afraid to ask for help to get the job done.
- Own up to errors or misunderstandings without rationalizing.
- Don't blame others when things get tough.
- If you see something wrong, stop and address it.
- When holding others accountable, first make sure they have been empowered to act.

We *support* each other to achieve our fullest potential.
- Set others up to succeed.
- Don't compete with peers and co-workers.
- Focus on building people's confidence by acknowledging their contributions, strengths, and successes.
- Team and company results are more important than your personal accomplishments.
- Make sure that employees have adequate resources and time to do their jobs.
- Think beyond your team or department. Look for opportunities to grow the greater good.
- Have an open-door policy with direct-reports.
- Actively offer assistance and advice to employees.
- Accept assistance or advice when needed.
- Hold regular meetings with your managers to review opportunities for improvement.
- Always look for opportunities to develop individuals' capabilities.

We *act responsibly* to support a sustainable future for the *communities* and *environment* in which we operate.
- Consider potential impacts on the community and environment when making decisions.
- Understand through ongoing dialogue how the Trail community perceives us and our impact on them.
- Be role models for environmental sustainability and stewardship.
- Personally act to minimize waste and pollution.

- Be a good neighbour. Be good citizens.
- Be proactive and do what's right.
- Personally participate in and support worthy community programs and events.
- Take time to attend community meetings to identify and understand others' perceptions of us.
- Be transparent about community donations and activities.
- Challenge yourself and others to improve the status quo.
- Take a longer-term outlook on business decisions.

---

nies treat environmental and CSR issues as separate from their internal working relationships. One of the behaviours aptly sums up what is needed on both fronts: 'Be a good neighbour. Be good citizens.'

To make these behaviours as concrete as possible, the senior managers also offered one or two personal stories about how they had recently used each of the guiding principles. Some of these stories are presented in figure 5.2. You can see their usefulness as a communication tool in discussions of the guiding principles with managers, supervisors, and staff. Through telling these stories, senior managers modelled how other managers could positively reinforce the guiding principles by telling their own stories and encouraging their team members to do the same.

Figure 5.2 Teck Cominco's Trail Operations: senior managers' stories about living the guiding principles

---

We act with *integrity*, treating all with *dignity*, *fairness*, and *respect*.
- 'At recent bonus reviews, a reference was made to some employees who were close to retirement as 'floaters.' I referred to our guiding principle of respect and suggested we not talk about older employees this way.'

We commit to everyone going home *safe* and *healthy* every day.
- 'I observed workers working on a suspended load while touring the WHS worksite. Three levels of supervision and [a] safety coordinator were present. Initially I felt that if this was a safety issue one of the supervisors or the safety coordinator would speak up, as they are all more experienced with this type of field work. On second thought, I quickly concluded that my level of experience was irrelevant. I started

walking over to talk to the workers. Before I opened my mouth they recognized the issue, stopped work, lowered the load onto the ground then resumed work.'

We take *personal responsibility* for our actions and results.
- 'I was recently overloaded with action items and did not have enough time to complete them. As a result, one item that I had committed to doing for an employee in my group was not done in the expected time and I knew I would not be able to get it done. I met with the employee and told him my situation, saying that it was my fault to commit I could get it done that quickly. He accepted and appreciated the communication and we agreed to a new date (that I better deliver on!).'

We *support* each other to achieve our fullest potential.
- 'Rather than judging and labelling some employees, I have been focusing more on trying to find ways to make them more successful by training, feedback, and different job opportunities.'

We *act responsibly* to support a sustainable future for the *communities* and *environment* in which we operate.
- 'White sturgeon living in the Columbia River have been listed as an endangered species. We have decided to voluntarily provide resources including funding and employee time to the white sturgeon recovery effort. We do this because our operations are located on or near the Columbia River and we benefit greatly from the river. Therefore we feel it is appropriate to put some energy into taking care of the river.'

Storytelling is a powerful way to sustain a culture. It is used by many companies on the best workplaces lists created by the Great Place to Work Institute. Whether it is telling new hires about the culture or recognizing at a weekly team meeting how an employee used one of the values to get through a difficult situation, stories are timely reminders of how organizational life ought to be conducted.

Leadership to Build Supportive Workplaces

Several years ago, the City of London, Ontario, embarked on a journey to strengthen the organization's culture by making it more supportive and values-based. As in Teck Cominco's Trail Operations, there was nothing 'broken' at the city administration. Instead, the challenge was getting managers, supervisors, and employees to do things a bit differently, at least enough to make a real difference in work experiences and service quality. Over time, these improvements also would enhance the city's reputation as an employer of choice.

The City of London's vision is to 'inspire pride and confidence in every Londoner.' In fact, 'inspire' was a theme that ran through most of the city's strategy for public service. Talking about inspiring Londoners in their city raised the obvious question: how can employees also be inspired to deliver even higher-quality public services? Part of the answer lay in finding ways to live the city's two corporate values: individual responsibility and collective accountability. These values are about as compact and as basic as an organization can get in defining its values. But they worked for the city. Rather than creating a longer list of values with descriptions, the city opted to use the values as broad guidelines for creating a more supportive workplace. In fact, this became a strategic priority.

A Supportive Workplace Committee, consisting of managers, led a variety of initiatives to implement this strategic goal. Most important, it consulted widely with employees and managers about the ingredients of a supportive workplace and the behaviours that were required to create and sustain this sort of culture (their term). Basically, everyone in the organization had an opportunity to contribute to these discussions. Two main sources of input were a leadership development program for managers, run in partnership with the University of Western Ontario's Ivey School of Business, and round-table consultations with employees and managers during an employee appreciation week. These consultations first asked people to identify the key dimensions of a supportive workplace. Then the discussions turned to specific behaviours consistent with each of the corporate values that contribute to a specific dimension of a supportive workplace.

I participated in the employee appreciation week consultations and heard the same words being used repeatedly to describe what employees and managers wanted in their jobs and workplaces. Prominent themes in the discussions of supportive workplace behaviours were pride, trust, and 'standing together' – which refers to a common purpose achieved through teamwork and a sense of belonging. Sifting through the mountains of transcripts from these consultations, the Supportive Workplace Committee connected supportive workplace dimensions, corporate values, and behaviours. Figure 5.3 lists some of the

Figure 5.3 Examples of leadership behaviours to build a more supportive workplace and live the values, based on City of London consultations

Supportive workplace dimensions	Examples of how to live the corporate values	
	Individual responsibility	Collective accountability
Honest communication	Practise open, honest, clear, meaningful, timely, consistent, respectful, two-way communication with all employees.	Communicate division and department goals and direction across the organization.
Support each other	Follow through with your commitments to employees.	Actively encourage collaborative workplace relationships in which people support each other to achieve division and department goals.
Fairness	Have a positive and welcoming attitude towards the diverse experiences, backgrounds, and personal characteristics of your employees.	Ensure that the processes for recruitment, promotion, job assignments, and training opportunities are fair and equitable across the organization.
Work/life balance	Model balance in your own work life.	Understand employees' work/life balance needs and support them to achieve balance.
Recognize and celebrate contributions	Help each employee see how their job contributes to the City's Mission and Vision.	Share stories about individual and team successes within and across departments.
Fun environment	Encourage and support actions by employees to socialize and have fun together.	Hold regular events that celebrate people's contributions, strengthen the 'standing together' feeling – and that are fun!
Opportunities for training and development	Openly and regularly share your knowledge, expertise and ideas with others.	Facilitate access to appropriate training and development for each employee in ways that best meet their job and career goals.
Freedom and empowerment	Trust employees to do their job and provide them the resources they need to succeed.	Expect each employee to decide how to 'do the right thing' to achieve department and corporate goals.

Accessible management	Be approachable and available for employees to talk with you about their ideas, concerns and suggestions.	All managers and supervisors are visible and accessible to front-line employees.
Pride	Care about your work and take ownership for doing the best you can to serve the citizens of London.	Expect other employees to be ready, able and motivated to do their job to the best of their ability.
Respectful relationships	Personally show that you value each employee's input and job contributions.	In every interaction, treat others how you would like to be treated.

behaviours that enable supervisors and managers to create and maintain a more supportive workplace. The figure also links these behaviours to the corporate values of individual responsibility and collective accountability.

The city took a sequenced approach to leadership development. The intent was to incorporate leadership behaviours, like those listed in figure 5.3, into the system used to annually evaluate the performance of individual managers. Over time, the behaviours would also be reinforced in policies and practices, including revised criteria for recruiting people into supervisory positions. In other words, the leadership behaviours in figure 5.3 are meant to be not prescriptive but developmental. More than anything, they are an invitation to further reflections and conversations about how managers, individually and as a collective, can live the values as they build supportive workplaces.

Leading Change

To recap, leadership in a healthy organization is a shared responsibility. Everyone has a role to play. While senior management support and actions are major enablers of progress, the quest for a healthier organization must provide opportunities for all employees to become involved in that process. We have seen how healthy organizations approach leadership in inclusive ways, empowering employees down to the front lines to take ownership of work environment improvements. Managers and supervisors set the tone and direction for this involvement to happen. Reflecting on how Teck Cominco's Trail Operations and the City of London used guiding principles and values to define behaviours – starting with leadership behaviours – you can find opportunities in your organization for managers to encourage others to lead.

As Michael Fullan reminds us, leadership is all about bringing people together to achieve purposeful change. But here is the catch: someone has to take the initiative. That is why leadership is one of the basic building blocks of a healthy organization. Otherwise, an organization is beset with inertia, suspended in a state of limbo where any talk of creating a more vibrant workplace and improving employee experiences remains just that – talk. To avoid this inertia trap, change agents at all levels of an organization must understand the change process itself. This will equip them to play the most constructive role possible, working with others to implement improvements. Chapter 6 takes a close look at the dynamics of change involved in creating healthier organizations.

6 Healthy Change

Several years ago, the Canadian government's department of health asked me to write a report on healthy workplace change strategies. I discovered just how little tactical information is available on the actual processes for successfully introducing changes leading towards healthier workplaces.[1] In the five years since writing the report for Health Canada, I have observed dozens of organizations in different industries and countries develop healthy workplace strategies. Each strategy, in its own way, sought to forge stronger people – performance links. Yet despite careful planning, results often were disappointing. Somehow, the strategy could not get traction.

These experiences gave me a better understanding about *how* to bring about healthy change. This chapter offers practical lessons from a wide range of organizations that are in the midst of creating more vibrant workplaces and positive cultures. What I do not offer is a step-by-step guide. Organizational change is too contextualized and complex to follow a straightforward, project-management, one-size-fits-all approach.

A relatively small number of organizations have achieved remarkable overall health. Indeed, these companies have been recognized for this achievement on lists of best workplaces, best employers, best-run and most admired businesses, and most environmentally and socially responsible corporations. While much can be learned from this top tier, their so-called best practices are not easily copied. So this chapter mainly is directed at the large middle group of organizations that are neither dangerously unhealthy nor exceptionally healthy in terms of the vibrancy of their workplaces, the resonance of their culture, or the level of inspiration experienced by their employees. Mostly, my examples are very good organizations striving to become truly excellent. Their journeys provide tips that you can use to help to seize opportunities, navigate twists and turns, avoid pitfalls, and make progress on your healthy organization journey.

There are many theories of organizational change. The one that I find most helpful for understanding healthy change is proposed by Richard Beckhard, a pioneer in the field of organization development (OD).[2] OD practitioners plan and implement system-wide changes in an organization's processes. They often focus on how people work together and with customers and community stakeholders. Beckhard suggests that it is possible to design change to improve organizational health, as long as the focus is on the change process as well as the change goals. The usefulness of an OD approach to healthy change has been reinforced through my work with managers and employees. As we will see in the examples below, many types of change can be designed to strengthen the organization's capacity to collaborate, learn, innovate, adapt, and live its values.

Watching many workplaces advance towards their vision of a healthy organization, I have taken away five basic lessons, which this chapter describes:

1. Get your organization on its own healthy organization trajectory that fits its needs, strategy and unique circumstances.
2. Most organizational change can be designed as a healthy experience for those involved and for other stakeholders.
3. Consistent with the idea of inclusive leadership, find ways to personally influence healthy trajectories and processes.
4. A healthy change process will provide opportunities to put in place two healthy organization building blocks: inclusive leadership and a positive culture.
5. Five principles can guide action: understand your organization's readiness to change; align structure and culture; link people initiatives to the business strategy; widen the circle of involvement; and make time for learning and innovation.

Getting on a Healthy Change Trajectory

There is no standard recipe for creating a healthy organization. Rather, your challenge is to co-create with others in your workplace the most suitable way to connect employee well-being, working conditions, and performance. A customized approach to the changes needed must be tailored to the unique circumstances, culture, and needs of your organization. This requires creatively mapping out an appropriate healthy change trajectory and taking steps to get on it.

Focusing on the Journey

Becoming a healthy organization is more of a journey than a destination. Yes, the 'what' is important, but so, too, is the 'how.' Indeed, you need to set specific goals for the short, medium, and long terms. Yet, as we have seen, the attributes of a vibrant workplace and positive culture emerge and take root over time. Thus, each organization will be at a different point along a healthy organization trajectory, looking for opportunities to take the next step. What healthy organizations have in common is a commitment by employees and managers to achieve optimal results for all stakeholders. Everyone understands that results depend most of all on a positive work environment that supports employees to thrive.

Consider the following examples of organizations in which change agents are making concerted efforts to move down a healthy trajectory. These first-hand examples show that different paths can lead towards similar well-being and performance goals.

- A telecommunications company launched a new customer service strategy in its six call centres. The call centre that went furthest to implement supportive coaching and team-based learning achieved the highest customer service performance ratings, lowest turnover, and highest employee satisfaction. Employees at this centre experienced less stress in their jobs because they had more autonomy to meet customer needs and more support from co-workers to get the information required to resolve customer problems. This approach to teamwork was encouraged by the regional vice-president, whose motto was 'do what ever you can to meet customers' needs, just don't give away the store!'
- Anticipating a wave of retirements, a city administration developed a detailed HR plan. But this was not enough to renew management ranks. Rising workloads, overly bureaucratic reporting structures, and difficulty in setting priorities had taken the fun out of work. Promising employees and supervisors turned down promotions

to avoid high levels of stress and burnout. After wide discussion, there was collective realization that the solution lay in more flexible career paths, giving employees and front-line supervisors authority and accountability for decisions, and a more supportive culture.

- A logistics company measured its performance by how long it took to pick up, ship, sort, and deliver a package. Work was fast paced. Consultations with employees identified stress and work/life balance as major concerns. Leadership training was revised to help managers address these issues. The director of health and safety saw an opportunity and championed a pilot project that added to the corporate report card organizational health measures, such as lost-time injury, short-term disability, turnover, and overtime utilization. These metrics caught the attention of operations managers because they saw how healthy work environments affected the number of workers available on any given shift.

Employees and managers in each of these organizations took decisive steps towards healthy organization goals. Keeping up momentum requires putting firmly in place two of the healthy organization building blocks we discussed earlier: a positive culture and inclusive leadership.

The Role of Culture and Leadership

The culture building block of a healthy organization supports ethically responsible behaviours, including how people should be treated. The same values also offer guideposts for any type of change in response to volatile business conditions. The recent global economic crisis pushed employers into uncharted waters with few navigational aids. Trico Homes, as we saw in chapter 1, relied on its five core values to find a way to survive the collapse of the housing market in 2008.

Some companies also responded to previous market shocks in healthy and sustainable ways. In the aftermath of the 9/11 terrorist attacks on the World Trade Center, businesses providing or reliant on air transportation were especially hard-hit and nobody knew at the time what the outcome would be. Two major companies directly affected – FedEx and Four Seasons Hotels – approached these tough business decisions guided by their core values. FedEx's philosophy of 'people, service, profit' has shaped its character, one that includes generosity, caring, and helping others. The company's 'no layoff philosophy' kicked into gear. While people were reassigned immediately after 9/11, nobody was let go. Similarly at Four Seasons, the hardest-hit resorts re-assigned staff to redecorate the premises instead of laying them off. As CEO Isadore Sharp observed, the test of a culture and its values is not what it is like in good times, but what it is like in tough times.

Examples of healthy change reveal that what is needed is not bet- ter change management – an overly popular concept among managers – but change leadership from many groups and individuals. Healthy change requires considerable effort by numerous and diverse champi- ons. Change agents need to till the ground, providing fertile conditions for new ways of thinking and acting to take root and eventually flour- ish. Improvements become a shared responsibility – what I described in the last chapter as 'inclusive leadership.'

If you have a personal commitment to a healthier workplace, then you are an agent or champion of healthy change. As such, you should always be on the lookout for the language, opportunities, and allies to help make this happen. You likely will have a personal vision of a healthy organization or workplace. You probably do not accept the sta- tus quo but, at the same time, you understand that positioning change depends a great deal on timing and organizational politics. You may even describe your approach as 'change by stealth.' This is a term one champion used in a healthy workplace strategy workshop, because he moved one opportunistic step at a time, without the benefit of an of- ficial healthy workplace strategy. I certainly have seen change agents quit their job in frustration. But in my experience, most people who truly believe in the importance of healthy organizations remain tireless advocates and influencers of change.

Groups also can be powerful engines of change, diagnosing work- place needs and proposing action plans. Groups can troubleshoot and solve problems that fall outside the scope, mandate, or resources of existing organizational arrangements. For example, a task force, com- mittee, or project group can break through red tape, bridge function- al areas, and do end runs around resistant managers. Organizational change experts recommend that groups leading change need a clear purpose, a design that fits this purpose, links to other parts of the or- ganization, and a group culture that supports risk-taking and learning.[3] Change team leaders should coach team members to focus simultane- ously on performance and culture. The goal of a change team is not to 'manage' a new project but to stimulate organizational development and innovation through the actions of others.

Let us take the case of a new wellness committee in a large police services organization. Members spent several day-long sessions fleshing out goals and timelines. What really energized committee members was a discussion of the benefits each of them wanted to see result from committee efforts. It also helped that senior management left it to the committee to come up with its own definition of 'wellness.' The committee put its own stamp on wellness by identifying five organizational benefits (reduced costs, team effectiveness, productivity, retention, and morale) and five individual benefits (satisfaction, engagement, individual effectiveness, personal health, and work/life balance) that its wellness-related actions should achieve. By communicating these wellness benefits to co-workers, the committee encouraged others to think more about organizational health goals rather than just individual wellness.

Five Principles for Healthy Change

My approach to healthy change can be summarized in five broad principles, a synthesis of my practical experience filtered through relevant research evidence. They highlight the issues that change agents will need to consider as they move from thinking to action:

1. Understand your organization's readiness to change.
2. Align structure and culture.
3. Link people initiatives to the business strategy.
4. Widen the circle of involvement.
5. Make time for learning and innovation.

I launch this discussion by providing a change readiness assessment tool that can be adapted for use in your organization. It is intended to stimulate thinking and discussion among change agents about the best current opportunities to move forward, enablers of success, and barriers that will need to be addressed.

I then use case studies of organizations that I have worked with as a consultant to illustrate principles 2 through 5. Actually, you can see most if not all of the four principles illustrated in each case. The principles are intended as guideposts for individual change agents, from executives to front-line employees. They also are useful discussion points for committees or working groups charged with designing and implementing a quality of work life, performance improvement, or healthy workplace initiative.

Understanding Change Readiness

A basic insight from the field of health promotion is the importance of a person's readiness to make changes in their health-related attitudes and behaviours. A person's readiness to change determines what will be realistic goals and timelines for them – and whether they will make any progress at all. Readiness assesses past actions, knowledge and awareness about change benefits, and the motivation to adopt new lifestyle practices.

Organizations also can be assessed for their readiness to change in a healthy direction. Use the basic model of a healthy organization presented in chapter 1 to develop a vision that you would like to see your organization aspire to achieve. Use language in the vision that suits the character of your organization (e.g., healthy organization, healthy workplace, employer of choice, inspiring workplace).

Now use that 'draft' vision (at some point you will need to validate it with co-workers) to assess your organization on the change readiness continuum using the twenty-five criteria listed in figure 6.1, as applicable. Not all criteria may apply, so you will need to adapt the assessment tool to fit your circumstances. Enter a check mark in the appropriate box to indicate if each of the organizational characteristics listed in figure 6.1 fits one of these criteria:

- A current or potential source of resistance to introducing changes to realize your healthy organization vision.
- A source of inertia created by the weight of tradition and/or indifference that will have to be overcome.
- Ready to be tapped as actual or potential sources of support for healthy workplace change.
- Already generating momentum for healthy improvements in the workplace environment, the culture, or organizational processes and systems.

If you checked either the 'Resistance' or the 'Inertia' boxes, think about what you can do to move this factor to either 'Readiness' or 'Momentum.' Use the assessment tool in a group or committee that has a mandate to implement change, discussing the results as a prelude to identifying a change process and setting change goals. This is a diagnostic tool, not a test – there are no 'right' answers. This type of assessment should be one of the initial steps in planning a healthy workplace intervention.

organization change readiness assessment

ıcteristics	Resistance	Inertia	Readiness	Momentum
alues				
vision statement				
3. Orgaɪ_____ mission statement				
4. Organization's strategic plan				
5. Organization's dominant culture				
6. Your department, unit, or team's culture culture				
7. Organization's social responsibility commitments				
8. Performance management system				
9. Other rewards and incentives				
10. The Board				
11. The CEO				
12. Senior managers				
13. Line managers				
14. Your manager				
15. Your coworkers or team				
16. Your staff (direct reports)				
17. HR professionals/managers				
18. OD, OHS and labour relations professionals and managers				
19. The organization's structures and systems				
20. Corporate communication				
21. Work unit communication				
22. Employee consultation and feedback				
23. Local union representatives				
24. Union leadership				
25. Professional groups or associations				
TOTAL CHECK MARKS				

Tailor the change strategy – including the evaluation component – to fit the picture that emerges. Whatever your readiness profile, the objective is to leverage the sources of 'readiness' and 'momentum,' find ways to reduce resistance, and break free of the inertia.

Successful implementation requires putting in place enabling conditions to help make the organization change ready. Doing so first requires identifying and removing barriers. This is an important step towards closing 'the knowing–doing gap.'[4] A common barrier to change is inertia: the deadweight of traditional practices that have gone unchallenged. Lack of information about alternatives contributes to inertia. Remarkably, when larger organizations put employee development, engagement, and retention goals on their agendas, they often discover pockets of internal excellence. Lessons that help other units to improve can help to overcome inertia. Thus, shared learning is a vital part of healthy change.

Heavy workloads and time scarcity also are major change barriers. In my discussions with managers or employees, these barriers invariably are identified as holding them back from doing more to promote a healthy organization. Overworked employees won't embrace a new change initiative, even one aimed at improving their work environment. It will be dismissed as 'just one more thing on my plate.' For managers and supervisors, lack of time is reinforced by incentives that give priority to operational and business goals, not people goals. One way for managers to make time is to involve more employees in the process – in other words, practising inclusive leadership.

Resistance among front-line supervisors and middle managers can be the Achilles heel of organizational change. Historically, the greatest opposition to redesigned work systems came not from workers, but from supervisors who perceived a threat to their limited power base. Similar scenarios are played out today if supervisors read into the change greater responsibility, more accountability, and increased work demands. Supervisors also may lack the skills needed to enable change, so managers at all levels need to be equipped to make constructive contributions. The best way for supervisors and managers to become enablers of healthy change is to directly involve them in improving drivers of health and performance for themselves and their team.

With these considerations about change readiness in mind, we now turn to four case studies to describe the remaining healthy change principles.

Aligning Structure and Culture

University of British Columbia Okanagan (UBCO) is Canada's newest university campus. Located amid the vineyards and orchards of the scenic Okanagan valley, the university was founded in 2005, when the world-class University of British Columbia took over the academic programs previously offered by a local degree-granting community college. UBCO has what it takes to succeed: part of the highly reputed University of British Columbia, a mandate to develop innovative interdisciplinary programs, unprecedented enrolment growth and faculty recruitment, and a brand new campus in a spectacular natural environment.

UBCO illustrates a general principle of healthy change: the importance of aligning culture and structure. As a new institution, UBCO cultivated a culture that would support an intimate learning community, with the ultimate goal of becoming the best small university in Canada. Other features of what UBCO executives, HR professionals, and others guiding these changes called a 'healthy workplace culture strategy' show how one organization put the cultural foundation in place as a new organizational structure – in this case, a new university – took shape.

GETTING OFF TO A GOOD START

For UBCO to seize the opportunities created by location, size, and UBC connection, clear leadership and active participation of faculty and staff were essential. Leadership came from a number of change agents in administration, human resources, faculty, and from those at the executive levels at UBCO. The acknowledged challenge was to forge a distinctive culture that captured the spirit of a new, rapidly growing university. A 'healthy workplace culture' was how Dr Doug Owram, the deputy vice-chancellor (the head of UBCO), and other leaders described the workplace component of a larger vision of a healthy and sustainable organization. Solidifying the culture was all part of the process of building a campus community that connected staff, faculty, and students with each other and with the Okanagan region.

Those leading the culture-building took a participatory approach. Most staff were new to the organization, but some had worked for years at UBCO's college predecessor – which had its own culture. So it was critical that the entire workforce had opportunities to shape the future culture. A number of linked initiatives helped in this effort. A full-time workplace health promotion coordinator launched an annual health symposium that brought people together to share what they were doing to create health promoting environments. The executive created a Healthy Workplace Culture Strategy that set the direction and, over time, would brand UBCO's unique working and learning environment. A Healthy Workplace Culture Working Group fleshed out strategy, beginning with consultations involving academic and non-academic staff. These consultations were jointly led by the provost (a senior academic leader) and the campus health promotion coordinator.

The Work Group's consultation took two forms: an online survey and five consultation sessions. The survey asked about health and wellness activities and needs, the UBCO Academic Plan, and attitudes about the workplace. Results showed a high level of interest in participating in a variety of health promotion activities or issues, ranging from community service to fitness, health screening, charity fund raising events, future health conferences, and community organic gardening. This immediately broadened the scope of what healthy activities meant to employees. The survey also revealed a need to connect people with UBCO's goals as laid out in its Academic Plan. Finally, the survey validated what informal discussions had identified as the bedrock of a healthy workplace culture, including mutual respect, supportive co-workers, fair treatment, helpful feedback, and work/life balance.

The community consultations were facilitated, open-invitation, ninety-minute discussions on three questions: What would a healthy workplace culture look like at UBCO? What are its characteristics? and What are the key values? Two major themes emerged: the importance of providing people with the supports and resources they need to do their jobs well (a clear link to UBCO's mission) and strengthening the feeling of community on the campus. Other important themes were the need to create a strong UBCO identify; the importance of valuing, respecting, and rewarding people; and improved corporate communication.

The consultations helped to articulate and strengthen the features of UBCO's healthy workplace culture. Above all, the process helped to foster a sense of community. Faculty, administrators, and support staff identified many potential actions that would help a positive culture to evolve. Follow-ups to the culture consultations included installing more bike racks, more regional outreach, enhanced childcare options, and workplace health promotion resources.

INSIGHTS ABOUT THE PARADOX OF WORKPLACE CHANGE

The UBCO story highlights a basic paradox of workplace change. One of the great truisms of twenty-first- century workplaces is that change is relentless. But if this is accurate, then why does research show that most major organizational change initiatives fail to achieve their intended goals? What stands in the way of the workplace changes needed to foster innovation and productivity or to create the kind of vibrant work environments that drive well-being and productivity?

To resolve this paradox, it helps to view workplace change in terms of yin and yang, with complementary but opposing forces in constant tension. These forces are structures and cultures, the hard and soft sides of every workplace. Structures are visible in organization charts, headcounts, job classifications, information technology, and rules about how work should be done. Culture is the organization as a community – the workplace's social glue created by shared meanings of how life in the office, at the service counter, or on the production line ought to be lived. If you want your organization to get on or stay on a healthy change trajectory, changes in structures or operational processes must be balanced with the values and other elements of culture.

In practice, however, structural change goals usually trump cultural change goals. I often hear senior managers acknowledge, after the fact, the need to 'fix the culture piece' in the wake of disruptive restructuring or downsizing. I also hear managers describe their struggles to create better workplaces that deliver better results. Their goals vary – recruitment and retention, employer of choice, employee wellness, workforce development, employee engagement. But the big roadblock is designing a change process that balances the yin and yang, aligning structures and cultures so they become complementary, not opposing, forces.

A case in point is health care, a sector that has experienced much consolidation and organizational restructuring. The merger of different hospitals and other facilities can cause turmoil on the front lines of care delivery. As one hospital administrator described a government decision to redraw organizational boundaries for a second time, 'they just blew us up again.' No wonder the goal of creating better workplaces that support the delivery of better patient care gets sidelined when health care managers are preoccupied with figuring out how they fit into new structures. The 'culture piece' gets left aside as the dust settles and, with it, the chance to tap into the cultural energy that comes from each unit's distinctive values and history.

A good alignment between structure and culture also contributes to successful corporate mergers and acquisitions. Encana, Canada's largest energy company, took this approach. Calgary-based Encana was created in 2002 when Alberta Energy and PanCanadian Energy merged. The new company set out to create a new, high-performance corporation with a culture supportive of this vision, blending the best from its predecessors and adding some. The centrepiece is a corporate constitution, which, according to founding CEO Gwyn Morgan, would 'foster complete, transparent accountability' for acting out the values as a means of achieving Encana's vision. The new culture is rooted in a shared set of 'moral principles' defining specific values that guide behaviour.

Similarly, successful acquisitions must draw on the strengths of the acquired company. Take, for example, a Houston-based energy firm that was acquired by a larger multinational. The Houston company had a hard-driving entrepreneurial culture that encouraged employee recognition and fun. On the day a big deal was signed, the president threw an employee party, complete with a mariachi band and margaritas. While the new multinational owner's head office recognized the need for overarching corporate values, it also realized that Houston's exuberant culture contributed to the firm's growth – a major reason for the acquisition.

To emphasize: it is important to view your organization holistically as a finely balanced system. The next time your organization refines its mission or revises its strategy, synchronize structure and culture. UBCO provides insights about how culture and structures must mutually evolve. The initial momentum described above picked up recently when the entire University of British Columbia system implemented a 'Focus on People' HR plan, placing priority on developing sustainable and healthy workplaces. A new strategic plan, *Place and Promise*, included sustainability as one of its pillars.[5] This plan opened up opportunities to explore the university's role in shaping a desirable ecological, social, and economic future. One of the university's commitments is to create fulfilling, values-based work environments. Leveraging these developments, UBCO's vision of a thriving learning community now rests on a culture of health and embraces a wider conception of health and sustainability.

Linking People Initiatives to the Business Strategy

Preserve (not its real name) is a government agency providing services directly to the public in many locations. It employs several thousand people in a wide variety of occupations, some part time and/or temporary. Although government regulated, it has considerable scope to be flexible and innovative in its people practices. However, saddled with an expanded mandate for service delivery, rising public expectations for service access, and a reduced budget, the organization has struggled to rally its managers and employees around a renewed business strategy.

How Preserve approached this challenge illustrates another general principle of healthy change: the importance in any organization of closely linking all people initiatives to the business strategy. The agency faced three common issues. First was an urgent need to implement a new business strategy within budgetary constraints. Second, the executive team had a mindset and leadership style inconsistent with its newly espoused people goals. And third, Preserve had too many separate people initiatives, resulting in confusion and inefficiencies. From a healthy organization perspective, the solution is to incorporate people goals, supports and actions at the centre of the business strategy.

MOVE DOWN YOUR OWN HEALTHY TRAJECTORY

Preserve's CEO emphasized in her communications with employees the importance to the corporate mission of creating 'one community' that would have a 'positive culture.' Some of the pieces were already in place. For example, the organization had a human resources plan. At executive retreats and employee forums, lengthy discussions took place about strengthening the culture so that employees would feel more empowered to respond to new goals and service delivery requirements. And the organization had good data on where the greatest needs and opportunities for positive change were, having conducted an employee survey and followed up with focus groups to identify priority action areas.

But, like many other large organizations, Preserve was attempting to do too much at once to advance its human resources goals. There were too many separate 'people' policies and initiatives; each time a new one was 'rolled out,' HR staff in the field and line managers would baulk at the added work. There also was a profusion of terminology and change initiatives, with dozens of different words being used to describe the organization's people priorities and goals, and separate strategies on leadership, healthy workplaces, engagement, change management, and learning. As a result, it was difficult for even the 'champions' of these initiatives to see how all the strands tied together, never mind to convince line managers of their strategic relevance. So, while there was readiness and some momentum, finding a path forward required cutting through all this dense underbrush or language and initiatives.

Key members of the human resource group recognized these challenges. But they also were well aware an effective process for moving forward had to address the executive's traditional style of managing, rather than leading. As one HR staff member put it, the executive focuses on 'fixing not building' people and culture. However, at one of its retreats, the executive compared its current leadership style with the kind of culture it wanted to create in the organization. This raised awareness of the importance of being less operationally focused and directive and more supportive of line managers and employees taking initiative and using their creativity. At subsequent meetings, the executive settled on a way of connecting strategy, culture, and work environments, a solution that emphasized employee engagement, defined as 'the energy of employees and the strength of their connection to Preserve.' This definition prompted follow-up discussions at which managers identified the key 'drivers' of engagement, which all managers were expected to improve.

HR took this as a signal to do something it had wanted to do for years: mine the organization's human resource data sources, including the employee survey results, to identify a handful of meaningful indicators to help managers to track progress on the HR strategy. The mapping exercise also involved an analysis of employee survey data to validate the executive's intuitive model of engagement drivers and outcomes. The upshot was a small set of key indicators that could be used in future to guide management actions in areas that mattered most. The organization was on the path to a more coherent, integrated – and certainly more efficient – focus on people initiatives, with built-in accountability for managers. The stage was set for what the executive team wanted in the first place: shared responsibility for a positive work environment and performance excellence.

INSIGHTS ABOUT LINKS TO THE BUSINESS STRATEGY

Preserve is not alone in struggling to find the best way to connect its people support system to the corporate strategy. I want to use Preserve's experience to revisit a point made in chapter 2: workplace wellness and health promotion initiatives can be springboards to a healthy organization if they become integral to the corporate strategy. In this regard, healthy workplace advocates should heed the advice of HR experts, who argue that people practices must be directly linked with business goals if they are to impact performance.[6] This insight is missing from the studies of workplace health promotion return on investment discussed in chapter 2.

Workplace health promotion and wellness programs can be effective launching pads for deeper change, especially if they have a comprehensive scope. These features enable practitioners to address underlying organizational and workplace conditions that are prerequisites for achieving employee health goals and productivity. A major hurdle is encouraging more expansive thinking among employees and managers about how intangibles, such as quality of work life, are powerful drivers of tangible results, such as productivity, growth, and profits. In a healthy organization, managers view employees' well-being as an important goal in its own right that directly contributes to business success. Thus, actions required to create a healthy organization must address all aspects of work design and people management. Programs that deliver measurable improvements in employees' work experiences and performance cannot simply be 'added on.' They need to be woven into the business strategy.

A strategy-focused approach to healthy change must address three issues head on. The first issue emphasizes the *risk factors*, or the underlying job characteristics and organizational conditions that enhance or impair health and performance. The second zeroes in on an integrated set of desired *outcomes*, in terms of employee health, organizational results, social and environmental impacts, and the organization's long-term sustainability. The third highlights the *actions* required to address these underlying factors and achieve the desired outcomes.

In terms of risk factors, healthy change must target as required the relationship, job, team, and support factors identified in figure 3.1. These would include physical working conditions, ergonomics, temporal aspects of the workday and tasks, job content, job autonomy, co-worker relations, quality of supervision, and financial and economic aspects.

Outcomes will vary by the scope and objectives of the planned change or intervention. Among the outcomes to consider are improved employee health, which may help to convince senior managers that investing in employee wellness makes business sense. Reduced absenteeism and utilization of employer-provided health benefits are common in this regard. If the focus is more comprehensive, looking at the performance of the organization as a whole, a balanced scorecard approach that includes employee experiences – such as job satisfaction, commitment, and morale – are worth considering. If your organization is ready to adopt its own version of a healthy organization value chain, then you also can link employee experience measures with your customer or client experience metrics. And, as we will see in chapter 8, assessing an organization's impact on society and the environment is a fast-emerging area of social responsibility reporting.

In terms of actions, even though the process of creating healthy workplaces is not well documented, we can identify common features, based on assessments of comprehensive workplace health promotion initiatives in various countries that attempt to address environmental conditions and individual health behaviours. In most instances, these reviews did not jump to the next level – the healthy organization – because health outcomes and organizational results were not directly linked. Making that leap requires a clear understanding of these success factors.

Looking at cutting-edge human resource management practices provides insights about what works. 'Best practices' were a major preoccupation in the human resource management community during the 1990s. Academic researchers thought differently, debating whether 'best practices' exist. Viewed as especially troublesome was the implication in 'best' that there are objective standards for judging the effectiveness of practices and, furthermore, that such practices are universally applicable. A more nuanced view emerged. While researchers agree on the features of high performance work systems, whether they outperformed traditional systems was viewed as depending on the strategic fit within a firm's context and goals. For healthy organizations, this 'fit' factor must apply to all people initiatives and programs.

Widen the Circle of Involvement

The National Research Council's Institute for Fuel Cell Innovation (NRC-IFCI) is at the forefront of clean energy research and development. The institute works in partnership with industry and universities to develop hydrogen fuel cells. Located in Vancouver, Canada, its new facility meets the latest 'green' building design standards and is home to over 100 scientists and support staff as well as several hundred students, visiting scientists, and guest workers, who spend some time in the facility each year.

The NRC-IFCI provides an instructive story about how senior managers' initial discussions with employees about what they needed to achieve new performance goals in a revised business plan opened the way for participatory workplace improvements. By designing a change methodology in which groups of managers and employees identified root causes of performance and quality of work life problems, jointly crafted solutions were easier to find. And a true sense of shared responsibility for the future success of the institute was embodied in the work-

Figure 6.2 Institute for Fuel Cell Innovation's workplace vision

---

We are committed to collaboratively creating a high quality and safe workplace that supports all employees to contribute fully to the Institute's success. Achieving excellence in our research and external partnerships requires an excellent work environment. This is defined by:

- *Team work* based on the values of respect and trust.
- *Communication* within teams, among teams and between employees and management that is open, honest, and two-way.
- *Decision-making and business processes* that are based on the values of integrity, flexibility, transparency and accountability.
- A *culture* that puts people first, embraces diversity, is inclusive and friendly, celebrates success through recognition, and builds commitment to the Institute.
- *Support* for success by ensuring each employee has the resources, equipment and training they need.
- An overall *employee experience* that is personally rewarding, enjoyable and motivating.

---

place vision that employee task groups presented to the organization as a catalyst for change.

MOVING TO HIGHER GROUND

With a new business plan that raised the performance bar, the institute's senior managers realized that the organization had to 'move to higher ground.' Critical to success were basic elements of a high-performing organization, such as team work, cooperation, clear priorities, and effective communication. Through employee consultations, senior management established five task groups that focused on what were generally recognized as priority issues: communication, safety, human resources, workload, and equipment. Each task groups was co-led by a manager and a front-line employee, whose role included coordinating their work with that of the other groups.

At a day-long planning session, group members discussed creating what several participants called a 'dream workplace' at the institute as a framework for future success. To provide a common reference point for group deliberations, task group co-leads created a shared vision of what this workplace looks like (see figure 6.2). It was intended as a tool for priority-setting, coordinating recommendations from the group, and keeping everyone focused on the actions that would most effectively contribute to workplace improvements. This vision was validated by other task group members, then communicated and discussed among all staff. It turned out to be an invaluable organization development tool.

The five task groups went on to make dozens of specific recommendations for improvement, with follow-up action sequenced over the coming months and years. But the workplace vision helped everyone to see the importance of the common themes in these recommendations: improved communication, coordination and cooperation, learning and development opportunities, and sustainable workloads. Perhaps the biggest contribution of the groups to moving the institute onto a solid healthy organization trajectory was the emphasis they gave to getting the improvement process right. What the groups demonstrated was that employees and managers could work together to set realistic goals and design change processes that would continually improve the institute's ability to help bring to market cutting-edge fuel cell technology.

INSIGHTS ABOUT INVOLVEMENT

The NRC-IFCI case highlights critical insights about the collaboration required for successful change. Healthy change processes move organizations forward because they provide ever-expanding opportunities for others to become involved. Change is an opportunity for employees to be engaged in solving problems and taking ownership for results. While leadership from the top of the organization is a big plus, employees throughout the organization can become change agents and contribute to making it healthier.

Like leadership, the topic of organizational change has sparked much talking and writing by management experts. One prominent model of change suggests that senior managers can manage change just the way they would any corporate project. The widely used term 'change management' implies that managers are the ones in the driver's seat. However, the major weakness of this traditional approach to change is a reliance on top-down, executive-driven plans. Avoiding the limitations of change management requires balancing top management support with employee involvement, in other words, combining top-down and bottom-up approaches.

Richard Axelrod, an organizational development expert, argues that when top managers are the change cheerleaders, negative consequences for the organization's structure and culture can result.[7] The main

drawbacks include greater cynicism, resistance, bureaucracy, and rein-
forcement of top-down control – what Axelrod calls the 'Dilbert organization,' named after the hapless character in Scott Adams's comic strip
about a seriously dysfunctional office. The failure of many change initiatives can be traced to the change management process used, because
it 'disengages the very people whose support is essential to success.' As
a solution, Axelrod recommends 'widening the circle of involvement'
by using democratic principles of participation that create the trust and
confidence needed for change to succeed.

Axelrod's observations are backed up by academic experts on organizational change, two of whom state: 'The more people are involved,
the more the change effort is their change effort. The more individuals
can see that they can succeed in the future state, the more empowered
they feel.'[8] It is on this key point that organizational change intersects
with health promotion thinking. People need to be involved in creating a health-promoting environment that supports improvements in
personal health and well-being. Applied to workplaces, this requires
designing change processes in ways that contribute to healthy workplace goals.

My assessment of award-winning healthy workplaces identified
strong commitment from top management, reinforced by their individual behaviour, as a key success factor. Equally essential is the
meaningful involvement of all groups – front-line workers, all levels
of management, unions, and professional associations – in the organization. This key ingredient of organizational change resonates with a
core idea of health promotion. The World Health Organization's widely
used definition of health promotion suggests that worker involvement
in the process of creating and maintaining healthier working conditions
is a prerequisite of a healthy workplace. As the NRC-IFCI example so
clearly shows, real progress is possible when the impetus for change
comes from the bottom and middle of the organization, not just from
the top.

People cannot become enthusiastic participants in a change process if
they do not know about it. Open and constant communication is a key
success factor in any organizational change initiative. Creating healthier workplaces is no different. One of the complaints I often hear from
workplace health promotion or wellness coordinators is the low level
of uptake in available programs. It usually reflects two weaknesses: a
lack of continual communication, using language that is meaningful to
the diverse demographic groups, and designing programs so that em-

ployees actually feel some ownership over them – through committees, councils, or active consultation mechanisms.

It is equally important to keep everyone in the organization informed about the goals, strategies, and progress milestones for change. Traditional change initiatives driven from the executive suite often suffer from communicating too little, too late. As change expert John Kotter warns, most corporate change initiatives under-communicate by a factor of ten.[9] If change is flowing from the front lines of an organization, change agents must keep senior management informed about the impact of the initiative and use multiple channels to communicate progress to co-workers. Also important is helping all managers to adjust their thinking about what drives performance, so that workplace and cultural factors become part of their thinking in this regard.

Shifting thinking is an important step in changing action patterns. Effective communication is the means to this end. New thinking can come about only if a common language can be found for talking about health and performance within your organization. After a recent workshop I facilitated on how to improve job quality, one of the participants, who was a workplace wellness coordinator at a mental health NGO, raised the importance of language. She noted that different labels – healthy organization, healthy workplace, quality jobs, engaged employees, health and productivity – all point to similar determinants and outcomes. Depending on the type of organization, one label will work better than the others, so change agents need to find language that fits the context of their workplace. Using local language, they will be able to expand the possibilities for how decision-makers think – and take action – about the impact of the work environment on organizational performance.

Words such as *collaboration, adaptability, capabilities, productivity,* and *innovation* need to be paired with words such as *wellness* and *health*. If you are a workplace health promotion advocate and a member of a healthy workplace or wellness committee, focus on finding language that resonates with front-line employees as well as senior management. That may include creating a committee vision of a healthy workplace that uses words such as *capabilities, collaboration, change,* and *innovation* to describe the benefits of having healthy employees working in a vibrant environment.

Make Time for Learning and Innovation

EnerProf (not its real name) provides professional services to the energy sector. Its workforce of several hundred is located at a corporate office and many employees spend considerable time working off-site with clients. The workforce includes engineers, project managers, lawyers, auditors, and IT experts. EnerProf is a revealing example of an organization that didn't rush into a healthy organization strategy. Instead, it took stock by auditing what worked well and what needed fixing in its people practices, culture, and work environment.

Conducting an audit may not suit your organization. However, it gave the engineers and professionals in this business time in their schedules to identify, share, and discuss lessons learned about effective people practices that could propel the organization to a higher level of customer service. An audit was a formal process, so it took priority on people's agendas, thereby overcoming what is one of the major barriers to healthy workplace innovation: a shortage of time due to heavy workloads and competing priorities. EnerProf underscores the importance of these basic activities – reflection, discussion, and learning – for making workplace innovation happen.

CONDUCTING A HEALTHY ORGANIZATION AUDIT

Several years ago, EnerProf was at a critical juncture. As one of the managers put it, many of his colleagues were asking: 'how can we energize the organization to bring it to the next level?' Nothing was seriously wrong with EnerProf's culture, working conditions, or performance, but there was a growing recognition that to fulfil its client service mission and renew its workforce, which included replacing many baby boomers who were retiring, it had to do much better in terms of both people practices and performance. Above all, the organization needed to tap into employees' creative potential.

Converging circumstances brought this issue to the forefront. In response, the executive team requested an 'audit' of the organization's health. This approach was consistent with how it did business. The audit was designed to assess opportunities to improve in two areas: organizational effectiveness and working conditions. As they discussed what it meant to be a healthy organization, employees and managers came to see how the organization's mission depended on its culture, people practices, and work environments. Through these discussions, the company was able to identify a future change trajectory that would more tightly connect people and performance.

The idea of a healthy organization audit was initiated by the CEO, who pointed out that he was responding to several changes and opportunities in the organization. EnerProf had launched a high-profile work/life balance program several years earlier to improve its hiring of and retaining female professionals. This initiative succeeded to a point, in terms of increased recruitment of females. However, a recent employee survey found that heavy workloads and high stress threatened to undermine work/life balance. Employees feared reprisals if they spoke out about these conditions, in part because of a few unsympathetic executives, who left the organization shortly after the survey. Furthermore, the survey also identified needs in the areas of recognition, open exchange of ideas, and an environment more conducive to learning and creativity. These issues were acknowledged at a board/ executive retreat and reinforced in employee survey follow-up committees within each department.

As they talked openly about these issues, managers and employees across EnerProf identified several barriers to progress. The corporate values were dormant and needed to be revisited and revived. Managers had too many priorities competing for their time and attention. The executive team's 'action tracker' was cluttered with over sixty items. The performance management system was ineffective at focusing people on the results that mattered most for the future success of the organization. The human resource unit was slow to adopt a strategic view of its role. One of the five strategic goals referred to people, but in a confusing way that was difficult to translate into action. This made it hard to measure and report progress on people goals in the same clear way as was used for other operational and client service goals in an annual report card.

The actual process of auditing the health of the organization was healthy. It gave employees and managers time to reflect, openly discuss solutions, and consider options for next steps. When the project was completed, there was general recognition that it was unlike other 'projects,' because the organization had gained greater collective understanding, clarity, and focus on how to simultaneously make progress on people and performance.

INSIGHTS ABOUT THE NEED TO LEARN AND INNOVATE
EnerProf created what was, for it, the ideal opportunity for collaborative learning and, through the process, set new directions for workplace innovation. This custom-designed approach is necessary because, as I have emphasized, there is no standardized model for healthy change. There is no easy-to-follow checklist or template for bringing about the changes needed to create a healthy workplace or the more ambitious

goal of a healthy organization. Off-the-shelf programs may work in specific areas, such as smoking cessation, nutrition improvement, or employee assistance. However, a generic approach does not work for primary workplace interventions that address the underlying, systemic determinants of health and performance.

The big insight provided by EnerProf is to avoid a 'paint-by-numbers' approach to creating healthy organizations in which change is a step-by-step program. Successful implementation of change requires ongoing reflection and learning by the groups and individual change agents involved. This dynamic approach to change requires continual feedback loops and adjustments to the initial plan. In this regard, we can extract some useful lessons from research on the diffusion of innovation. Indeed, a healthy organization strategy is an innovation because it introduces something new, institutionalizes its use, and diffuses the healthy practices and their supporting values more widely. After all, the goal is to make healthy practices a routine part of daily workplace activities. In this sense, not only is the content of the change innovative, but the actual strategy for carrying it out also has to be innovative. Thus, the creative part is designing and implementing change that fits an organization's unique history, culture, market conditions, and employee characteristics.

Furthermore, the organization's learning capacity is critical for successful innovation. Learning and innovation go hand-in-hand as defining characteristics of a vibrant workplace. I have closely observed dozens of organizations develop and implement their own healthy organization strategies. To varying degrees, they linked a vibrant work environment with HR goals and bigger strategic goals, from customer or client service to operational excellence. I recall a learning network meeting, where managers and training professionals from major corporations agreed that 'getting results is what it is all about, but equally important is *how* you do it.' These companies acknowledged that more time was needed for 'collective reflection' on how the company goes about achieving its goals. Learning requires time to reflect on what has been done – a very healthy behaviour for any organization to encourage.

Experts on learning organizations generally agree that people learn in workplaces through a process that extends over time, is collaborative, and is based on continual knowledge acquisition and dissemination. Learning helps workers to avoid repeating mistakes and to reproduce successes. Management expert Michael Beer, using a health-related metaphor, argues that 'the capacity to learn and change' is organizational fitness.[10] Especially important in this regard is learning through ongoing and rigorous reviews of change initiatives. By reflecting on the experiences of implementing change, then refining and readjusting the action plan, it is possible to make change a process of continual organizational learning.

Effective bundles of healthy workplace practices are hard to imitate. Diffusion is limited because there is no easy-to-follow checklist or template for bringing about the changes needed to create a healthy workplace, or the more ambitious goal of a healthy organization. While standardized programs may work in specific areas, such as smoking cessation, a generic approach does not work for primary workplace health interventions that underlie drivers of wellness and performance. A healthy workplace strategy is an organizational innovation because it introduces something new, making it the new status quo. Learning and innovation go hand-in-hand; both are defining characteristics of a healthy organization. A healthy work environment contributes to business success by encouraging learning and adaptability.

Measuring progress is an essential component of learning and innovation. Your efforts to monitor and evaluate healthy workplace programs, changes, and interventions must be viewed in this light. Monitoring and evaluation are often weak links in the chain that connects organizational change interventions to desired outcomes. Yet the information gained through these measurement activities is critical to making change a dynamic learning process. Good measures can help decision-makers to view workplace health initiatives as investments in people that build the human capabilities needed for high performance. Change can provide learning opportunities for employees and managers about how to do things better, but only if evaluation data are converted to useable knowledge that can inform decisions and actions. Healthy workplace advocates also need to document the cost of inaction, as this could be a message that captures the attention of senior management. Chapter 8 pursues these issues. For now, the key point is that evaluation and measurement should be viewed not as separate activities, but as resources for learning how you are doing on your healthy organization trajectory.

Change as Renewal

This chapter has covered a sweeping landscape – change – from a healthy organization perspective. My intent has been to provide a practical framework and guiding principles that you can use in your workplace. I have emphasized that the change process itself must contribute to healthy workplace goals. In short, how people experience the journey is what builds towards your vision of a more vibrant and inspiring workplace. That experience must be positive overall, personally engaging, and clearly tied to a better future. If people experience change as stressful, imposed from the top, or inconsistent with the organization's people goals and values, then both the process and end results will be unhealthy.

Healthy organizations are built through gradual and cumulative changes over time. Ideally, look for that next step – however small – that with few resources can boost morale, well-being, and performance. There can be big pay-offs from small improvements. As management experts Felix Barber and Rainer Strack, writing in *Harvard Business Review*, observe: 'Because employees represent both the major cost and the major driver of value creation, people-management moves that lead to even small changes in operational performance can have a major impact on returns.'[11] The trick, of course, is to identify those small steps along your healthy organization trajectory. The suggestions in this chapter are intended to help you to find ways to do this.

The trap lies in getting stuck simply thinking and talking about a vision of a healthy workplace – or the label that best fits your trajectory. Almost every organization has strengths to build on and opportunities to take bold new steps forward. Building incrementally on these strengths and seizing present opportunities, however small to begin with, can start making the vision a reality. As we will see in chapter 7, the pressures for workforce and workplace renewal and for strengthening community relationships offer many opportunities to progress down a healthy organization trajectory.

7 Sustainable Success

Nexen is a North American-based independent energy company with operations in western Canada, the Gulf of Mexico, Colombia, West Africa, the North Sea, and Yemen. The company finds, develops, produces, and markets crude oil, natural gas, and power. Its philosophy is to 'build sustainable businesses.'[1] Nexen takes a long-term view of its energy assets, stakeholders, and the environment. Corporate decision-makers strive to balance shareholder value, social and economic benefits, and environmental impacts. In many ways, Nexen exemplifies how the healthy organization value chain introduced in chapter 1 actually works. The makings of sustainable success are found in Nexen's long-term focus, values-based approach to ethical business practices, and genuine concern for the well-being of employees, society and the environment.

Achieving a sustainable business requires the infusion of social responsibility principles into corporate operations, people practices and community relations. In this regard, Nexen is guided by its commitment to 'behave ethically and contribute to economic development while improving the quality of life of the workforce and their families as well as the local community and society at large.'[2] The company's annual sustainability report to stakeholders provides accountability for how well it is living up to this commitment. The company wants to do more than minimize its carbon footprint or further reduce lost-time injuries among its employees – although both goals are important, of course. So it builds social and environmental goals into its energy products, for example, by adopting the Canadian Chemical Producers' Association's Responsible Care approach to safe and environmentally sound management of its products over their entire life cycle.

Also central to Nexen's vision of a sustainable business is the belief that its future 'is in the hands of its employees.' This belief guides actions on many fronts. For example, an ethical work environment is one of the drivers of the company's sustainability vision. Its Integrity Resource Centre provides staff training on integrity and ethical practices and investigates reports of any breaches of company policies. Over the course of one recent year, almost all of its 4,000 employees attended a workshop on integrity. The company also has tightened the links between its health, safety, environmental, and social responsibility policies and practices. A member of the executive team provides oversight for this integrated approach. Employee safety and health are not a separate set of goals and practices, but are embedded in the company culture and work environment by valuing trust, respect and cooperation. Since one of Nexen's core principles is investing in people, during the recent global recession the company was financially able to commit to no layoffs and it actually recruited new talent critical to its future plans.

Now that we understand the building blocks of a healthy organization, we can turn our attention to the top of the healthy organization value chain: sustainable success. This chapter examines sustainable success and its implications for an organization's social, environmental, and human resource practices. I have argued that workplace health promotion activities can be launching pads for addressing the underlying drivers of well-being and performance. By the same token, as your organization articulates its social responsibility commitments, the stage is set for you and other change agents to pose a fundamental question: in the future, how can we thrive in ways that benefit all stakeholders?

I believe that sustainable success depends in large part on how organizations go about renewing relationships with stakeholders, including employees. In this chapter, therefore, I focus on these two big drivers of sustainable success. First, I examine the quality of the relationships with customers, business partners, local communities, and society as a whole. Then I consider how to develop the future workforce capabilities needed to achieve the organization's goals and realize its long-term vision. I expand the discussion of healthy change in chapter 6 by addressing issues such as revitalizing relationships with customers, other stakeholders, and communities; developing workforce capabilities for the long term; and tapping the synergies between socially responsible business practices and internal people practices.

To summarize, here are the chapter's key sights for achieving sustainable success:

1. Organizations become more sustainable by taking a long-term approach to success, balancing the needs and interests of all stakeholders.
2. Healthy organizations have strong core values that guide the treatment of employees, communities, and the environment.
3. Social responsibility commitments open opportunities to embed social and environmental goals into business strategy, inspiring employees in the process.
4. Human resource strategies such as workforce diversity and flexible work arrangements benefit employees, the organization, and society.
5. Long-range workforce planning is a useful tool for aligning workforce capabilities with the future needs of the business and society.

What Makes Success Sustainable?

What actions can you take today to ensure your organization's success decades into the future? This question is central to plotting an organization's healthy trajectory. To answer it, we need to think beyond financial health and consider the social, environmental, and human resource dimensions of an organization's sustainability. We need an integrated approach that unites internal and external practices. Whatever actions you decide will move your organization down a healthy trajectory, their implementation requires a values-based corporate philosophy that is applied rigorously in all relationships, inside and outside the organization. This is the basic lesson from Nexen, Four Seasons, Trico Homes, Teck Cominco Trail Operations, and other organizations I have described. At the heart of sustainable success is the integrity with which board members, managers, and employees apply the organization's core values in all decisions and actions. Consistency in this regard expands the possibilities for positively shaping the future of your organization – and society.

Social and Environmental Dimensions

Sustainable success connects the building blocks of a healthy organization to social and environmental responsibility. Because corporate social responsibility (CSR) has an external focus, its internal supports often get overlooked. I propose that a company's external CSR practices depend on an enabling work environment, culture, and leadership. Equally necessary is how employees themselves contribute to and perceive these CSR practices. When companies showcase their carbon neutral footprint or close monitoring of human rights among Third-World contractors, we also need to understand the role employees played in these accomplishments. And when an organization receives an outstanding employer award, we need to determine if this recognition squares with its treatment of external stakeholders. This chapter presents a unified perspective on human resource, social, and environmental practices as the basis for sustainable success.

Here is what is needed to achieve sustainable success. For a start, the gap between rhetoric and practice regarding social responsibility must be closed. According to a global survey of CEOs conducted by McKinsey, a consulting firm, most believe their companies should embed responsible approaches to environmental, social, and governance issues in their strategy and operations.[3] However, far fewer are able to report actually doing so.

One company that has made progress over the past decade is athletic gear maker Nike. It has taken significant steps to protect human rights throughout its global supply chain, which employs over 800,000 people, although it is the first to admit that challenges remain. Perhaps more significant for closing the gap I just referred to is Nike's increasingly creative environmental practices. The company uses 'considered design' in the manufacture of its running shoes, rating each model according to a sustainability index based on waste reduction, reduced use of toxins, use of recycled materials, and the environmental impact of each ingredient.[4] However, what is missing from these stories (but could be easily added) is how Nike's employees went about these innovations, the supportive internal conditions, and the results in terms of a heightened sense of pride, satisfaction – and future inspiration.

Providing an employee perspective on CSR applies the same approach I used to describe the building blocks of a healthy organization. This makes sense, given that workers increasingly want green and responsible employers. For example, in a recent online poll of young Canadian workers, most would consider leaving their current job for a more environmentally friendly employer.[5] The kinds of companies that will be attractive are moving at an impressive rate to 'embed' human and environmental criteria in their methods of conducting business and in every step in the product or service chain. Sustainability becomes a design feature. Design consultant Valerie Casey at the California-based design house IDEO has written a 'Designers Accord.' Companies such as Johnson & Johnson, Adobe Systems, and others who sign on are making a public commitment to sustainable design and to tracking their carbon footprint.[6] While recruitment, retention, and talent development goals may not be central to the Designers Accord, it surely will bolster these companies' human resource strategies.

Human Resource Dimensions

What is critical about the human resource dimensions of sustainable success is how the organization goes about cultivating people capabilities for the future. Capability is a person's actual and potential ability to do something and, at an organizational level, collective capabilities are greater than the sum of individual capabilities. Human resource experts Dave Ulrich and Norm Smallwood call capabilities intangible assets. 'You can't see or touch them,' they argue, 'yet they can make all the difference in the world when it comes to market value.'[7] In today's uncertain economy, an organization's future depends more than ever on its capabilities to adapt, learn, lead, innovate and be resilient.

Many managers view talent management as getting the right people into the right jobs, and doing it quickly. While this is important, also needed is a 'big picture' view of the capabilities that will be required in five or ten years. As IBM discovered from interviews with over 400 HR executives in forty countries, boards and senior executive are paying more attention to long-range workforce issues.[8] Three priority areas for improvement identified by the IBM study were predicting future skill requirements, identifying and using existing talent, and encouraging collaboration. The study concluded that future organizational success depends on agile and adaptable workforces. These are the very attributes required to anticipate and effectively respond to emerging social and environmental challenges.

Most large corporations now publish CSR reports to demonstrate accountability and transparency in the eyes of stakeholders.[9] After all, to do well by doing good – the basic principle of CSR – an organization not only must apply ethical principles and incorporate social and environmental goals into business strategies. It also must be seen to do so by investors, employees, and the public. Increasingly critical to a company's reputation in this regard are its internal people practices.

For example, Vancity has been widely recognized for how it has combined CSR and HR within an ethical business framework.[10] Vancity – a credit union on Canada's west coast – has three values: integrity, innovation, and responsibility. It defines the latter as follows: 'We are accountable to our members, employees, colleagues, and communities for the results of our decisions and actions.' Living up to this commitment happens each and every day through even the smallest interactions involving employees, customers, and local communities. Everyone in Vancity's world – employees, customers, suppliers, and communities – is a partner in shaping its future. The employee value proposition also is the community value proposition.

There is talk now of a 'sustainability advantage' flowing from environmental policies and practices that contribute to human resource goals.[11] As such, a company's brand and reputation are becoming an integral part of future workforce planning. I am suggesting that any sustainability advantage could just as accurately be called a healthy organization advantage, because it rests on workplace, cultural, and leadership foundations.

Ingredients of Sustainable Success

To summarize this integration of the social, environmental, and human resource dimension of sustainability, we can identify four ingredients of sustainable success:

1. Applying long-term, holistic thinking to what success means for the organization. This thinking shapes vision, mission, and strategic plans, providing greater value to stakeholders through ethically sound business practices.
2. Using strong corporate values and ethics to guide all relationships, whether among co-workers, between senior managers and front-line staff, with customers, or with the communities touched by the organization's products or services.
3. Adapting vibrant workplace attributes – particularly collaboration, employee input, open communication, developing potential, and encouraging learning and innovation – to external stakeholder relations.
4. Regenerating the organization's human capabilities by renewing employees' talents and creatively seeking out mutually beneficial relationships with customers and communities.

Renewing Relationships with Society

So far, I have illustrated the importance of a long-range and integrative view of the organization's success. As such, the organization's vision – its ideal future – is realized and sustained by balancing the needs and interests of customers, employees, and society. Calibrating this balance is ongoing. In this regard, what steps can you take to renew your organization's relationship with society? To help you answer this question, I want to highlight the potential to simultaneously strengthen external stakeholder and workplace relationships.

Corporate Social Responsibility Evolves

As labels go, corporate social responsibility (CSR) has been criticized as heavy on rhetoric and light on action. But the basic idea is catching on in the corporate world. A global survey by the *Economist* found that CSR is moving up as a priority for executives.[12] More companies are looking for ways to 'get it right' – and some are leading the way.

CSR has developed in three waves. The traditional, first-wave approach is corporate philanthropy. For example, Imagine Canada is a national registered charity that sets standards in this area on behalf of the non-profit and charitable sector. Imagine Canada's 'Caring Company Commitment' encourages organizations to lead in the community by example. This initiative has seen over 100 companies make a commitment to dedicate 1 per cent of domestic pre-tax profits to support charities and non-profit organizations. The commitment also involves a pledge to encourage and facilitate employee volunteering and giving, championing and sustaining at least one community investment project with CEO support that leverages the company's expertise to make a difference in the community, and publishing an annual report describing the company's community investments and citizenship actions.[13] Many good causes providing community benefits rely on this philanthropy.

Over this decade, risk management has become a second wave of CSR, as corporations try to mitigate the negative impacts of their practices on communities and the environment. Now a third wave is fast emerging, which uses a CSR lens to identifying new business opportunities that are socially and environmentally responsible. This more 'strategic' approach to CSR goes beyond an awareness of a business's impacts on communities and a willingness to change practices that have negative consequences. It moves the CSR starting line forward, beginning with the premise that businesses can operate in ways that build in social and environmental benefits.

The Changing Face of Social Responsibility

CSR's third wave aligns with a healthy organization perspective. It shows the potential for actively engaging employees in providing sustainable products and services. Yet earlier waves of CSR also can contribute to more vibrant and inspiring workplaces and demonstrate core values. Let us briefly consider some examples of how organizations are linking philanthropy, employee volunteering, and environmental practices in ways that build healthier organizations.

Home Depot's approach to social responsibility reflects its founders' personal values.[14] A core corporate value is 'giving back.' One way Home Depot does this is through its Team Depot program in all of its stores. Employees give their own time to work together on projects that benefit communities, and they address broader issues such as environmental problems, at-risk youth, and affordable housing. Each Home Depot retail outlet has one Team Depot representative who is assigned two hours per week to initiate projects in local communities and receive special training on how to hold and run successful projects and volunteer events. Each store selects the issues or projects that are of particular importance to their communities. Working on Team Depot projects helps to further the team spirit among employees at Home Depot and gives individuals the opportunity to develop or demonstrate skills that might not be apparent in their regular jobs. Many of Home Depot's managers who have risen through the ranks have developed their leadership skills through close involvement with Team Depot projects.

TNT Express, an Amsterdam-based global logistics and express company, has been recognized for its ongoing efforts to be socially responsible. The company's 'Moving the World' program involves a team of fifty employees on standby at its corporate headquarters in Amsterdam to respond within forty-eight hours to help out in disasters anywhere in the world. This is a partnership with the World Food Program (WFP), the UN agency that reduces hunger. It has responded to dozens of emergencies, including the Asian tsunami in 2004 and the floods that wrought destruction to Bangladesh in 2007. Volunteers also work around the world on secondment to WFP and raise money for the program. In a staff survey 68 per cent said that pro bono work gave them pride in working for the company and that it helps in recruiting new graduates. According to the director of the Moving the World program, 'It's providing a soul to TNT.'[15]

Environmental sustainability goals typically are part of an organization's social responsibility commitments. Toronto-based Environics

Communications Inc. launched a comprehensive program to reduce its impact on the environment – largely at the instigation of its employees. When the company committed to becoming carbon neutral by 2008, it switched to Bullfrog Power (which sources power from generators that meet strict environmental standards), reduced paper usage, and used recycled paper. Environics has sought out environmentally responsible vendors for catering and provided all staff members with a refillable water bottle to avoid unnecessary plastics in the office. And every employee is eligible to receive $250 towards the purchase of a bicycle. These environmentally friendly moves did involve extra (although not significant) costs, but there also were big investments on a personal level. An important lesson is that managers and employees need to get behind environmental initiatives, or they risk being dismissed as 'greenwashing.' This is how an inclusive approach to leadership can not only improve the workplace, but also directly benefit society.

Good Corporate Citizen, Outstanding Employer

Investors are scrutinizing corporate citizenship more closely than ever. A company's reputation on CSR issues can influence its market valuation. Public fury over executive compensation in the wake of massive job losses and government bail-outs essentially is a debate about corporate ethics. Some companies are trying to raise public and investor awareness of how their CSR efforts contribute to society and corporate performance. Jeff Swartz, chief executive at Timberland, the U.S. outdoor footwear and clothing company, stated that 'commerce and justice don't have to be antagonistic notions.'[16] Timberland was among the first to measure the impact of its social and environmental initiatives. Increasingly, companies such as Timberland understand that they must act responsibly in all areas to build a sustainable business.

For TNT Express, sustainability refers to the environment, while social responsibility refers to employees, customers, investors, and society. They are combined into corporate responsibility, which is how TNT presents its rigorous annual reporting of performance in these areas.[17] TNT was the highest-scoring company on the Dow Jones Sustainability Index in 2007 and 2008 within their industry sector. In 2009 it was awarded a CSR Leadership Excellence Award.[18] Actually, what the practices of companies like TNT show is that sustainability extends beyond environmental impacts to include the renewal of human resources and community connections.

Like Timberland and TNT, a growing number of companies are being recognized for their socially responsible employment, environmental, and community practices. For example, in 2007 and 2008 the following organizations (most are large publicly traded companies, as required by some of the CSR awards) were selected based on cross-referencing organizations that have made it onto the 100 Best Corporate Citizens and/or the World's Most Admired Companies and/or the Corporate Knight's 50 Best Corporate Citizens lists with organizations that have made it onto one or more of the following outstanding employer lists: 100 Best Companies to Work For In America, 50 Best Workplaces in Canada, and the 50 Best Employers in Canada:

- Adobe Systems Inc.
- American Express Co.
- Cisco Systems Inc.
- FedEx
- General Mills Inc.
- Google Inc.
- Herman Miller Inc.
- Microsoft Corp.
- Nexen Inc.
- NIKE Inc.
- Procter & Gamble.
- Starbucks Coffee Co.
- Texas Instruments Inc.
- Timberland Co.
- Vancity Credit Union

I recently chaired a panel at the Health, Work and Wellness Conference, a large annual gathering held in Canada. Executives from three companies – Ernst & Young, Trico Homes, and Environics Communications – participated on the panel. The panellists described the ways their companies support employees to give back to the community and protect the environment. The topic was a big step beyond employee health promotion, but it responded to growing recognition that healthy organizations also benefit communities and the environment. The three companies have common fundamentals. Each was recognized as among the 50 Best Workplaces in Canada in 2008 by the Great Place to Work Institute Canada. (None is publicly traded, so would not meet CSR award criteria.) They have strong, trust-based cultures that value employees' contributions to customers and the community. And they have made social responsibility central to their operating philosophy, business plans, and employee engagement strategies.

The panel theme was 'moving forward by giving back.' Here are some of lessons from these three companies on how to do so:

- Involve employees in selecting charity and community partners as a way to create engagement. Also provide opportunities for employees' families to be involved in community activities, and seek employees' advice on how to make these activities fun.
- Support employees to give back. Provide the policies, practices, and resources needed to encourage employees to take initiative, make the time, and fully benefit from volunteer experiences.
- Lead the way for the entire organization to get involved. Senior managers must provide ongoing support, actively participate, and regularly communicate how community and environmental actions demonstrate honest, ethical, and responsible business practices.
- Learn from the process of giving back. Volunteering, charity support, and reducing the organization's carbon footprint provide ideal opportunities for employees to learn, grow, and find innovative ways to work together and with partners.
- Embed the principle of giving back in the corporate culture as way of extending workplace values (such as respect, fairness, and integrity) into society. This is how social and environmental responsibility becomes part of a corporate brand that will resonate with prospective recruits, customers, and community partners.

Environics Communications, Ernst & Young, and Trico Homes have developed successful practices for engaging with employees, the community, and the environment. These practices are woven into their people strategies. All are open to new approaches to volunteering, giving, and environmental sustainability and no doubt will rely on employees' input for creative solutions.

Making Sustainability Strategic

I mentioned earlier that third-wave CSR dissolves the lines between social, environmental, and business goals. As business strategy experts Michael Porter and Mark Kramer explain, 'the more closely tied a social issue is to a company's business, the greater the opportunity to leverage the firm's resources – and benefit society.'[19] Social and environmental benefits are designed into products and services. And companies taking a strategic approach to CSR map the social and environmental impacts all along the value chain. Strategic CSR also can have positive implications for employees and people practices, although this dimension needs more attention. Ideally, a company must consider the social and community impact of all its people policies and practices.[20] Just think of the potentially positive community spin-offs from corporate investments in training and education, safety and health, diversity, and decent compensation.

In other words, strategic CSR raises the bar for good corporate citizenship at the same time as it sparks innovation. Porter and Kramer's example is the Toyota Prius, whose hybrid engine produces environmental benefits and a competitive edge. Two other global corporations practising strategic CSR are GE and Boston Consulting Group, and we can learn much about sustainable success from their approaches.

GE is one of the world's largest and most diversified corporations. Its website states: 'At GE, we consider our culture to be among our innovations. Over decades our leaders have built GE's culture into what it is today – a place for creating and bringing big ideas to life.'[21] GE believes that 'a company can do well even as it does good.' This belief guides the philanthropic work of the GE Foundation and employee volunteering. More significant for a sustainable future, however, is that GE is greening its business. Each business unit has to cut carbon dioxide emissions in order to reduce overall greenhouse gas emissions by 2012 to 1 per cent below 2004 levels. There is also a remarkable change in direction, reflected in a new strategy called 'Ecomagination.' Jeffrey Immelt, the CEO, has a vision of clean technologies as GE's future. GE now promotes clean coal technologies and wind power and is investing heavily in other breakthrough green technologies – no doubt offering inspiring challenges to the scientists, engineers, and other employees involved.[22]

Boston Consulting Group (BCG), a global management consulting firm, is ranked third on *Fortune's* 2009 list of 100 Best Companies to Work For In America. BCG created a Social Impact Practice Network to have a lasting positive impact on society.[23] The network's efforts are guided by the UN's Millennium Development Goals of combating poverty, disease, illiteracy, and other problems afflicting the poorest individuals. Through partnerships and projects, 11 per cent of global employees participate in the network. This activity helps society, enriches the professional experiences of BCG staff, and helps the firm to attract and retain talented staff. BCG's community knowledge also gets transferred to its corporate clients, to meet its CSR objectives, and benefits BCG's ongoing philanthropic work with NGOs such as World Food Program, Bill & Melinda Gates Foundation, and Save the Children. The network is open to any employee and a global staffing team ensures that opportunities are distributed across the organization's locations. BCG also offers longer-term opportunities, such as six- to twelve-month secondments with a global NGO partner while remaining a BCG employee as well as social impact leaves of absence for up to twelve months. These socially responsible corporations place a high priority on open channels of communication with stakeholders. Toyota listens to its customers, GE consults with its partners and communities about wind power, and BCG plays an important information broker role. Interestingly, open communication is a pre-eminent quality of vibrant and high-performing workplaces, so here is a good example of how sustainable success results from applying the same effective people practices internally and externally.

Vibrant Workplaces Support Social Responsibility

The examples of CSR I have provided clearly show the opportunities in CSR to build more vibrant workplaces, positive cultures, and a shared responsibility for success. Authentic CSR is not a public relations exercise; it has real substance and credibility in the eyes of all stakeholders. When authentic, CSR has the potential to instil pride and foster team spirit among employees. It also can provide new outlets for employees' creativity, further demonstrate core values, and reinforce the organization's reputation as caring and responsive to community needs and concerns. Indeed, CSR and HR goals converge. Evidence of this can be found in the research for Great Place to Work Institute Canada's (GPTW) 2007 list of 50 Best Workplaces in Canada, published in *Canadian Business* magazine.

A major part of the Best Workplaces assessment process involves surveying a random sample of employees using GPTW's fifty-seven-question Trust Index. Using results from this survey, I ranked the 2007 list companies by average scores on this question: 'I feel good about the ways we contribute to the community.' For all fifty organizations on the list, positive employee responses to this question ranged between 85 per cent and 90 per cent, and some companies achieved 100 per cent positive ratings. I then looked for common themes in the highest-ranking workplaces on another survey question, which asked employees to describe in their own words what made their company a great place to work at.

Two conclusions jumped out. First, what makes these workplaces great is the people. Employees care and support each other, take part in fun activities, and feel that senior managers or owners genuinely care about them. Words such as *team* and *family* are frequently used. Second, employees view these workplaces as thriving communities in which internal and external relationships are mutually reinforcing. The support, respect, and caring that staff show for each other reach into the community through volunteering, corporate philanthropy, environmental sustainability and ethical actions, and relations with suppliers and partners. The result is a deep sense of pride.

To illustrate, here are representative quotes from employees in several companies in which *all* employees surveyed felt positively about 'the ways we contribute to the community':

- Everyone that works here makes a point of getting to know each other. We participate in events during and outside of company hours.
- The people. Everybody works together as equal members of a team toward common goals, and treats one another with respect. Management has people-oriented values and responds to staff input. We provide a valuable community service.
- I am blessed to have found such an incredibly generous company to work for. They encourage me to be the best that I can be by offering continual personal growth opportunities, fabulous benefits and perks and a tremendously positive, nurturing work environment. In addition, the employees and management are actively involved in giving back to the community regularly.
- I truly get the feeling like I am part of a family here at —— which makes for a fun working environment. I am compensated fairly and am made to feel like my contribution is worth something.
- I work for an amazing company that is very active in the community (over 3000 hours of community service last year). I love that they have onsite fitness classes, a wonderful (inexpensive) cafeteria and a beautiful facility.
- It feels like a happy family here. There is no discrimination towards me with my hearing loss, quite opposite everyone is aware of my hearing loss and accommodates it. Also that we care for the community makes

it special. We also have a monthly international lunch, which we learn about other cultures and food. There are too many positive things to write.

- The emphasis on giving back to the community is astounding. Blows me away every time we do another event. Also, the staff appreciation activities are truly one of a kind. The family BBQ really hit home as something wonderful for us.
- The special events we put on and take care of make a big impact on the community and employees. The events make everyone feel like they are helping and get everyone together to talk and feel more welcome.
- Right from the beginning of my employment with —— I was welcomed as 'one of the family.'
- Everybody in this organization believes in team effort and treats everyone just like a family. We all believe in contributing back to the community.
- We have a unique culture of team and community and our respect toward diversity makes us proud to come to work.
- A genuine concern for its people and community.

Renewing Workforce Capabilities

I am encouraging an integrative approach to organizational sustainability, which taps the synergy between internal people practices and relations with external stakeholders. Thus far, I have focused externally on the social and environmental dimensions of sustainable success. To complement this approach, I now will shift the attention to what you can do internally to recruit, develop, and retain the future workforce. After all, a capable workforce is what drives sustainable success.

There also is demographic pressure to give workforce renewal high priority. Looking at the global economy's meltdown and the sudden threat of mass unemployment, some may conclude that the intense competition for talent that peaked in 2007 is yesterday's concern. I believe they are wrong. Economic cycles do not alter the demographic facts. In North America, Japan, and most of Europe, workforces are aging and there are fewer new workers than will be needed to replace retirees. For example, over half of the workers in Canada are over the age of forty-two. Japan's population is actually shrinking. Across Europe, deaths will outnumber births by 2015. By 2030 people over sixty-five will comprise almost half of Germany's adult population. Even if some older workers postpone retirement in order to make up for savings lost when financial markets tumbled in 2008, the reality is that workforce renewal will seriously challenge many organizations.

If anything, the global recession has provided breathing space to develop longer-term workforce plans. Even firms that were forced by the recession to cut jobs need a long-term strategy to rebuild their workforce capabilities around a repositioned business strategy – just as Trico Homes did. The remainder of this chapter explores different ways that workforce renewal and social responsibility converge, providing ideas for how your organization can build the basis for sustainable success in three areas:

- Workforce diversity strategies dovetail with many organizations' commitment to reflect the changing demographic profile of their customers and communities.
- Meeting the challenge of addressing the needs of three generations of employees offers new opportunities for flexible work arrangements which benefit society.
- Developing long-range workforce plans opens up creative possibilities for aligning workforce capabilities with the future needs of society.

Workforce Diversity Strategies

One socially responsible solution to workforce renewal expands the search for new sources of talent by recruiting a more diverse workforce. Doing so requires a barrier-free work environment that is welcoming and accommodating to individuals from a wider range of backgrounds. The foundations for an inclusive workplace are the organization's people values and a commitment to reflect in its workforce a changing society.

In North America, a workforce diversity strategy enables an employer to better reflect the make-up of society and ensure that all potential sources of talent are being tapped. It's also the socially responsible thing to do. For example, immigrants made up 20 per cent of Canada's workforce in 2006. However, 42 per cent of large employers do not have a strategic plan to foster diversity.[24] The labour shortages prior to the global recession were a big incentive to overcome these barriers. Increasingly, employers in Canada recognized that they would fall short of meeting their recruitment goals unless they created a more welcoming work environment for persons with disabilities, Aboriginal persons, immigrants, and women in male-dominated areas such as construction.

Moving in this direction has the added advantage of forming stronger community ties. I noted in chapter 4 that, for TD Financial, diversity goes beyond a commitment to good corporate citizenship and has become how this North American bank does business. In addition to its Diversity Leadership Council, TD has a workplace accommodation policy that gives job applicants and employees access to an inclusive and barrier-free workplace. The Dedicated Assistive Technology team and accommodation fund support persons with disabilities (1,700 of whom are employed by the bank), providing sign language interpreters, text readers, large screen monitors, and workstation modifications. The bank also adjusts work hours and job scope so that everyone is able to contribute. Diversity managers and coaches work with other managers and supervisors to raise awareness of diversity issues and provide skill development to achieve inclusive workplaces.

Other firms have developed similar approaches, designating managers to lead corporation-wide action plans. Ernst & Young is a leading professional services firm with about 4,000 employees across Canada. The company has a full-time manager of inclusiveness, who is responsible for creating and implementing career development strategies and programs that ensure an inclusive environment. The manager of inclusiveness works closely with the CEO, who chairs the Inclusiveness Steering Committee. Inclusiveness awareness workshops are mandatory for all managers and partners. Recruiters also receive specific training on inclusive hiring practices. Advisory groups monitor and guide gender equity and ethnic diversity practices. To ensure the effectiveness of diversity-related initiatives, Ernst & Young is committed to reviewing diversity data, setting goals, and conducting ongoing focus groups to measure progress.

A diversity strategy also strengthens ties with the community. At a diversity workshop, I recall a Home Depot manager describing how this happened at his store. It used to be, he explained, that hiring persons with disabilities was seen simply as 'the right thing to do.' The few such individuals recruited were given special treatment, with the assumption that they could not do a regular job. So hiring a person with a disability was like a charitable gesture and probably seemed that way. Through closer involvement with community agencies trying to find meaningful employment for persons with disabilities, the store managers and HR team realized that everyone could benefit from a different

approach. Rather than trying to fit persons with disabilities into existing job slots, they asked a new question: what can this person do and
where in the store do they have the greatest potential to contribute?

This attitude meant rethinking what a job is and altering performance expectations to fit what people can offer. Co-workers' attitudes
also had to change so that their idea of a team was more inclusive. The
store manager described it as a 'capabilities' approach. One example
he provided was the necessity of giving hundreds of in-store plants
the required amount of water at regular intervals. This was a task that
seemed difficult for high school student part-timers, most of whom had
never had to care for plants. The solution came through a community
employment agency, which referred to the store an individual with a
developmental disability who loved plants, knew exactly how to care
for them, and could carefully focus on this one task. She quickly became a valued member of the greenhouse team.

Many other organizations also have incorporated diversity goals into
their business philosophy and strategy. At Campbell's Company of Canada, which makes soup and other foods, a strong focus on workforce
diversity and inclusion defines its business partnerships. Campbell's
believes that creating relationships with minority and women-owned
businesses is vital to the company's overall success and makes a contribution to the global economy. The company's mission is to increase
their diverse supplier base by providing equal access to those suppliers
interested in doing business with Campbell's. The result is a stronger
supplier base with a broader representation of vendors that better reflects the markets they serve.

In these examples, diversity was one strand in an integrated people
strategy that connected employees and the local community. Some of
these companies, notably Campbell's, TD, and Ernst & Young, are recognized on lists such as the 50 Best Workplaces in Canada. This reinforces the vital links up the healthy organization value chain, showing
in particular how leadership, culture, and vibrant workplaces contribute to sustainable success.

Inspiring Three Generations of Workers

A question frequently asked by HR professionals is 'how do we manage three generations in the workplace?' The three generations most
commonly discussed in North America are baby boomers (born 1946–
65), Generation X (born 1966–79), and Generation Y (born 1980–95). I

believe you will have a far more effective workforce renewal strategy if you understand the needs of these different generations and, rather than 'managing' them, find ways to inspire them over the long term.

As each generation ages and matures, it loses some of the features that labelled it in the first place. That happened with baby boomers. Commentators in the 1960s and 1970s feared that the 'peace and love' ethics of the baby boomers would unleash havoc inside workplaces, weakening the foundations of capitalism. A more accurate assessment is provided by historian Doug Owram, who concludes that the youth revolution of the 1960s was over by 1975, 'with the front edge of the baby boom approaching the magic age of thirty.'[25] Owram quotes one student radical as observing that he had given up his cause in the 1970s because 'it was time to get a job.'[26]

Similarly, Gen-X's initial image was later recast. During the recession of the early 1990s Gen-X was widely described as alienated, powerless, and cynical in the face of hard times. This 'new' generation apparently had scaled down its expectations and rejected many of the values and institutions of its parents. These themes were dissected in academic studies with titles such as *Generation on Hold* and in novels, such as Douglas Copeland's iconic *Generation X*.[27] Yet by 1999 Gen-X had lost its rudderless slacker image. The internet boom was on and many Gen-Xers had ridden the wave. So there were plenty of examples of thirty-year-old entrepreneurs whose eighty-hour weeks were reaping huge dividends.[28]

Generation Y followed the Gen-Xers into the workforce. A recent PricewaterhouseCoopers report of these young graduates in forty-four countries offers a balanced view of what Gen-Y means for workplaces.[29] The report discovered they wanted similar returns from work as older generations, including steady employment with a few employers; they did not want constant job-hopping. What they do bring into the workplace are generation-specific skills and interests, being IT savvy, social networking, globally oriented, and willing to travel. These attributes can benefit employers. For example, consumer electronics retailer Best Buy asked a consultant to price a new employee internet portal. After a quote for several million came back, a group of young employees assembled an informal team of developers and made the portal for $250,000. Now, facing falling sales and profits, Best Buy is looking for novel ideas from its Gen-Y employees to apply the latest technology to marketing and sales.[30]

But the question remains: are there fundamental differences in work

aspirations across the generations? The Rethinking Work survey compared employees age thirty or younger with those over forty-five.[31] Not
surprisingly, younger workers more highly value career advancement
opportunities and older workers put somewhat more importance on
benefits, a sense of pride and accomplishment, and freedom to make
decisions. However, a core set of features that defines a vibrant workplace is important to all age groups: a work environment that is healthy,
safe, and free from harassment and discrimination; training and other
opportunities to develop skills and abilities; friendly and helpful co-
workers; challenging and interesting work; good pay; and flexible
work arrangements.

Employers who are preoccupied with the needs of young recruits
are missing a chance to address the quality of work needs of all their
staff. Understanding the full spectrum of workforce needs is critical to
organizational renewal. Feedback from employees or prospective recruits could reveal, for example, that quite different needs lie behind
the high value placed on training. For young workers or new managers,
it may mean expanding their skills repertoire. For experienced workers,
it could mean adapting existing skills to new roles such as coaching
or mentoring. Similarly, 'good pay' means very different things to a
twenty-five-year old and a fifty-five-year old.

So, too, does 'flexibility.' Young workers are the least tied down of
any age group. Those who are not saddled with large student loans
may want time for travel or further education. Flexibility for them also
involves teleworking and spread out work time, rather than the traditional 9-to-5 schedule. Middle-aged workers with families are going
to want flexibility to meet children's needs. Older workers want hard-
earned and long-deferred time for travel, leisure, and volunteer activities – and for some, grandchildren. According to one survey, workers
fifty-five and older would prefer to work Tuesday, Wednesday, and
Thursday from 9:00 a.m. to noon and to have over six weeks of annual
vacation.[32]

Given that baby boomers far outnumber Gen-Y, employers should be
enabling a smooth and possibly delayed departure of the boomer generation. In fact, of all the areas where flexibility in workplace policies
and practices are required, this presents the greatest opportunity. Finding innovative ways to maximize the contributions of this huge pool of
experienced workers means redesigning retirement.

The coming wave of baby boomer retirements has been on employers' radar screens for well over a decade. Yet surprisingly few have

taken the steps needed to prepare for this new demographic reality. Employers' human resource policies and practices, workplace culture, and related work environment factors influence decisions by older workers to stay, retire and not work, or retire and re-engage in the workforce. The aging workforce also poses significant risks to employers in terms of lost knowledge, which again requires strategic responses. As U.S. demographer Ken Dychtwald and his colleagues observe: 'In an ideal world, flexible retirement would allow employees to move in and out of the workplace seamlessly, without ever choosing a moment to retire.'[33] By jettisoning traditional notions of retirement, you also will be opening up flexible options for all workers.

There is another urgent reason to do this. Beyond older worker retention and recruitment, a compelling business case for redesigning work-retirement transitions is reduction of the risk of losing core knowledge when experienced baby boomers retire. Retaining the tacit knowledge of retiring workers in critical positions requires more than succession planning for senior management positions. Vital knowledge can be possessed by any worker, from the front lines up.

What I am talking about preserving is tacit knowledge. This is the 'know-how' or 'how-to' knowledge gained from years of doing the organization's tasks, and it usually is not written down. Even sophisticated knowledge management systems do not fully capture tacit knowledge. Solutions require an integration of a firm's knowledge management and human resource strategies.[34] Long-range workforce planning is part of the solution, helping to identify what kinds of tacit knowledge need to be preserved to meet future business goals. It also opens the door to redefining the roles of experienced workers with vital knowledge, giving them time and support to be coaches and mentors to junior staff. Furthermore, the redesign of project teams to include workers with different experience levels also speeds up knowledge transfer. These kinds of innovations often are welcomed by workers of all ages.

Decisions to stay employed or retire are strongly influenced by job quality – as are younger workers' decisions to join, stay, or quit. Among the workers in the Rethinking Work survey, those who are stressed out or dissatisfied with their jobs planned to retire at least a year earlier than co-workers who had a good quality of work life. Furthermore, the biggest incentive for employees to keep working beyond their planned retirement is not money, but the opportunity to do what they are really good at. Flexible hours and schedules, including part-time work, are big attractions. Many are seeking greater personal rewards, such as making a useful contribution to society and having opportunities for challenging and interesting work. Another criterion is a healthy work environment, especially one that is low stress.

A good number of employers soon could be at a disadvantage in the labour market if they do not respond to workforce aging with appropriate action plans. You can start by asking what flexible retirement (if not already in place) would look like in your organization and, more broadly, how the principle of flexibility could be adapted to careers and work arrangements for all workers. As for social responsibility, just think about the potential to improve the quality of life for employees and their families.

Long-Range Workforce Planning

Whether it is flexible phased retirement, empowering Gen-Y workers to contribute their IT skills, or inclusive workplace practices, each of these initiatives will be more effective when they are part of a comprehensive, long-range, workforce plan. Workforce planning may sound dry and technical. But, in fact, it is a sound method for engaging today's workforce to envision and develop tomorrow's workforce – a process that meets all the requirements of healthy change outlined in chapter 6.

The private sector makes extensive use of long-range business planning. A good example is Royal Dutch Shell's 2050 energy scenarios. 'More energy, less carbon dioxide' sums up the global challenge for energy.[35] In one scenario, called 'Scramble,' little action is taken to encourage more efficient energy use or reduce greenhouse gases. The other scenario, called 'Blueprints,' sees the spread of local actions to address three interrelated challenges: economic development, energy security, and environmental pollution. A price is put on carbon emissions, and new green technologies lead to alternative and more efficient energy sources. CO_2 levels go down as a result. Such future scenarios can be used to test corporate strategies in any sector and expanded to anticipate future workforce requirements.

Most large employers have talent management strategies focusing on high-performers and succession plans for senior management positions. However, few have long-range workforce plans that take a broader and future-oriented perspective on organizational renewal. From what I have observed, long-range workforce planning may be more widely used in the public sector, where the workforce is older and heading for retirement sooner than in the private sector. A good example is Edmonton, a western Canadian city of 1 million people and capital of the energy-rich province of Alberta. The city government's approach to workforce planning combines a straightforward process with vision and imagination.

Positioning an organization for future success requires a clear vision of an ideal future and the capacity to adapt plans and goals as the actual future unfolds. Municipalities are big thinkers in this regard, creating planning frameworks that provide direction for their physical, economic and social development.[36] Edmonton's plan is for ten years, but it uses a thirty-year time horizon. Most major cities have such plans and some, such as Seattle and San Francisco, use 100-year time horizons. Edmonton's new municipal development plan, *The Way We Grow*, uses extensive community input to identify the values and growth scenarios that best fit citizens' changing needs and future aspirations. Interestingly, this ongoing work is expected of a city administration, but when a corporation does it, the CSR label gets applied.

To ensure that it will have the right capabilities to guide the municipal plan, the City of Edmonton also created a long-range workforce plan. In a nutshell, workforce planning is a strategy-focused, evidence-based approach for ensuring that an organization has people with the right capabilities in the positions it needs to achieve long-term success. The workforce planning process started with a ten-year assessment of the external and internal environments. The ten-year community plan calls for dramatic changes in roles and skill sets. For example, there will be less need for building management and maintenance expertise and much more environmental knowledge and skill required. Each department identified the implications of the ten-year community plan for its operations, focusing on workforce and workplace changes that would support future roles and goals. The departments' workforce plans were rolled into the corporate workforce plan.

Edmonton launched its workforce planning process in 2003, and it is now embedded into the business planning cycle. The city's three-year HR strategies are guided by the overall workforce plan. The plan has resulted in increased focus on succession planning, leadership development, and talent management as part of an integrated strategy.[37] Successful workforce planning requires HR to play a greater consulting role, supporting operational departments to develop and implement their own workforce plans. HR staff who had focused on program delivery now had to embrace a far more strategic role, and HR provides more data and analysis regarding current and future workforce needs. In short, it adopted an evidence-based approach to identifying and developing the future competencies needed by departments. Workforce planning has its drawbacks. It works best in larger organizations and it can be expensive and time-consuming. But the potential advantages for organizational renewal are significant. Consistent with a healthy organization perspective, it provides a long-term, holistic, and strategic approach to developing the people capacity needed for future success.

Making Progress

This chapter has tied together organizational renewal in terms of the workforce, the workplace, and relationships with society. A healthy organization evolves organically, so it is in a constant state of renewal. But it does so with an eye on the distant horizon, not just on today's challenges. It also seeks innovative ways to balance the needs and aspirations of customers, shareholders, employees, and community stakeholders.

One of the key points made in the chapter is that new directions in strategic CSR have the potential to reposition businesses in ways that benefit all stakeholders. This approach, in my view, is what a sustainable organization is all about. Another key point is that internal and external renewal strategies need to be merged. The long-range workforce plans, inclusive workplace, and flexible employment practices I have described should be viewed as enablers of business strategies that embrace the ethics of environmental and social responsibility.

Measurement also is a prominent theme in the chapter. Workforce planning, as practised by the City of Edmonton, requires the analysis of workforce demographics and skills. Responding to the needs of an increasingly diverse workforce and tracking progress on inclusiveness require that organizations use employee surveys, as TD does. A focus on generational differences in work values inside your organization requires employee consultations or surveys, so you can understand where there is convergence and divergence within your workforce. Socially responsible companies such as Vancity, TNT, and Nexen use annual reporting systems, set targets, commit to improvement actions, and hold themselves publicly accountable for progress. And many of the organizations profiled in this chapter have undergone rigorous independent vetting in order to earn a place on one or more of the lists that recognize ethical, responsible, and sustainable business and people practices. In short, a purposeful use of metrics can inform decisions and actions required to build sustainable organizations. This is the subject of chapter 8.

8 Measuring Progress

Hilti's power tools are prized by professional builders for their durable quality and are much coveted by serious home do-it-your-selfers. What most of its customers may not know about is the Austrian-based manufacturer's rigorous approach to organizational health. Hilti sees the link between employee and customer satisfaction being forged within healthy environments. According to Hartwig Eugster, plant manager at Hilti, 'we have found that satisfied staff are synonymous with improved customer satisfaction and an upward trend in profitability. By means of the measures implemented in the field of corporate culture and workplace health promotion, we have been able to sustainably increase the level of satisfaction among our employees.'[1] Staff and customer satisfaction are measured with different instruments, but by putting these separate indicators side by side, Hilti is able to connect actions on the people side with business results.

Executives at Genentech, one of the world's leading biotech firms, made a discovery of a different kind a few years ago. Stephen Juelsgaard, an executive at Genentech, explained to a conference in 2007 how the biotech company had experienced 20 per cent annual growth since 2001. Throughout that period, it was on *Fortune* magazine's list of 100 Best Companies to Work For In America. Executives realized that the company's improved ranking on the *Fortune* list tracked its stock price. Essentially, they connected two big performance dots. When employees were asked to write down what makes it a great workplace, three qualities stood out: commitment to science and creating innovative treatments, dedication to patients, and valuing and respecting employees – all drivers of performance. What sparked the executive team to connect these data points was their belief that culture lies at the heart of the company's continued success.

In the public sector, a leader in the use of healthy organization metrics is Britain's National Health Service (NHS). The annual NHS Staff Survey measures what staff identified as key drivers and outcomes of healthy work environments. What is notable is how the survey feeds into a comprehensive framework for ongoing improvements in operational and patient outcomes – what really matters to the public. The 600 NHS organizations must take follow-up actions on survey results in order to meet government targets for twenty-four core performance standards. The reporting and monitoring of survey results are the mandate of the Care Quality Commission, an independent regulatory body. Staff survey results are integrated into a comprehensive performance report card, the Annual Health Check.[2] Adding even greater public accountability, complete survey results for every NHS organization are reported on the Care Quality Commission's website.[3]

Hilti, Genentech, and the NHS illustrate, in different ways, how to piece together relevant data to paint a more complete picture of a healthy organization value chain. These organizations have ventured into the frontier of organizational health, creatively using selective metrics to improve the links between people and performance. HR dashboards, balanced scorecards, health promotion return on investment, and 'triple bottom line' report cards – these topics are the focus of growing numbers of management conferences and featured articles in practitioner publications.

This trend is promising, because it opens up more possibilities for making better decisions that contribute to vibrant workplaces, healthy change, and results that are sustainable. Meaningful HR metrics help an organization to track its progress on people goals by creating accountability for the required actions – at least in theory. If it were that easy, more organizations would have a robust system for measuring the human side of performance. But there are many pitfalls to using metrics. One of the biggest risks is that organizations can drown in their own data. Managers can become immobilized trying to make sense of numbers that are meaningless, inaccurate, or overwhelming in quantity. Metrics can become the tail that wags the dog, displacing the original intent: 'learn how we're doing and where we need to do better.'

In this chapter, I examine the promise and pitfalls of measuring progress along your healthy organization trajectory. Throughout the book, I have drawn on various types of data – surveys, qualitative consultations, corporate information, and published research findings – to build a case for investing in healthy organizations. Having the relevant metrics available contributes to healthy change and a positive culture. Now I will help readers to identify what they can do to improve the use of data relevant to their organizational improvement goals. To this end, the chapter addresses five questions:

1. How can you make better use of evidence to plan, implement and monitor organizational improvements?
2. What measurement tools are available to you and how can you adapt them to your needs?
3. What are successful practices for using surveys as catalysts for healthy change?
4. What must you consider when integrating people metrics into a corporate performance reporting framework?
5. What are the basic guidelines you need to follow in order to measure workplace progress effectively?

Using Evidence for Action

The healthy organization model adds an important new dimension to business performance reporting. At the heart of a healthy organization is the relationship between vibrant work environments, employees' capabilities, and results. Once senior managers grasp this connection between individual well-being and productivity, the next step is to use work environment quality and well-being as performance indicators. This puts employees' experiences right next to customer satisfaction, profits, growth, operating efficiency, and social and environmental impact as key performance measures.

From a risk management perspective, unhealthy and unsafe work environments can impose large costs on an employer. These range from lost productivity and overtime costs due to absenteeism to all the direct and indirect costs of a demoralized workforce and underutilized talent. The costs and risks of an unhealthy work environment for employers should be clear by now. Workplace health research does a good job of quantifying the extent of the problem, using measures such as absenteeism rates and costs, health benefit plan costs, the burden of long-term disability, turnover, and the like. But if these measures are flipped 180 degrees, we have positive indicators of well-being, performance, and sustainability. So, as measures go, retention replaces turnover, days at work replaces absenteeism, injury-free days replaces lost-time injuries, and return to work success rates are used instead of long-term disability rates.

This positive approach to people metrics is most consistent with a healthy organization model. However, we cannot assume this sort of information will have any impact, beyond keeping HR staff busy collecting it.

Practical Challenges of Using Evidence

Jac Fitz-enz, the guru of human resource metrics, makes a convincing case for a focused effort to collect, analyse, understand, and use HR data in organizational decisions: 'Information is the key to performance management and improvement. Without it, we have only opinions with no supporting facts and no directional signals ... Human data show us how the only active asset, people, are doing in their quest to drive the organization towards its goals.'[4] Fitz-enz encourages managers and other change agents to share and use the best available evidence in their decisions and plans. However, this presents practitioners with numerous practical challenges.

Monitoring and evaluation are often the weakest links connecting work environments to healthy outcomes. The information gained through these activities can generate a dynamic learning process that contributes to organizational renewal. Data must spark ideas about how to do things better. This is possible only if monitoring and evaluation data are converted into useable knowledge to inform decisions and actions. Fitz-ens calls it an 'information sharing culture,' with a strong emphasis on knowledge for action. Otherwise, measurement and evaluation turn into meaningless organizational rituals that do nothing but waste resources.

We do not have a handy organizational equivalent of a weigh scale or blood pressure gauge for assessing whether a company is healthy. Thus, organizations have no choice but to come to grips with why they need healthy organization measures, what measures are needed, and how to make the fullest use of them. While it is a good idea to incorporate monitoring and evaluation into any change initiative, putting all the pieces together into a more complete picture of organizational health performance takes time. In U.S. firms widely recognized as leaders in linking health and productivity, data integration happened later in the process of creating a healthier workforce and more productive work environment once actions were under way.[5]

Thinking Ahead

Selecting relevant metrics is more than a technical exercise. You need to think ahead to who will use these data, for what purposes, and what barriers stand in the way of effective use of evidence for decision-making. I invite you to use the following examples I have observed to reflect on the challenges of using data in your organization:

- Using metrics takes time and commitment. A meeting of senior management to address the results of an employee survey had to be rescheduled, because only one person had read the survey report. This shaky start to survey follow-up reinforced employees' cynicism that managers do not care about their views.
- Organizations adopt performance reporting systems without helping the intended users understand them. I have seen managers in organizations with balanced scorecards role their eyes, throw up their hands, and make bad jokes about dashboards as 'dartboards' when asked 'what's it like using a scorecard?'
- Many managers need to feel an emotional connection to employee feedback and numbers do not do that. So, when the sceptical CFO sees dozens of anonymous comments from an employee survey saying 'I love working here,' the positive impact of the firm's people strategy suddenly becomes real.
- Managers want to focus on what they can most influence. In a conference discussion of healthy outcomes, senior managers recognized that there are two levels of health drivers, individual and organizational, and that employers should focus on only the latter.
- Some organizations have consistently measured the wrong things. A strategic goal of a natural resources company was the efficient use of human resources. It struggled to find meaningful indicators of this. Advice from HR to change 'efficient' to 'effective' went unheeded by senior management.

In sum, there are big gaps in management's use of evidence for decision making.[6] These gaps partly stem from the failure of academics to transfer knowledge in understandable ways or to examine what matters most to practitioners.[7] Practitioners, for their part, lack time and motivation to distil the relevant implications from a deluge of academic research. And, when presented with recommendations based on solid internal evidence, managers may ignore them or not require data to

Figure 8.1 Key issues identified in a healthy workplace assessment

Wellness strategy success factors	*Major needs*
1. Commitment from senior management	1. Reduce injury risks and absenteeism
2. Collaboration between management and unions	2. Mental health and stress
3. Participation of employee groups in the design and implementation	3. Health trends in an aging workforce
Strengths to build on	*Barriers to change*
1. Solid foundation of health and safety programs	1. Some employees do not feel valued
2. Lost-time work injury reduction	2. Managers perceive employee dissatisfaction
3. On-site Health Centre	3. Post-strike mood of general distrust
4. Employee and family assistance program	4. Perceived lack of recognition among senior managers that improvements are required
5. Joint Health and Safety Committee	

justify a particular people investment. Still, as more senior managers understand the strategic value of work environments, culture, and human resource practices, we can be sure that better use will be made of people metrics.

The Value of Qualitative Consultations

But let us not get carried away with metrics just yet. Obviously, to make progress and even be thinking about how to measure it, you need a starting point and a clear direction. In fact, some of the most useful information for planning actions is qualitative, obtained through employee consultations. The added advantage of employee consultations is that people come to better understand each other, develop shared goals for their workplace, and have opportunities to take ownership for solutions. Change agents at earlier stages of planning healthy change may find useful lessons in the following examples of how two organizations used consultations in the early stages of developing their healthy organization trajectory.

Senior managers and health and safety professionals at Teck Cominco's Trail Operations had been considering the launch of a workplace wellness strategy. In the wake of a strike by production workers, there was a heightened sense of mutual distrust on both union and management sides. However, rising disability costs, an aging workforce, and an intensely competitive market for skilled trades underscored the urgency of expanding the traditional health and safety focus to a more comprehensive approach to total wellness. Some 80 per cent of workers were in skilled manual jobs and many were nearing the end of long careers with the company. As a first major step, informal discussions were held with key individuals – managers, union representatives, occupational health and safety experts – to define wellness and identify priority needs and opportunities for progress. This was 'phase 1' of the wellness strategy. A 'phase 2' would implement actions around specific improvement goals. The organization approached any major change initiative in this way.

Figure 8.1 provides a summary of what the phase 1 assessment found and shows how simple and direct the messages were. Consultations identified key points in four areas: factors that would ensure success of the wellness strategy; existing strengths the organization could build on; major needs; and the biggest barriers to moving down the wellness path. This information provided a solid foundation from which to launch a joint union-management wellness committee to coordinate, plan, and implement specific initiatives to address the three major needs. The importance of taking stock before moving forward is clearly illustrated and must be done in a way that is consistent with how the organization goes about problem-solving. It also must build a common change agenda around a few consensus needs.

As a new university committed to creating a healthy workplace culture, UBC Okanagan established a Healthy Workplace Advisory Group comprising administrative and service staff, faculty, unions, and the executive. One of the first things the group did was to consult with co-workers to identify what they saw as the elements of a supportive culture at UBCO. Students with training in qualitative research were involved as note-takers for the consultation sessions. This input was then used to define the core values that will guide UBCO to achieve its distinctive mission and vision. An online survey asked respondents to provide written responses to three open-ended questions:

1. What values do you believe are essential to achieve a healthy workplace culture (list up to 3)?
2. What is the best thing about your current workplace?
3. Describe one change that would make your workplace better.

A thematic analysis of the written responses were both validating and revealing; it provided a clear picture of the most important features of a healthy culture. Four value themes emerged, the most widely mentioned one being respect. This was followed by quality of work life, mainly expressed as work/life balance and flexibility in work arrangements. Third-ranked was a supportive community, referring mainly to supportive relationships and a supportive environment. Fourth was communication, which, like respect, was usually stated as a single word. A total of twenty categories were created, in order to capture the diverse language and wide scope of the values provided by survey respondents. In the end, some categories were combined. For example, the value of respect also could include tolerance, openness, diversity, fairness, caring, and compassion. Similarly, the concept of a supportive community included a positive atmosphere, professional development, appreciation and recognition, and services and facilities.

This qualitative consultation and the list of values that emerged helped to energize ongoing conversations about the culture. One clear result was a collectively understood shortlist of healthy workplace culture building blocks. These provided solid ground for ongoing initiatives with wider involvement from employee groups.

Measurement Tools

In this section, I offer suggestions for how you might approach healthy organization measurement. I start with an overview of what needs to be measured, then share some ideas on measurement tools and research design, and end with a brief discussion – and some cautions – about calculating returns on investment in workplace wellness initiatives.

Measures

Healthy organization indicators measure a range of social, psychological, organizational, and physical determinants (drivers); processes (factors or activities that influence how determinants affect outcomes); and outcomes (effects). Figure 8.2 organizes measures by their level of analysis and their position in the causal sequence. Indicators can provide information that enables action at four different levels: individual, job, work unit or team, and the organization as a whole. Individual-level data can be aggregated and reported at the work unit or organizational level to obtain a diagnosis of performance and quality of work life out-

Figure 8.2 Examples of evaluation measures by level of analysis and position in the causal sequence

| Level of analysis | ⇨ Position in the causal sequence ⇨ | | |
	Determinant	Process	Outcome
Individual	Employee's sense of job autonomy	Timeliness and usefulness of performance feedback	Self-reported health and well-being
Job	Challenging and meaningful tasks	Job scope and design	Job satisfaction
Unit or team	Mutual respect	Policies and practices to support and recognize team effectiveness	Team morale
Organization	Leadership commitment to people development	Annual hours of training per full-time equivalent employee	Career development opportunities

comes such as morale and work/life balance. It is important to clearly distinguish these outcomes from their underlying 'causes.' Factors influencing employee experiences are the vibrant workplace ingredients outlined in chapter 3, in four broad categories: relationships, job, teamwork, and supports.

As also noted in chapter 3, the characteristics of an inspired employee suggest relevant outcome indicators, although the most basic measures here would include employee satisfaction, commitment, pride, and sense of accomplishment. To round out the assessment of performance, at the organizational level it is possible to use employee surveys either to assess performance-relevant outcomes – such as perceived team performance or actual use of skills and initiative – or to rely on other data sources, such as customer satisfaction surveys.

In terms of process, referring back to the healthy organization value chain, we see there is a layer in that model that I called 'effective people practices.' These are the systems, resources, and programs that ensure the determinants will, in fact, have a positive impact on outcomes.

Tools

An important decision in planning an evaluation is whether to create your own measures, use measures from external sources, or use some combination. Existing measures could be extracted from administrative data (e.g., absenteeism, voluntary turnover, and overtime). Building your own evaluation tools could involve developing an employee survey or adding new questions to an existing survey. You could also review existing tools available in published academic research, through licensing arrangements or from consultants. Regardless of whether you borrow or build or buy, it is important to assess the accuracy of the measures and the usefulness of the data they generate for decision-making and action within your organization.

Academic researchers offer various tools for assessing culture, work environments, quality of work life, workplace health and safety, and other relevant topics. Usually, measurement tools published in academic journals are in the public domain and can be used with no cost as long as you credit the source. Advantages of using assessment tools created by academic researchers include the following:

- Documented validity (they measure what they are intended to measure) and reliability (they measure the same thing across different groups and over time).
- Clear definitions of the concepts being measured.
- A solid theoretical foundation, explaining how the concepts measured are interrelated.

However, there are trade-offs. Academic tools can create technical and conceptual overload, giving more than you need to meet your immediate organizational goals.[8] And measures designed to test academic theories may not have practical applications. Still, you might find what you need or get good ideas for adapting measures to suit your purposes.

Qualitative information is a complement or alternative to the quantitative evaluation methods described above. Examples include open-ended questions in surveys, focus groups, other forms of in-person or Web-based employee consultation, and individual interviews. These techniques can be useful at an early stage of planning an intervention, for example, to identify areas of concern or needs. Or they could be a follow-up to a quantitative evaluation to further probe and explain findings or to develop solutions. For some organizations, a qualitative approach is a more personal way to connect with employees and involve them in the change process than conducting a survey.

Design Options

Actually, there is no 'best practice' to conduct evaluations in workplaces. Practically speaking, the best method is the one that fits your context and meets your objectives. Become acquainted with the pros and cons of the evaluation approach you are considering. And, most important, do not go overboard trying to find the perfect methodology. It may be useful to search scholarly e-journals and practitioner publications, on-line databases (e.g., Medline, ABI-Inform), and Google Scholar for recent publications relevant to your plans. Partnerships with universities can help to tap available expertise on methods. Also useful are informal communities of practice, comprising practitioners who share a similar vision or approach to workplace improvements.[9] If you decide to hire an external consultant to conduct the evaluation, being well informed will ensure you get what the organization most needs in terms of actionable information.

Using rigorous scientific evaluation methods is possible, but often not practical. Here are three examples showing how teams of researchers and practitioners have carried out this type of evaluation. As you read these examples, think about whether these methods would provide value-added to your organization's healthy change process.

Reducing musculoskeletal injuries is a goal of all health care organizations. The Occupational Health and Safety Agency for Healthcare in British Columbia (OHSAH), Canada, evaluated in partnership with employers and unions an integrated injury prevention and return to work process.[10] The goal of the program (called PEARS, which stands for Prevention and Early Active Return to Work Safely) is to reduce the incidence, duration, time loss, and related costs of workplace musculoskeletal injuries through early intervention and the implementation of preventative strategies such as ergonomic assessments and workplace accommodation. Evaluation of pilot sites tracked incidence rates for injuries and the duration of associated time loss.[11] While results showed no reduction in incidence, the program was effective in returning to work more quickly injured nurses and health science professionals. The evaluation calculated savings in time loss and compensation, providing support for expanding the program. It also demonstrated the benefits of union - management cooperation on healthy workplace issues.

Randomized controlled trials (RCT) – considered the 'gold standard' in evaluation research methods – are rarely used to assess organizational change. This is because of the commitment of time, resources, and management required and the disruption of workplace routines. Here is how RCT was used to assess the efficacy of nurse-manager consultation and problem solving meetings for improving staff morale and care quality and reducing absenteeism.[12] Thirteen in-patient units were randomly assigned to treatment and control groups, and the experimental group received training from university experts in a cooperative form of problem solving. Outcomes were measured through a survey of employee morale and absenteeism. Incident reports and patient satisfaction were used to assess the quality of care. The results showed significant improvements in perceptions of the work environment and working relationships in the experimental groups, compared with the control groups.

An entirely different approach to implementing and evaluating workplace change is 'participatory action research' (PAR). PAR combines research with organizational development, with a big emphasis on stakeholder participation. Some organizations, for example, UBC Okanagan, use the approach without labelling it PAR. Employees (and sometimes customers or community stakeholders) are actively involved in defining common problems or they change goals, designing a plan to bring about improvements, then reflecting on the changes and adjusting the plan accordingly. PAR can utilize standard qualitative or quantitative data-gathering and analysis tools to enable learning.[13] The experience and practical knowledge of front-line employees are as important to the process as 'expert' knowledge obtained from scientific research. PAR is an interactive cycle of collective observing, reflecting, and acting. The approach includes a wide spectrum of grass-roots, team, or committee-led change initiatives with a research or evaluation component.[14]

Return on Investment

The U.S. Centers for Disease Control and Prevention (CDC) offers useful guidelines for assessing the financial impact of workplace illness prevention and health promotion programs.[15] This is referred to as 'return-on-investment,' or ROI. The CDC defines the cost effectiveness of an intervention as the ratio of an intervention compared with an alternative as the net costs divided by net health outcomes. Cost-benefit analysis assigns a monetary value to all program outcomes. Realistically, cost-benefit information should be only one of many inputs for decisions about resource allocations in workplaces.

When asking for ROI data, managers need to be aware that providing such information can be an onerous task. Not surprisingly, many organizations shy away from ROI analysis on HR programs because of the volume and quality of data required, lack of in-house research expertise, and the long-term commitment needed to both the program and the evaluation process. Even when 'business case' data are required, there can be a double standard of evidence required by employers for investing in workplace health interventions that are proactive and preventative. Employer-sponsored health plans fund expensive medical treatments that are based on evidence of efficacy, rather than on ROI data. As a team of U.S. workplace health experts observed: 'The health promotion field, however, is continually challenged to prove something medical researchers cannot – that the financial benefits of health promotion exceed its costs.'[16]

What is more, some decision-makers do not need to be convinced of the benefits of healthy workplaces. An organization's core values may be the rationale for setting and meeting people goals. Just think of all the organizations that invest heavily in employee training. Very few systematically evaluate their return on training investment, assuming that training is a necessary human capital investment for both the firm and its employees. The same is true for healthy workplace investments. For example, as the manager of Health and Productivity at Chevron Corporation in California commented about the company's disability management system: 'The return we have achieved has not always been well documented from a financial point of view, but the consensus from our management is that health promotion has added to Chevron's financial success by helping achieve Chevron's goals.'[17]

My intent is not to steer you away from ROI analysis, but rather to offer a word of caution: know what you are wading into. Change agents should be especially sceptical when asked for an ROI-based business case *before* they proceed with a change. It is far more realistic to incorporate an evaluation component into the implementation strategy, using the results as part of the learning and improvement process. This will provide a home-grown business case that will be difficult for senior management to ignore.

Using Surveys for Healthy Change

More organizations are using surveys to evaluate work environments and obtain employee input. Doing a survey is the easy part. A greater challenge is learning from survey results. Look at surveys as one tool for building a better workplace through staff engagement and communication. Surveys are opportunities to involve staff in planning and implementing changes based on survey findings. Surveys also open up communication channels with employees. Effective follow-up requires extensive two-way communication so decision-makers can hear employee reactions to the survey findings and their ideas for improvements.

Survey Guidelines

Expanding on these points, I list below detailed guidelines to help you and other change agents translate results from surveys or other evaluations into action.

1. A senior manager, project team, or committee needs a clear mandate to 'champion' or sponsor the survey from start to finish, especially by involving others in the follow-up process.
2. Recognize that no survey can be definitive. Treat the survey as one mechanism for getting employee feedback. There may be few surprises. Chances are the findings will reinforce what you already know intuitively or from other sources of information.
3. A constructive focus can be achieved by reporting only the percentage of positive responses for evaluative questions on the survey. This also makes results easier to interpret.
4. Follow-up actions are a shared responsibility and should involve employees, unions, supervisors, managers, human resources, occupational health and safety or wellness, corporate communications, and the executive team.

5. Human resources departments must be prepared to assess and readjust current human resources policies and practices in light of survey findings.

6. Consider a sequential approach to reporting, beginning with the executive, followed by managers and supervisors, employees at company forums or team meetings. Consultations give the committee and survey champion opportunities to refine, focus, and validate the priority action areas and key messages.

7. A survey without concerted follow-up action is an expensive and demoralizing waste of resources. To enable follow-up, employees need time to undertake action planning and implementation. The executive must make this a priority.

8. The survey committee should review the results and identify areas of strength and two or three opportunities for improvement. Present these key findings as the committee's view, and ask others for their interpretations.

9. Action planning has to happen within each work unit, so data need to be reported in this way to enable meaningful discussions and action. Give units their results in a form that compares them with those of the rest of the organization. Balance corporate-wide priority action areas with unit-specific actions.

10. Most medium-size and large organizations have 'pockets of excellence' – a few work units in which employees are truly inspired. The survey can help to identify such units, so their 'story' can be shared across the organization.

11. The committee should also examine the data for variations by demographic groups, looking for groups that stand out as being considerably higher or lower than average. Targeted or corporate-wide improvements can be planned based on this group analysis.

12. Coordinating actions at the organization-wide, work unit, and individual levels is an important ongoing role, often taken on by human resources, the survey committee, or the survey champion.

13. If you used open-ended questions, categorize the responses by theme and use the results to amplify and give a human face to the numbers in the survey. All senior managers should read these written responses.

14. Share the complete survey findings with any employees who are interested. This is easily done on an intranet site, but hard copies should be available to employees who do not have computer access.

15. If you are repeating a survey, distil the key trends for communication and follow-up purposes. Where are you making progress, holding your own, or backsliding? Did you achieve or exceed any improvement targets set previously?

Finding a Clear Direction from Survey Data

I have seen many organizations launch a survey only to become immobilized by the results. Several years later, they still lack a clear sense of direction. If this is your experience, consider stepping back and taking another more focused look at the survey findings. One organization I worked with was inundated with people concepts. These sounded similar – positive culture, supportive relationships, workplace community, engaged employees – but were not clearly defined. As a result, it was difficult to find a clear direction for follow-up to a recent employee survey. Working with HR, the executive team took a step back and organized all the concepts it was using into three categories: drivers (i.e., implied 'causes' or enabling conditions); outcomes for employees; and outcomes or goals for the organization. It consolidated the concepts, creating a compact and actionable strategy statement that linked people and performance:

> We aspire to be a high-performing organization, fulfilling our mandate by providing excellent services through teamwork and leadership. The key to excelling at our mission is a highly capable workforce. This requires all employees to be engaged in their work and feel commitment and pride towards the organization. A capable, engaged, committed, and satisfied workforce is only possible if we create and sustain positive work environments and supportive people management practices. Each workplace must strive for positive working relationships guided by core values of fairness, respect, and competence.

Then the HR team revisited the employee survey findings in search of key indicators of employee engagement and its main drivers. The survey contained ten questions that measured aspects of engagement (and led to endless debates about which one was most important). Statistical analysis reduced the ten items to four items that were combined into an Engagement Scale, which simplified reporting by using a single score. The scale score provided a meaningful key performance indicator for tracking and reporting progress on this strategic goal. These scale items are as follows:

- I am proud of the work carried out in my work unit.
- I feel committed to the work that I do in my job.
- My job gives me a feeling of accomplishment.
- Overall, how satisfied are you with your job?

The re-analysis of survey data was pushed further, identifying which of the many potential drivers of engagement had the biggest 'net impact' (i.e., after taking into account other drivers, along with employee demographics) on the new engagement scale score. Again, multiple indicators were combined into four distinct scales measuring people leadership, work unit relationships, training and learning, and job resources. By far, the biggest influence on engagement is people leadership, capturing the quality and consistency of corporate-wide communication, values, and culture. All four of these driver scales contained between three to seven survey questions, each with clear action implications for managers and employees.

Having a model of drivers and outcomes of a healthy organization will help to guide decision-making about which human resource investments, policies, and practices would be most beneficial for the employer and its employees. Most organizations have implicit models that link people and performance. So a useful whiteboard exercise for senior managers as a group is to map this out, guided by a simple question: 'what drives our business results?' This model can then be validated in discussions with middle managers, front-line supervisors, and employees. It should be built from all the major pieces of the HR strategy.

Using Survey Results for Leadership Development

The federal governments in the United States and Canada are among their nations' largest employers. In each country, they also carry out extensive employee surveys in terms of the numbers surveyed and the scale of the follow-up actions. Canada's Public Service Employee Survey (PSES) has been conducted since 1999, most recently in fall 2008. Public service-wide results are published online, in a model display of government transparency.[18] Trends over time show some improvements in the work environment, career development, satisfaction, and commitment. Anyone considering a public service career can use the data to identify the best federal government workplaces. And existing federal public servants can see which department or agency would be a better place for them to work.

The Canada Public Service Agency, the central government HR unit, facilitates survey follow-ups at the department and agency level. It also supports a range of ongoing initiatives to develop an engaged, high-performing workforce and healthy and supportive workplaces across the public service. Faced with a serious demographic crunch due to the large number of retiring baby boomers, many of whom are managers, for the past decade the public service has emphasized leadership development and succession planning.

Worth noting is how indicators on the PSES can be directly linked to the leadership behaviours that are cultivated and rewarded in the public service. Figure 8.3 shows on the left side the percentage of employees responding to the 2005 PSES who were positive or most positive on six basic measures of effective supervision. These include keeping promises, being open to different opinions without reprisal, keeping employees informed, providing recognition, discussing results expected, and providing feedback. When positive and most positive responses are combined, all scores are in the 70 per cent range. But the goal is to increase the 'most positive' part of the bar in the figure. Now, looking at the right side of the figure, you will see ten of the leadership skills and abilities that are the focus of leadership training programs. There is not a direct correspondence between all the survey items on the left and the leadership skills on the right. However, we can assume that any supervisor who had all these skills in abundance likely would be rated 'most positive' by her or his direct reports on the survey. For a large and very complex organization, this basic use of survey indicators to track and inform leadership development shows what is possible and practical.

Integrated Performance Reporting

Most large and mid-sized organizations conduct employee surveys, but relatively few use indicators from these surveys in corporate report cards. Yet there are promising developments in this regard, as some organizations expand their existing balanced scorecard, executive dashboard, or annual reporting to include people and social responsibility metrics. A balanced scorecard guides an organization to measure how well it is implementing its strategy by giving equal emphasis to financial, operational, customer, and employee development goals. An executive dashboard or report card is a similar but simpler reporting method. The triple bottom line – referred to as 'people, profits, and planet' – expands

Figure 8.3 Measuring how supervisors support employees to succeed

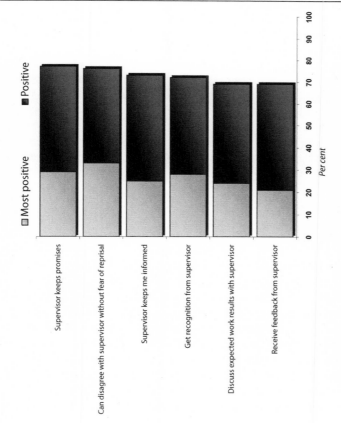

Examples of the leadership skills, abilities, and characteristics needed in the federal public service, guided by integrity and respect:

– Fosters a climate of transparency, trust and respect
– Builds a safe and healthy work environment
– Teaches and learns from others
– Shares information
– Promotes collaboration
– Encourages open constructive discussion of diverse views
– Follows through on commitments
– Solicits and listens to input
– Communicates with clarity and commitment
– Coaches, challenges and provides growth opportunities

Source: Canada Public Service Agency, Key Leadership Competencies, 2006. www.psagency-agencefp.gc.ca

Note: Response categories on all items are 'strongly agree' and 'agree' for most positive and positive, respectively.
Source: Government of Canada, Public Service Employee Survey, 2005 http://www.tbs-sct.gc.ca/pses-saff/2008/index-eng.asp.

business success criteria to include social and environmental objectives. Compared with traditional financial reports, these approaches are more integrated, holistic, and comprehensive. With the inclusion of the appropriate people, community, and sustainability metrics, these types of integrated performance reporting systems become powerful tools for achieving and sustaining healthy organization goals.

Examples of Effective Performance Reporting

I now want to provide lessons from research and practice in organizations that have included HR metrics in corporate performance reporting systems. Keep in mind, though, that the 'art and science' of organizational performance metrics is evolving, so it is more appropriate to extract lessons from organizations known to have created integrated performance reporting systems that are tied to managers' incentives and rewards. These organizations have taken that extra step to hold decision-makers accountable. Other users of people metrics are not there yet.

Following the basic idea of a balanced scorecard or a triple bottom line, each organization must find its own way to translate its strategy into a compact dashboard of key performance indicators. Metrics become integrated when their interrelationships are known. Metrics become meaningful only when managers, in particular, know exactly what actions make these metrics go up or down. The actual measures in the following examples differ, reflecting the distinctive contexts and goals of these organizations. Here are three examples of different approaches to integrated performance reporting:

- *Ernst & Young.* This global professional services firm developed a system for measuring the impact of work environments on the bottom line as part of its People First strategy. Three pillars refreshed their corporate strategy in the late 1990s: people, quality, and growth. At the global level, each executive must have two people goals. Accountability is achieved using a balanced scorecard approach. The tool they use is People Point, an online rating by any employee for each executive. One item, 'Fosters a positive work environment and helps people grow,' tells what behaviour supports the rating. This system has changed executive behaviour more than any prior performance management system used by the firm. It is now applied to all managers. A Global People Survey with thirty worldwide questions and local supplements also is used. A Business Effectiveness Index, comprising eight survey items, correlates with business performance. Ernst & Young also developed a People Commitment Index, which correlates with performance.

- *ArcelorMittal Dofasco.* Dofasco views its 'innovative, productive and empowered workforce' as critical to being the most profitable steelmaker in North America. It carefully tracks health and wellness, safety, engagement, and productivity at the individual and organizational levels. The following composite indicators are used: job satisfaction; overall health, fitness, and energy levels; productivity and efficiency levels; and absenteeism rates. These metrics are derived from quarterly employee feedback surveys, annual employee satisfaction surveys, focus groups, cost benefit analyses, health audits, program attendance and evaluations, and fitness improvements. Management responsibility for health and wellness has been integrated into Dofasco's existing performance management system and department-level business plans. Dofasco also is committed to the triple bottom line of sustainability (environment, community, profitability) and makes an annual Report to the Community.

- *Vancity Credit Union.* This financial services institution based in the Vancouver area, with 2,000 employees, uses performance indicators to assess how well it is living up to its Statement of Values and Commitments. All high-level performance indicators are publicly reported using a balanced scorecard framework. One of the five commitments is 'We will ensure that Vancity is a great place to work.' This is reported annually with improvement targets, using these metrics: (1) Overall employee satisfaction, measured by a six-item 'engagement index' reported for the organization as a whole, operating divisions, and major employee demographic groups. (2) Percentage of employees agreeing that Vancity's statement of values and commitments provides meaningful direction in their work. (3) Staff turnover. (4) Percentage of employees agreeing the balance between their work and personal commitments is right for them (an 'employee health and safety' measure). Vancity pioneered in Canada the 'social audit' process, which is how it annually assesses its economic, social, and environmental performance and presents the results to the public in accountability reports.

The above examples describe developed systems, so it is useful to look behind the scenes at how organizations go about creating integrated performance reporting. I will use the example of a major logistics and transportation company I worked with. The company spent several years developing and introducing HR metrics into its operationally focused performance report card. Some executives and line managers saw the need to put key people indicators alongside operational metrics, which the company had spent considerable time in perfecting. The challenge was identifying what people outcomes to measure, then how to roll them into a single indicator. As the executive team realized the complexities of measuring and reporting – the company had dozens of key performance indicators 'owned' by different managers and teams – it opted for simplicity.

Basically, HR and operations managers took several runs at trying to create a high-level HR indicator that could be used in quarterly corporate performance reports. The search for a single measure was consistent with how operational performance was measured; for example, a team had recently developed a customer service quality index reported monthly. The goal was to create an HR metric that was a business driver and could be used to calculate the cost of a lost day of work. Working with operations managers who created the service quality indicator, the HR team implemented a workplace health index on a pilot basis. Designed for use at the work unit level, the index includes lost-time injury frequency and severity, short-term disability, turnover, and overtime. Several pilot work units used the index to take action on psychosocial work environment issues related to stress, absenteeism, and turnover. No doubt the index will evolve as work units provide feedback. But for now, the organization has found a way to use HR metrics to create wider responsibility for work environment improvements.

Triangulating Your Existing Data

These examples show what is possible when an organization is diligent and purposeful about using a people-focused measurement and reporting system. But you do not need a sophisticated corporate report card system to put together a bigger picture of performance. Rather, look for easy ways to 'triangulate' existing data – basically, connect the dots (see figure 8.4). Triangulation taps into existing sources of administrative data and combines these data with information from employee and customer surveys. The key to data triangulation is using a standardized reporting category for all data, such as department, functional unit, or worksite. Using a Microsoft Excel spreadsheet, you can present data

Figure 8.4 Triangulating existing data for learning and improvement

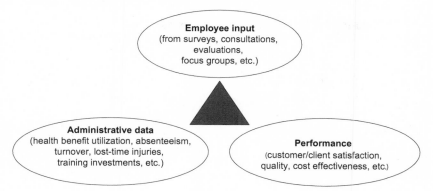

from different sources side by side and look for patterns. When you look at these patterns, ask questions such as 'are units high in employee satisfaction also low in overtime utilization and absenteeism as well as above average in customer satisfaction?'

As you consider your organization's readiness for integrated performance reporting, there are several points to bear in mind. Effective corporate performance measurement systems transform data into information. This makes it critical to understand how the corporate strategy has been translated into dashboard metrics. Furthermore, there needs to be a group within the organization that 'owns' the metrics and dashboard, communicates to the CEO and executive the strategic and operational issues identified in the dashboard, and identifies the supports and resources required by line managers to use the metrics to take action. Metrics must foster learning. For example, dashboards are a powerful tool for internal benchmarking and learning from your own centres of excellence. It is necessary, of course, for the dashboard to be used constructively as a diagnostic tool for learning and improvement. Dashboards also are accountability tools and should be linked to annual performance appraisals and performance-based compensation, as Ernst & Young has done.

Guidelines for Measuring Improvements

To summarize our discussion, below I list guidelines for you to consider when planning, evaluating, and tracking change. I encourage you to adapt these guidelines to fit your healthy change trajectory. They can be usefully applied to a new program, practice, or initiative intended to improve work environments, employee health and wellness, or organizational performance. They can be narrow or broad in focus, aiming to create positive outcomes for individual employees, teams, and the organization.

1. *Be Goal-Focused*. Always keep your objectives front and centre. It helps to create a shared vision of the kind of work environment you are striving to create. If you are having difficulty figuring out how to evaluate a program, perhaps it has too many goals or fuzzy goals. Do not let the tools or methods drive the process. Rather, always keep your eye on the objectives of the changes or interventions and use only evaluation tools that specifically address them.
2. *Model Your Vision*. Every step of the intervention process must contribute to your organization's vision of a high-quality work environment. Evaluation is not simply data collection, but an opportunity for collaborative learning and organizational development. A robust evaluation process will give managers, employees, and teams more control over improvements in their environment. It also contributes to their ongoing learning.
3. *Take a Positive Approach*. Evaluation should help the organization to improve. It should encourage group learning and workplace innovation. Avoid the use of measures for punitive actions. Examples of what to avoid are using absenteeism data to target specific individuals through an absenteeism management program that does not address underlying causes, or inferring that the managers of specific units where survey results show low morale are poor managers. Evaluation data should encourage constructive discussions among stakeholders, beginning with the question: 'how can we better support the employees in this team or work unit?'
4. *Create a Model*. A model maps out your common-sense understanding of how specific changes should improve quality of work life and contribute to other organizational performance goals. Establishing a 'causal relationship' in scientific terms is difficult, but you can still build a convincing case and a model will help to do this.
5. *Integrate*. Look for opportunities to integrate different kinds of measures, creating a composite picture of how the intervention contributes not only to employees but also to organizational goals such as the quality of customer services or products and operational excellence. Connecting the data dots in this way makes your evaluation far more compelling to decision-makers.

6. *Make Metrics Meaningful and Actionable.* Think of the end-user. Collect and analyse only the data you need – and are prepared to act upon. Report your findings in ways that support learning, action planning, and change implementation. Who will use the evaluation information and for what purposes? The knowledge generated by the evaluation must be a catalyst for actions in support of high-quality work environments. To this end, consider translating some of the indicators into costs, such as calculating overtime costs, costs of lost-time injuries, and the cost of replacing an employee who voluntarily leaves.

7. *Mine Existing Data.* Most organizations have data that can be useful for evaluations on outcomes such as absenteeism, time-loss injuries, incidence and length of disability, and voluntary turnover. Try to analyse and report these data in ways that assess the impact of an intervention. Look for ways to link surveys of employees, and customers or clients – which is most easily done by using a uniform reporting unit, such as worksite, functional unit, or employee group.

Healthy Organization Measures Are Good Public Policy

Good measurement tools and reporting frameworks for progress on organizational health goals also can be developed at the sector, regional, or national levels. If a group of employers sees mutual gains by raising the floor for workplace health promotion or the overall quality of the work environment, they can collaborate to create shared approaches.

A leading example of this approach to create healthier organizations is found in the United Kingdom, where the Health and Safety Executive (the national body responsible for occupational health and safety) developed evidence-based good management practices to reduce the risks of work stress.[19] Industry was a partner in the development and dissemination of the standards and related assessment tools. The business case was clear-cut: 36 per cent of sickness absenteeism due to work-related illness or workplace injuries in the United Kingdom is caused by stress, depression, and anxiety. As a result, between 30 per cent and 40 per cent of the direct costs of sickness absenteeism can be attributed to these causes. The Confederation of British Industry estimates that the average direct and indirect (including reduced customer satisfaction, lower productivity, and higher staff turnover) costs of work stress to be approximately $3,000 per worker per year.[20]

The Health and Safety Executive's (HSE) preventative approach aims to promote healthier outcomes for employees and organizations by establishing 'management standards.' Its six evidence-based standards for reducing work stress address work demands, employee control over their work, support, relationships at work, role clarity, organizational change, and culture. Consistent with the healthy change model I laid out in chapter 6, the HSE advocates a bottom-up approach to changes required to reduce stress risks. Standards define the future state the organization should strive to achieve; risk assessment identifies the hazards that need to be reduced.

The standards are not legally enforceable but are principles designed to help employers to meet their legal obligation to provide employees with a hazard-free workplace. This is a continual improvement process. Baseline measures are established and progress is tracked using an employee survey tool that asks a series of questions derived from each of the standards. The standard is set for 85 per cent for each indicator (e.g., 85 per cent of employees saying they are able to deal with the demands of their jobs). Standards are considered an effective, practical way to reduce work stress.

The HSE approach resembles the United Kingdom's successful human resource management standard, the Investors in People program. However, experience with the Investors in People standard shows the limits of a voluntary model. One study of its impact suggests that some organizations that attain a standard for people practices may already have these in place. Furthermore, as a result of following the standards, these already high-performing organizations may have ended up linking training to business needs rather than employees' developmental needs, as they had done previously.[21]

The overall sustainability of organizations will surely become the focus of corporate and government leaders in the coming decade. If anything, the global economic crisis may speed up this process, having focused collective attention on organizational survival. We can expect rising health care costs to prompt employers to find solutions by promoting healthier work environments. A promising step in this direction is the proposed Healthy Workforce Act, before the U.S. Congress in 2009, which would give tax incentives to businesses that introduce comprehensive workplace wellness programs.[22] As one of the components of the Obama administration's health care reform plan, the goals are to improve the health of the workforce and reduce health care costs.

As I have argued, workplace wellness programs are ideal launching pads for more far-reaching strategies to create healthy organizations. Continued labour and skill shortages in some occupations and sectors will put a premium on finding better ways to unleash workers' productive potential. So will the steady stream of new information technologies. Strains on the environment and communities will only heighten the pressures on organizations to 'do good' and 'give back.' If we can measure a company's carbon footprint, calculate the value of its human capital, and feed a wide range of performance data into corporate balanced scorecards, surely we can construct meaningful metrics for tracking the overall health of an organization and its people.

My recommendation to governments is to collaborate with employer groups, employee organizations (e.g., professional associations and unions) and university researchers to create a Healthy Organization Index. Just as measures of Gross Domestic Product for the economy have evolved and expanded to include environment and society, it is entirely possible to create a composite of existing employee, workplace, and organizational measures that any organization can use to self-assess progress. This is already happening in Europe in the area of job quality, using the European Survey of Working Conditions conducted biannually in all member states of the European Union. In Canada, it would be feasible to include a select set of workplace and organizational indicators in the Canadian Community Health Survey. This Statistics Canada survey already has good measures of work-related stress and employees' overall health. However, unlike the organizational changes discussed throughout the book, this public policy initiative requires something different to get off the ground: political will.

9 Designing a Healthy Organization Strategy

This final chapter provides an action-oriented summary of key insights and practical suggestions provided throughout the book. My intent is to offer readers a guide for planning and implementing a healthy organization change strategy in their workplace.

To reiterate one of my opening points, I am aware that organizations are at different places on a healthy organization trajectory. And for each of you, that trajectory looks somewhat different, reflecting the distinctive circumstances of your organization. Some of you will already have a healthy organization strategy mapped out, so you will be thinking in more tactical terms about implementation. Others will be looking for ideas than can help to launch a strategy. So I'm not offering a prescriptive guide. Rather, I present issues and pose questions for your reflection, discussion, and, most important, action. I firmly believe that you have to find your own way forward; coming up with answers to the questions I raise below can be a catalyst – in keeping with the organic nature of change in a healthy organization. It is also a good way to collaboratively design a change strategy.

I encourage the flexible application of the suggestions below, as well as the tools and resources presented in earlier chapters. Please use them in any way that is helpful, adapting entire sections, using figures or checklists as organizational development tools, or pulling together pieces from different sections to meet your particular needs. As you and your co-workers tailor these suggestions to fit your organization's immediate needs and challenges, you will find there is considerable room for creativity. As I have shown through examples, regardless of your formal position, as a change agent you have the scope to exercise positive influences within your own sphere of the organization.

What follows are invitations to ongoing discussions that lead to action. In fact, I like to think of this chapter as a general guide for extended conversations that you could have with your co-workers or employees. Another way to use the suggestions I offer is personal reflection on the current health of your organization and the possible roles you could play in moving it to the next level.

I have taken this approach here because of the positive experiences I have had with numerous organizations, watching what happens when employees and managers are collectively challenged to envision a healthy path forward for their organization. When designing these workshops, I try to learn as much as I can about the organization, its goals, and the challenges faced by change agents. So the starting points and direction of the strategy design process would look different, reflecting these particular realities. In fact, the people in the organization co-design the workshop with me. For example, if you have just refreshed your corporate values, there is a natural stepping stone to framing a vibrant workplace vision (or healthy workplace, if you prefer). Or, if you have before you results from a recent employee survey, then a helpful starting point is the discussion of survey follow-up. For organizations that have robust social responsibility frameworks, the timing and opportunity may be right to forge closer links with HR. And so on.

Additional resources to help you to design your own healthy organization strategy are available on the book's website, www.creatinghealthyorganizations.ca. I invite you to visit the site, make use of these resources, offer suggestions for further resources, and join an online discussion about what you and your co-workers are doing to move down a healthy organization trajectory.

1. *Use the Healthy Organization Model as a diagnostic and planning tool.*
   - How can you leverage existing workplace health and wellness initiatives to incorporate healthy organization thinking and goals?
   - Using the Healthy Organization Model as an assessment tool, what pieces of it are already operative in your workplace? What are the strengths? Use these strengths as a foundation to build on.
   - Are there teams, units, or departments in your organization that have their own version of a Healthy Organization Model?
   - To expand the case for investing in a healthier work environment, how could you make the connections (using the Healthy Organization Model) to employee engagement, workplace learning, and collaboration?

- How closely does the Healthy Organization Model resemble the strategy model used in your organization to link people with results?
- What language and thinking is used in your workplace to describe how people and performance are connected? Try modifying the Healthy Organization Value Chain to fit your context, looking for new insights about your organization's links in the value chain.
- How can your organization's social responsibility commitments and practices (including philanthropy, community partnerships, support for employee volunteering, and environmental practices) be integrated with people practices? Look for new synergies through this sort of integration. Also look for ways to ensure the consistency of corporate values and ethical commitments made to stakeholders.

2. *Use the idea of a vibrant workplace to get at the 'drivers' of health and performance.*
   - What is the evidence-based 'business case' in your organization for investing in employee and workplace health promotion programs? If there is no business case, is that because your organization has strong people values, making these investments the right thing to do? Or is it because no one has taken the time to calculate the costs associated with employee health and wellness? Regardless, you need to be able to explain convincingly to senior managers and co-workers the strategic impact of a vibrant work environment.
   - Does the concept of a vibrant workplace help to address current or future challenges your organization faces? If the word 'vibrant' does not fit your context, what would you replace it with, being careful not to loose the holistic focus on workplace ingredients of a healthy organization? You need to find language that is comfortable for co-workers to use and, at the same time, is sufficiently compelling that they will be mobilized to take further action.
   - Use figures 2.1 and 2.2 as assessment tools – or at a minimum, a stimulus for discussion – to understand where your workplace is on the health promotion / healthy organization continuum. What specific dimensions of your workplace health promotion initiatives are on the healthy organization side of the continuum? What actions are needed to expand other aspects of workplace health promotion to an organizational perspective?

- What is the need in your organization for the following types of health promotion programs: healthy lifestyle programs, helping employees with chronic health conditions, and comprehensive programs targeting high-risk employees? If the answer to the question is not available, how realistic is it to assess these needs? If you did obtain this information and acted on it, how would that advance you towards healthier organization goals?
- What would be the value to your organization of having a full discussion of the causes and consequences of absenteeism and presenteeism? Do you currently have indicators that suggest either undermines organizational performance and employee quality of life?
- Using insights from the discussion about job stress and work/life balance, how psychologically healthy is your workplace? Would addressing the root causes of stress and work/life imbalance be a good next step to improving overall health and performance?

3. *How can you move beyond engagement to create a truly inspired workforce?*
   - What is your own personal vision of a vibrant (or your own term, as suggested above) workplace? Think about how these conditions would inspire you in your work.
   - Identify an appropriate time and venue for your work group, or management team, to develop a shared vision of a vibrant workplace. If managers were to develop a vision of the ideal 'fully engaged' employee, how would the elements of that vision 'map' onto an employee vision of a healthy or vibrant workplace? The point here is to find ways to help others, particularly managers, connect workplace features with performance-related outcomes, most notably employee engagement.
   - After you have had the discussions just described, write a unifying vision for your organization that clearly describes the six to eight key elements of a vibrant workplace that will inspire employees. This is the 'big picture' of the kind of workplace your organization has the potential to achieve. What would enable actions to strengthen, or create, these workplace elements?
   - Would employees in your workplace view the elements of a vibrant workplace as the major contributors to their overall well-being while at work? If not, what is missing?
   - If employees in your organization were asked to describe one improvement in their workplace that would have the greatest

positive impact on their well-being, what do you think the top three improvements would be? If it is realistic to do so, add this question to an employee survey or conduct consultations or focus groups. The results could generate ground-up initiatives to improve the workplace.

- How might your organization benefit from identifying the biggest gaps between what employees highly value in a job and their current experiences in this regard? What is the most effective way to gather this information and ensure that it will be acted upon?

4. *Talk about your culture and become aware of its power.*

- Create an overall picture of your organization's culture. Is it strong or weak? Is there a widely understood set of core values? What are the main unwritten assumptions or beliefs that underlie workplace behaviours? Do specific groups have their own subcultures? The point of this exercise, which can be done by a team or committee, is to identify the aspects of the culture that are the most and the least healthy.

- Do senior managers in your organization talk about culture (or elements of the culture) as providing a competitive advantage? If they do, how can this discussion be expanded so that everyone gains a clearer understanding of how culture contributes to performance (as outlined in figure 4.1)? If managers do not view culture this way, what action can you take to help them to see these links?

- How does culture influence day-to-day working relationships among co-workers, between managers and employees, and with customers and other external stakeholders? How would you rate the level of trust in all these relationships? As a way to build a healthier organization, what concrete steps could be taken to build trust?

- If in the recent past your organization has tried to change the culture, reflect on this experience through a healthy organization lens. What are the key lessons that can help you and others to create a healthier culture?

- Values or guiding principles are powerful catalysts for moving down the healthy organization path. For your organization, would revisiting the values or creating more behaviourally focused guiding principles be a good next step towards a healthier organization? If not, when would be the right time to do so, how would you position such an initiative, and who would champion it?

5. *Make healthy leadership something everyone does.*
   - How is the term 'leadership' used in your organization today? Is its use exclusive, inclusive, or in-between? What opportunities exist right now to take a more inclusive approach to leadership? Consider the implications of moving in this direction for employee and supervisor training and leadership development programs.
   - To what extent do the leadership competencies promoted in your organization (either through formal leadership development programs or implicitly through promotions, succession planning, or talent management) foster healthy values, behaviours, and relationships? Consider the best ways to go about making these connections between leadership and culture visible and stronger.
   - Actions to create healthier organizations can be led from many places and positions. In your workplace, who has taken this kind of leadership? What support have these change agents had? Extract the key lessons from these experiences that can inform more grass-roots change in future.
   - Specifically, what does your executive team need to do in order to empower and mobilize others to take healthy workplace actions? Realistically, is there anything you can do to help the executive team become champions and enablers of healthy workplace change, so that improvement goals become more of a shared responsibility?
   - Take another look at the six elements of inclusive leadership. Think of ways you and your co-workers could use the six elements as an organizational development tool. Options include using it as a basis for assessment and discussion at workshops, management or team retreats, at workplace wellness committee meetings, or HR department meetings. If your organization invests in leadership development, this opens up possibilities for discussing the benefits of inclusive leadership.
   - Try approaching the concept of healthy leadership from another angle: supervisors' people skills and behaviours. Look at current supervisor selection criteria, training, and performance incentives. How can these systems be revised to include concrete skills and

behaviours that cultivate healthy and productive working relationships?

6. *Design any change to be a healthy experience.*
   - Reflect on your organization's healthy change trajectory. Is it on a pathway that will raise health and performance standards and outcomes? If your answer is 'no,' collaborate with co-workers to map out an ideal healthy change trajectory for your organization.
   - Do executives, people professionals, and line managers in your organization understand the importance of making change a healthy process? If not, how can you or your team raise awareness about this issue?
   - Groups can be powerful engines of change. Which groups (e.g., teams, committees, and informal networks) are best positioned, and have the capabilities, to positively influence change, moving it along a healthy trajectory?
   - After reviewing the five principles for guiding healthy change, write down a list of 'guiding principles for healthy change' that would resonate with your colleagues. These principles would apply to any change, resulting in more successful implementation.
   - Take a recent healthy workplace, wellness, safety, or HR initiative and assess it using these criteria: How effectively were changes in structures, processes and culture aligned? Did everyone involved and affected understand how this change contributed to the business strategy? How well did the organization learn from this change experience, and have these lessons contributed to more innovative practices?
   - Try using the Change Readiness Assessment tool (figure 6.1) to identify sources of resistance, inertia, readiness, and momentum for any planned healthy organization change.

7. *Adopt an integrated approach to renewing your stakeholder relationships and workforce capabilities.*
   - Examine your CSR approach through the healthy organization lens. Assess three things: How firmly connected is CSR to the organization's culture, especially its values? Have the potential synergies between CSR and the organization's approach to HR been tapped? What are the best opportunities for taking a 'strategic' approach to CSR, building social and environmental goals into products or services?

- What would sustainable success look like for your organization? Identify current practices that are not sustainable over the next five to ten years. Then identify the practices and other organizational features, including culture, that already contribute to sustainable success.
- What capabilities has your organization developed for renewing the workforce? Do you have processes, systems, expertise, and other resources that effectively meet employee recruitment, retention, and development goals? Look for ways to more closely link workforce renewal with workplace improvements that move in the direction of a healthier organization.
- How inclusive is your workplace? What steps could be taken to implement some of the healthy organization changes above (e.g., especially focusing on culture, values, and relationships) with the specific goal of making a more welcoming environment?
- Identify an effective and easy way to document the needs of different age groups in your workforce. This might be accomplished by re-analysing existing survey data, adding new questions to your next employee survey, running an online pulse survey, or conducting focus groups. Look for both similarities and differences, focusing on ingredients of vibrant and inspiring workplaces.
- Is your organization taking appropriate steps to retain older workers with critical competencies and to transfer their essential knowledge to junior colleagues before they depart? How can the concept of 'flexibility' be adapted to HR policies and practices to meet the needs of all age groups, particularly older workers?
- Long-range workforce planning is a significant commitment and often becomes an umbrella for all people-related plans, programs, and practices. Consider the pros and cons of developing a long-range workforce plan in your organization. If there are significant advantages, how would you go about getting such a plan on the senior management agenda for consideration?

8. *Develop and make full use of meaningful metrics.*
   - Consider how effectively managers in your organization make use of internal and external evidence when planning change. Does the culture support evidence-informed decision making? If it does, then your challenge will be to elevate HR metrics to the same level of quality and relevance as other business performance data.

- Identify your specific short-, medium-, and long-term healthy organization goals. For each goal, develop a meaningful indicator that will help to track progress (or select from among existing people metrics). The key criterion for the selection of any indicator is its ability to generate learning and further action.
- There are many examples throughout the book of how organizations use internal data, usually from administrative databases or employee surveys, to document needs, find strengths to build on, identify gaps that need closing, and plan improvements. These examples provide reference points for reviewing how your organization uses its existing employee data to achieve healthy organization goals. Based on this review, what are the best opportunities to better mine these data?
- When you look at your current HR and other people metrics, including safety, how integrated are they in your corporate performance reporting system? If you have a balanced scorecard or performance report card, what relatively easy modifications could be made to incorporate one or two new people metrics?
- Healthy cultures are built around values, relationships, and behaviours. How can existing people metrics be used to create accountability among managers at different levels for living the values, cultivating healthy and productive relationships, and personally demonstrating healthy behaviours? What would be the implications for your organization's performance management system? How can this model of accountability be extended to all employees?
- Employee surveys are useful tools for obtaining employees' assessments of the 'drivers' of organizational health. All the ingredients of a vibrant workplace can be measured in well-designed surveys. Assess your existing employee survey to determine how well it measures the drivers of organizational health. Do the relevant questions in the survey provide actionable results? If your survey lacks such questions, consider making the appropriate modifications. And if you do not conduct an employee survey, now is a good time to start.

Moving an organization further along a healthy trajectory, plotting its future course, and keeping it moving in that direction – this is hard work. That is why I have emphasized the importance of inclusive leadership, healthy change as a shared responsibility, and the need for managers and employees to co-create vibrant workplaces. As your next step, why not take the ideas from this book that resonated most with you back to your co-workers, start a discussion, and collectively explore the possibilities.

Notes

Introduction

1 De Smet, A., Loch, M. and Schaninger, B. (2007). Healthy organizations. *Executive Excellence*, 1 September.
2 Beer, M., and Eisenstat, R. (2000). The silent killers of strategy implementation and learning. *Sloan Management Review*, 41 (4), 29–40.
3 Karasek, R., and Theorell, T. (1990). *Healthy Work: Stress, Productivity, and the Reconstruction of Working Life*. New York: Basic Books.
4 Ibid., 2.
5 Dutton, J.E., and Glynn, M.A. (2007). Positive organizational scholarship. In *Handbook of Organizational Behavior*, edited by Cooper, C., and Barling, J. Thousand Oaks, CA: Sage.

1. The Healthy Organization

1 Malzon, R.A., and Lindsay, G.B. (1992). *Health Promotion at the Worksite: A Brief Survey of Large Organizations in Europe*. Copenhagen: World Health Organization, Regional Office for Europe. European Occupational Health Series No. 4, 9.
2 Lim, S.Y., and Murphy, L.R. (1999). The relationship of organizational factors to employee health and overall effectiveness. *American Journal of Industrial Medicine* Supplement, May, 64.
3 European Network for Workplace Health Promotion (2003). *Healthy Employees in Healthy Organisations*. Essen, Germany, 6 (www.enwhp.org).
4 Becker, B.E., Huselid, M.A., and Ulrich, D. (2001). *The HR Scorecard. Linking People, Strategy, and Performance*. Boston: Harvard Business School Press. Pfeffer, J. (1998). *The Human Equation: Building Profits by Putting People First*.

Boston: Harvard Business School Press. Huselid, M.A. (1995). The impact of human resource management practices on turnover, productivity, and corporate financial performance. *Academy of Management Journal*, 38, 635–72.

5 Rucci, A.J., Kirn, S.P., and Quinn, R.T. (1998). The employee-customer-profit chain at Sears. *Harvard Business Review*, January, 82–97.

6 Quoted in Macey, W.H., and Schneider, B. (2008). The meaning of employee engagement. *Industrial and Organizational Psychology*, 1, 7.

7 Prost, M. (2007). Failure to inspire. *Human Resource Executive On-line*. 1 November. http://www.hreonline.com/HRE/story.sp?storyId=43275541

8 *Economist*. (2007). Something new under the sun: Special report on innovation. 13 October, 4.

9 Garvin, D.A. (1999). *Learning in Action*. Boston: Harvard Business School Press, 42.

10 Gephart, M.A., Marsick, V.J., Van Buren, M.E., and Spiro, M.S. (1996). Learning organizations come alive. *Training and Development*, December, 35–45.

11 Senge, P.M. (1990). *The Fifth Discipline. The Art and Practice of the Learning Organization*. New York: Currency Doubleday.

12 Marosszeky, M. (2005). Best practice in the construction supply chain. *ASQ World Conference on Quality and Improvement Proceedings*, 217–28.

13 Adler, P.S., and Heckscher, C. (2006). Towards collaborative community. In *The Firm as a Collaborative Community*, edited by Heckscher, C., and Adler, P.S. Oxford: Oxford University Press.

14 Phua, F. and Rowlinson, S. (2004). How important is cooperation to construction project success? A grounded empirical quantification. *Engineering, Construction and Architectural Management*, 11 (1), 45.

15 Berry, L.L. (2004). Leadership lessons from Mayo Clinic. *Organizational Dynamics*, 33, 228–42.

16 Stubblefield, A. (2006). The Baptist Health Care Journey to Excellence: Creating a culture that WOWs! Presentation at the Great Place to Work Institute Conference. Boston, 7 April.

17 Stubblefield, A. (2005). *The Baptist Health Care Journey to Excellence*. Hoboken, NJ: John Wiley, 95.

18 Russell Investment Group data courtesy of Great Place to Work Institute.

19 Fulmer, S., Gerhart, B., and Scott, K.S. (2003). Are the 100 Best better? An empirical investigation of the relationship between being a 'great place to work' and firm performance. *Personnel Psychology*, 56, 965–93.

20 Edmans, A. (2007). Does the stock market fully value intangibles? Employee satisfaction and equity prices. Unpublished paper. Wharton School, University of Pennsylvania. http://ssrn.com/abstract=985735.

21 Harter, J.K., Hayes, T.L., and Schmidt, F.L. (2002). Business-unit-level relationship between employee satisfaction, employee engagement, and business outcomes: a meta-analysis. *Journal of Applied Psychology*, 87, 268–79.

22 Wagner, R., and Harter, J.K. (2006). *12: The Elements of Great Managing*. New York: Gallup Press.

23 Sirota, D., Mischkind, L.A., and Meltzer, M.I. (2005). *The Enthusiastic Employee: How Companies Profit by Giving Workers What They Want*, Upper Saddle River, NJ: Wharton School Publishing.

24 On high performance workplaces, see Pfeffer, J. (1998). *The Human Equation: Building Profits by Putting People First*, Boston: Harvard Business School Press; Appelbaum, E., Bailey, T., Berg, P., and Kalleberg, A.L. (2000). *Manufacturing Advantage: Why High-Performance Work Systems Pay Off*. Ithaca, NY: Cornell University Press.

25 Pfeffer, *The Human Equation*, 90.

26 From the International Finance Corporation, which is part of the World Bank. http://www.ifc.org/ifcext/economics.nsf/content/csr-intropage.

27 Verma, A., and Gomez, R. (2008). Does employee relations occur in a vacuum? Recent evidence on corporate social responsibility and employee relations in Canada. Paper presented at the Second International Workshop on Work and Intervention Practices. Laval University, Quebec City, 27–29 August.

2. Beyond Workplace Health Promotion

1 For information see: http://www.hpb.gov.sg/hpb/default.asp?pg_id=2115.

2 Buffett & Company Worksite Wellness Inc. (2009). *National Wellness Survey Report* 2009. Whitby, Ontario: Buffett and Company Worksite Wellness Inc.

3 For the evidence see Engbers, L.H., van Poppel, M.N., Chin, A.P., and van Mechelen, W. (2005). Worksite health promotion programs with environmental changes: A systematic review. *American Journal of Preventive Medicine*, 29, 61–70; Pelletier, K.R. (2001). A review and analysis of the clinical- and cost-effectiveness studies of comprehensive health promotion and disease management programs at the worksite: 1998–2000 update. *American Journal of Health Promotion*, 16, 107–16; Ozminkowski, R.J., Goetzel, R.Z., Santoro, J., Saenz, B., Eley, C., and Gorsky, B. (2004). Estimating risk reduction required to break even in a health promotion program. *American Journal of Health Promotion*, 18, 316–25; Shain, M., and Kramer, D.M. (2004). Health promotion in the workplace: Framing the concept; reviewing the evidence. *Occupational and Environmental Medicine*, 61, 643–8; Belkic, K., Schnall, P., Landsbergis, P., and Baker, D. (2000). The workplace

and cardiovascular health: Conclusions and thoughts for a future agenda. *Occupational Medicine: State of the Art Reviews*, 15, 307–21; Pelletier, K.R. (2005). A review and analysis of the clinical and cost-effectiveness studies of comprehensive health promotion and disease management programs at the worksite: Update VI 2000–2004. *Journal of Occupational and Environmental Medicine*, 47, 1051–8.

4 Max, W. (2001). The financial impact of smoking on health-related costs: A review of the literature. *American Journal of Health Promotion*, 15, 321–31.

5 Kuyumcu, N. (2008). Helping employees butt out generates big savings. *Benefits Canada*, 22 April. www.benefitscanada.com.

6 World Health Organization. Obesity and overweight Web page. http://www.who.int/dietphysicalactivity/publications/facts/obesity/en/

7 Canadian Institute for Health Information (2006). *Improving the Health of Canadians: Promoting Healthy Weights*. Ottawa: CIHI. http://secure.cihi.ca/cihiweb/products/healthyweights06_e.pdf .

8 DiNubile, N.A., and Sherman, C. (1999). Exercise and the bottom line: promoting physical and fiscal fitness in the workplace: A commentary. *Physician and Sportsmedicine*, 27 (2), 37-43.

9 Briner, R.B. (1997). Improving stress assessment: Toward an evidence-based approach to organizational stress interventions. *Journal of Psychosomatic Research*. 43:61–71. Barling, J., Kelloway, E.K., and Frone, M.R., eds. (2005). *Handbook of Work Stress*. Thousand Oaks, CA: Sage.

10 Burton, W.N., Conti, D.J., Chen, C.Y., Schultz, A.B., and Edington, D.W. (2001). The impact of allergies and allergy treatment on worker productivity. *Journal of Occupational and Environmental Medicine*, 43, 1–16.

11 Riedel, J.E., Baase, C., Hymel, P., Lynch, W., McCabe, M., Mercer, W.R., and Peterson, K. (2001). The effect of disease prevention and health promotion on workplace productivity: A literature review. *American Journal of Health Promotion*, 15, 167–90.

12 Bertera, R.L. (1990). The effects of workplace health promotion on absenteeism and employment costs in a large industrial population. *American Journal of Public Health*, 80, 1101–5.

13 Goetzel, R.Z., Anderson, D.R., Whitmer, R.W., Ozminkowski, R.J., Dunn, R.L., and Wasserman, J. (1998). The relationship between modifiable health risks and healthcare expenditures: An analysis of the multi-employer HERO health risk and cost database. *Journal of Occupational and Environmental Medicine*, 40, 843–5; Powell, D.R. (1999). Characteristics of successful wellness programs.' *Employee Benefits Journal*, 24(3), 15–21; Leonard, B. (2001). Healthcare costs increase interest in wellness programs. *HRMagazine*, 46 (9), 35–6; Goetzel, R.Z., Juday, T.R., and Ozminkowski, R.J. (2005).

Estimating the return-on-investment from changes in employee health risks on the Dow Chemical Company's healthcare costs. *Journal of Occupational and Environmental Medicine, 47*, 759–68; Brown, D. (2001). Wellness programs bring health bottom line. *Canadian HR Reporter*, 17 December.

14 White, J. (2008). Companies signal an active approach to employee health. *Benefits Canada*, 4 April. http://www.benefitscanada.com/benefit/health/article.jsp?content=20080404_150857_2232.

15 Marshall, A. (2004). Challenges and opportunities for promoting physical activity in the workplace. *Journal of Science and Medicine in Sport, 7* (1).

16 See for the United States: Hutchins, J. (2001). Optimas 2001 – Partnership: Labor and management build a prescription for health. *Workforce, 80* (3), 50. In Canada, Chrysler and the Canadian Auto Workers Union have successfully introduced the Tune Up Your Heart program and other wellness initiatives. www.workingtowardwellness.ca.

17 O'Donnell, M.P. (2000). Health and productivity management: The concept, impact, and opportunity. Commentary to Goetzel and Ozminkowski. *American Journal of Health Promotion, 14*, 215.

18 Murphy, R., and Cooper, C.L. (2000). *Healthy and Productive Work: An International Perspective*. London: Taylor and Francis.

19 Sainfort, F., Karsh, B.T., Booske, B.C., and Smith, M.J. (2001). Applying quality improvement principles to achieve healthy work organizations. *Journal of Quality Improvement, 27*, 469–83.

20 See the QWQHC website. http://www.qwqhc.ca/indicators-healthy-workplaces.aspx.

21 Canadian Institute for Health Information. (2006). *Improving the Health of Canadians: Promoting Healthy Weights*. Ottawa: CIHI. http://secure.cihi.ca/cihiweb/products/healthyweights06_e.pdf. Also see http://www.husky.ca/.

22 Edington, D.W. (2001). Emerging research: A view from one research center. *American Journal of Health Promotion, 15*, 341–9.

23 Health and Safety Executive, United Kingdom. (2006). HSE press release E009:06 – 31 January. http://www.hse.gov.uk/press/2006/e06009.htm.

24 Recovre Corp Health. (2009). *Well Aware Absence Management*. http://www.recovre.com.au/LinkClick.aspx?link=brochures_pdf%2FWell+Aware+DL_Web+view.pdfandtabid=270andmid=972.

25 Ruiz, G. (2006). Tallying the true cost of absenteeism. *Workforce Management*, 19 April. http://www.workforce.com/section/00/article/24/33/85.html

26 Statistics Canada (2007). *Work Absence Rates, 2006*. Ottawa: Statistics Canada, Catalogue No. 71-211-XIE.

27 U.S. Department of Veterans Affairs, Office of Inspector General. (2004).

Evaluation of Nurse Staffing in Veterans Health Administration Facilities. Report No. 03-00079-183, 7.

28 Davey, M.M., et al. (2009). Predictors of nurse absenteeism in hospitals: A systematic review. *Journal of Nursing Management*, 17, 312–30. Lovell, B.L., Lee, R.T., and Frank, E. (2009). May I long experience the joy of healing: Professional and personal well-being among physicians from a Canadian province. *BMC Family Practice*, 10, 18.

29 Edington, Emerging research, 346.

30 Hemp, P. (2004). Presenteeism: At work – but out of it. *Harvard Business Review*, October, 49–58.

31 Schultz, A., and Edington, D. (2007). Employee health and presenteeism: A systematic review. *Journal of Occupational Rehabilitation*, 17, 547–79. For an overview of return-to-work best practices, see Institute for Work and Health. (2007). *Seven 'Principles' for Successful Return to Work*. Toronto: Institute for Work and Health.

32 Goetzel, R.Z., Long, S.R., Ozminkowski, R.J., Hawkins, K., Wang, S., and Lynch, W. (2004). Health, absence, disability, and presenteeism cost estimates of certain physical and mental health conditions affecting US employers. *Journal of Occupational and Environmental Medicine*, 46, 398–412.

33 *Canadian HR Reporter*, 21 April 2008. www.hrreporter.com

34 Karasek, R., and Theorell, T. (1990). *Healthy Work: Stress, Productivity, and the Reconstruction of Working Life*; Siegrist, J. (1996). Adverse health effects of high-effort/low-reward conditions. *Journal of Occupational Health Psychology*, 1, 27–41; Maslach, C., Schaufeli, W.B., and Leiter, M.P. (2001). Job burnout. *Annual Review of Psychology*, 52, 397–422.

35 Rethinking Work was conducted by Ekos Research Associates Inc. and The Graham Lowe Group Inc. In the fall of 2004 a worker survey was conducted using a random sample of 2002 individuals who were either employed, self-employed, or unemployed (but who had held a job at some point in the past twelve months). The sample is considered to be representative of the Canadian workforce and has a margin of error of up to +/−2.2 per cent, nineteen times out of twenty.

36 See Eby, L.T., Casper, W.J., Lockwood, A., et al. (2005). Work and family research in IO/OB: Content analysis and review of the literature (1980–2002). *Journal of Vocational Behavior*, 66, 124–97.

3. How Vibrant Workplaces Inspire Employees

1 Ford, R.C., Wilderom, C.P.M., and Caparella, J. (2008). Strategically crafting a customer-focused culture: An inductive case study. *Journal of Strategy and Management*, 1, 143–67.

2 Ibid., 157.

3 Allen, J., Hamilton, B., and Reichheld, F.F. (2005). Tuning in to the voice of your customer. *Harvard Management Update,*10 (10). http://hbswk.hbs.edu/archive/5075.html.

4 See http://www.health.qld.gov.au/qhafe/htm/mr090425.asp.

5 See http://www.authentichappiness.sas.upenn.edu/seligman.aspx. Seligman, M.E.P., Steen, T.A., Park, N., and Peterson, C. (2005). Positive psychology progress: Empirical validation of interventions. *American Psychologist*, 60, 410–21.

6 Helliwell, J.F., and Huang, H. (2005). How's the job? Well-being and social capital in the workplace. National Bureau of Economic Research (NBER), Working Paper No. W11759.

7 Sharp, I. (2009). *Four Seasons. The Story of a Business Philosophy.* Toronto: Viking Canada.

8 Aaserud, K., Cornell, C., McElgunn, J., Shiffman, K., and Wright, R. (2007). The golden rules of growth. *Profit*, May, 72.

9 Ipsos MORI. (2008). *What Matters to Staff in the NHS.* Research study conducted for Department of Health, England.

10 Lowe, G.S., and Schellenberg, G. (2001). *What's a Good Job? The Importance of Employment Relationships.* Ottawa: Canadian Policy Research Networks. www.cprn.org.

11 This section draws on Lowe, G.S., Schellenberg, G., and Shannon, H.S. (2003). Correlates of employees' perceptions of a healthy work environment. *American Journal of Health Promotion*, 17, 390–9.

12 I also have called this a 'job quality deficit' score. See Lowe, G. (2007). *21st Century Job Quality: Achieving What Canadians Want.* Research Report W-37. Ottawa: Canadian Policy Research Networks. www.cprn.org

13 There are other ways to do this. You can add together the positive responses (the fourth and fifth categories) on both response scales and make the gap calculation that way, or you can use average scores on the response scale.

14 Gaps are calculated using the most positive response category (response category 5 on the five-category 'agree' and 'importance' scales used to answer the questions).

4. Positive Cultures

1 Johnson, J., Dakens, L., Edwards, P., and Morse, N. (2008). *SwitchPoints: Culture Change on the Fast Track to Business Success*, Hoboken, NJ: John Wiley.

2 Liker, J.K. (2004). *The Toyota Way: 14 Principles From the World's Greatest Manufacturer.* New York: McGraw-Hill.

3 Heskett, J.L., Sasser, W.E., and Wheeler, J. (2008). *The Ownership Quotient: Putting the Service Profit Chain to Work for Unbeatable Competitive Advantage.* Boston: Harvard Business Press.
4 For an overview of the Walkerton tragedy, see Wikipedia. http:// en.wikipedia.org/wiki/Walkerton_Tragedy#cite_note-Walkerton-part-1-1. This quote is from that website.
5 DeCloet, D. (2007). Sweat luxury. *Report on Business Magazine*, April, 42.
6 Dofasco news release, 17 September 2002. http://www.dofasco.ca/bins/ content_page.asp?cid=2347-2349-2534.
7 Sutton, R.I. (2007). *The No Asshole Rule: Building a Civilized Workplace and Surviving One That Isn't.* New York: Business Plus.
8 http://caib.nasa.gov/news/report/pdf/vol1/full/caib_report_volume1. pdf.
9 Solomon, R.C., and Flores, F. (2001). *Building Trust in Business, Politics, Relationships and Life.* New York: Oxford University Press, 5.
10 Colquitt, J.A., Scott, B.A., and LePine, J.A. (2007). Trust, trustworthiness, and trust propensity: A meta-analytic test of their unique relationships with risk taking and job performance. *Journal of Applied Psychology*, 92, 909–27.
11 Quoted in Pitts, G. (2007). Community-ship v. the decision maker. *Globe and Mail Report on Business*, 30 October, B2.
12 Kanter, R.M. (2008). Transforming giants: What kind of company makes it its business to make the world a better place? *Harvard Business Review*, January, 43–52.
13 Collins, J.C., and Porras, J.I. (1994). *Built to Last: Successful Habits of Visionary Companies.* New York: HarperCollins.
14 www.vancouver2010.com. Also see Brethour, P. (2007). Shaped by the crucible of culture. *Globe and Mail Report on Business*, 28 May, B3.

5. Inclusive Leadership

1 Mintzberg, H. (2004). Enough leadership. *Harvard Business Review*, November, 22.
2 Dinham, S., Aubusson, P., and Brady, L. (2008). Distributed leadership as a factor in and outcome of teacher action learning. *International Electronic Journal For Leadership in Learning*, 12 (4). http://www.ucalgary.ca/~iejll/ volume12/dinham.htm.
3 Baker, G.R., MacIntosh-Murray, A., Porcellato, C., Dionne, L., Stelmacovich, K., and Born, K. (2008). Trillium Health Centre. In *High Performing Healthcare Systems: Delivering Quality by Design*, edited by Baker, G.R. et al. Toronto: Longwoods.

4 Kouzes, J.M., and Posner, B.Z. (2007). *The Leadership Challenge*. 4th ed. San Francisco: John Wiley.
5 Ibid., 338. Emphasis in original.
6 Covey, S.M.R. (2006). *The Speed of Trust. The One Thing That Changes Everything*. New York: Free Press, 40.
7 Fullan, M. (2001). *Leading in a Culture of Change*. San Francisco: Jossey-Bass.
8 Wheatley, M.J. (2005). *Finding Our Way: Leadership for an Uncertain Time*. San Francisco: Berrett-Koehler.
9 Ibid., 88–9.
10 Goleman, D. (2006). *Emotional Intelligence*. New York: Bantam, 149.
11 Rethinking Work. 2004 worker survey and 2005 employer survey.

6. Healthy Change

1 Lowe, G. (2004). *Healthy Workplace Strategies: Creating Change and Achieving Results*. Ottawa: Health Canada. www.grahamlowe.ca.
2 Beckhard, R. (1997). The healthy organization: A profile. In *The Organization of the Future*, edited by Hesselbein, F., Goldsmith, M., and Beckhard, R. San Francisco: Jossey-Bass.
3 Hackman, R.J., and Edmondson, A.C. (2008). Groups as agents of change. In *Handbook of Organization Development*, edited by Cummings, T.G. Thousand Oaks, CA: Sage.
4 Pfeffer, J., and Sutton, R.I. (2000). *The Knowing-Doing Gap. How Smart Companies Turn Knowledge into Action*. Boston: Harvard Business School Press.
5 The relevant reports and documentation can be accessed at http://www.ubc.ca/; http://web.ubc.ca/okanagan/welcome.html.
6 Becker, B.E., Huselid, M.A., and Ulrich, D. (2001). *The HR Scorecard. Linking People, Strategy, and Performance*. Boston: Harvard Business School Press, 9.
7 Axelrod, R.H. (2000). *Terms of Engagement: Changing the Way We Change Organizations*. San Francisco: Berrett-Koehler.
8 Tushman, M., and O'Reilly III, C.A. (1997). *Winning Through Innovation: A Practical Guide to Leading Organizational Change and Renewal*. Boston: Harvard Business School Press, 200.
9 Kotter, J.P. (1996). *Leading Change*. Boston: Harvard Business School Press.
10 Beer, M. (2003). Building organizational fitness. In *Organization 21C: Someday All Organizations Will Lead This Way*, edited by Chowdhury, S. Upper Saddle River, NJ: Financial Times Prentice Hall, 311–28.
11 Barber, F., and Strack, R. (2005). The surprising economics of a 'people business.' *Harvard Business Review*, June, 84.

7. Sustainable Success

1 See Nexen, *Balance: 2008 Sustainability Report*. www.nexeninc.com/about_us/corporate_profile.
2 Nexen's Community Investment Policy: www.nexeninc.com/files/Policies/CommunityInvPolicy.pdf.
3 Franklin, D. (2008). Just good business. A special report on corporate social responsibility. *Economist*, 19 January, 4.
4 Levenson, E. (2008). Citizen Nike. *Fortune*. 24 November, 165–6.
5 Johne, M. (2007). Show us the green, workers say. *Globe and Mail*, 10 October, C1.
6 Reingold, J., and Tkacyzk, C. (2008). Ten new gurus you should know about. *Fortune*, 24 November, 153.
7 Ulrich, D., and Smallwood, N. (2004). Capitalizing on capabilities. *Harvard Business Review*, June, 119.
8 Lister, T. (2008). What keeps HR executives up at night? *Canadian HR Reporter*, 7 April, 17.
9 Blackwell, R. (2008). The double-edged sword of corporate altruism. *Globe and Mail Report on Business*, 10 November, B5.
10 https://www.vancity.com/MyBusiness/AboutUs/.
11 Johne, Show us the green, workers say.
12 Franklin, Just good business.
13 http://www.imaginecanada.ca/en/node/49.
14 http://www.fivewinds.com/uploadedfiles_shared/CSRCaseStudy-HomeDepot.pdf.
15 Franklin, Just good business, 6.
16 Maitland, A. (2004). Corporate care in the global community. *Financial Times*, 8 January, 12.
17 TNT. *Sure We Can. Corporate Responsibility Report 2008*. http://group.tnt.com/Images/tnt-corporate-responsibility-report-2008_tcm177-427051.pdf.
18 TNT recognised for consistent contributions to community. (2009).*Traffic World*, 16 January.
19 Porter, M.E., and Kramer, M.R. (2006). Strategy and society: The link between competitive advantage and corporate social responsibility. *Harvard Business Review*, December, 88.
20 Ibid., 86.
21 www.ge.com.
22 A lean, clean electric machine. (2005). *Economist*, 10 December, 77–9.
23 Boston Consulting Group. (2008). *Making a Difference: BCG's Partnerships and Projects for Social Impact*. http://www.bcg.com/impact_expertise/publications/files/Making_a_Difference_Dec_2008.pdf.

24 Conference Board of Canada. (2007). *Report on Diversity.*
25 Owram, D. (1997). *Born at the Right Time: A History of the Baby Boom Genera-tion.* Toronto: University of Toronto Press, 281.
26 Ibid., 306.
27 Côté, J.E., and Allahar, A.L. (1994). *Generation on Hold: Coming of Age in the Late Twentieth Century,* Toronto: Stoddart; Coupland, D. (1993). *Generation X: Tales for an Accelerated Culture.* New York: St. Martin's Press.
28 Miller, M. (1999). Gen-X working its 'lazy' label off. *Edmonton Journal,* 17 October, E10 (reprinted from the *Los Angeles Times*).
29 Cited in Generation Y goes to work. (2009). *Economist,* 3 January, 47–8.
30 Ibid.
31 Lowe, *21st Century Job Quality.*
32 *The Competition for Canadian Talent.* (2008). RBC Survey conducted by Ipsos Reid. http://www.rbc.com/newsroom/20080415survey.html.
33 Dychtwald, K., Erickson, T., and Morison, B. (2004). It's time to retire re-tirement. *Harvard Business Review,* March, 55.
34 DeLong, D.W. (2004). *Lost Knowledge: Confronting the Threat of an Aging Workforce.* New York: Oxford University Press. On the importance of tacit knowledge for firms, see Dixon, N.M. (2000). *Common Knowledge: How Companies Thrive by Sharing What They Know.* Boston: Harvard Business School Press.
35 http://www.shell.com/home/content/aboutshell/our_strategy/shell_global_scenarios/shell_energy_scenarios_2050/shell_energy_scenarios_02042008.html.
36 http://www.edmonton.ca/city_government/city_organization/plan-edmonton.aspx.
37 City of Edmonton, Office of the City Auditor. (2008). *Human Resources Branch Audit.*

8. Measuring Progress

1 European Network for Workplace Health Promotion. (2003). *Healthy Em-ployees in Healthy Organisations.* Essen, Germany, 10. www.enwhp.org.
2 http://www.cqc.org.uk/_db/_documents/0708_annual_health_check_overview_document.pdf.
3 http://www.cqc.org.uk/usingcareservices/healthcare/nhsstaffsurveys/2008nhsstaffsurvey.cfm.
4 Fitz-enz, J. (2000). *The ROI of Human Capital: Measuring the Economic Value of Employee Performance.* New York: AMACOM (American Management Association), 22.
5 Riedel, J.E., Baase, C., Hymel, P., Lynch, W., McCabe, M., Mercer, W.R., and

Peterson, K. (2001). The effect of disease prevention and health promotion on workplace productivity: A literature review. *American Journal of Health Promotion*, 15(3), 167–90.

6 Pfeffer, J., and Sutton, R.I. (2000). *The Knowing–Doing Gap. How Smart Companies Turn Knowledge into Action*. Boston: Harvard Business School Press.

7 Editors' Forum on the Research–Practice Gap in Human Resource Management. (2007). *Academy of Management Journal*, 50(5).

8 For job and organizational assessment tools, see Field, D.L. (2002). *Taking the Measure of Work: A Guide to Validated Scales for Organizational Research and Diagnosis*. Thousand Oaks, CA: Sage.

9 For resources on communities of practice, see www.co-i-l.com/coil/knowledge- garden/cop/index.shtml.

10 OHSAH website: www.ohsah.bc.ca.

11 Davis, P.M., Badii, M., and A. Yassi. (2004). Preventing disability from occupational musculoskeletal injuries in an urban, acute and tertiary care hospital: Results from a prevention and early active return-to-work safely program. *Journal of Occupational and Environmental Medicine*, 46, 1253–62.

12 Weir, R., Stewart, L., Browne, G., Roberts, J., Gafni, A., Easton, S., and Seymour, L. (1997). The efficacy and effectiveness of process consultation in improving staff morale and absenteeism. *Medical Care*, 35, 334-53.

13 Hughes, I., and Seymour-Rolls, K. (2000). Participatory action research: Getting the job done. Action Research E-Reports, 4. www.fhs.usyd.edu.au/arow/arer/004.htm; Reason, P., and Bradbury, H., eds. (2001). *Handbook of Action Research: Participative Inquiry and Practice*. London: Sage.

14 A useful guide to participatory ('high involvement') organizational change is Axelrod, R.H., Axelrod, E.M., Beedon, J., and Jacobs, R.W. (2004). *You Don't Have to Do It Alone: How to Involve Others to Get Things Done*. San Francisco: Berrett-Koehler.

15 Harris, J.R., Holman, P.B., and Carande-Kulis, V.G.. (2001). Financial impact of health promotion: We need to know much more, but we know enough to act. *American Journal of Health Promotion*, 15, 378–82.

16 Anderson, D.R., Serxner, S.A., and Gold, D.B. (2001). Conceptual framework, critical questions, and practical challenges in conducting research on the financial impact of worksite health promotion. *American Journal of Health Promotion*,15, 281–8.

17 Whitehead, D.A. (2001). A corporate perspective on health promotion: Reflections and advice from Chevron. *American Journal of Health Promotion*, 15, 367–9.

18 PSES results for 2005 are available at http://www.psagency-agencefp.gc.ca/arc/survey-sondage/2005/index_e.asp. The 2008 PSES results will

be released online in 2009. http://www.psagency-agencefp.gc.ca/svdg/pses-eng.asp

19 Mackay, C.J., Cousins, R., Kelly, P.J., Lee, S., and McCaig, R.H. (2004). 'Management Standards' and work-related stress in the UK: Policy background and science. *Work and Stress*, 18, 91–112.

20 Henderson Global Investors. (2005). *Less Stress, More Value. Henderson's 2005 Survey of Leading UK Employers.* www.henderson.com.

21 Grugulis, I., and Bevitt, S. (2002). The impact of investors in people: A case study of a hospital trust. *Human Resource Management*, 12, 44–60.

22 See http://www.uswwa.org/portal/uswwa/legislation/default. Pear, R. (2009). Congress plans incentives for employers that offer wellness programs. *New York Times*, 10 May.

Index

FOX ISLAND

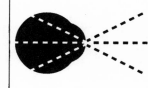

This Large Print Book carries the
Seal of Approval of N.A.V.H.

Fox Island

Stephen and Janet Bly

Thorndike Press • Thorndike, Maine

Published in 1999 by arrangement with Servant Publications.

Thorndike Large Print ® Christian Fiction Series.

The tree indicium is a trademark of Thorndike Press.

The text of this Large Print edition is unabridged.
Other aspects of the book may vary from the original edition.

Set in 16 pt. Plantin.

Printed in the United States on permanent paper.

Library of Congress Cataloging in Publication Data

Bly, Stephen A., 1944–
    Fox Island / Stephen and Janet Bly.
        p.   cm. (Hidden West Series Book I)
        ISBN 0-7862-1679-4 (lg. print : hc : alk. paper)
        1. Married people — Washington (State) — Fiction.
    2. Large type books. I. Bly, Janet. II. Title.
    [PS3552.L93F69   1999]
        813′.54—dc21   98-42035

*For the
Class of '62*

1

Until recently, Fox Island's fame was limited to a footnote in art books, as the home of reclusive and mysterious 1930s artist Jessica Davenport. But the Northwest population flood of the late twentieth century has bridged its way into every corner of Puget Sound. Situated in the southern reaches of the Sound, Fox Island still offers residents and guests a sylvan retreat, only seventeen miles from Tacoma and forty-eight miles from Seattle.

Of course, it is 1,454 miles from Scottsdale, Arizona.

Tony Shadowbrook stormed into the kitchen in stocking feet. His long-sleeved black-and-red Brooks & Dunn western shirt dangled, unsnapped and untucked. He waved a magazine in his left hand. "Did you read this? This clown in *Publishers Weekly* never even read my book. Did you see this review?"

"Tony, do you think these earrings are too flashy for going on a plane? You know, daytime travel and all?" Price held the ornaments to her ears, pulling back the shoulder-length ash-brown hair streaked with highlights, some natural, some not.

"But listen to this. . . ." Tony's eyes squinted close to the flying pages, his tanned face framed by a slight line where his cowboy hat usually perched.

"Daddy, that's homemade oatmeal raisin chewies you're smelling." Kathy's long blond hair slightly straightened as she whirled around, then folded again in tucked, perfect waves.

"Oh, thanks, kiddo, my favorite. But why do you think . . . ?"

Price, with a soft scent of roses and musk, slipped between her daughter and her husband. "Have either of you seen Kit? She does know that we're about to leave, doesn't she?"

Kathy took a bite of cookie. "She's out in the garage, I guess. Do you want me to put these things in a bag or in a tin?"

"You didn't have to do that," Price protested as she buzzed her daughter's cheek. "Put them in a bag. They won't take up as much room." She marveled at her daughter. Hair in place, spotless white shorts, crisp denim blouse, not a sign of flour splotches anywhere. She wondered how many times Kathy had changed clothes already this morning.

Tony jammed on his steel-rimmed glasses as he circled the oak-topped kitchen island. " 'Shadowbrook's latest offering is like looking at the Black Hills after you've seen the Rockies. It's nice . . . but lacks stature. It should cause Louis L'Amour to rest easy in his grave. The mantle has certainly not been passed . . . yet.' What does he mean, 'lacks stature'? Who is this guy, Albert Cummings III? Teaches English at some junior college, no doubt, and moonlights to make ends meet by writing nonsense garbage like this. I know the type. A frustrated writer masquerading as a literary critic."

Kathy wiped off the sink and refrigerator with a desert-rose dish towel. "Oh, Daddy, come on . . . teachers aren't that bad. Mother teaches English."

"Well, sure, at Arizona State! That's different. Besides, your mother happens . . ."

"She happens to like your books!"

Price stepped closer. "The earrings. Tony, what about these silver-and-gold feather earrings?"

He grabbed the wall phone. "I'll call Liz. She'll be indignant. Probably will want the publishing house to voice some public protest. I'm not about to let . . ." He stopped as Kathy motioned to him to look over at his wife. Price's almond-shaped eyes and full lips flashed warmth his way. "They're stunning, absolutely stunning. You look classy, as always. And such a young lady. Now, what about . . . ?"

"But are they overdone for daytime travel?"

"No, no, no . . . I love 'em! Hey, what time is it?"

"It's 9:10." Kathy quickly tied back her honey-colored hair with the woven southwest belt she pulled from the waist of her shorts and scooted through the kitchen picking up scattered sections of the Scottsdale *Progress Tribune* and *The Wall Street Journal*.

Tony hung up the phone. "When should we be at Sky Harbor?"

"No later than 9:50. I do think I'll wear them. They sort of soften the gray, don't they?"

"Mother, you don't look a day over thirty-five and you know it."

Price felt a sudden stab of emotion. *I'm going to miss my girls. Why isn't it ever easy to let my kids go?*

"You're the sweetest liar in this whole family, Kath, but I feel every bit of forty-nine, especially with my babies in college."

"I can't believe you're going to be fifty next year."

"Is anyone going to listen to this cheap review of *Shotgun Creek* or not?" Tony slammed down the magazine on the countertop and tried to snap his buttons and tuck in his shirt at the same time. His face was blotched with streaks of red. Price gently patted his cheek.

"I promise to read it on the plane. How's the temp outside?"

"It's June 10 in Scottsdale! What do you think? Somewhere over a hundred. Where's Kit? She'll blow a gasket when she sees this."

"Kristina's in the garage, but you'd better finish getting ready first. Is your suitcase packed?"

"Packed? Oh, yeah. Just a couple more things. I've got the batteries charging for our laptops." Tony shoved the magazine in his mouth and finished tucking in his shirt.

"Daddy, did you pack your gun?"

The magazine dropped to the counter.

"Gun? Why would I need a gun?"

"I read one of those clippings in your Fox Island file, about the two prisoners who escaped from the federal prison and held a family captive."

"That was forty years ago."

"But the prison is still on that neighboring island, isn't it?"

"Yes, but I am not taking a gun. They're all locked in the safe." He looked her in the eye. "And they better stay that way. I'll go get the laptops. Price, be sure and pack that lousy review. It will keep my adrenaline pumped for a week."

Price packed the cookies and the magazine in her purse.

As if you need your adrenaline pumped, Tony Shadowbrook. This is the summer you promised to slow down and take it easy, remember?

One last time she glanced around the kitchen at the white walls and white cupboards and red tile floor. The only color accent showing was the turquoise pottery dishes Kathy left to air dry on the white drainboard and fresh-picked blooms of Indian Blankets, marigolds, daisies and a few paintbrushes bursting from a white ceramic pitcher on the oak board center island. "To remind us this is a cheery going away," Kathy had explained at breakfast.

Price looked at her watch. "I hope we're not forgetting anything."

Kathy hugged her. They could hear doors slamming from the direction of the master bedroom. "We can ship it to you, if you did.

Fox Island sounds like such a peaceful place. I bet you and Daddy have a really tranquil time writing this new book."

"Well, it won't be as hectic as last summer in Utah."

"You mean when Kit decided to rebuild that diesel engine in the family room of that house we rented?"

"Actually, I was thinking about all those Saturday nights that blond Adonis couldn't seem to get you to the house before 3:00 in the morning."

"Nicholas is the only guy I ever dated who spent more time looking at himself in a mirror than he ever did looking at me."

"It seems strange to be leaving you and Kit for the entire summer."

"Mom, we're going to be sophomores in college. We're eighteen years old. We'll be fine. We'll make good choices. We're mature women now." Kathy opened the cupboard door under the sink to toss a paper towel into the trash. "Oh, yuck!"

"What is it?"

"There's water running out of that crooked pipe!"

"Oh no!" Price moaned. "Tony!"

With one Justin cowboy boot jammed on his left foot, he hopped and hobbled to the kitchen trying to pull on the other.

"We've got a leak!" Price pointed to the chrome trap under the sink.

"You've got to be kidding!"

"Daddy, what am I going to do?"

"Stick a bucket under it, and don't use that side of the sink until the plumber comes. I'll call Dewitt." Then he looked at Price and shook his head. "That's a ten-dollar job that will cost a hundred bucks for a plumber to fix."

"Do you know what time it is?"

"Right. I'll call, then I'll load up the luggage." Tony mumbled his way back down the hall.

Price placed a bucket under the leak and glanced at her earrings again in the small mirror next to the kitchen sink. "Kath, you'd better go get Kit. What's she doing out there, anyway?"

"I think I'd better let her explain."

By the time Price and Kathy traipsed in, Tony had all four suitcases and two briefcases stacked on the red tile entryway.

"Honey, you better go talk to your daughter."

"What's Kit up to?"

Kathy straightened the collar of her father's shirt. "She's replacing a water pump on your car."

"She's what?"

"You said that we ought to take your Cherokee to the garage this week and get the water pump checked. So, Kit decided to replace it herself."

Tony groaned. "Tell her to clean up and come on. We've got to go."

Price nudged him in the ribs. "You need to talk to her, Tony."

Clutching his straw cowboy hat, Tony Shadowbrook rambled through the scattered cacti and succulents of the front patio toward the three-car garage.

Price attempted to lift the luggage. "You know you girls can call us anytime, day or night, don't you?"

"Don't worry so much, Mom! Mark and Josh both promised they'll check on us."

"Yes, but a married brother in Tucson won't get by too often and Josh . . ."

"He's just a few minutes from here," Kathy reminded her.

"Unless he's hang gliding in the Canyon, or jet skiing on the Colorado, or ballooning in Yuma."

Kathy giggled. "Or falling off some building at Rawhide. Isn't that new stunt totally awesome?"

"I refuse to even think about it! It makes me angry to know several thousand people pay money to watch my son almost kill himself four times a day."

She stared across the patio, expecting a husband and daughter to appear.

Lord, when do they get on their own so much that Mom and Dad can relax? It seems like other people have normal children . . . peaceful, simple, easy care. I know, I know . . . I'm the one who wanted to marry him, and he's not peaceful, simple, or easy care. I really do love them the way they are — most of the time.

Kit led the way across the patio.

"Kristina!"

Kit reached out to hug her mother, then pulled back. Her hands, her clothes, her freckled face and bobbed brown hair were smudged with grease and dirt. "Hey, I like the earrings, Mom. They really bring out the pretty gray strands in your hair, don't they?"

Price grimaced. "Did you finish with your father's car?"

"Almost got the sucker done. It's a lot easier than I thought."

"Almost?"

"She's really doing a pretty good job," Tony bragged. "Maybe I should let her fix that drip under the sink. Kit, you can buy one of those traps at Wal-Mart and . . ."

"Tony! How are we getting to the airport now?"

"I guess we'll have to take one of the other cars."

"All that luggage won't fit in my Neon," Kathy wailed.

"Well," Price insisted, "it certainly won't cram into the Mustang convertible."

Kit wiped her hands on her faded Wrangler jeans. "No big deal. We can take my truck. Grab a suitcase, Kath. Let's get 'em loaded up."

"Tony, we can't all fit in that pickup," Price objected.

Kit threw up her hands. "I can ride in the back."

Price gave her husband her best "You'd better do something quick, Shadowbrook" look.

"Honey, you and Kathy ride in the Neon. I'll load up the luggage in the truck; Kit and I will meet you at the Alaska Airlines terminal."

Price studied her silver-and-gold watch. "You realize we've only got twenty minutes leeway, don't you?"

Kit grabbed a bag and scooted for the garage. "We'll probably beat you there."

Flight 670, nonstop to Sea-Tac, was scheduled to depart the Phoenix Sky Harbor International Airport at 10:25 A.M.

17

At 10:05 Price and Kathy Shadowbrook paced the sidewalk in front of the Alaska Airlines sign.

"I never should have put the two of them in the car together! They have absolutely no sense of time."

"If only they'd at least wear a watch . . ."

Price studied the steady surge of hotel shuttles, busses, cabs and cars. "It wouldn't make any difference. Neither would bother looking at it. But how could they possibly get lost from home to here?"

"There they are!" Kathy shouted. "They've got someone with them."

"Who on earth . . . ?"

"No, not who. It's a what, a dog or something."

"Good grief. It's a cow."

The rusted blue '58 Chevy pickup rolled up to the terminal with a jolt. A slightly smudged and wrinkled Tony Shadowbrook jumped out and signaled for a skycap.

"What happened?" Price called out.

"Pop knew a shortcut by the riverbed," Kit explained as she hauled out their baggage.

"What's with the cow?" Kathy ventured.

"It's a calf. It was on the highway about to get smashed. We chased it down. I'll go find its owner soon as we see you off. Want

18

us to go in with you?"

Tony rushed up and began tugging Price inside. "The skycap says we'll have to check in at the gate. I guess we're a little late."

"You're a mess, Shadowbrook," Price said.

"Thanks for the lift, girls. We'll call you when we get to Fox Island." Tony threw them a kiss.

Price turned for one more quick look. Kathy was waving both arms. Kit's were buried in her pockets. "Remember the list I left," Price called out. "One copy's in the kitchen, the other's . . ."

"Go on, write your book," Kit hollered.

"We're okay, Mother," they heard Kathy say as Tony scooted them through the automatic glass doors. Then he ran back. "Kit! The calf! He's jumped out!"

"I'll get him, Pop! Kath will help me."

Katherine Shadowbrook jammed her hands on her designer shorts clad hips. "Me? You've got to be kidding!"

Their last view of the twins was Kit dashing in front of a parked tour bus to grab the frightened calf while fending off the attacks of a cane-wielding senior citizen. Kathy stood locked in place on the sidewalk, her hands clutching the top of her head.

★ ★ ★

At 32,790 feet, somewhere over Susanville, California, Tony Shadowbrook returned to Row 14, seat C.

"You look much more presentable, Mr. Shadowbrook."

"And you look elegant and fashionable, as always." He leaned over and kissed her cheek.

"It really feels different not bringing the girls along."

"They have jobs, summer school classes, trips of their own planned. They're growing up, Mama."

Tony and Price stared at each other, then a smile broke across their faces.

"Do you know that Kath told me not to worry, that they were mature women now? How long do you think it will be until we get a 'Daddy, you won't believe what Kit did!' phone call?"

"Not until we get to Sea-Tac. How in the world did we ever produce such unidentical twins?"

"I always figured it was your fault or that it was proof of God's sense of humor. But we'd better get our minds on this new book."

"Yes, the waiting public wants to know: What will the Shadowbrooks do for the

20

fourth installment in their 'stunning' Hidden West series?" Tony glanced up the aisle. "But first, I think we'll eat lunch."

The flight attendant handed them two small baskets — turkey and swiss sandwiches on rye, coleslaw, bags of chips, apples, pear juice and granola bars.

Price pried out a small slip of paper from the bottom of the basket and read it aloud. " 'For the Lord watches over the way of the righteous.' I really appreciate these psalm cards on Alaska Airlines. . . . Oh, rats!"

"What?" Tony mumbled through his turkey sandwich.

"We forgot to pray with the girls. Everything was so hectic. How could we forget something so important?"

"We prayed at breakfast."

"But I wanted something more. . . . I'll just have to write it all out for them. Maybe that's better. That way they'll have something more permanent to read whenever . . ."

"No preaching."

"Who, me? I'm a wimp when it comes to preaching and you know it. I'll just be sharing honest concerns from a mother's heart."

Lord, why can't I ever get it right? The kids are practically grown, and there's still so much I need to tell them and teach them, and now I won't even be with them this summer. They really need you in this world, Lord. I need you. The boys need you. Tony needs you. And we're all so busy and disconnected. It's a crazy way to start the summer.

They were somewhere over central Oregon when Price retrieved her notebook. "Book planning time, Mr. Shadowbrook. How about opening with a different slant? Don't you think we're getting into a rut?"

Tony flipped through an airlines magazine without reading it. "But it's a highly successful rut. 'If it ain't broke . . . don't fix it.' "

"Not even if it's routine and predictable?"

"Predictable? Are you calling *Promontory* predictable? *Sunset Magazine* called it 'The must-read book for any trip to northern Utah.' "

"You're right. It was fun. But I want us to stay creative."

"Look, my western novels are creative. Poetry is creative. Cowboy music is creative. In a nonfiction historical series you want . . . consistency . . . continuity . . . a familiar, homey pattern."

"But I don't think it will be a homey book. We've got a history there of escaped convicts, gangland murders plotted from beachfront mansions, Japanese submarine invasions, the Chain Saw Militia . . . not to mention the possibility of an interview with Jessica Davenport Reynolds, the first she's allowed in fifty-five years. I'm really hyped about this book. But we've got to convey that excitement to the readers."

"You're right about one thing. We have more background on this place ahead of time than any of the other books in this series."

Price gazed out the window at a brilliant sun-flocked drift of clouds as wing shadows darted across them. "So, if we follow our format, I presume we'll open with the United States Exploring Expedition of 1841 and Lieutenant Charles Wilkes naming the Island after the expedition's assistant surgeon, Lieutenant John L. Fox?"

"Yeah, we could do a lot with that. The drama of twelve bronzed and sea-tough men nobly paddling across the strong and dangerous currents of the Tacoma Narrows against all odds to land on a deserted, heavily forested island . . . struggling against the severe elements and the violent dissension among the tattered band of renegade sailors, with only the unflagging bravery and audacious stubbornness of one man holding the whole party together."

"But we do intend to stick close to the historical truth, don't we? Tony, it's supposed to be a travelogue, not an adventure novel."

"It is *not* a travelogue. We are not writing a series of travelogues. We're writing a history of some of the most fascinating out-of-the-way places in the great American West."

Why does she keep saying that? Anthony Shadowbrook does not write travelogues.

Price shifted the arms and back of her seat and tried to relax. "You've been reading the cover copy too long," she said. "I think we ought to consider opening with the Indian legend of the Clay Babies."

"And I think we can wait until we're settled in before we make any such decisions. You know the trouble with writing? You never get a vacation. Even when you're on vacation, you constantly work through scenes, stories, characters, plots, ideas. Come on, babe, for the first time in over twenty-six years we have a whole summer to ourselves. We can write that book tomorrow."

Price felt the tension ease from her neck and shoulders. She pushed her glasses to the top of her head. "We've waited a long time for this, haven't we?"

"Remember when we first got married? We were going to raise the kids, and then travel and write."

"That was forty-six books ago. You've been busy, Mr. Anthony Baldwin Shadowbrook."

"Two doctorates, a professorship, and a dozen books with your name on them . . . you've been busy, too, Dr. Priscilla Carey Shadowbrook."

"A married son still in graduate school, another son who's trying to scare his parents to death as a stuntman, and twin daughters who get along about as well as a mongoose and a snake . . . we've *both* been real busy, babe!" She reached over and slipped her fingers into his.

"Are you ready for a quiet summer?"

She nodded. "I believe we deserve it . . . and Melody said Fox Island is delightful in the summer."

"Melody?"

"Tony . . . Melody Mason, my former student."

"The Melody whose aunt is Jessica Davenport, right?"

"No, it's her grandmother, Jessica Davenport Reynolds."

"I read somewhere that she's called 'the Garbo of the Northwest.' "

"Sounds like a real adventure, doesn't it? Did you know she wants to be a writer?"

"The grandmother?"

"No . . . Melody. I told you all this before. Weren't you listening?"

"I was probably lost somewhere along *Shotgun Creek*." Tony leaned back and closed his eyes.

"You really get absorbed in your own stories. Do you suppose all writers are that way?"

"All except Stephen King, I suppose. When I was young I used to wonder what it was like to be a writer. Nowadays, I keep wondering what it would be like *not* to be a writer."

"You'd hate it . . . trust me."

"Is this Mason girl going to meet us at the airport?"

"Yes, she'll drive us to the Island."

"I don't think we've ever rented a place that was furnished with a car. What will we be driving all summer, an old Oldsmobile?"

Price reached up and turned off the lights above their seats. "What difference does it make? The Island is only five miles long and one and a half miles wide. We could do the whole thing with bicycles."

"It's an old white Oldsmobile, isn't it?"

"I'm not sure of the color."

"How old is this grandmother Davenport?"

"Reynolds. She's in her seventies."

"It's white."

"Dr. Shadowbrook! It's me . . . Melody Mason. I can tell from your face I look different, don't I? And you must be Anthony." A long, thick switch of black hair and huge loop earrings swinging, she clutched his hand with both of hers. "Wow! This is something I've dreamt about . . . meeting Anthony Shadowbrook face-to-face. And all this time I thought of you as an old man. Boy, was I wrong! You look just like those rugged rodeo cowboys on ESPN. Before I read your books I didn't know a tapadera from a Winchester. Now I'm into the whole . . ."

Price tugged Tony away from her grip and steered through the terminal toward the baggage claim department. Melody scooted ahead of them. She didn't look at all different than Price recalled. The same dark, straight hair, the bushy eyebrows that touched when she smiled, the nervous chatter, the brown eyes always begging for approval. Walking backward, she kept talking.

"I'm a writer, too. Oh, not that I have any

books published yet . . . you know, the struggling years? That's me. Actually, they've been the struggling years ever since I graduated from ASU."

"Eh . . . when was that?" Tony managed to ask.

"Class of '92, with a degree in interpretative writing."

"Interpretative writing?" Tony glanced over at Price.

"It was an experimental major in the communications department, as I remember. Melody, is everything ready for us at your grandmother's house?"

"Oh yes! You'll love it, really. It's right on the water overlooking Carr Inlet. On a clear day you can stand at the end of the dock and see the Olympic Mountains. And the sunsets on the Sound are legendary. Talk about secluded. Well, you know the reputation my grandmother has."

Price shifted the straps of her patchwork leather purse to the other shoulder and slowed the pace. She already regretted wearing heels. "We really appreciate being able to rent the house. Everything we've read about Fox Island mentions the Davenport house. Your grandmother and her sister made lots of news in the thirties and forties. You said your grandmother's in a

28

care facility. Has the house been vacant long?"

"Oh no. I've been living there the past several years. But like I told you in my letter . . . I just thought if I could talk the Shadowbrooks into setting their next Hidden West book on Fox Island, then they should stay in Grandma Jessie's place. It's part of the Island's history too. Our family was among the early settlers."

"That's very generous of you," Tony said in his "I don't like the sounds of this" voice. "Where will you be living this summer?"

Price stopped to catch her breath at the top of the stairs. "Melody's staying with her mother in Gig Harbor. How's your mother doing? Severe depression, wasn't it?"

Melody pulled sunglasses and mints out of her purse. "Oh, thanks for asking. Yeah, I think Mom's feeling pretty good this summer. But, there's been a little change in plans."

"Oh?"

"Yeah, I'm not exactly staying with my mother. You see, I moved my stuff over there three days ago so I could bring in some professional cleaners and really have Grandma's place first rate for you. But, well, Mom and I got in this sort of argument, and I decided . . . we decided . . .

actually . . . she told me I'd better find some other arrangements."

"If we're causing you any problems, we can go straight to a realtor and find something else," Tony plugged in.

"That might be difficult at this late date," Price mumbled.

Is this whole housing thing falling apart? We really don't need any complications now. Please, Lord, just a smooth, peaceful summer.

"Oh, don't worry," Melody assured. "I have it all planned out. See, I'm going to spend the summer with my friend, Kim. She's an artist, a really good one. Not as good as Grandma, of course, but she has this thing about angels. Even her seascapes have them."

"Oh . . . that's nice," Price said.

"A struggling artist, if you know what I mean. Anyway, she lives in a cabin out on Gibson Point."

"Well, I'm glad it all worked out for you." Tony parked his briefcase next to the baggage claim carousel.

"Actually, it hasn't quite worked out. Kim has this sort of boyfriend living with her. He's a jerk. Really. That's what Kim says. And she's going to kick Amigo out this weekend."

Tony raised his eyebrows. "Amigo?"

"That's the guy's name."

"Then, when he's gone, you'll stay with her?" Price questioned.

"Yep. It'll be cool. I'll write in the den and she'll paint on the deck. We've got it all planned out. She'll do all the cooking and laundry and I'll do the rest. Did I tell you I'm working on a book of short stories?"

Tony examined the bags revolving on the carousel. A whiny voice on the loud speaker droned flight information about a flight to Anchorage. "Eh . . . no, I don't think you mentioned it."

"Well . . ." Melody rocked back and forth on her black velcro strapped sandals. "See, I call it *Endangered Species*, but it's not about animals. It's about people. People whose occupations are being phased out by the unrelenting technological progress of the late twentieth century. My first piece is called *The Last Hot Dog Stand in America*. Isn't that title great? It came to me in a dream one night."

Price scooted the two briefcases to the side as Tony fished out a large blue suitcase from the carousel. "So, you're not staying with your mom, or Kim, for a few days. Where does that leave you?"

"Well, here's what I thought . . . and you two feel perfectly free to squelch the idea.

31

. . . Grandma has this small apartment above her garage. Mainly just storage, but it's really quite comfortable. Has a little balcony and everything. So, if it would be all right, I'd like to stay there until Kim's place opens up. It'll just be for a few days. Now, I know you paid for the whole place for all summer . . . but I thought I could spend the weekend driving you all over the Island and introducing you to the people you'll need to talk to. You know, sort of in exchange for bunking in the garage loft?"

"N-O. Absolutely not!" Tony mouthed to Price behind Melody's back.

No, no, no. This is the summer that Price and I get reacquainted. No emergency runs to the hospital for injured kids. No pizza wedged behind the couch cushions. No one busting into our bedroom early in the morning because they thought they heard us talking. Just me and Price.

"What do you think, Dr. Shadowbrook?"

"Well . . . I think . . ." Tony shook his head at Price. "Just for a few days . . . I suppose that would be . . . but we really have to have privacy in order to complete this project. I think I explained all this in our correspondence."

"You got it. Believe me, you won't even know I'm out there."

Tony huddled the suitcases between them. "Melody, why don't you get your car and we'll wait out front. These are too heavy to carry to the parking garage."

"Oh, sure. Wow, you really have a lot of baggage. I've just, you know, never been around famous writers before."

"Do you have room?" Tony quizzed. "We could rent a vehicle."

"Oh no. We'll make it. VWs hold a whole lot more than most people think."

Melody Mason scurried out the front door of the terminal and disappeared in the confusion of cars, taxis, hotel vans and temporary Seattlites.

"A Volkswagen?" Tony sighed. "This doesn't look good. We can't load this in a little car. And then she's going to stay with us? It's not fair. We had this all planned out. What will we do with a girl in our garage?"

"She isn't a girl. She's twenty-five years old, in case your old eyes didn't notice, an attractive young woman who spent entirely too long holding your hand."

"Whoa! I feel a shoot-out scene coming on. But I'm not the one who told her, 'Oh, sure, stay at the house for the weekend.' "

"What could I say? But she'll be out of the

33

garage by Monday, or we'll just make other arrangements."

"I don't think it would hurt to start searching for an alternative." Tony pulled off his cowboy hat and ran his fingers through his close-cropped sandy brown hair. He took a deep breath. "Then again, maybe we're getting worried over nothing. Let's get to the Island and set up camp. I'm anxious to get started on that book."

"Tony . . . they're calling your name!"

"Who?"

"The public address system."

"Really? How can you hear that?"

"Because I'm not nearly as old as you are!"

"Three years, that's all, kid. Where's the house phone?"

"One of those white ones over there. But who would call you here?"

"Probably Miss Mason. She lost her way and can't find her '55 Bug."

Tony scooted across the polished tile terminal to a wall phone. "Tony Shadowbrook . . . is there a call for me?"

"Are you the writer?"

"Eh, yeah . . . who is this?"

"Are you the one who wrote *Lonesome Dove*?"

"No, that was Larry McMurtry."

"I know I've heard of you. What did you write?"

"Who is this?"

"One of the airport operators."

"Did I have a phone message?" Tony asked.

"Yes, just a minute. Say, you wrote *Talking God*, didn't you?"

"That was Tony Hillerman. . . . What about my call?"

"Your daughter wants you to call home, Mr. Shadowbrook. Come on, now, what did you write?"

"My latest novel is called *Shotgun Creek*."

"Never heard of it."

"Yeah . . . well . . . it's pretty new."

"Mr. Shadowbrook, is it true that you know Tom Selleck?"

"No."

"Oh . . . well . . . good day."

With the scent of strong espresso drifting through the terminal, Tony retraced his steps, lizard cowboy boots pounding over the sounds of passing loafers, tennies and hiking boots.

"Sorry for the delay. I got waylaid by a fan . . . well, sort of a fan."

"What was the urgent message?"

"One of the girls called."

Price slumped her shoulders. "I can't believe they've already had a spat. I'll bet it's about that cow."

"No, it's not. Well, maybe. Let's scoot these bags over to the pay phones. You'll probably have to mediate."

The phone rang four times before he heard a familiar voice.

"Hi, Pop, how was your flight?"

"Fine. What's the emergency?"

"Wait, Kit wants to talk, too. I'll go get her. She's out in the garage."

"What is it, Tony?" Price prodded.

"Kath went to get Kit."

"I knew it was Kit."

"Hey, Pop! How's the world-famous writer?"

"Kit, what's going on?"

"Did you tell him, Kath?"

"No, I was waiting for you. . . ."

"Tell me what?"

"About an hour ago a man named Terrance Davidian came by the house to see you."

"I don't know any Terrance Davidian."

"We know. Now, listen, Daddy, Terrance Davidian used to work for Michael Ovitz."

"Who?"

"Oh, Pop, you know, the Hollywood superagent who's now at Disney. Disney . . .

36

as in Walt, as in Mickey Mouse, as in mega-bucks."

"Okay, so what?"

"Well, get ready for this. Davidian said he thinks *Shotgun Creek* is one terrific western. He wants to take it to the studios!"

"What?"

"He's going to get them to make a movie out of your book, *Shotgun Creek*! Can you believe it? And . . . there's a chance of sequels for the rest of the River Breaks series. Daddy? Are you there?"

"What studio did you say he's from?"

"I didn't. I think he's an agent."

"Well, then, he's looking for his cut, no doubt."

"Pop, this is serious. He's got your address there on Fox Island. I think he's flying up to see you."

"He's flying up here? When?"

"It sounded like today. Didn't it, Kit?"

"Yeah, but," Kit paused, "don't trust him too far, Pop."

"Oh, Kit, come on. He really, really likes your book, Daddy. He said you were the next Luke Grey or Zane Short or something."

"What's the problem, Kit?" Tony asked.

"Look, the guy drives up here in an old beat-up Datsun. Come on, even our paper boy can afford a better car than that!"

"Who's coming to Fox Island?" Price demanded.

Tony waved his hand her way. "Is that all, girls?"

"Yes, aren't you excited? I know Mom will be. This could be that big break you've always talked about needing."

"Speaking of big breaks," Kit broke in, "I busted a bolt off the block. Do you have any Easyouts in your toolbox, Pop?"

"No, but why don't you buy me one?"

"Bye, Pop!"

"Hey, Daddy . . ."

"Kath?"

"Kit's off the phone now. You'll never guess what she's got in the backyard!"

"The calf, right?"

"Yeah . . . how did you . . . ?"

"It's okay, Kath. Thanks for telling us."

"Bye, Daddy."

"Talk to you later, sweetheart."

Melody Mason, all five feet one inch of her, beamed innocence and cheer beside a pouting Price. "Well, what are those two up to?" his wife asked.

"Besides raising a calf in our backyard?"

"I told you!"

"Also, some Hollywood agent stopped by to talk about a scheme to make *Shotgun*

38

Creek into a movie."

"Really? Oh, wow, this is terrific," Melody blurted out. "I've always thought Keanu Reeves would make an excellent Jake Houston. Can't you see that? He's a natural."

"Let's get to the Island, ladies. We can talk on the way. Where's your car, Melody?"

"The green VW bus. Over there with the Deadhead poster covering the broken window. I'm going to get that fixed before winter. But it kind of gives it character, don't you think?"

2 Indians called the Island "Bu Teu," which means "sea person." Fist-sized clay pebbles washed ashore on the west end of Fox Island often resemble the shapes of birds, fish, animals and even infants. Legend labels them Mud or Clay Babies. According to Indian legend, a beautiful princess spurned her own kind and married the handsome son of the Old-Man-of-the-Sea. Underwater lifestyle so changed her that she could no longer visit her parents on land. So, when she is homesick for her former people, she tarries near her favorite beach, forming small clay figurines that wash ashore. She leaves her artwork behind to be found by adventurous pilgrims who scout along the sand and mud.

But then, not everyone sojourning on Fox Island has time to explore the beaches.

Tony burst through the kitchen doorway, still dressed in his all-black running gear. Sweat streamed down his face. "What time's that interview?"

Price glanced up from her Hannah Whitall Smith devotional book. "So what do you think of this? 'Man's part is to trust, and God's part is to work.' "

Tony grabbed a red-and-yellow striped beach towel and twirled it into a twist. "Of course, that depends on the context," he shrugged. "If you're talking about salvation, it's on the money. But if someone uses it as an excuse never to do anything, to just sit on his duff and wait for his 'welfare blessings' from the Lord, then it's kind of shallow."

"Thanks for the theological lesson of the morning."

"Do I hear a twinge of sarcasm?" Tony briskly wiped his face and neck. Tufts of hair stood up, making him look like a middle-aged light heavyweight boxer after a tough first round.

Price sighed deeply. "For as long as I've been a Christian, I feel like I do so little for God. I do a lot of busy work for the church, but I never seem to talk about Him to others. I guess I keep looking for some grand God-given task."

"I'm not sure we all get something grand, spiritually speaking. But we keep busy, that's for sure." He tossed the beach towel across the deck railing. "Is that interview at 10:00?"

"What are you going to wear today?"

"What difference does that make? It's on radio."

"But we're going to the Yacht Club luncheon benefit. I don't want us to clash."

"Honey, I absolutely don't care. You pick something out." He flung open the refrigerator door and stared at a half-empty gallon of nonfat milk and a dozen radishes floating in a container of water.

"I'm going to wear my teal skirt and silver blouse . . . and maybe my silver boots," Price informed. "How about you putting on that teal green shirt with the southwest design and your silver Apache scarf?"

"Nah, I don't want to wear that."

"Tony, you just said it didn't matter!"

The back door squeaked open and slammed shut. Tony and Price stared down the hall.

"Hi, guys! It's just me. I'm headed downstairs to the shower." Robe-wrapped in royal blue, Melody Mason disappeared down the knotty pine stairway. A scent of something sweet and sour from the kitchen followed her.

"One weekend. She was only going to live in the garage one weekend!" Tony growled as he hauled out a nearly empty carton of orange juice hiding behind the nonfat milk.

Price grabbed his arm and ushered him to the bay window. "It's only been eight days," she shushed. Sea gulls circled the narrow strip of rocky beach stretched beyond the lawn. A boy and dog chased the birds with a stick, then quickly ran next door.

Tony plopped down in a brown canvas director's chair, took a swig of juice, and untied his running shoes. "When she said 'garage apartment,' I figured there would surely be a bathroom out there. Day and night we never know when she'll pop in."

"It is rather distracting." Price stood behind him and rubbed his neck and shoulders. "But she said she's moving in with Kim on Wednesday, whether or not this Amigo guy leaves."

"What time was that interview?"

As Tony quaffed the last of the juice, Price stepped back into the kitchen and returned with a bright pink notepad.

"Here's what Liz gave me. Ten o'clock with WBAC from Boston. The host is Shari LaPointe. . . ."

"Do we know her?"

"You remember Shari . . . last April at the booksellers convention? She's the one who wore the dress made of book covers."

"Oh . . . that Shari!" Tony raised his eyebrows.

"Yes, the bleached blonde who batted her eyes and said, 'Oh, Tony . . . I want you to know that I purposely put the cover of *Shotgun Creek* close to my heart!' "

He jumped up, shoes and socks hanging from his fingertips. "I can't believe she's in radio."

"Well, I can't believe I'm letting you do this interview."

"When did you say she's going to call?"

"In twenty-five minutes."

Tony poured Rattlesnake Blend coffee into a blue enamel tin cup. "You want to listen in on the extension?"

"Nope, but thanks for the offer. I'll be tied up . . . going through the old newspapers. I read the book on the Jessica Davenport paintings. It's strange reading about famous pieces of art with the originals hanging on the walls all around you. Of the dozen samples they mentioned, ten are here and two are at the museum."

"What are you finding so far? Anything we can use?"

"You mean, besides the fact that the great prisoner escape of 1952 happened on Anderson Island instead of Fox Island?"

"I still can't believe that."

"We made the mistake of going by the newspaper account. The story broke during the night. The Seattle papers got word the standoff happened on Fox Island. So that's the way it was printed. The news services picked it up before the retraction appeared."

"But how did it get in that book we read?"

"The author must have read only the Seattle paper account. We happened onto a first printing that had the error. They say all subsequent printings have it changed over to Anderson Island."

"But that was one of the strong points of coming to Fox Island," Tony complained. "It provided us with an angle, an entry, a little excitement. Now that whole scenario's gone."

"We'll find another hook. I just get the feeling there's something here we haven't discovered. There's plenty of potential here."

"I think I like writing fiction better than nonfiction. Did I ever tell you that?"

"You mean in the last ten days?"

"No, I mean in the last ten minutes." Tony banged several cupboards and drawers. "Where's the foil?"

"Above the refrigerator."

Price pulled half a bagel from the toaster

and smeared it with strawberry preserves. "Hey, I did find a place called Smuggler's Cove, but no one really knows why."

"I'm sure I could make something up."

"Oh, no you don't, Shadowbrook," Price laughed, brief but hearty. "I'm sure when the world-famous novelist Anthony Shadowbrook gets through with *Fox Island*, the place will sound as intriguing as . . . say, *Fall River Mills*. Every summer it's the same thing. We wonder if we'll ever find enough fascinating data for a book. But somehow we manage. 'Man's part is to trust, and God's part is to work.' "

"That's exactly how that phrase can be misused. We've got to do our work . . . and trust God to do his work."

"You fell for that bait, didn't you?"

"Are you going to flog me with that line all summer?"

"Maybe," she grinned. "Now, what are you going to wear to the luncheon, Mr. Shadowbrook?"

"I decided on the green shirt with the southwest print. How do you think that silver Apache scarf will look with it?"

"Stunning, I'm sure. Did anyone ever tell you what excellent taste in clothes you have?"

"Never." He kissed her on the forehead

and turned toward the door. "I think I have time for a shower before that radio interview."

"You better not. Melody's downstairs. You know there's not enough water pressure for two showers at once."

He threw up his hands. "Sort of like bringing the girls along after all. Guess I'll drag the laptop out to the deck and clean up that section on the Indian occupation of the Island."

"Take the remote phone. You can do the interview out there. Only . . ."

"Only what?"

"Watch out for dive-bombing sea gulls."

Anthony Shadowbrook, barefoot and still wearing black jogging shorts and black T-shirt that read "Cheyenne Frontier Days," studied the strip of McNeill Island appearing out of the distant fog across Carr Inlet.

I can't believe they didn't escape over here. I can see it now: armed and desperate men fighting the currents . . . breaking into a small cabin dripping wet . . . in the dark of night. Terrified, pajama-clad children clutch to their mother's gown as a frightened father gropes for his now-broken glasses so that he might see his attackers and face a violent challenge to protect his children and defend his wife's honor. Why didn't that happen on Fox Island?

I could have written a chapter like that in four hours. Now it'll take a week of research and writing to replace it. Lord, sometimes I need to be reminded just why it is I'm writing this book. I mean, besides having some time to be alone for the summer with the most beautiful woman in the world.

Come to think about it . . . maybe that's a good enough reason.

"Isn't it great out here?"

Melody Mason suddenly stood beside him, wrapped in royal blue and head turbanned in white.

"Summer's a great time. How's the rest of the year?"

"Foggier. Colder. But each season has its beauty. Say, did you get a chance to read my story yet?"

"The one about the hot dog stand?"

"Yeah."

"Eh . . . I think Price is reading it now. Listen, Melody, I don't want to sound rude, but I'm doing a radio interview in just a minute. So, I'll need a moment to collect my thoughts."

"Oh, wow! What station is it? Maybe I could tune in."

"I don't think so. It's WBAC in Boston."

"That is so cool! Isn't it great being a

writer? I can't think of anything I'd rather do. Tell Dr. S. I'll be ready to go in about forty minutes."

"Oh? This morning?"

"This is the morning I give her a Davenport tour of the Island . . . all the places that have been connected with my family."

"You're not going to interview your grandmother today, are you? I wanted to sit in on the first public visit with Jessica Davenport in fifty years."

Melody rubbed her hands together, then tried to wind the turban tighter around her head. Several dark locks of hair sprawled from the top and she nervously tried to stuff them back in.

"Actually . . . I know I told you about getting an interview. But Grandma Jessie just hasn't been doing too well. Old age and crankiness and such. I'm not sure she's up to the interview."

Tony shrugged. "I understand. We do have all summer."

"Yeah, well . . ." Melody stuck one crimson-nailed foot out of her navy slippers and reached down to scratch a toe. Then she peeked back at Tony. Her lips pinched tight together. "I told Grandma Jessie about you guys wanting to talk to her, and she sort of, you know, blew up. She started yelling and screaming and stuff."

Tony's eyes narrowed. "I'm sorry it disturbed her so much."

"It's okay. Really. She has her good days and bad days. I'll just have to wait for a better one. When she's okay, she remembers the old days real good. Isn't that weird? She can't remember what happened yesterday, but she can describe every moment of June 2, 1942."

"What happened on June 2, 1942?"

The telephone rang. Melody spun around and ran down the stairs. "I'll tell you later, Mr. S. Have a good interview!"

"Hi, Daddy . . . it's me."

"Kath? What's up, sweetheart? I've got a radio interview any minute now. . . ."

"I'll make it quick. Did Josh call you last night?"

"No. Was he supposed to?"

"Well, he said he would, but I knew he wouldn't. He promised to call from the hospital."

"Good grief. What happened?"

"Some props gave way or something out at Rawhide, and he broke his arm. Only a slight fracture, that's all. He's okay, and their insurance covers the whole thing. I

50

thought you'd want to know. Talk to you later . . . have a good interview."

"Kath . . . wait. . . ."

He gaped at the buzzing instrument.

The sliding glass door rolled open. "Is your interview over?" Price stood there, brushing her hair, which looked dark brunette in the shadows.

"They haven't called yet. That was Kath. . . . Josh had an accident at Rawhide last night and busted his arm."

"I knew it. I hate when I'm right about impending disaster. Where is he? I'll call him."

"Kath said it was minor. Could we wait until after the radio interview?"

"We need two phone lines."

"You want the phone? Go ahead and use it. Listen, babe, I couldn't care less about this interview. Who wants to talk to some blonde in a cardboard dress?"

Price grabbed her purse off the kitchen counter. "I need to buy some bread and juice at the market. I'll call Josh from the pay phone."

"Melody said her grandmother wasn't up to an interview. I guess she even got hostile about it."

"Oh, brother. You mean we aren't going to get a Jessica Davenport scoop?"

"Well, not today. But Melody figures sometime in the next few weeks it will work out. I guess her grandmother sort of bounces in and out of reality."

"Don't we all?" Price dug in her purse and pulled out her car keys.

The phone rang again from the railing of the deck.

"That will be WBAC," Tony said.

"I'll be back in a few minutes."

"Tell Josh I'll talk to him later. Find out what doctor he went to. Maybe we can call and find out what really happened."

"Answer your phone. Your public is waiting." Price blew him a kiss and stepped back into the house.

"Hello, Tony Shadowbrook here."

A male voice on the other end startled him. "Tony . . . Tony! Man, am I glad I finally caught you."

"Are you with WBAC in Boston?"

"No, I'm just your stepping-stone to incredible fame."

"If you're selling something, we're definitely not interested. I either already have it, or don't want it. I'm really busy."

"Wait, this is Terry Davidian!"

"Who?"

"Terry Davidian of Terrance Davidian and Associates. I talked to your son and daughter last week."

"Son and daughter?"

"I was at your house in Scottsdale. I guess I just missed you. Kathy and Kit, if I remember."

"Daughters. They're both girls."

"Oh, my, well, one was, eh, one was under the car. There was grease and . . ."

"No problem. Look, Davidson, I need . . ."

"Davidian. Terry Davidian. Formerly with Michael Ovitz."

"Davidian, I'm scheduled for a radio interview right now. I'll have to call you back."

"I'm on the road, so let me call you. I'm just north of Portland . . . driving up I-5 . . . how about us doing lunch on Fox Island? You name the restaurant and I'll meet you there."

"No restaurants on this Island, Davidian. Besides, I have a previous commitment. Maybe you ought to talk to my publicist. Her name is Liz. . . ."

"No, no, no! Tony, my main man, I didn't drive over twelve hundred miles to talk to a publicist. This is big, real big. I'll check back with you later. Save me some time in your afternoon schedule."

"Yeah, right."

★ ★ ★

Tony Shadowbrook pecked at his laptop computer on top of the redwood table. The cordless phone lay on the bench beside him. He flipped through the pages of a locally published book entitled *How the U.S. Government Covered Up a Japanese Submarine Invasion of Fox Island*, written by a man named Harvey Peterson, who claimed the credentials of "Supreme Commander of the Fox Island Chain Saw Militia." Which, as far as Tony could determine, had a membership of one.

This guy ought to be writing headlines for tabloid ragsheets. Who reads this boring stuff? Surely no one believes it, do they? But he probably sold more copies than my latest novel.

Lord, why is it that writing with integrity never seems to sell as well as garbage? I mean, they keep telling me if I'd just write my stories to be more violent, sexy and vulgar I'd sell more copies. But I won't do it. That's my goal in life. To write the last, decent best-seller. A book you can read aloud to a sixth grade class and not be ashamed. Maybe after the River Breaks series, I'll do a historical saga to end all sagas.

A good five minutes later he glanced up to stare across the waters of Carr Inlet. He could faintly hear the water sloshing and bubbling against the driftwood and beach. An acrid vegetable smell stung him, like stewed chard and pot herbs, like rancid sea plants.

"Radio! Where is that interview?" he muttered, then punched familiar numbers into the phone.

"Liz? This is Tony."

"Where are you?"

"On Fox Island."

"You're supposed to be on the radio."

"Yeah, that's what I thought. They never called. Check it out for me, would you?"

"I confirmed it with LaPointe just yesterday. Don't go away. I'll see what's happening."

"Liz? Hey, do you know anything about some agent named Terrance, or Terry Davidian?"

"Book agent?"

"Movie agent."

"Never heard of him."

"Yeah, well, give me a call about the interview."

"Right."

He was pouring another half cup of Rattlesnake Blend when the phone rang.

"Tony, it's Liz. Shari LaPointe got fired last night from WBAC, and no one knows anything about the interview."

"Fired?"

"Yeah, isn't that nice? And you won't believe what for!"

"I don't want to know."

"Good. Anyway, they offered to rebook you next week. What do you think?"

"Tell them to forget it. I'm too busy with this Hidden West project."

"How's it coming?"

"Slow. By the end of summer I'll be ready to write *Standoff at Rifle Ridge*. Listen, I've been thinking about . . ."

"That reminds me, Brock said he needs a story synopsis and some cover ideas for *Standoff*."

"Tell him I have no idea in the world what's going to be in that book until late September."

"I'll tell him you're working on it."

"Liz, I'm not working on it yet. But I'll meet the deadlines. Don't I always?"

"In your fashion, Tony. Look, if you can jot down just a paragraph on a couple possible scenes, it will keep them happy for a while."

"Have a grubby Houston riding a Tobiano horse pointing a '73 Winchester carbine at some unseen enemy."

"What kind of horse?"

"A paint. You know, basically white, with dark patches."

"We've already done that one, so send me a little something when you get a chance. Meanwhile, if an agent shows, remember the publishing house and I both need to be brought in on the deal."

"Right."

"One other thing. They finally got a photographer hired for *Fox Island*. Fax me a possible photo shoot. I'll line it up."

"I'll tell Price. She handles that."

"Have a good week. Boy, I envy you two. Famous writers spending every summer at some different remote exotic resort, while I slave away in the hot, humid city. Bye."

A sea gull swooped over the patio and deposited the unusable parts of its breakfast in the middle of the redwood table.

"Lord, there are lots of ways you can keep me humble. That's not one of my more favorite ones."

Tony gathered up the phone and computer and scooted back into the house. He headed straight for the shower.

The Yacht Club benefit was peopled mainly by Tacoma and Seattle socialites who owned a cabin or boat slip on Fox

Island. The buffet style luncheon featured piles of smoked clams; baked oysters; shrimp jambalaya; hot crab dip; open-faced sandwiches; tiny, slimy hors d'oeuvres; long wooden bowls filled with seaweed pudding; and double chocolate mousse shaped like sail boats.

Tony had just finished his sixth "Oh, I've never met an author before" conversation when Price tugged at his elbow.

"Excuse me, Mr. Shadowbrook." She tilted her head and batted her blue eyes. "But you remind me so much of . . . my father."

"Come on, you. We're going for a walk."

"What, and leave all your adoring fans?"

"There aren't three people here who've ever read one of my books, and that includes you and me."

"Where are we going?"

"To look at the boats."

A slight breeze pushed fluffy white clouds out Hale Passage toward the Narrows. The air reeked of fish and salt and clean sweat. Sipping from plastic glasses of lemonade, they wandered along the rough wooden docks and boat slips.

"Tell me what Josh said," Tony quizzed.

"It happened in the stunt where Josh chases Paul to the top of the barn and they end up with the somersault into the wagon."

"Yeah?"

"There was a scrap two-by-four tossed on the gigantic air mattress, and Josh caught the board when he landed."

"But he's not going to take some time off?"

"No, he insists he's fine. He'll wear leather cuffs and that will cover the brace."

"I don't suppose his mother could talk him out of it?"

"Not a chance. He did mention there's a new girl in the act. She has an awesome smile."

"Oh, joy, another sweet young thing who's going to try to keep up with Josh Shadowbrook. You know what I don't understand, babe? How did two sensible, reasonable, rational people end up with a daredevil son?"

Price slipped her arm into his. "I told you. Josh believes every one of his dad's books. He intends to live just like your heroes do."

"He should read *Fox Island*. That should calm him down some. I still haven't captured a heartbeat for this place. But there might be something to all the Prohibition-era guests that stayed at the Longhouse."

"You think it was a West Coast organized

59

crime retreat center?"

"I guess I'm hoping it was. In the old days it was fairly simple to smuggle goods into the Sound. Lots of fog. Lots of islands. Lots of harbors. What about your trip with Melody?"

"I don't think it looks too good about getting the interview with Jessica Davenport. Now I find out she's really ticked at Melody for renting the house to us."

"Oh, that's great."

"The whole family seems dysfunctional, bordering on tragic. She's an identical twin, you know."

"Melody?"

"No, her grandmother."

"Mr. Shadowbrook!"

Tony shaded his eyes toward the dock. A tall, thin woman with a black hat, black silk stirrup pants and heels approached them. A wide silver bracelet above the elbow reflected darts of sun rays. A squat, balding man with a yellow bow tie followed behind, munching pretzels in the shape of Mount Rainier.

"Mr. Shadowbrook? I'm Sheila Lenore from Bellevue. This is my Richard . . . he's in enviro-safe sludge removal."

Without giving Price a glance, she huddled close to Tony, like a vulture moving in on its prey. "Could I get you to sign my copy of *Shotgun Creek*? Just put, 'To my good friend Sheila, love Tony.' I read all of your books, and I have to say that *Shotgun Creek* is my favorite. I especially like the way you bring Jake and that Indian girl . . . What's her name?"

"Tukawa."

"Yes, well, their little scene up in that aspen grove . . . oh, my, it makes my heart flutter just to think of it. Doesn't it, Richard?"

"Yes, dear. It sort of reminded me of when we were on the cruise to . . ."

"Thank you so much, Anthony. You know, I once stood in line for three hours to get John Grisham's autograph. This is much easier, isn't it, Richard?"

"A trifle, yes. Of course, Grisham was in New York and it was . . ."

"Well, I'll leave you alone. Who did you say this young lady was? Is she related to you?"

"Yes, she is." Tony slipped his arm around Price's shoulder.

"Oh, my, I'll bet you are very proud of your father, dear!"

She dawdled toward the clubhouse as Richard turned back to whisper, "Keep writing those books! It keeps her busy!"

Tony shook his head. "Sometimes I wonder who I'm really writing these westerns for."

Price held a cup of ice to her forehead. "I think she was a delightful woman, with quite a discerning eye."

"That's not the first time someone's called you my daughter. Makes me feel like a lecherous old man . . . or an extremely lucky one. Now, tell me more about Mrs. Davenport."

"Mrs. Reynolds. That's her married name. Jessica and her identical twin sister, Jill, were born and raised right here on Fox Island."

"Identical twins. That would be different. Do you think we'd have gotten two like Kathy or two like Kit?"

"Two Kits, and I certainly wouldn't look nearly so young, Mr. S. Anyway, as Melody tells it, Jill and Jessica always dressed identical. They were the darlings of the Island folks in the twenties and thirties. They were co-queens of the Fox Island Fair and Pageant from 1932 to 1941. That's when Jessica did most of her paintings.

"I did learn something very fascinating. You know how most of them are 'Two Girl . . .' paintings?"

"What do you mean?" Tony asked.

"The titles. 'Two Girls in a Mirror,' 'Two Girls at the Lake,' 'Two Girls Shopping.' There's always a full view of one girl and her reflection in every one?"

"Yeah, that's what made them so popular."

"Well." Price whirled around to face him. "It really is two girls. Jessica painted herself as the girl and her sister, Jill, as the reflection."

"That's an interesting touch. I'd never heard that before. That will give us some previously unpublished data. That's great, babe. This is more like it. Anything else?"

"They went to college at Radcliffe."

"Somebody had some bucks."

"Their father once owned most of downtown Tacoma. Anyway, they were going to school in the East, and one June, on their way home from college, they were in a car wreck in Council Bluffs, Iowa."

"Hey, that wouldn't happen to have been on June 2, 1942?"

"How did you know that?"

"Melody mentioned her grandmother could always remember what happened on that date."

"Jill was thrown from the car and killed. Jessica was driving, and I guess she still blames herself for her sister's death."

"And she's been reclusive ever since?"

"Yes. She even refused to paint anymore."

"Because there was no more reflection? This is good stuff, darlin'."

Price glanced up toward the clubhouse. "Looks like someone else has spotted you." A man in a navy blazer waved a nautical hat at them from the patio, thick hair blowing slightly, left hand cupped to his mouth.

"Shall we return to the party, Dr. Shadowbrook?"

"Do you need me to help you . . . Father, dear?"

"Mr. Shadowbrook?" the man on the patio called again.

"He seems quite insistent." She waved to the man and gently tugged Tony along the dock.

At last they stepped up to the awning-covered deck adjoining the clubhouse. The man hurried up to them; his blazer boasted anchor brass buttons.

"Sorry to disturb you, Mr. Shadowbrook, but there's a telephone call for you. Said you should call back immediately."

"Who was it?"

"A Mr. Davidian. Terrance Davidian of Hollywood."

"Honey, did I tell you he called from

Portland this morning?"

"He's quite tenacious."

"How in the world did he know where I was?"

The man with the brass buttons pointed to a burgundy phone sitting on a metal table next to a purple and blue Japanese iris arrangement. "You can take the call out there."

"I can call him some other time," Tony told him.

Price nudged him. "Maybe you'd better check it out. He must have thought it was important to track you down at the Yacht Club."

Tony sighed and plopped down in the metal deck chair, almost tipping over the bouquet. He pulled off his sunglasses and strained to read the slip of paper. Price rearranged the flowers.

"Verne's Garage and Espresso, where getting an oil change never tasted so good! This is Verne, Jr. What can I do for ya?"

"Eh, maybe I dialed the wrong number. Is there a Terrance Davidian there?"

"Who?"

"I must have misdialed. I'm calling Terry Davidian."

"Oh, yeah, that Hollywood guy. Just a

minute. He's eating lunch out of the candy machine."

Tony signaled for Price to join the other guests.

"Hey, Tony, big guy . . . Terry, here. Sorry to pull you away from the social scene, but your research assistant said I could find you here."

"Research assistant?"

"Yeah, a Miss Mason, I believe. Here's the deal. I wouldn't think of putting a bind on you like this, but wouldn't you know it, my car busted just as I was coming across the bridge. Now old Verne, here, said he could have the thing fixed by dark, but I said,

'Hey, why waste time waiting in a garage, even though the espresso is every bit as excellent as that on Rodeo Boulevard.' So, if I could talk you into coming over here and giving me a lift to your beach cabana, we could spend the afternoon going over the details of that movie deal."

"I have the afternoon scheduled. Maybe you should talk to my publisher first."

"Tony, baby . . . whew! Don't get me wrong. I'm on your side. There's no reason for you to give them the lion's share of this deal. If you got just two hours, I can show you how you can spend next summer in your own house in Malibu. Comprende? Are you listening, Tony?"

"And you need a ride from the bridge?"

"Right. I'll be waiting here at Verne's."

"I don't remember a garage on the Island. Just where is this Verne's?"

"Stone Drive exit right as you come down off the bridge."

"Exit? What bridge are you talking about?"

"Hey, Verne, what's that bridge called? Oh yeah, it's the Tacoma Narrows Bridge."

"The Narrows Bridge?" Tony groaned. "I thought you meant the bridge to Fox Island."

"Thanks, partner. I'll treat you to a cup of mocha supreme. How long before you'll be here?"

Tony looked at his watch. "At least an hour. Maybe two."

"What?"

"I'm in the middle of a benefit, remember?"

"Oh yeah, right, one hour it is."

"Or longer. I'll send my research assistant. She'll pick you up."

"That's cool. But, Tony, I wouldn't tell her what's happening here. I wouldn't want this to leak out to the media. Not yet anyway. You know what I mean?"

"Sure. No problem. Miss Mason will be driving a big Oldsmobile."

"What color?"

"White."

Tony found Price surrounded by several men, big diamond rings sparkling. All seemed to be talking at once. They continued blustering even as she slipped away.

"Who's the guy with the camouflage jacket and the handpainted tie that looks like a giant redwood?" he asked.

"Harvey Peterson, the one who wrote the book."

"The coverup of the Japanese invasion?"

"Yes, we do have that, don't we?"

"Oh yeah, it's pretty weird."

"Well, I thought we did, but Harvey said if we'd stop by his bookstore he'd give us an autographed copy."

"He has a bookstore on the Island?"

"From what I could tell, it's in his garage. Mr. Peterson says they sell through the mail and at gun and militia shows all over the country. So, what about the big movie deal?"

"The only thing we agreed upon was to pick up Davidian at the Narrows bridge."

"Pick him up? Is he hitchhiking?"

When Tony explained the scenario, she suggested, "We could always send our 'research assistant' in her VW bus. I don't think it would make it back over that bridge again."

"Wouldn't help. He's on this side. He's only going to be here an hour, an hour and a half tops. Then we'll have Melody take him back to good old Verne's. At least I'll get him out of our hair."

They left the party a little past 2:30 P.M. Within minutes of their arrival at the Davenport house, Melody Mason backed the big Olds out of the tiny garage onto the narrow, steep driveway. She rolled down the window as she braked just short of the rosebushes.

"Thanks, Mr. S., for not getting mad about the research assistant thing. It just seemed like the right thing to say at the time."

"That's all right, Melody. We appreciate your doing this for us."

"I'll hurry right back."

"No. Take your time and be careful."

They watched her chug up the steep drive and then turn left on Third Avenue. Then they sauntered to the deck, arm and arm.

"Do you feel like a writer today, Mr. Shadowbrook?"

"Yeah, like a frustrated writer with no time to write. I'll be glad when things settle down and we can get some serious days' work in. Remember when we used to think that all a writer had to do was write?"

"This summer will be different. The girls are at home. We've got a beautiful view of the Sound. I look forward to good days on the book and long sunset walks hand in hand along the shoreline. Do I need to fix dinner for this Davidian guy?"

"Absolutely not. Tell you what. We'll sit here on the deck. After an hour if I get to pulling on my right ear, you get up and come over and say, 'Tony, don't forget you have another appointment in five minutes.' "

"What other appointment?"

"Mrs. Shadowbrook, would you like to hike with me down to the point to look for Clay Babies?"

"Certainly, Mr. Shadowbrook. When do you want to go?"

"About five minutes after I start pulling on my right ear."

3 As is much of the land west of the Cascades, Fox Island remains an evergreen paradise of firs, pines and spruce. At times looking as if methodically landscaped by a Grand Gardener, the wild blackberries and grapes blend artistically with the daffodils and dahlias. Flamboyant red-barked Madrona trees clamor to be seen in every vista before they shed their bark, leaves and berries.

But after a while, even the magnificent Madronas don't catch everyone's attention.

Tony sprawled on a chaise out on the deck. Three pelicans dove into the Sound, their large beaks handy fishnets as they plunged for underwater meals. Two settled for surface feeding. The third soared on a rising thermal, its white body dulled gray by the sunless inlet. Price carried out a tray with a mug of steaming tea and two toasted bagels.

"It's foggier than usual," she announced as she wiped off the metal chair with her napkin and sat down.

"Makes it seem even more remote out

here. I definitely like this side of the Island better. There's no narrow passage or bridge to cut down your imagination of being in a part of the hidden West."

"What did you decide about Davidian?"

"He's a flake."

"I mean, besides that." She sipped her tea and tightened the soft blue chamois robe more securely under her chin, glad she had followed her impulse and bought it their last trip into Tacoma.

"The guy's a phony. He drives all the way up here, has car trouble, and winds up bumming at our house for three days. Then he wires home for money to repair that old junker. And after all that, he has the audacity to ask me to give him a $10,000 advance to take my book to ten Hollywood studios."

"Twelve studios."

"Ten, twelve, it doesn't matter. I can't believe the nerve of some guys."

"Yes, but he did call back last night and say he'd do it for free if you'd agree to a 15% agent fee. He might just have the kind of nerve that lands him in the right place at one of the studios. What do you have to lose?"

"Self-respect. I don't want to be represented by some Westwood ding-a-ling. If the studios think my books are good enough for movies, then they can come beat at my door. I've got an agent."

"A book agent in New York City. Liz admits she doesn't know anything about Hollywood."

Tony slammed his hand on the table. "I'm not going to run around tossing my novels to the wolves to be destroyed and rejected."

"Well . . . you might be right, of course." Price paused and sipped on the Earl Grey. "But if you had waited until a publishing house beat down your door, you'd never have gotten that first novel in print."

"That's different. That's the publishing business. Sure, you have to keep sending your manuscript until you find the right house. But now they can pick up the book, check out my publishing record."

"How are they going to get a copy to look at unless someone shoves one in their face?" she insisted.

"Not Davidian. He's a windbag! I don't trust him."

"I wonder what type agent it does take to get Hollywood's attention? Besides, behind all that wind and the Vuarnet sunglasses seems to be a guy who's well connected. And he sure has an air of confidence about him."

"I don't want to talk about it."

Price crunched into the toasted bagel smothered edge to edge with melted butter and wild black cherry preserves. "So, let's move to a more enjoyable subject. Did you get a chance to look at my work on chapter one?"

Tony flipped open his portfolio and yanked out twenty-five double-spaced typed pages. "I think it's starting to take shape, don't you?"

"Yes I do," she nodded without lifting the manuscript. "What do you think about my idea to open each chapter with an italicized section on geographical description, and transition into the text? I thought it would . . ."

"Oh, well, we talked about that. Like I said, it just doesn't seem right. Nice idea, though. Maybe I'll use that sometime in a novel. I just deleted those openings and . . ."

"You did what?" Price picked up the first chapter and stared at the front page in disbelief.

"Look, honey, that idea was a little too distractive. I think keeping in pattern with our other . . ."

"You don't mean you deleted the entire opening paragraph?"

"Only the stuff in italics."

"That *stuff* in italics was my part! What was wrong with it?"

"Oh, it was nice writing. You always do a superb job. But it's the concept, it just . . ."

"It just didn't meet your present needs? Is that what you're trying to tell me?"

"Babe, look."

"Don't 'babe' me. Tell me, Mr. Famous Author, just exactly what was wrong with those openings, other than the fact you didn't think of it yourself?"

"Surely you don't think . . . ? It was just . . ."

"Just what?"

"Well, for one thing," he cleared his throat and drummed his fingers on metal, "the transitions were rough and . . ."

"Then rewrite the transitions. The opening is what gives me ownership in that chapter. Take it out and I'm nothing more than a copy editor."

Tony stood up and walked to the deck railing. The fog seemed cold and heavy, rather than restful. "I thought we solved all of that last summer. You remember those long talks we had? Now, you've got to trust me on this. I've written a number of books and . . ."

Price stood up and slammed her hands on her hips. "I am well aware of your book list,

Mr. Shadowbrook! I was working under the assumption that this project would be co-written."

Tony gently placed his hand on her shoulder. "Hey, there's no reason to get in such a tiff."

Shoving his hand away, she stormed back into the house. "I am NOT in a tiff!" she barked. "And I don't want to talk about it."

When the sliding glass door slammed shut, Tony turned and peered into the fog-bank for some sign of life. He was surprised to see the pelicans had moved far down the inlet. The shroud of silence shut him into his own private world.

Why can't we just calmly talk about it? We're both adults. We're both professionals. Why does she have to take it so personally? I'm a reasonable man. All she has to do is logically explain, step by step, line by line. . . .

He gathered up Price's tray and tiptoed into the house.

"Honey, let's talk this out," he called out.

"We did," she finally answered from the bedroom. "I'm going to take a shower."

"Priscilla!" The bathroom door slammed. He could hear the turn of the lock.

"Whoa! I've never seen Dr. S. so upset."

Melody Mason stood at the front door clutching a large yellow plastic basket.

"Maybe this isn't a good time to do my laundry. I'll do it this evening."

"Oh, well," Tony stammered, "it's just some . . . eh, creative differences."

"Is Dr. S's name Priscilla? I've never heard anyone call her that before."

"Well, I don't normally call her that."

"You only call her that when you're mad?"

"Something like that."

"Well, at least you're human. For a while I figured you two were the last perfect Christian couple."

Tony took a deep breath. "Well, Melody, I'm afraid we're a long way from perfection. But that doesn't mean we're not trying. Actually, it was just a little artistic misunderstanding. You see, she mistook my . . ."

"Hey, Mr. S., you don't have to explain to me. I've often wondered how two literary masters can get along in the same household at all. Kim and I get into hairy arguments all the time over our pieces, and she's an artist and I'm a writer, and we don't even live together. Tell Dr. S. I'll be over at my place whenever she's ready."

"Oh? More interviews?"

"Yes. Mrs. Nelson's mother is visiting this week. She lives in Spokane. But in the thirties she worked at the Longhouse."

"Then maybe she could tell us something about the type of guests they had. Make sure you two ask her about the Thirty-sixth Avenue Slayings."

"When that Chinese restaurant was shot up?"

"One account I read said it might have been planned at the Longhouse on Fox Island. Also, find out if there are some other people from those days we can interview."

"Why are you telling me? Shouldn't Dr. S. know this?"

"Communication isn't too strong between the Shadowbrooks right at the moment."

"Harvey Peterson flagged me down yesterday. He's really anxious to have you come visit with him. Says he has information that will knock your socks off. But he insists that you be the one to do the interview. It's a man thing, he says."

"Does anyone take Harvey seriously?"

"Harvey does."

"I tell you what would knock my socks off . . . if a fake Japanese invasion of Fox Island was staged by Tacoma mob bosses to cover up a great escape of prisoners from McNeil Island. Now that would be a story."

"Wouldn't that be cool? Maybe you could write a novel about Fox Island someday."

"Well, don't line me up with Harvey just yet. I want to do a little more investigating before I take him on."

"Did you know that Mrs. Mackay got back from Ohio on Saturday and she'll have the museum open today?"

"Yes, I have an appointment with her at 10:30."

"It seems funny you've been on the Island three weeks now and haven't seen the museum. Are you going to look through all the documents and stuff filed in the back room?"

"Most definitely."

"Well . . ." Melody waved, then balanced the basket on her knee and shoved open the screen door. "Hope you get it all worked out with Dr. S."

Tony and Price dressed without a word.

I ought to ask Price if this tan pullover Henley shirt is too casual for the museum assignment, but I don't dare. Maybe they're right. Having two authors doesn't really work. Maybe I should just let her do whatever she wants with the manuscript. But it's got to be right. Maybe I could . . . how long is this going to last anyway? This is ridiculous.

Price slipped on her fuchsia nylon jacket, grabbed up her briefcase and tugged her purse strap over her shoulder.

"You'll have to make your own lunch," she finally said.

He stretched his arms out to block the doorway. "We've got to work this thing out."

"What's there to work out? Obviously, you've already made up your mind."

He put down his arms and backed up a few steps. "No I haven't, but I have my reasons for wanting to keep the same format."

She didn't move. "And I have my reasons for wanting to change."

"So, let's sit down and rationally talk this out right now."

"Tony, in case you have forgotten, you don't operate on reason. You fly by instinct. You shoot from the hip, like most of your heroes. And, like them, you are usually quite good at it. But this time you missed the mark."

"Give me one good reason to open each chapter with an italicized section."

"Because the contrast in both style and form gives warmth and closeness to your part of the text, that's why."

Why do the crow's-feet always disappear around her blue eyes when she's angry? Those deep azure eyes.

"Oh, well, you could be right on that. But

that surely doesn't mean . . ."

The phone jarred them.

"Tony, baby, it's me, Terry Davidian. Say, I was double-checking on . . ."

"I'm busy . . . call me later."

"How about five-ish?"

"How about August-ish?" He hung up the receiver. "Now, where were we?"

A smile began to ease across her face. For some reason Tony remembered the first time he ever saw her. She was a summer tour guide at the Grand Canyon, and he was leading a string of mules.

That incredible smile snared me. Everything about her seemed to glow. That's all I could think about all the way down into the Canyon and all the way back.

"You were about to tell me I was completely right."

Tony rubbed the back of his neck. "What I meant was . . ."

The phone rang again.

"If that's Davidian . . ." He pounced on the phone. "Shadowbrooks."

"Daddy, it's me. You've got to do something with Kit."

"Darlin', slow down. What's the matter?" He motioned for Price to grab the phone in the kitchen.

"Mother, it's about Kit."

"What's up, Kath?"

"She didn't come home last night."

"What do you mean?"

"She went to a drag race out at Quartzite, and she didn't come back."

"Who'd she go with?" Price asked.

"Who else? Travis. He asked her to be on his crew."

"She's still not home?"

"She walked in the door only a few minutes ago. Mother, I've been awake all night worried about her."

"Put her on the phone."

"She's in the shower."

"Take the portable to the bathroom and put her on. You listen in, too."

"She's going to be mad that I called you."

"Yes, she will."

There was a long pause. Price paced around the kitchen.

I told him they were not mature enough to be left alone. One of them, sure. But together? No way. We should have brought them up here.

Tony traipsed back and forth the length of the phone cord.

Surely she didn't do anything dumb. Kit's a smart girl, Lord. They're both smart girls. It's just that Kit's . . . a lot like me. Surely she didn't do anything dumb.

"Hi, guys, I can't believe Kath called you!"

"Kit, she called because she was worried. Where were you all night?" Price asked.

"I went to the drags, that's all. Travis kept winning, so we stayed late. He finished second and won $145. Isn't that cool?"

"You were there all night?"

"No! The tow car broke down on the interstate. It took us until almost daylight to get it fixed."

"Who's we?" her father quizzed.

"Travis, Ken, Brad and Punky."

"You spent the night with four boys?" Price gasped.

"I spent the night underneath an '82 Chevy pickup while four guys held the light."

"Kristina, why didn't you call Kathy?"

"Mom, there wasn't a phone for fifty miles. You know how deserted that part of I-10 is."

"Well, when you got it fixed, you could have called her then."

"I thought she'd be sleeping. I didn't want to wake her. How was I to know she was having a private all-night swim party?"

"A what?" It was Tony's turn to gasp.

"That's not true!" Kathy protested. "I asked Bryson to come over and wait with me because I was worried sick."

"You waited in your bathing suits?" Kit sneered.

"It was a hot night, so we went swimming. Just for a little while. We didn't go in the house, Mother. We sat out in front and waited. That's all. We were right out front on the patio waiting when you got home, Kit."

"Sure, waiting underneath a blanket."

"A what?" Tony sputtered.

"Look, Mom and Pop, I have no idea why Kathy had to call you. I won't be late next week. I've got Travis' rig repaired, so I'm sure it won't break down again."

"Kit," Price lectured, "if you don't get home at the prearranged time, you will have to find a phone and check in, without exception."

"Take your mom's cellular phone next time."

"Really?"

"Yes, but only make emergency calls. Any other calls that are listed on that phone will come out of your paycheck, is that clear?"

"Yes, sir, Pop."

"Katherine?"

"Mother?"

"When we said no male company after

dark, we meant in the pool, in the yard, in the driveway, at the curb."

"Oh, is that what you meant?"

"Oh, is that what you meant?" Kit mimicked.

"Kit!"

"Sorry, Pop. Can I finish my shower? I've got to get to work in less than an hour."

"How can you work after being up all night?"

"I could lube cars in my sleep," she insisted. "Bye."

"Mother and Daddy, I'm sorry if I disappointed you."

"Kathy, you call us whenever you need to. Now, you and sis try to get along."

"We'll be fine. Bye."

"Bye, darling."

Price strolled into the hallway. Tony stared out the back window at a pot of hanging geraniums.

"It's going to be a long summer," she sighed. "Do you think the two of them will ever become friends? Tony? Tony, what are you thinking about?"

"I think you might be right."

"Right about what? About Kit and Kathy becoming friends?"

"Oh, that, too. I was just thinking that you're right about opening each chapter with an italicized descriptive passage."

"Really? You like it?"

"I think so. It does tend to highlight the rest of the chapter, doesn't it? I say let's leave it that way for the whole book and then evaluate it when it's done."

Price whirled around, her hair whipping against Tony's face. "Great. I really do think it's creative and . . . hey, wait a minute, Shadowbrook!"

"What?"

"You aren't just trying to placate me and then toss the whole thing out later on?"

"Nope."

"Prove it."

"Well . . ." He pondered. "I promise we won't delete any of the opening paragraphs unless we both agree on it. How will that work?"

"Splendid!" Price leaned over and gave him a kiss on the cheek.

"And," he said with a wide smile, "you promise you won't delete any of my sections of the book without my approval, right?" He kissed her lips, long and full.

She finally pulled away and winked. "Dream on."

Price padded across the carpet toward the hall, then turned around. "You should change that shirt. It's too plain. You really ought to cowboy up a bit for that museum visit."

Dressed in beige shorts and a forest green sweatshirt shoved up to his elbows, Tony straddled a redwood bench on the deck with his laptop in front of him and reworked the opening two pages of chapter three. His sandal-clad feet were freezing. After hammering away on a single sentence for the fifth try, he stared at the fog hovering lower than ever, just above the water.

What if the Davenport sisters were runners for the mob, carrying great sums of money between Seattle and the East Coast? And maybe the car wreck in Iowa wasn't an accident, but payback for skimming off millions. Jessica has been hiding out waiting for . . . relax, Shadowbrook. Nonfiction. Historical tidbits, a traveler's delight. Flowers, fauna, wildlife. Annual mushroom festival. I wish they did have a mushroom festival.

He thought he heard the doorbell. He started back into the house, then stepped to the side of the deck and hollered, "Around back . . . I'm back here!"

The man who walked slowly toward Tony had a slight, apologetic smile. His silk gray stripe on gray suit fit like a seasoned tailor had studied his every move. Yet his face was thin, almost gaunt. He was bald on top, white hair cropped close to his head. His eyes and mouth formed identical slits, friendly but appraising, tentative. He leaned over one of the blooms. He reached down as though to pluck one, then patted it instead.

"Such a lovely pompon," he commented. "I'm so glad to find someone at home. I'm Lloyd Bennington . . . from Chestertown, Maryland. I'm looking for Jessica Davenport. I mean, I'm sure she's . . . I think her married name is Reynolds."

Tony had never seen such a starched white shirt. The collar seemed to scrape the man's neck a raw red. "Jessica is living in a retirement community now."

"Are you her son?"

"No, we're leasing the place for the summer."

The man stuck a finger into the neckline of his shirt and gently rubbed. "Oh dear, I was so hoping to speak to Jessica."

"She's not more than five minutes from here. Are you a friend?"

"Actually, I've never met Jessica. I'm really looking for her sister, Jill. It's been a while since I've seen her. I didn't know her address and was hoping to get it from Jessica."

"You're looking for *Jill* Davenport?"

"Yes, do you know where I might find her?"

"Mister. . . . eh . . ."

"Bennington . . . Lloyd Bennington."

"Mr. Bennington, Jill Davenport was killed in a car wreck in Council Bluffs, Iowa, on June 2, 1942."

The half slits in Lloyd Bennington's eyes closed, his head dropped, and Tony noticed a slight shudder.

"Would you like to come around and sit on the deck?" Tony offered.

"Yes, thank you. I am a little tired."

Bennington climbed the stairs slowly and slumped on the redwood bench.

"When was the last time you saw Jill Davenport?"

"May," he mumbled, staring down at the deck.

"When?"

"May of '42."

"That was well over fifty years ago. You must have considered the possibility that she might have passed on by now," Tony tried to console.

"Oh yes, of course. I knew she might be gone. But I never considered that it could have been so soon after we broke up."

"You were dating Miss Davenport?"

"Yes."

"And the family didn't notify you of her death?"

"Well . . ." the old gentleman coughed and stared out at the Sound. "None of her family knew about us, I suppose."

"Not even Jessica?"

"I'm not sure. Jessica had just married Reynolds, and he was about to go to the war, so they were busy with each other. Well, she probably knew."

A tear slid down the man's face. He pulled out a white kerchief.

"You must have really cared for her."

"Well, I was hoping that . . . it's difficult to explain."

This is incredible. He's been out of the picture for over fifty years, and he still has memories that bring tears? What has this guy been doing? Lord, which of my memories are going to bring tears even after fifty years?

Tony decided he liked the man. The hesitancy, the mood of melancholy, combined with the Brooks Brothers demeanor, encouraged his curiosity. "If I might ask, why now? After all these years, why come looking for Jill Davenport now?"

"Mr. eh . . ."

"Shadowbrook."

"Shadowbrook? Like the guy who writes those westerns?"

"Yes, that's me."

"No fooling? You're Louis Shadow-brook?"

"I'm Tony Shadowbrook. It's Louis . . ."

"You a brother to Louis?"

"There is no Louis Shadowbrook. There's Louis L'Amour and I'm Tony Shadowbrook."

"Right. I knew that. Where was I?"

"You were telling me why you waited so long to contact Jill Davenport."

"Oh, yes. Well, Mr. Shadowbrook, I'm seventy-six years old. Last April they found some colon cancer in me. They cut me open and sewed me right back up. Said there was nothing they could do. So, I'm just trying to settle up some unfinished matters before the Almighty calls me to account."

"And you had some unfinished business with Jill Davenport?"

"It's just the way a foolish, dying old man thinks, I suppose."

"Say, would you like to read the news-paper account of her death? My wife and I are writing a book about the Island, and we're researching the families and the Davenport sisters."

The man's face brightened. "If you don't mind. Maybe it would help some."

Tony returned with a stack of old newspapers in vinyl covers and two cups of coffee. Neither man spoke as Bennington read several articles. Then, he stood and shuffled toward the stairs. "I'm glad I came. I'll be going now."

"I'd suggest you go visit Jessica, but she's not seeing visitors these days. Seems like she never really recovered from losing her sister."

Bennington rested his hand on the railing, stared a moment at the Sound, then closed his eyes as though to memorize the view. "No need. No purpose to be served in that. I bought one of her paintings. Had to give it to a museum a while back. It was too realistic."

"She did all those before the accident, you know."

"I wasn't aware of that. Oh, I knew the 'Two Girls' motif had ceased. But I assumed she kept on painting."

"Not that we can determine." Tony searched for something else to tell the man. "Jessica sees the accident as her fault, so I hear. She's gotten worse the past few years. I guess identical twins are pretty close."

"Jill talked highly of her sister. Always said she was the talented one. Identical only in looks, she told me. Well, it's just as well Jessica's unavailable. It would probably just remind both of us of a painful past. If she remembered anything, she'd probably just get angry."

"Jessica's granddaughter lives in the apartment over the garage here. She's gone now, but maybe you'd like to talk to her?"

"Jessica's granddaughter? I suppose I could, but, actually, I really don't know what I'd say. An old, old friend of her grandmother's sister? There's not much to talk about. All that long trip out here and I finally see how foolish it was. It was a long flight and I'm tired. Think I'll head back to the hotel."

"Where are you staying?"

"The Airport Hilton."

"Could I pass that information to the granddaughter, just in case?"

"As you wish."

Tony stared at the man as he inched down the stairs.

Bennington scooted up the sidewalk toward the road before he turned back. "Thanks for your help, Mr. Shadowbrook. I'm glad you were here. I really didn't want to speak directly to Jessica, and you've been so helpful. I was risking an angry scene, not good for either of us. And keep writing those good books. I've read your whole Sackett series."

"No, that was . . ." Tony started to protest, but the stately gentleman slid into a tan Lincoln and backed it down the long, uphill driveway.

Angry? Why would anyone be angry?

Tony, Price and Melody ate turkey pasta salad, purchased from the local Food Mart, off white paper plates tucked into wicker holders. A low-hanging sun glittered off the salty waters of lower Puget Sound. Just as it sank beyond the Olympic Peninsula, a ring of wispy clouds tinged peach, then melon, then tangerine surrounded it. Tony tore a hunk of sourdough bread and smeared it with something that resembled margarine from a plastic tub.

"I don't believe it," Melody blurted out. "You actually talked to a man who dated my great-aunt Jill?"

"Your grandmother and her sister were extremely pretty ladies back then. I suppose they both had their share of dates," Price suggested.

"Grandma Jessie always said Jill was such a perfectionist. She refused to date any of the boys on the Island. Something to do with them not having the social standing she required."

"Well, all I know is this guy met Jill after

your grandmother's wedding and broke up with her a few weeks later."

"And now, he decides to come for a visit?" Price dug deep into a white cardboard carton and raked out the last square chunks of turkey.

"I guess at the end of your life you relive some 'what ifs.' "

"Speaking of what ifs," Melody broke in. "What if Grandma Jessie still lived here and went to the door. He might have thought it was Jill. The old guy could have had a heart attack. Whoa, you could have written that into your book."

"You're starting to sound like Tony," Price laughed.

Tony glanced up, his fork poised in the air. "What did you ladies discover about the Island's history?"

Price spoke between bites. "Arthur Murray once came for a short vacation here and met with the San Souci girls for a private dance lesson."

"The San Souci Club really were the Fox Island socialites, weren't they?"

"Still are," Melody reported.

Price set down her fork and wiped her mouth with a green calico napkin. "Mrs. Johnson reported that her father was one of the original members of the 'Law and Order

Society of Fox Island and Hale Passage.' "

"The vigilantes? I read a little something about that down at the museum. There were thirty members who contributed $134 for dues. Something about needing to stop the sneakthieves and footpads. But I haven't found any record of them doing anything."

"Well," Price added, "according to Mrs. Johnson, her father always said he figured the thief had joined the vigilantes in order to avoid suspicion, because the stealing stopped after the group was formed. Then the organization seemed to fade out of existence."

Price strolled to the railing and leaned her elbows on the gray cracked paint of a two-by-six, between a sundial and some clay baby ducks. She tossed her head back. A delicate sea breeze drifted against her tanning skin. "It's sort of sad."

"About there being no more crime?"

"No, about that Mr. Bennington. An old man who knows he's dying and tries to find a former girlfriend."

Melody jingled her long gold earrings. Her black hair shone with gold highlights in the evening sunset. "It does sound romantic, doesn't it?"

"I wonder . . . when you're old, will you go and look up all your old girlfriends?"

Price batted her eyes at Tony.

"All I have to do is look across the kitchen table every morning and I see all my old girlfriends."

Melody choked back a bite of salad and began to cough.

"Are you all right?" Tony asked.

"Dr. S. was the only girlfriend you ever had?"

"Yeah."

"How can that be? Were you raised in a monastery or something?"

"I guess I'm one of those rarities . . . a one-woman man."

"Anyway, that's what he tells me." The dimples deepened in Price's grin.

"That is so cool! And how about you, Dr. S.? Would you ever go look up your old boyfriends?"

"Eh . . . no." Price retrieved a navy cardigan sweater and pulled it over her shoulders. "I wouldn't know where to begin."

"Me either," Melody added. "Besides, most of my old boyfriends are a bunch of jerks."

Price turned back and looked at a stack of papers in a box next to Tony. "Well, what did you discover at the museum?"

"I've got quite a bit of stuff on organized crime in Tacoma, but I haven't found a Fox

Island connection yet. I'll keep searching. And Harvey Peterson keeps making news from time to time. You know, those local eccentric kinds of stories they use for filler on the evening news? Looks like I'll need to do that interview pretty soon."

Tony sorted through the papers in the box, then looked up at Melody. "Hey, kiddo, I did find an old article about a ferryboat wreck . . . which involved your aunt Jill."

Melody leaned forward. Her dark eyebrows tensed close together and almost overlapped. "You did? Are you sure? I never heard about that."

Tony spread the yellowed copy in front of her. "It's all right here . . . 'The Fox Island to Tacoma ferryboat, called the *Arcadia*, rammed the Sixth Street dock during a storm, and several people were injured, including high school freshman, Jill Davenport, who suffered fractures in both legs.' "

Melody grabbed the sheet. "Auntie Jill broke both legs? Why didn't Grandma ever tell me that story? I wonder if Mother knows?"

"Price, how about opening the book with a ferryboat scene?"

"You don't mean, 'It was a dark and stormy night. . . .' Do you?"

98

"Some sort of variation. Think of it. The drama of a child on a rough ferryboat ride to school. It might add the drama . . . and sense of distance and separation . . . that the Island portrayed back then."

"Perhaps," Price mused. "But they didn't have to take the ferry until high school."

"Okay, maybe it was a shopping trip . . . they could be traveling back home. . . ."

"Wishing they had never left the Island?" Price suggested.

Tony ripped off another hunk of bread. "Yeah, that would work. Sort of the way we opened *Promontory* with the railroad scene."

"Let's scout around and talk to folks who used to ride the ferries. I'll review my notes."

Melody looked up from the papers she was reading. "My mom. Talk to her. She rode the ferry until she was about ten."

Price gathered the leftovers on a wide wooden tray. "Great, why don't you call her? Maybe we could run over tonight. We need to go to a supermarket anyway. This is the last of the deli salads."

"Well, one of you ought to call her," Melody stammered. "She . . . we . . . well, see . . . she sometimes has friends over . . . and, you know, she doesn't like to be disturbed. I mean, that's why I didn't stay with her. And, well . . . it would just be best if you called."

Price patted Melody's shoulder. "Maybe we should wait 'til morning."

Melody's face relaxed. "Yeah, that's great. Only don't call her too early."

Tony glanced over at Melody. "We really need to talk to that grandmother of yours sometime."

"Yeah, I know. Maybe this article will help."

"About the ferry accident?"

"Yeah, I'll ask her about it, and maybe she'll start to open up about the old days. Then I'll say, 'Grandma Jessie, we ought to have the Shadowbrooks write some of this down,' or something like that."

"Maybe that will work. We really don't want to upset her," Tony said.

"I wonder what she'd say if I told her about that guy Bennington?" Melody pondered.

"He said she might get angry."

"I wonder why?"

Price spread notes across the blue variegated carpet in the living room while Tony studied topo maps on the oak dining table. Melody scampered up the stairs with a manuscript box under her arm.

"Hi, guys. I'm waiting for the clothes dryer. So I thought, you know . . . if you weren't too busy . . . you could give me some pointers on my book."

"We're kind of tied up at the moment," Tony said. "But sure, we could take a break."

"That would be great. For six months now I've been dreaming about this day."

"Oh?" Tony glanced at Price.

"I kept thinking, 'If only the Shadowbrooks could read this . . . if only the Shadowbrooks could read this.' So, what do you think? Be honest. I can take it, really. Does it have a chance? Do you know of a publishing house taking this kind of thing? It's important to me to get the right house, you know? I don't want just anyone publishing this."

Price gathered up her notes into several piles. "Well, Mr. Shadowbrook, why don't you go first?"

Tony began to pace the room. "Melody, I can sense how important this work is to you and. . . ."

"I've been working on it over four years."

"Four years?"

"Yes, I started it as a senior with Dr. S. Remember our senior project was to submit a book proposal to a publisher? Putnam rejected it, of course, but I got an A in the class. Boy, am I glad they didn't want it. I write so much better now than I did then."

Tony's boot clunked against an end table.

"I would hate to be stuck with a first novel that I wasn't happy with later on," she continued. "It's better to wait until your writing's matured, don't you think? Anyway, what about the novel?"

"Melody . . ." Tony paused. "People write for many different reasons. Sometimes it's to explore a new talent. Sometimes they have a need to express their thoughts and ideas. Sometimes it's just practice, so that they can get better. Sometimes, like a person who enjoys sitting alone and playing the piano, they enjoy the creative exercise. It's an outlet. Then there are those who write in order to be published."

"That's me. I definitely write to be published. I was born to be a writer. It's all I've ever wanted to be. It's my calling, my God-given talent, you know?"

"I can tell you surely have the desire to write. Did Price ever explain how we got into the writing business?"

"You mean, with articles in small circulation magazines, stories in Christian youth papers, things like that?"

"That's where it all began."

"See, here's the neat thing. I have learned so much from Dr. S.'s classes, and reading all of your books, I feel like I've already passed that preliminary stage. Anyway, what about my novel? Don't you just love the way it starts? The detailed description of that alpine flower on top of the huge granite rock? Have you ever read anything more, you know, in depth than that?"

"It might have been a tad extended. How long did that scene last?"

"Oh, just the first six pages or so, that's all. Then it transitions right into the blind girl at the hot dog stand. Everything I ever learned about transitions I learned from Dr. S."

Tony pulled off his boots and rubbed his toes. "I think Price is better qualified to talk about structure and form. I'm more an idea man myself, better for looking at the overall project. Price, maybe you two would like to talk about the details. I think I'll go print up that chapter I reworked today."

"Oh, sure . . . but really, Mr. S. What's your overall opinion? Tell me the truth; I can take it. Do you feel that the book is publishable the way it now stands?"

Tony scratched his forehead, then rubbed his cheek and chin. He peered into Melody's expectant eyes. Her head tilted just like a cocker spaniel puppy's, the kind you bring home from the pound and then discover it has distemper.

"No," he said.

Melody bit on her lip and pulled her arms tight over her head, like Kathy did when Kit chased the calf at the airport, a universal gesture by the young for warding off evil. "But . . . but I'm sure I have some more work to do. Don't we all? But the idea . . . the plot . . . it's workable, wouldn't you say?"

"Nope. Frankly, Melody, I want to be real honest. I just don't think it's publishable."

Tony felt Price's hand jab at the small of his back as Melody's dark brown eyes filled with tears.

4

As the consequences of the Medicine Creek Treaty of 1854 became obvious to the various Native American tribes in the southern Puget Sound region, many protested the injustices. The discovery of gold in the territory brought hordes of argonauts. Tension, hostilities and violence increased between the two cultures. Trying to keep the peace, Governor Isaac I. Stevens converted Fox Island into a temporary Indian reservation. Within a few years, however, the tribes were allowed to return to their homelands in the Nisqually and Puyallup Valleys. Indian artifacts are still occasionally discovered on the Island.

As, periodically, are native Fox Islanders.

Tony sat in the big white Oldsmobile and scanned his notes, scribbled on a yellow legal pad. Both windows were rolled down and a cool, but not cold, breeze rolled through the car off the Narrows. He glanced up and stared at the crystal clear sky. Mount

Rainier hovered behind the skyline of Tacoma across the water. Its immense size made it seem like God himself looking down from the heavens.

Everything is so small in comparison. That mountain's huge. It's close. And yet many days man's pollution makes it seem remote, removed. Maybe it does symbolize you, Lord. Always close. Always mighty. But a world of blinded people just can't see.

He cleared his throat. "Now, what do I know about good old Harvey Peterson?"

His eyes again reviewed each line on the notepad.

Born, Fox Island, Washington, 1934. Graduated from high school in Tacoma in 1951. Served two years in Korea. University of Washington degree in engineering, 1959. Worked for Boeing, 1960 to 1990. Retired to pursue political causes. Island's leading reactionary.

He was against building the bridge, building the acoustic range, and closing the school. Ran for Pierce County Commissioner four times. Never received more than 269 votes. Wrote a book in 1992. Never married.

Tony tugged on his black felt cowboy hat, rolled up the windows and took one last look at Mount Rainier.

"Well . . . here goes."

The big poster in Harvey Peterson's front window read "Insured by Smith & Wesson: Policy 357." A crudely painted sign in the yard boasted "Book Store In Garage." Tony glanced in that direction but saw a "Closed" sign in the window. He hiked up the concrete and rock steps and rang the doorbell.

Peterson came to the door dressed in faded camouflage fatigues and worn combat boots. He stood a few inches shorter than Tony. He was stocky, but with no flab.

"Come in, Shadowbrook. Been lookin' forward to meetin' ya!"

The bachelor's large living room was neat and orderly. The variegated leaf pattern in the rug coordinated with the upholstered furniture. Fish decor hung from the walls and adorned throw pillows.

"Pull off your hat and sit a spell. Tony, I got to tell you that scene when Houston was reloadin' those .44-.40 shells as he was ridin' to Fort Laramie with the entire Cheyenne nation on his tail, that was almost as tense as being there. Keep up the good work."

"So you like the River Breaks series?"

"It's your best yet. In fact, nobody describes the guns and gunfights of the Old West like Tony Shadowbrook. That's a fact. Anyone who's got an ounce of brains knows that. Now, can I get you a Coke? I'd offer you a beer, but I don't drink."

"Coke is fine."

While Peterson stepped to the kitchen Tony glanced at rows and rows of bookshelves. He browsed the titles. *The Butane Lighter Hand Grenade. Home-Built Claymore Mines. Survival Poaching.*

"You find any good books?" Harvey asked as he came back into the room carrying two cans of Coke.

"Pretty rough stuff here, Harvey."

"That's my research. Mostly published by big companies who are interested only in making money. Most of it is useless. We might as well sit down over here." He motioned Tony toward a leather chair. "Sure do appreciate you comin'. Hope the little woman didn't get offended when I told her I didn't do interviews with women."

"She was delighted to send me."

"Shadowbrook, I'll tell you what's wrong with women interviewers. They just don't know the right questions to ask. I had a gal sit right there from the *Times* and ask me, 'Why do you always look angry?' Can you imagine that? Why do I look angry? Who gives a squat how I look? Then she went back and wrote an article about how I was advocating the overthrow of the U.S. government. I advocate the recapture of the U.S. government by democratic means. It belonged to the people and it's been stolen by politicians and bureaucrats. Anyway, that's not why you came. Go ahead, ask your questions."

"I'm interested in your theory about a Japanese invasion of Fox Island during World War II."

"Theory? The Japs were here. That's no theory. I saw them with my own eyes. I was only about eight at the time."

"What exactly did you see?"

"I was up island about a mile from here trying to hunt coons."

"You were doing what?"

"Huntin' raccoons. Me and Pee Wee Mack used to hunt about every night. I had a 06 Winchester .22, and Pee Wee had a miner's lamp he'd borrowed from his grandpa. We set off to be the big hunters. Only had one bullet that night, so we were determined not to waste it. Well, down there just where they claim a F-94 crashed in '53, we spotted some men snoopin' around in the woods. Pee Wee blew out the lamp, and we crawled on our bellies until we were close enough to see. They were Japs, all right. We counted two dozen of them."

"What were they doing?"

"Either they were lost, and thought they were on a different island, or they were practicin' night maneuvers. We just lay there in the weeds and watched them. We were close enough to see the Japanese army insignia on their uniforms when the moon reflected right."

"They did this all night?"

"Nope. After about an hour, they hiked down to Big Rock and got in a rubber raft. Then they rowed out into Carr Inlet, and as they went we saw a submarine surface. It was a Jap sub . . . even at night I could tell that. And that's the last I saw of them.

"Me and Pee Wee stood guard at Big Rock with our one bullet the rest of the night. Nothin' happened, except we got whipped the next mornin' by our folks. Never read one word of it in the paper. Not one word."

"And you never heard anything more about a Japanese invasion of the Northwest?"

"Not a word. Even though me and Pee Wee searched the ground and discovered several Japanese items. In fact, for years I just figured me and Pee Wee were the only two who knew about it. But when I got back from Korea, there was all this talk about an accidental jet crash. It wasn't any accident."

"What do you mean?"

"They crashed that sucker on purpose in order to bring in a hundred people and comb the ground. That would erase any trace of the Japanese."

"Seems to me, Harvey, a couple dozen Japanese troops on Fox Island for a few hours one night wouldn't leave enough impact on the place to have anything left to spot ten years later."

"Tony, I like your way of thinking. See, that's the kind of question a woman never seems to ask. I'll bet you know the answer to that question."

"I'd like to hear yours first."

"Well, what if . . . just what if . . . that Japanese patrol's purpose was to cache some weapons or supplies for a land invasion that was in the works?"

"Land invasion?"

"Sure, what if the battle of Midway had gone the other way? There wouldn't have been anyone in the Pacific to stop them. A hard hit to the American mainland might have caused the American people to want a peaceful settlement in the Pacific. Maybe they cached supplies all up and down the coast . . . who knows? I met a man in Oregon one time that saw over five hundred Japs land on the beach just below Seaside."

"But since there was no invasion, and since we did win the war, why do you think the government still wanted to cover this up?"

"I figure that during the early fifties everyone was so paranoid about a Soviet war that some of them must have figured the public would panic if they were told the truth about how close we came to an invasion."

"How about now? It's fifty years later. The Cold War has eased. Why would they hide things now?"

"Because the government is riddled with cover-ups. If they admit this, it might open up a can of worms about other incidents. They surely don't want you to know the real reason General Patton got killed, or how many Communist missiles were positioned in Mexico, or the Soviets' chemical warfare, or the space program that backfired and blasted a hole in the ozone layer, or the United Nations' secret plan for dividing up America after it falls under the control of a One World Government. And you can quote me on those, if you want."

"If you don't mind, just for the sake of my book project, I think I'll stick to just talking about Fox Island. I'll leave these other themes for you to develop in your own writings."

112

"Right on, partner. Now, let me show you around the bookstore, and then I'll drive you down to where we saw the Japs. How much time do you have?"

"I've got to meet my wife at noon."

"Well, that's not much time but we'll hustle. I'll get the Jeep. Meet you out front."

Tony walked to the front door and slipped it closed behind him.

Where does a guy like Peterson get all these ideas? He should write fiction. I'm not sure I can use any of this, but there's usually a kernel of truth buried under the manure. Lord, I'd sure like to know what it is and whether it's worth digging to find it.

After thirty minutes of rapid-fire shouting from Harvey above the roar of the engine, and the constant jarring of the Jeep careening off potholes and boulders, Tony was ready for the smooth, quiet ride of the Oldsmobile. When he arrived home, Price and Melody were relaxing at the table in front of bright yellow linen napkins and whole wheat tuna sandwiches.

"How'd your interview go?" Price asked.

"Interesting. How about yours?"

"So-so."

"Well, give me the scoop. What did you learn about Fox Island's notorious Longhouse?"

"Anita Schaff worked there for two years and never once saw anyone she thought was a mobster stay there. But she wasn't sure what a mobster looked like. There were a number of working girls who came over for R and R."

"That's something I never thought of before," Melody pondered. "What does a woman who works in a brothel do for vacation? Have you ever thought about that?"

Tony loaded a plate with a sandwich and chips. "Was Anita Schaff working there at the time of the Tacoma gangland massacre?"

"No, that was before her time, but she did say there were always rumors of such things. There was also a rumor that the longshoreman's union officials held some high-level discussions at the place. But there doesn't seem to be any confirming evidence."

"So what do we end up with?" Tony pressed.

"Some very colorful rumors." Price circled the table refilling each glass of ice tea. "That ought to make your fiction-writing brain buzz. How about Mr. I-Don't-Do-Interviews-With-Women Peterson? What did you learn there?"

"He's quite a character."

"He's a fixture on the Island," Melody

added, "but sometimes he can be an embarrassment. Did he talk about what he thinks of environmentalists?"

Tony shook his head. "We didn't get to that subject, but I can imagine."

He spent a good twenty minutes filling them in on Harvey Peterson's theories while munching an entire bag of red jalapeño corn chips.

Price cleared the table as Melody used the phone in the hall.

"So, what, if anything, can we use from good old Harvey?" Price quizzed.

"I'd like to get some other opinions first. So far as I can tell, Harvey is the only one who believes his story. I was right about this Chainsaw Militia thing. Harvey's the only member."

"What about that boyhood friend, Pee Wee? Is he still around? He could confirm that wartime story."

"Nope. Harvey said Pee Wee moved to Alaska and drowned soon after that big event."

"So, do we just forget Harvey?"

"Probably. But I think I'll check around. Wade Miller's father was a career man in the navy and stationed at Farragut during the war."

"Farragut?"

"In Idaho. He knows submarines. I think I'll talk to him."

"What does Idaho have to do with submarines? Last I looked it wasn't close to an ocean."

"They had a huge submarine training base on Pend Oreille Lake. They were afraid to set it up on the West Coast. Figured the Japanese might try to bomb it or something."

"Now, that sounds a little like Harvey Peterson."

"That's my premise. Behind every crackpot theory is a . . ."

"Crackpot?" She flashed a dimpled smile.

". . . is a nugget of truth. Perhaps totally misunderstood or distorted . . . but it's there. Anyway, I'll check it out."

"It's all set," Melody called out from the hall. "Mom's expecting us this afternoon."

Price scooted toward the bedroom to comb her hair, while Melody ran up to her loft for her purse. Tony wandered to the front-room window. He stared out at the Sound and sipped Chuckwagon Blend Cowboy coffee from his blue tin enamel cup. White foam ruffled the inlet waters. The apple tree branches swayed in the stiff wind.

"Well, Tony," Price greeted him as she strolled back into the room. "What are you contemplating? A new fictional series on how the U.S. was almost invaded during the war? Or a tome on what soiled doves do on their days off?"

"Neither. I was contemplating a nap on that chaise lounge."

"You're showing your age, Shadowbrook."

He detected a feisty sparkle in her blue eyes. "And you aren't. Come on, doctor, our research assistant is waiting."

After they crossed the bridge it took them twenty-five minutes to reach Barbara Mason's home, just north of Gig Harbor. The stucco house looked as though it had been built in the 1940s . . . clear glass blocks wrapped around the southwest corner, a porthole window adorned each side of the front door. Overgrown rosebushes and junipers and ivy and ferns hadn't been pruned in years.

"Remember, Mom's either really happy or really depressed. There's never any in between," Melody cautioned.

"How long has she been that way?" Price asked.

"Ever since my father left."

"When was that?"

"1979."

"Do your mother and your grandmother get along very well?"

"Horrible. It's like they blame each other for their own misery. I pray for them every night."

Barbara Mason had Melody's dark hair, only blacker, as though it had been sponged with shoe polish, and shorter, hanging limply to the sagging shoulders. Heavy makeup emphasized the puffiness around the tired, worn eyes.

"You must be the writers." She held out both her hands to them. She wore large rings on every fleshy finger.

Price took on her English professor manners. "Thanks for giving us some time, Mrs. Mason."

"Melody's told me all about you." She turned to Tony. "I hear you think Melody's book stinks."

"Mother!"

"Your daughter has great enthusiasm for writing. I'm sure she'll find her true niche someday. Frankly, a stream of consciousness series of short stories about handicapped people in dying American vocations would be difficult for any writer to pull off."

"Melody has been a great help to us on

our book, Mrs. Mason," Price inserted.

"Call me Barbara. Come in, come in. Excuse the mess. I, eh . . . just can't seem to find a good steady housekeeper these days. Can I get you something to drink?"

"Mother!"

"Lemonade, would you like some lemonade?"

"That would be nice," Price said.

"Melody, honey, go out there and make us some lemonade. I'm sure there's some concentrate in the freezer."

"Oh, you don't need to do that," Price insisted.

"Nonsense, it will only take her a few minutes. Do you like tropical fish?"

Tony trailed behind the ladies as they entered a large dining room. Here and there pieces of gold-and-white striped wallpaper peeled away to reveal an undercoating of green paint. A mahogany Duncan Phyfe table was piled with stacks of unopened mail and catalogues.

"So, you have fish?" he asked.

"Let me show you my babies," Barbara Mason cooed as she pulled open a tattered Hawaiian print curtain doorway into the living room.

A six-foot-tall tank filled with milky water, a filter, pump, lights, thermostat and

dozens of darting shapes and colors dominated one wall. A dusty bookcase filled the
other. For the next hour Tony and Price
sipped lukewarm lemonade and learned the
habits of silver-and-black angelfish, emerald
Emperors, long-snouted yellow butterflies,
Siamese fighting fish and kissing gourami.

The drapes were drawn. The only light in
the room shone from the aquarium and one
brass floor lamp with a three-way bulb
turned to the first setting.

"Tell me, Mrs. Mason," Tony said
during a brief lull, "what was it like growing
up on Fox Island in the forties and early fifties, before the bridge was built?"

And for the next hour, she told them.

Price was relieved to see that Tony was
also taking notes because her mind kept
wandering.

*It's like Barbara just stopped living. Her
body trudges along, but there's no life. No purpose. No joy. No goals. Lord, I just want to
shake her and scream 'Wake up!' But that's
your job, isn't it? I don't know what my job is,
but I don't think I've seen many women more
miserable.*

By the time they left, Melody had washed
and dried the dishes, mopped the kitchen
floor, vacuumed every room but the living
room, taken out the trash and done a load of

laundry. It was only when they reached the supermarket parking lot on their way home that Melody managed to say, "You'll have to forgive my mom. She didn't used to be so sloppy. She's had a tough life."

"You don't need to apologize," Price quickly assured her.

"No, really. My mom's had lots of disappointments. Grandpa was lost at sea when she was only eight."

"I think I read about that," Tony mentioned.

"Well, my mom once said that Grandpa sat her down the night before he disappeared. He told her he was going away and wouldn't see her again, but that someday maybe she would understand."

"You mean he committed suicide?"

"Or just left. Grandma Jessie always insisted that he was lost at sea. I confronted her with Mom's account one time, but she claimed it was a lie. Mom figured the war must have changed Grandpa, because after he came back he and Grandma argued a lot."

"And your grandmother never remarried?"

"No. She taught school for a while. After she retired she would just sit out on the deck and read. Great-grandfather left a good inheritance. Anyway, she read and read and read. That's why there are so many boxes of books piled in the garage. I guess that's why I grew up wanting to be a writer. I spent a lot of time over there. In fact, Mom and I lived with Grandma Jessie for five years."

Price led the trio into the supermarket and shoved a grocery cart ahead of her as they swung over toward the vegetables. "So your mother felt deserted by her father?"

"Yeah, well, dear old Dad didn't help much either. Did I ever tell you about him?"

"You mentioned you hadn't seen him in years."

"When I was thirteen, he packed a suitcase and shoved off to Alaska with papers to recover great-grandfather's gold mine."

"What happened?" Price asked.

"We haven't seen him since. Oh, I get a package every once in a while from him, but it's always from a different address, and he never writes back when I send him a letter."

"Did your mother divorce him for desertion?"

"Nope."

"So she drinks a little too much?" Tony inserted.

"Yeah . . . Would you believe she reads her Bible and drinks? Weird combination, huh? She thinks that God's punishing her for something. Do you think God does things like that?"

Tony took over pushing the cart as Price piled in fruits and vegetables. "Well, there are certainly consequences for our actions, the law of cause and effect, but I don't think God means us to suffer continual physical and mental anguish."

"I wish you'd tell my mom that. I wish someone would sit her down and confront her, face-to-face."

As they crossed the slightly humped bridge back to the Island, they admired the stretch of shoreline view. Pines and firs ran to the water's edge, down and around landscaped houses and docks. A few fishing boats trolled the still surface.

Melody let out a deep sigh. "I'm really sorry for crying and making a big scene last night after what you said about my book."

Tony peered into Melody's round brown eyes through the rearview mirror.

"Price let me have it for my complete lack of tact. I'm afraid I didn't do a good job of expressing myself. I should have said . . ."

"No, really, it's all right. This morning I woke up and realized I really didn't like that book myself. It bores me to tears. It's just that . . . I want to be a writer so bad. And it's, sort of, the only story idea I ever had. I guess I'm afraid to give it up. I wouldn't know what else to write."

Tony tapped Price on the leg as if to say, "There's your cue."

"Melody, what was the first week's lesson in Advanced Creative Writing?" she began.

"Let me think. It's been a while. Something about 'write about things you know . . . people you know.' "

"Write within your world. Now, where is your world?"

"Fox Island?"

"Bingo!" Price exclaimed. "Why not write a short story about your grandmother and grandfather . . . ?"

"Or your mom and your dad and how you felt when he took off to Alaska?" Tony urged.

"Or write about the mysterious Mr. Bennington who suddenly shows up after fifty years looking for Jill Davenport."

"Oh, wow, sure! I was thinking about him. What if he jilted Auntie Jill for a girl from the Ziegfeld Follies whose family owned property in Texas? But after making millions in the oil business, he's left a widower and remembers his one true love. So he hurries out to Fox Island, only to find out she died soon after he left her!"

"Now, that's a start," Price urged. "Why

not write that scenario? It would make a good basis for a short story."

"Or even a book," Tony added. Now Price poked him. "Just keep asking 'what if?' "

"What do you mean?"

"What if Bennington and your Auntie Jill had purchased a lot together to one day build a house, and he's kept the property in her name all these years, and now it's worth millions to a real estate developer?"

"Oh, wow!" Melody said.

"Or what if the reason they split up was because he had run across your Grandma Jessie and her husband, thought it was Jill, and figured she was two-timing him."

"And by the time he figured it out, he couldn't find her. Yes!" Melody rejoiced. "I need a pencil to write this down. This could be a great story."

"Go for it," Tony said. "Enthusiasm for the story is half the battle of writing."

"I think I will," Melody bubbled. "I can hardly wait to get to my computer."

Tony spent most of the week digging through boxes of papers, letters and diaries stacked in the back room of the Fox Island Historical Museum. Price interviewed several more longtime residents of the

Island, including two former ferryboat captains. Neither saw much of Melody, who seemed content, secluded in her loft apartment.

With cups of hot chocolate and French roast coffee in their hands, Tony and Price converged on the deck on a sunny-skied Monday morning.

"It's been a month, babe. Do you miss Scottsdale?" Tony asked.

"I miss the girls. I guess I'm not ready for them to be on their own."

Tony sipped his brew from a dark blue porcelain mug with the word Seattle inscribed in gold. "Kathy calls just about every day. I think we're still needed."

"I hope Kit calls today. I'd like to find out how she got along working with those kids in Mexico last week."

Tony laughed. "She probably taught them how to tune up a V-8. I really figured she'd have outgrown that by now. A daughter with grease under her fingernails and a twin with designer nails. It must drive the behaviorists wild. Same identical environment, totally different personalities."

"The boys aren't exactly the same either," Price reminded him.

"Have you talked to our eldest recently?

I caught Josh at home last Thursday, but I missed Mark."

"We should call him tonight after he gets off work."

His coffee cold, Tony stepped back into the house for a refill just as the phone rang. Price trailed along behind.

"Shadowbrook here."

"Tony, hang on to your cowboy hat, dude. Have I got great news for you."

"Who is this?"

"This is Terry . . . Terry Davidian."

"Is it August yet?"

"Wait 'til you hear what happened last night. I was at this party in Malibu, one of the beach blasts everyone attends. So I'm talking to David Irving Silvers . . . THE David Irving Silvers . . . and he mentions that the studio is taking a look at a couple of possibilities for doing a western. But he said all the material he's seen is so stilted to political correctness that it's lost its zip and fun, and I say, 'Have I got a story for you.' "

Do people actually talk this way in real life?

"What's the bottom line here, Davidian?"

"Wait, wait. I mentioned *Shotgun Creek*, and Silvers said he was familiar with your work and would take a look at the story."

"He did?"

"He even asked if you were a member of the Screenwriter's Guild. You are, aren't you?"

"No."

"No problem. I can take care of that. What he did want to know was if you had representation, so naturally I made it sound like we were working together. Now, here's the thing. I've got an appointment with Silvers, but I can't go in there without being an authorized agent. So, what do you want me to do? Is that 15% thing a deal?"

"Ten percent, and you don't get a penny until I have money in hand."

"But, Tony, baby, I can't work all day and not get paid until way down the road."

"I do. Every day of my life."

"Listen, make it 15% and we'll go from there."

Tony glanced over at Price. She mouthed the words, *"Get it in writing."* "Make it 10%. When I get paid, you get paid."

"You're a tough man, Shadowbrook. But we've got a deal. I'll call you after I talk to Silvers."

"No, we don't have a deal. I want to see the agreement in writing first."

"What?"

"I want a written contract with all the terms and limitations spelled out."

"But, Tony, this is hot. I need to. . . ."

"No contract, no representation."

"OK, OK. Give me your fax number and I'll get you something to review by noon."

"Davidian, I want a contract in the mail. FedEx it if you want. I want the real thing. Then I'll send it to my publisher and my book agent. After the lawyers have looked it over and we settle with them, then I'll sign it."

"You've got to be kidding. We don't have time for that now. Let me get this in the saddle with Silvers, then we can plow through the paperwork."

"I don't do business that way, Davidian. Send me up the papers and I'll see they get shipped to New York."

"Tony, Tony, Tony. You can't make it down here unless you play by the rules. The rules of Hollywood."

"Davidian, I play by a lot higher rules than the rules of Hollywood. I'll look for the contract in the mail."

"Tony, you're kissing off hundreds of thousands. Maybe millions here. You think it over and I'll call back this afternoon."

"Don't bother."

"Wait . . . listen . . ."

"Bye, Davidian." Tony hung up the phone and glanced over at Price.

"You did good, Shadowbrook." Price flashed dimples on both sides of her well-tanned face; the silver earrings reflected the afternoon sun.

"You don't mind if I pass up millions?"

"Potential millions," she corrected. "We do all right the way it is."

"I thought you wanted me to hook up with Davidian?"

"Not if you have to cut corners."

"The whole deal keeps sounding a little thin. You know what I mean?"

"Maybe you should let Liz and the lawyers at Atlantic-Hampton handle it."

"That's my feeling exactly."

Melody Mason burst through the front door, swinging her brown leather purse with one hand and her car keys with the other. Her gold dangle earrings hung almost to the strap of her dark green tank top.

"Hi, guys. Can you get along without me the rest of today?"

"We'll manage," Tony piped back.

"I've got to go talk to a psychologist at the convalescent home. She called to say Grandma Jessie's been in a severe depression for several days. She wants to talk to the family about it. Mother has agreed to go with me, but I figure it will be a long session."

"Be sure and give us a report," Price urged. "We'll be praying for you."

"Yeah, thanks. I'll need it."

They both stared out the glass panels of the front door until Melody's car chugged up the steep driveway to the road.

"I hope we haven't been the cause of Melody's grandmother's setback," Tony sighed.

"She's never made peace with her past."

"Did you ever notice how this happens every summer?"

Price glanced in the hall mirror, admiring the gold filigreed frame as she brushed her hair back from her face. She remembered she'd forgotten to put on perfume. "What happens?"

"We try to slip unobtrusively into some little out-of-the-way spot for a summer of research and writing, then we get tied up in the lives of the people there."

"Maybe that's part of the Lord's plan for us," she mused. "How do you think I would look with earrings like Melody's?"

"You'd look gorgeous."

"You say that about everything I wear."

"It's true. I married a beautiful woman."

"And I married a man with poor eyesight."

"Are we going to continue this ridiculous conversation or get to work?"

"You've got a book to write."

"I've got a book to write every day of my life."

"Shadowbrook, are you bragging or complaining?"

"Did I ever tell you that your eyes sparkle when you go authoritarian?"

"I know, I'm gorgeous." Price raised her eyebrows in the semblance of a young Lauren Bacall imitation, then strutted back to her desk.

Midafternoon Price heard a shout from the deck. She looked out in time to see Tony clutching his head with both hands.

"What's wrong?" she called out.

"I can't believe this!" he bellowed.

"Are you all right?"

"No, I'm not all right! This laptop just ate chapter four."

"Oh, good. I mean, how terrible. How much did you lose?"

"The whole chapter! Why in the world did we ever start using computers, anyway? I don't have time for this!"

"Did you check your backup files?"

"I can't find any backup files!"

"Maybe there was a power surge."

"Power surge? I'd like to power surge Bill Gates, that's what I'd like to do!"

"Hey, here's chapter four on a backup disk."

"Oh, sure," Tony groaned, "but I've lost the last six hours of editing. This can't be happening to me. I don't need this!"

"Where's the manual?"

"In Scottsdale."

Price scooted a metal chair close to him. "Let me look at it."

While Tony prowled back and forth on the deck, Price punched the keys of the laptop.

"There it is," she shouted.

He leaned over her shoulder. "You got it back?"

"Look . . . on this auxiliary file . . . isn't that the backup document?"

"What's it doing over there?"

"Nothing. I can't bring it up."

"What?"

"I've got it listed, but it won't come up on screen. Maybe you can print it out."

"Great . . . that's just great! Then I'll have to punch it all back in again."

"Why don't you call tech support?"

"Oh, sure, and get stuck on hold for four hours?"

"What choices do you have?"

"Yo, Dudes! Can you lead me to Melody?"

Tony and Price spun around.

A huge man with shaggy full, tightly curling black beard, wild flying hair and a black leather jacket flung across one shoulder bulged through the sliding glass door. "I'm just lookin' for my woman. Does my Melody Tunes still shack up here?"

"You mean Melody Mason?" Price inquired, eyes on the man's massive arms.

"Yeah, I call her Melody Tunes. Where is she?"

"We're renting her house for the season."

"Now, ain't that a bummer? Where did that little spitfire move to?"

"Why don't you leave your name and number, and we'll have her call you when she gets back," Tony offered.

"So, she does live here?"

"In the garage apartment, but she's gone for the day."

"That's cool. I'll just wait."

The man lumbered across the living room and plunged down on the sofa. "You got anything to eat?"

Price and Tony looked at each other.

"Look, mister," Tony began.

"Everyone calls me Stud."

"I don't. If you want to wait for Melody,

that's up to you. But she might be gone quite a while. Now, we've got work to do, so you aren't waiting for her in our living room. You can park yourself out on the road by the driveway, or you can give us your phone number and I'll have her call you."

His burly face cowered like a wounded dog as he pulled himself off the couch. "Talk about lacking the gift of hospitality!" He rolled to his full six-foot-six frame and lumbered toward Tony, who had stepped back out on the deck. Tony backed against the deck railing.

The man stopped in midstride. "I think I'll cruise around the Island. Is Melody Tunes still driving that green VW bus?"

"Eh, yes."

"If I miss her, tell her I was looking for her." He glanced down at the laptop. "Looks like your Toshiba Turbo 75 is locked up."

"Well . . . yes."

He held down two buttons with his left hand and punched two others with his right. "Hey, there you go. Chapter four."

Price and Tony gawked in amazement. "How did you do that?"

"Fifteen years with Microsoft taught me a little bit. Retired on my thirty-fifth birthday.

Shoot, how much money does any one human need?"

Price studied the screen. "What did you do?"

"Nothin' to it. Here, I'll show you." He took Price's left hand in his and placed her fingers on the keyboard. Then he reached around her shoulder with his right hand and placed those on the laptop, still holding both hands. He caged her like a helpless puppy in one smooth movement.

"You can show me," Tony demanded, yanking the man's hands away from Price. "It's my computer. I really ought to be the one who learns."

"My, he's a bit insecure, isn't he?" the big man roared. "That's what you get for marrying such a foxy younger woman." He backed away from Price, gave her a wink, led Tony through the steps, then turned back into the house.

"You're leaving now?" Tony asked.

"Yep, just need to pick up my helmet. Tell Melody Tunes I'll catch her later. Say, did she ever tell you about the time we took my Harley to Alaska?"

"Eh, no, she didn't."

"Well, come to think about it, maybe it wasn't her. Don't tell her I said that."

"We won't," Tony assured him. As soon

as the man was safely out in the carport, he added, "Thanks for the computer help."

"Is Captain Renfold still down at the Acoustic Lab?"

"We haven't met anyone down there yet."

"Think I'll go down and swap lies with the navy. I built 'em a system once and they never used it. It didn't employ enough of their appropriations, I figured."

The roar from the motorcycle deafened the air. Tony and Price both stared at each other until the noise subsided.

"Did some biker just appear at our house and fix my computer?" Tony asked.

"How in the world did we not hear him drive up?"

"Next summer, we definitely need a house with more privacy," Tony insisted.

"I don't know. If we get too remote, who will fix your computer?" Price's blue eyes danced, a teasing, well-aimed dance, a dance learned through nearly thirty years of learning each other's rhythms.

Sunset splashed with washed orange and bright pink from the Olympics to McNeil Island when Tony lugged the research papers and computer into the house. Price leaned over the sink, peeling crisp, small cucumbers. "You going to call our oldest child tonight?"

"Yeah, I'll ask him to drive down next weekend and help Kit find a home for that calf. Kathy said the flowerbed's about eaten up and the backyard's drawing horseflies."

Price lowered her voice. "I think I hear Melody. Shall I invite her in for supper?"

"Depends. Is she alone, or is Goliath with her?"

"She's alone."

"Sure, invite her. I'll call Mark from the bedroom."

Tony returned to find Price and Melody huddled at the kitchen counter. Their faces glowed like sisters sharing a secret.

"I hear you met Kenny," Melody blurted out.

"Who?"

"The Stud? That's Kenny Mallard."

"So you do know him?"

"He's a jerk. He's only got one thing on his mind."

Tony raised an eyebrow. "Oh?"

"Yeah, computers. What a bore."

"He helped me out," Tony admitted.

"How were Mark and Amanda?" Price inquired.

"The internship's going good, but

Amanda was a little sick last week. She had to miss work and take some IV fluids. Everything's OK now. Mark said they'd drive down Saturday and check on the girls."

"Good. We'd better let Kathy know her brother's coming."

Tony piled a clear glass dinner plate high with shrimp salad and roquefort dressing and sat down next to Price. "How's your grandmother, Melody?"

"Still out in La-La Land. See, it all started the other day when I told her about this Bennington guy stopping by to look for Auntie Jill."

"I didn't know you told her about that. Did she get angry, like he said she would?"

"No, she just sort of froze up. She didn't want to talk about it. She mumbled something about it being 'too late now,' and has hardly said a word since. The psychologist wanted to know all about Bennington. She thinks it might be helpful for Grandma Jessie to face him."

"We're about a week late for that. I'm sure he's back home in Chestertown, Maryland, by now."

"Is that where he lives?"

"That's what he said."

"Maybe we could call him up?" Melody suggested.

"We?"

"I mean, maybe I could call him. Perhaps he'll be out this way again. I sure hate seeing Grandma Jessie the way she is now."

Price spread poppy-seed dressing on her salad and buttered a croissant, then sliced it in half and handed it to Melody. "I don't think it would hurt to call. The worst that can happen is you get some more material for your story."

"Oh, man, this new story is so cool. You two are really going to love this one. No fooling. It will knock your socks off. Wait until you read the opening line. But I'm not going to tell you any more. It's a surprise."

Tony glanced at Price and rolled his eyes.

5

In the late nineteenth century, the isolation of Fox Island forced the residents to live self-sufficiently. They cleared the land of evergreen trees and stumps that blanketed every knoll, plain and draw. This backbreaking task readied the soil for fruit trees, berry patches and vegetable gardens. To supplement the diet of salmon and clams dug at low tide, most every family raised chickens, milk cows or rabbits. Diversity was the key to survival.

It still is.

"It's way too cluttered, that's all," Tony insisted.

Price let the prescription computer glasses drop to her chest, held by the Navajo beaded strap around her neck. She rubbed her neck muscles and yawned. She had pulled her hair back into a large comb. Glancing around the room, she shrugged. "What's too cluttered?"

Tony eased beside her on the blue-flowered couch, then yanked out several throw pillows lodged in the small of his back. "Chapter five, of course. That's what

I've been reading."

"Do you mean parts of it, or the whole thing?" The soft wave of her hair emphasized her raised eyebrows.

"Well, in the first place, it's twenty-nine pages long. We need to cut it to twenty-five pages. Here, I've redlined some things I think we can delete."

Price pulled the pages out of his hand and flipped through them. "What is this?" She sat straight and tall on the full base of her authority as a seasoned university professor.

Tony Shadowbrook cradled his stocking feet into her lap. "You'll have to admit there is such a thing as too much detail. Didn't we talk that through last summer in Utah?"

Price squeezed out from under his legs and stood to gaze out the living room window. A lone sailboat gently bobbed in the waters in the distance. "I do remember a very heated discussion."

"And what was our conclusion? That we would jam in all the details, then thin it out a tad to make sure the material still retained its crispness."

Price leaned against the windowsill and tucked a hand under her chin. She brushed her lips and noticed they were chapped again. "I recall that it concluded in your buying me those cloisonné earrings and a dozen roses."

A grin broke across Tony's face, then receded as quickly as the tide. "Yeah, well, that's what I did in chapter five . . . I thinned it out a tad."

"A tad? In places you clear-cut it. If it were a forest, it would be an environmental disaster."

"But it's right at twenty-five pages, and I believe it reads pretty good."

She spread the twenty-five double-spaced typed pages in a fan on his legs, still sprawled full length on the couch. "Why was all the 'thinning' done on the part I wrote?"

"That's not true. I didn't even consider who wrote the original. If it needed to be chopped, I chopped it."

"I find it rather amazing that it's always my additions that need to be deleted."

"I don't know what you're talking about. Look . . . look . . . right here on page 123. See? I was describing the difference between loganberries, blackberries and boy-senberries. But it's not needed, so out it went."

"Show me one other place."

"What?"

"Where's one other place in the chapter

where you removed your own work?"

"Oh, well . . . I'm sure . . . it's just a matter of . . ." Tony shuffled through the pages. "Here! How about here? 'The pink cotton candy newborn clouds hung like wash on the baby blue sky.' I took that out too."

"That was my line."

"It was?"

"Yes."

"Oh, well . . . I'm sure there's more . . . it's just . . . maybe over. . . ." Tony sorted through the chapter, then began again.

"Good morning, Shadowbrooks. I'm headed for Mom's to make some phone calls. Need anything from the store?" Melody Mason swung into the room, her teeth shining whiter than ever.

"Not really, thanks," Price said as she dropped into the navy side chair. She ran her finger over the glass ginger jar front of the lamp stuffed with shells and starfish. She traced the scalloped shells motif on the footed resin base.

I told him four years ago he wasn't the kind to cowrite anything. I knew this would happen again. And we've got five more summers of this? We can't even fight in peace. Next year, no kids. No house-guests. No interruptions. Just the two of us, slugging it out.

"I'm going after Lloyd Bennington today.

I'll try the Airport Hilton and see if I can get his phone number from them. I've got a friend who works at the desk part-time. What was the name of that eastern town again, Mr. S.? I want to make sure I get as much of this story as I can."

Tony kept flipping through the pages and muttering to himself.

"What's he doing?" Melody whispered as she stepped a little closer.

"He's struggling with whether to allow someone else to have input into this book project or not," Price said.

"That is not true and you know it!" Tony snapped.

"Whoops, I'm out of here. The resolution of creative differences scene is a little too intense for me."

"I just hit on a touchy nerve," Tony tried to explain.

"Touchy?" Price scowled.

"It's a minor thing."

She stood and braced both hands on her hips. "Minor? An entire chapter?"

"Bye, you all. Have a nice fight." Melody scampered out the front door.

"We're not fighting!" Tony yelled after her.

"I'm going for a walk along the shoreline," Price announced.

"That sounds like a wonderful idea. I'll get my shoes and we can. . . ."

"Alone."

Within minutes Price had pulled on her cardigan sweater, grabbed a tape and her Walkman, and departed. Tony watched her from the window as she marched down the sidewalk past a dwarf apple tree, past the neighbor boy and his dog, past the boat shed. He watched until she disappeared around the point of the shoreline. Then he turned back and glanced at chapter five lying on the table.

Lord, I don't know if this gets tougher, or easier, every year. I want this to work. Maybe she's right. Maybe I just don't know how to work with someone else. But I hear the story in my head. I see it with my eyes. Any other account feels like a distortion, like I've lied to the readers.

Help me to hear her story.

And see her visions.

Price stretched out in her jade two-piece swimsuit on the chaise lounge, soaking in the afternoon sun. Tony, dripping with sweat from a run, waved a bright purple sheet of paper in her face.

"Have you seen these?"

Price propped herself up on one elbow

and pushed her sunglasses down on her nose. "What is it?"

"They've posted flyers all over the Island. There's a big meeting scheduled at the Community Center tonight."

"What for?"

"Planning for the annual Island Fair. I guess the organizers have invited someone to bring in a petting zoo . . . sheep, dogs, pigs, cows, burros, goats and all that?"

"So?"

"Some of the islanders feel this is cruel imprisonment and exploitation of animals. They're threatening to picket and boycott the Fair if the animals are brought in."

"Conflict in paradise? Sounds like a book chapter. Maybe we should attend the meeting."

"I couldn't agree with you more."

"I'm glad we agree on something."

"Look," he huffed, "we aren't going to go through that again, are we?"

"No. Let's just ignore chapter five. Maybe no one will notice that it's missing," she snapped. Not a hint of dimple showed on either cheek. "I'll get it," she said when the phone rang.

Tony had dried off and was jotting down notes on a steno pad when she returned.

"That was Liz. She's got an autograph

signing party set up at a grand opening of a bookstore in Seattle."

"When?" Tony asked.

"Next week . . . on Friday."

"Next week? What kind of notice is that?"

"Michael Crichton canceled and left them scrambling."

"Great! I get to be one of the subs off the bench again."

"Not you . . . us."

"Us?"

"*Promontory* was just picked up by the Traveler's Book Club. Liz thinks this will be a great way to have a second launch of the book. She wants us both there to do a signing. Besides, we can announce we're working on *Fox Island*."

"What about *Shotgun Creek*?"

"She insisted on *Promontory*."

"Well, sure . . . that's fine. We don't have anything else, do we?"

"Not on my calendar."

"Will Liz work it with us?"

"She's lined up a publisher's rep to handle the chores."

"Well, as long as we don't sit around talking to ourselves most of the afternoon."

"It should be good traffic. It's a grand opening and all."

"Well, go ahead and call her back. We

haven't been to Seattle much since we came up here."

"I already told her we'd do it, but we might not be speaking to each other."

"What did she say?"

"She said, 'Doesn't this happen every summer?' "

"It's really not that big a deal. You didn't have to go telling everyone in New York."

"I didn't. I only told Liz."

"Same thing."

Price adjusted the straps on her suit. "I know what's eating you, Shadowbrook. You feel slighted to be called after the big boys cancel out, right?"

Tony gazed out at the Sound. Canada geese soared like an arrowhead toward a large sailboat. "Think I'll go for a walk along the shoreline."

"I thought you just went running."

"I did. I just want a little walk."

"Let me pull on some shorts and I'll join you," she added.

"Alone."

Just once, Lord. Just once I'd like to know what it feels like to be the first one called. On the top of the list. There's nothing flatter than a low-on-the-rung writer having a mediocre day.

By the time Tony returned, Price had prepared broiled lemon almond chicken, brown rice pilaf and fresh green beans from the neighbor's garden, and was watching CNN Headline News on the small kitchen television set.

She glanced up. He thought he could detect a slight dimple. "How was your walk?"

"Good. I . . . eh . . . look, you were sort of right. I guess every once in a while I get a glimpse of myself from a distance. And . . . I get a little tired of finishing second or third. 'If you ain't the lead dog, the scenery never changes,' does it?"

"Come on, number two dog, eat your chow."

This time the dimples were obvious.

"Honey, listen, I really . . ."

"Hey, you two! Good, you're not busy. Are you?"

Melody Mason burst through the front door, bounded up the stairs and strolled into the kitchen.

"We were about to eat supper."

"Oh, no thanks. I'm not hungry. I bought a pizza and ate half of it on the way home from Mom's. Do you want to hear something really weird?"

"It won't ruin our meal, will it?" Tony asked.

"Oh no. It's not gross or anything. It's about that guy, Bennington. You know what? There's no Lloyd Bennington in Chestertown, Maryland."

"Maybe he lives out in the country?" Tony suggested.

"I checked out all of Kent County. Then I checked out Queen Annes County. I even looked at the town of Chester."

Tony shrugged. "Maybe I remembered the name wrong."

"Well, I looked up things like Floyd Bennington and even Lloyd Pennington. No luck."

"It had to be the right name. You said it got a strong reaction out of your grandmother," Price remarked.

"What about the hotel? What did your friend at the Airport Hilton find out?"

"All she could tell me was that no man by the name of Lloyd Bennington stayed at the hotel for the past month."

"Did anyone from Maryland stay at the hotel on the day that Bennington was here?"

"She can look up an individual name, but that's all. The rest is confidential." Melody opened the cupboard and retrieved a glass bowl. "That rice looks good. Think I'll just have a little."

She slipped into the chair at the table

between Price and Tony. "This thing is getting really weird. Some guy pops in here, gets Grandma stirred up by the mention of his name, then disappears off the face of the globe. I feel like I've stepped into *The Twilight Zone*."

"I suppose he could have given you a fictitious town," Price suggested.

"But why?" Tony eyed Melody heaping spoons of rice and tossing beans on top.

"Nothing like leaving conflict and confusion wherever you go. Hey, did you two get those 'creative differences' settled? Wow, those earrings are really cool, Dr. S."

"Thanks. Tony bought them for me last summer. I think they're hand painted, don't you?"

"I think you're avoiding my other question. But, hey, that's none of my business."

"Speaking of fights," Tony broke in, "what do you know about this meeting at the Community Center tonight?"

"Is that tonight? Wow, I forgot and I've got to go. It looks like the hippies are up to it again."

"You don't really call them hippies anymore, do you?" Price asked.

"Well, that's one of the nicer terms. When I was real little they moved out here on the Island in swarms. They camped in the trees, broke into summer cabins, rented old barns and moved in two dozen people. Now, that was a zoo."

"I suppose the same thing happened all up and down the coast," Tony said as he bit into a piece of juicy, done-just-right chicken. "Plenty moved into Arizona about then, too. It reflected the era we were going through."

"Yeah, well, up here they started growing marijuana and who knows what else? They really stunk, bad. As soon as you walked into a room or business, you could tell if one was there. I bought my VW from some of 'em, and I had to take it to get completely reupholstered and recarpeted to get the smell out. Once, Shelli Teasdale and me cut through the trees west of 11th Avenue toward the Inlet, and this grimy guy with a hatchet chased us all the way to 9th. I thought he was going to kill us. The Teasdales moved to Steilacoom right after that."

"But that was the '70s. This is the '90s," Price cautioned.

"Some of them moved on, but lots of them moved in and stayed. Most of them are cool, really. I've got some good friends that used to be heavy into that stuff. At least they have steady jobs and take baths now.

But look at this petting zoo thing. It's a classic example of misguided energy. It's meant to help kids love and appreciate animals, right? They get to pet a calf or a piglet. As a result, maybe they'll actually consider animals to be more than the main ingredient in a Big Mac or a hot dog. That sounds good to me. So why are they boycotting the Island Fair?"

"We thought we'd find out for ourselves."

"You're not going to mention this in your book, are you?"

"Oh, we don't know. Might be a little something we could use."

Melody's usual bright smile faded. Not one of her teeth showed. "I certainly can't think of any reason you would even want to consider writing about this."

"Could be we'll find out how remote communities solve conflicts . . . or something like that."

"If Harvey Peterson is there, you'll find out about settling conflicts."

"Peterson? What's Harvey have to do with a petting zoo? He doesn't think it's part of a government cover-up, does he?"

"Harvey is active in everything that happens on the Island. He seems to thrive on being in the middle of every conflict. He's the one who sawed down that big pine tree and shoved it into the Sound with two of the tree huggers still chained to it."

"What happened?" Price quizzed.

"Oh, they let him off with just a fine."

"No, what happened to the two chained to the log?"

"The Coast Guard rescued them. Last I heard they moved to north-central Idaho."

"So, Harvey Peterson is sort of a counter-activist?"

"That's a mild way of putting it."

"Sounds like you have a few extremists on both sides. This meeting will beat staying home to watch TV," Tony remarked.

"You two never watch TV anyway," Melody added.

"I'd always rather read a good book," Price said.

"Speaking of good books, I stayed up to 2:00 A.M. rewriting my opening paragraph. If I show it to you, you've got to promise not to use it in one of your books."

Tony held up a hand. "You got it, kid."

"Listen." Melody stared down at her half-eaten plate of rice and beans. "I've got some rotten news. Grandma Jessie kind of laid down the law at me today. She said she wouldn't do any interviews . . . ever. It's really unreasonable, and I don't know what to do about it."

"I wish we could just meet her and let her know we're not trying to exploit her," Price mused.

"Do you think she might change her mind?" Tony prodded.

"It's like Grandma is afraid of something. She's been a recluse so long, she's built up a fear of talking to strangers. Besides, she's getting real forgetful and it embarrasses her."

"What do you mean?" Price asked.

"Like last spring when Kim went with me to see Grandma Jessie. Remember I told you Kim's into painting? Well, she was thrilled to be able to ask about some techniques that Grandma used on the 'Two Girl' paintings . . . and Grandma Jessie couldn't even remember how she did them. That sort of thing really depresses her."

"We certainly don't want to depress her, but we'd really love to have her talk about the old days on the Island," Price added. "A few quotes from Jessica Davenport would be invaluable."

"Maybe you and Melody could just peek in the door and say 'hello' or something," Tony suggested. "That wouldn't be too threatening, would it, Melody?"

"Maybe. I could at least tell what kind of mood she's in and perhaps introduce Dr.

Shadowbrook. I was hoping she wouldn't be this way, since I know you guys and all. Anyway, I'll keep working at it. That interview is my summer goal, even if it doesn't look too promising." Melody scooped her fork into the rice and leaned over the plate to engulf the whole bite.

"Do you want to ride down to the community meeting with us?" Tony offered.

"Sure, we can take my car if you want," Melody mumbled.

"Oh no," Tony laughed, "if we show up in a VW bus they'll expect us to carry a protest sign."

"Really? Do you think a VW bus still makes a political statement? I wonder if I should buy a different car? Oh, man, I just remembered that pizza is still out there. I'll see you later. Go ahead and have a quiet supper."

Melody was out the door when Tony shoved his chair away from the table. "She's never going to move into Kim's cabin, is she?"

"Not until we make her."

"It's like having another daughter."

"She's sort of halfway in between Kit and Kathy, don't you think?"

"I miss our girls," Tony mused. "They both have their quirks, but at least we're used to them."

"Why don't you call our quirky daughters? You haven't talked to them in a week."

Tony dialed the Scottsdale number. A male voice answered.

"This is Anthony Shadowbrook. With whom am I speaking?"

"He ain't here."

"Who isn't there?"

"Anthony Shadowbrook. He's gone to Alaska or someplace. You want to talk to his daughter?"

"Please."

"Hello?"

"Kath? It's Dad."

"Oh, hi, Daddy! Hey, everyone, quiet down! It's my father."

"What's going on?"

"The college and career Bible study needed a place to meet. I knew you and Mom wouldn't care . . . right?"

"Yeah . . . well . . . I think so. Anyway, I'm just checking on you. Is everything going well?"

"Everything's great, Daddy. Really! There's this neat guy at work who sure is hanging around me a lot. He's totally cute."

"How about Kit? Did she get rid of the calf?"

"Not yet."

"Can I speak to her?"

"She's not home."

"Where is she?"

"She . . . went down to Mesa to look for a job."

"A job? She already has a job."

"She got fired from the Speedy Squirt place."

"Fired? When?"

"Who got fired?" Price interrupted.

Tony put his hand over the receiver, "Kit," then removed it. "What happened, Kathy?"

"She lubed the boss."

"She did what?"

"What did she do?" Price insisted.

Tony turned to his wife. "She lubed the boss."

Price flung her hand across her chest and coughed up a startled "What?"

"Kath, what exactly does that mean?"

"I think I'd better have her call you. Are you going to be there at the house tonight?"

"We'll be at a meeting until, oh, say, 9:00. Have her call right after that."

"Okay, Daddy. Are you and Mom having a neat time all alone up there?"

"It's a . . . we're getting . . . yeah, it's a nice location."

"I told everyone about the possibility of *Shotgun Creek* being a movie. We're all praying for you."

"Thanks, kiddo. You make sure to have Kit give me a call."

Tony hung up the phone and stared at Price.

"I have no idea in the world what it means that she lubed the boss. Not only that, but there are fifty college kids at a Bible study in our living room."

"The house will be a mess," Price groaned.

"Kath will clean it up. You know how addicted to neatness she is."

"Maybe we ought to go home," Price suggested.

"Are you kidding? The book isn't half done."

"I mean for just a few days to settle things down, then come back."

"We've got to turn them loose, Mama."

"In our living room?"

"Yep."

Price ate the last bit of green beans dunked in garlic butter sauce. "I feel very anxious and insecure being here when the girls need me at home."

"They didn't say they needed you," Tony reminded her.

"Well, they do, and you know it."

"Kit will have a good reason."

"For lubing the boss?"

"Yep."

"Well, we'll have to get home from that community meeting by nine."

"Sure." Tony speared another piece of chicken. "How long could it take to decide on a petting zoo?"

At 11:15 P.M., Price and Melody crashed through the front door of the house. Tony had just hung up the receiver.

"How long have you been on the phone?"

"Oh, Kit didn't call until ten minutes ago. How did the meeting go after I left?"

"Pretty wild. You missed the best part. What's the deal with Kit?"

"I learned what 'lubing the boss' means. What do you mean about the meeting?"

"Harvey Peterson showed up with a chain saw. Now, explain Kit."

"Wait, wait, wait!" Melody broke in. "This is worse than trying to watch a tennis match. How about one conversation at a time?"

"Okay," Tony began, "tell me about the meeting."

"No, that can wait. Tell me about our daughter."

"What did Harvey do with the chain saw?"

"What did Kit do to her boss?"

"That's it, I'm out of here," Melody asserted. "I've heard of plots and subplots in novels, but not in conversations. After that meeting and the hairy ride home, I need a little peace and quiet. Sorry to leave you without a moderator, but I'm going to bed."

They heard the front door click shut. Price put a pot of water on the stove's back burner.

"What did she mean a 'hairy ride home'? I thought you said there would be no problem catching a lift after I had to leave early?"

"There was no problem. Kenny Mallard brought us home."

"On his Harley?"

"Yeah."

"Both of you?"

"Yes."

"At the same time?"

Price laughed and ran her fingers through her hair. She noticed once again how long it was getting and determined to ask Melody to recommend a beauty shop. "It was quite an adventure."

"I don't want to hear about it."

She smiled and stuck a bag of Stash Licorice tea into her newly acquired Fox Island mug, the one encircled with Clay Babies. "Good. Tell me all about Kit, then I'll tell you about the meeting."

"No, I'll tell you about Kit. Then I'll tell you about Kathy. And then you can tell me about the meeting. Get your hot tea and come relax. We both need to sit down."

"Oh, joy. Kathy, too, huh?"

Tony stretched out on the carpet after folding scattered pages of *The Peninsula Gateway* and tossing them next to the fireplace. Price slunk into the navy stuffed chair and inhaled the licorice scent.

"Well, here goes. Mr. Conesco, Kit's boss, came back to work today after lunch and showed Kit the new uniform he wanted her to wear . . . hot pink shorts and halter. He told Kit he was giving her a raise and wanted her to work out front lining up the paperwork on the cars as they drove in."

Price plopped her tea next to the seashell lamp. "Wearing the hot pink shorts and halter?"

"You got it."

"But that's . . . that's sexual harassment or something, isn't it?"

"Well, Kit wasn't about to wear those clothes or give up any job that had to do with working on cars."

"So she quit?"

Tony waved his hand. "Just wait now. Kit was ticked off. She said she'd be happy to wear the shorts and halter as soon as all the men who worked there agreed to wear the skimpy hot pink outfits."

"Kit said that? Well, I guess she would, wouldn't she?"

"Conesco went into a tirade about how he was the boss and she would do what he said or get fired."

"Nice guy! So what did Kit do?"

Tony began to laugh. It started with a fit of chuckles and expanded to a full-scale, uncontrolled series of war whoops.

"Get a grip, Shadowbrook. This is serious."

"Then, she . . . he, she . . . shoved . . . the lube gun . . . into his Dockers . . . and . . . and . . . pulled the trigger!"

Price slid back against the chair's stuffed cushion and shut her eyes, tight.

Tony's guffaws slowly wound down. Tears streamed from his eyes. He wiped them with his shirt sleeve, the new Roper shirt with black horse silhouettes. "When she jumped into her truck and drove off, he was still screaming curses and running around like a snake bit him."

"Well, at least she didn't punch the guy's lights out this time."

"I guess she went home, changed clothes, drove straight to Mesa and promptly got herself a job at an auto parts store."

"I hope they didn't ask for references."

"It's owned by the father of someone she met at the drag races."

"Is she doing all right?"

"Well, she did tell me she spent some time out at South Mountain Park. She suspects the Lord wants her to apologize, but she's still too angry. She said she was going to write Conesco an apology and have Josh deliver it when he picks up her check."

"She talked to her brother? What did Josh say about all this?"

"I think his exact words were, 'I'd be happy to stop by and face down the sleazy creep.' "

"We need to be home."

"They'll survive, Dr. Shadowbrook. Kit thinks it'll all work out. She told us not to worry."

"Not worry? Yeah, sure. I've worried about those two since the day they were born."

"Mama, you've worried about Mark and Josh just the same."

But son worries fall into a whole different cat-

egory than daughter worries. The girls definitely need me to be there and coach them along.

"What's this with Kathy?" she asked.

"It seems this totally awesome guy at work came to the Bible study tonight. But he was having some kind of car problem with his new Camaro convertible, so Kathy invited him to stay until Kit came back, so she could look at it."

"But Kit got home late. . . ."

"At which time Kathy and this guy, Linc, were in the swimming pool."

"Doing what?"

"Swimming, I guess. Kathy said it's still over a hundred in Scottsdale. Well, Kit fixed his car, while this guy stood around dripping water off his bathing suit and visited with her. She said he was a pretty neat guy, but said he had poor taste in girls."

"And Kathy said?"

"She said Kit was trying to hit on Linc, and if she didn't stop, she would rip her lips off."

"Kit? Making a pass at a boy? And what did you say?"

"I said for Kit to write the apology to her former boss, for Josh to deliver it without commentary and pick up her check. Then I told Kathy it didn't look right to have a male guest over to swim after dark, no matter what the excuse."

"That's all you told them?"

"No, I said their mother would call them tomorrow and give them both a long lecture."

"Me?"

"Yeah, you're Dr. Mama, the professor." Tony took a deep breath and sighed. "Okay, now it's your turn. No more stalling. What happened at the community meeting?"

"Wait a minute . . . my head's still buzzing. Do you want me to warm up some coffee for you? I need another cup of tea."

"That would be great. You know what, babe? I'm trying to figure out which daughter we should be more worried about. I suppose that's why parents have gray hair, isn't it?"

"Yes, but gray hair looks distinguished on men." Price headed to the kitchen.

"Listen, kid, you're way too defensive over a couple of strands of gray. Why, you don't look a day over . . . say . . . fifty."

Tony didn't even see the square leather pillow that sailed toward his head.

They sat at opposite ends of the sofa. He chugged coffee. She sipped scalding tea. Price tugged both shoes off and tucked her legs under her. Tony used a *Time* magazine on the end table as a coaster for the heels of his cowboy boots.

"Okay," he began, "when I left, a short dynamo named Ms. Tulip, or Miss Tulip, stood up, with a braid as pretty as a bronc rein hanging to her knees. Tulip Somethingerother was protesting the inhumane treatment of animals by the Cascade Kids-Can Pet, Inc."

"Was that before or after Harvey Peterson ranted and raved about dismantling the bridge and bringing back the ferry?"

"He did what?"

She cleared her voice to the semblance of a deep bass. " 'Before the bridge came in, we didn't have scumbags like you polluting our island.' "

"Scumbags? He actually said scumbags?"

"Yes."

"How did that go over?"

"The animal rights crowd stood in unison, gave Harvey a 'Heil Hitler' salute and called him a fascist."

"I don't suppose that sat well with Harvey?"

"He turned red in the face and said the Fox Island cemetery held the graves of his oldest brother, his uncle and a cousin, who all died fighting fascists. Their outburst was an insult to the memory of many fine Fox

Islanders, and he'd gladly step outside with any or all of the . . . I think his words were 'puke-faced wimps.' "

"He called them all out?"

"Yes, but they reminded him they only practiced nonviolence."

Tony leaned his head on the back of the cushion. "That reminds me, we ought to spend a couple hours at the cemetery reading the tombstones. Could be a story there."

Price unfolded her legs from beneath her and set her cup on the coffee table.

"Go on," Tony urged. "What happened next?"

"Well, they finally got some order into the meeting, then the *Wild and Free* bunch made a . . ."

"Where does the *Wild and Free* title come from?"

"I think it's a national group or something. Several were from out of the state, I know. Tulip lives here on the Island, though. Melody says she's been here for years and years. Anyway, they made a big case over Ho Chow."

"Who?"

"A Vietnamese pot-bellied pig. They had a huge blowup of an article in a newspaper in Oregon when Cascade KidsCan Pet,

Inc., held their petting zoo in a shopping center at Beaverton. The charge was that they so neglected the animals that Ho Chow died of starvation."

"Could be they have a case. How did KidsCan Pet, Inc., respond to that?" Tony asked.

"Their representative insisted the person responsible had been fired and such a thing wouldn't happen again."

"Both sides have a point. Sounds like an impasse."

"For the next two hours everybody in the building gave their opinion on everything from the Vietnam War to the need to overhaul the income tax to the safe and sane disposal of nuclear waste."

"Were any decisions made?"

"They're against the IRS and divided over the war, and definitely don't want radioactive material stored at the Acoustic Range."

"But, what about the petting zoo?"

"Kenny Mallard finally settled that."

"Melody's buddy?"

"Yeah, Kenny said they should allow the petting zoo to participate, but they ought to appoint a committee to oversee the animal care while they're here on the Island."

"Ahhh, and who were the lucky ones drafted for such a thankless chore?"

"Four were chosen. Tulip, Harvey Peterson, Kenny Mallard, and . . ."

"You said four. Who was the other one?"

"They decided to get someone from off the Island who had an objective point of view."

"Surely not . . . ?"

"Me."

"You? But we're here to observe, not to get involved."

"Melody nominated me, and everyone seemed to be so enthusiastic about it. Frankly, I didn't know how to get out of it."

Tony stood up and stretched. "Well, I guess that's one way to get to know some people better."

"That's what I was thinking," Price agreed.

He reached down and tugged her to her feet. "Listen, kiddo, I've got a surprise for you."

"This isn't a dumb line to get me into your bedroom, is it, Shadowbrook?"

"I can't believe you'd think such a thing of me," he said as he nuzzled her neck. "While I was waiting around I did a little exploration downstairs."

"You mean, you sorted through Jessica Reynolds' things?"

"Well, kind of . . ."

"And you found something?"

He flipped on the light and led her downstairs to a large family room. The rest of the basement space was divided between a spare bedroom and a storage area.

"I think I found some additional Grandma Jessica paintings."

"Some more original Davenports?"

"But they're signed, 'Reynolds.' Look at these."

Tony pulled out half a dozen canvases from behind a tall mahogany bureau. None were framed.

"They don't look like the others," Price commented, "but they're good, aren't they? Very good."

"It's like she gave up on the 'Two Girl' motif. They sort of remind me of Norman Rockwell, that is, with the realistic detail and the family life themes."

"All the subjects are women," Price noted.

"But there's a hint of tragedy or sorrow in some of the faces, don't you think?"

"Hmmm, yes. Each one tells a story within a story. When were they painted?"

"They're all dated between 1965 and

1970. Isn't that strange? It's like she attempted a comeback twenty-five years later. How come there wasn't anything in the art book about these?"

"Perhaps no one knows about them." A slight chill ran up her back. Price picked up a large stretched canvas that showed a young girl in a heated argument with her mother over some lipstick.

"This is intriguing . . . a simple, universal theme, yet an overlay of haunting . . . poignancy. Such a winsome quality. It expresses the bond of family, but with all its potential for sudden . . . change and . . . sadness."

Tony picked up another and hauled it out toward the light, examining it more closely. "We've just got to talk with Melody's grandmother. We're not going to be happy with this project until we do."

After nearly an hour of studying the pictures, Tony and Price hiked back up the stairs to the bright lights of the kitchen.

"*If* we can get permission, how about including some photos of these paintings in chapter six or seven?" Tony asked.

"We haven't finished discussing chapter five." Price scooped the pages off the dining table. "I just can't believe you said this was too cluttered."

"It's too busy, too disjointed, too distractive. We just need to tighten it, that's all."

"I believe it reads quite nicely, just as it is."

"Everything ever written could be tightened some. You know that."

"Not this chapter. You know, Mr. Shadowbrook, I'm not quite sure why I'm even here. The girls need me in Scottsdale. You obviously don't need me here."

"Of course I do. Now look, honey, don't get so defensive. We're professionals and . . ."

"Tony, you really don't enjoy cowriting projects, do you?"

"That's not true. I love having you along. I absolutely detest researching a project on my own, you know that."

"Oh sure, you like having me come along. But I wonder, is it for my wit or my dimples?"

Tony walked into the living room and plopped back on the sofa.

"Well?" she asserted.

"I'm thinking."

"Then you can just sit right there until you decide. This doctor's going to bed."

What's wrong with me? Tony didn't totally deserve that outburst. It was something . . .

174

something to do with those paintings. They were troubling, unsettling in how they depicted so perfectly . . . the fragility of human relationships. Lord, protect me and Tony.

6 The construction of the bridge in 1954 brought an end to Fox Islanders' one hundred years of dependence on boats for their existence. In the early days most families had their own small craft, but everyone relied on the freight and ferry services of commercial companies to bring supplies ... and to deliver Island-grown produce to the Tacoma markets. The powerful currents of the Narrows ensured that larger boats carrying people and goods to the mainland would always be needed. From English-imported beaver in 1835 to the City of Steilacoom in 1954, supply boats and ferries formed an important part of the everyday cycle of life on the Island.

Many of those life cycles ended up at a grassy tree-lined knoll near the corner of Island Boulevard and 6th Avenue.

Price, Tony and Melody Mason meandered among the tombstones of the Fox Island Cemetery. Looking more like a park for picnickers than a resting place for the dead, the plot of ground was filled with pines and firs and bushes. It was rimmed with a low, loose railing of long, skinny tree trunks, a gentle semblance of a boundary.

The July sun was almost straight above them, yet the morning dew still clung to the grass. The toes of Price's purple-trimmed white tennies soaked in the moisture.

"When I was a little girl," Melody was saying, "I would cut through here on my way to Shelli's house. I thought it was a really brave thing to do, sort of a sign of maturity: 'I can walk clear through the cemetery by myself!' I wonder why kids are so afraid of cemeteries?"

Tony led the way, notebook in hand, careful to avoid stepping on markers or bumping monuments. "I suppose there's always a fear of the unknown . . . and death is the ultimate unknown. That is, if you choose to ignore the Bible's teaching on the matter. Melody, are these some of Harvey Peterson's relatives?"

"I think so."

"He really did lose several in the war."

Price shot some pictures of a tall centennial time capsule and the inscriptions on several gravestones, then rejoined Tony and Melody.

"You know, Dr. S., every time one of Grandma's friends dies, she refuses to go to the funeral. It's like she just won't admit they're gone."

"I think it's probably to Satan's advantage to keep everyone scared of death. If he can convince us that death is the worst thing that can happen to us, then he's got the leverage, the control in our lives."

Melody reached down and brushed some loose wet grass off her sandaled feet. "Dr. S., what's worse than death?"

"Hell."

"Oh . . . yeah." Melody tossed her long dark hair, her expressive eyes hidden behind smoke-gray glasses. "You're the only professor I've ever known who thinks of that as a literal place." She stopped at a large raised marker.

"Now here's a sad story. The Zimmers lived in that white house down from Grandma's. Mr. Zimmer was real sick for several years. He picked out this stone and had them put his name on one side and Emaline, his wife, on the other, so they could be buried side by side. Well, right after he died, Emaline moved to Bremerton and married a high school sweetheart. He died last year, and everyone says there's a big stone in Bremerton with his and Emaline's names on it. What we're all wondering is, which place will she be buried?"

Price took a photo of the marker. "Perhaps Emaline will get married again."

"Wow, I never thought of that! That would really make it complicated."

"Maybe they could cremate her and put a little of the ashes at each site."

"Tony!" Price squealed.

"Yeah, wouldn't that be something?" Melody pondered. " 'Where's your mother buried?' they'll ask her kids. 'Oh, at Seattle, Bremerton and Fox Island.' "

They hiked up the crest of the knoll and passed most of the flat markers. "I'd sure like to know all their stories," Price observed, "but a name and date don't tell us much."

"Did you see the Japanese marker over there?" Tony pointed back across the lawn. "I'll bet Harvey Peterson has a great explanation of that one."

"Auntie Jill's buried over there . . . at the wrought-iron fenced place. It's our family plot, you might say."

The fence stood almost five feet tall and the paint was peeling. The only section like it in the cemetery, it measured ten by twenty feet. Melody squeaked open the iron gate. "My great-grandpa and grandma are buried here. They both died of the flu in the late '30s, only four months apart."

Tony hunched down and examined the stone. "How old were the twins at the time?"

"They were in high school. They lived with an aunt for a while, then left for Radcliffe. Here's Auntie Jill's marker."

"So they shipped her body home for burial?" he quizzed.

"Oh yeah. Grandma Jessie said she had the undertaker in Iowa take care of Auntie Jill, then she accompanied the casket on the train. The car they wrecked was totaled, so she rode in the baggage car right next to the coffin all the way home. She said they were the longest two days of her life."

Tony jotted a few lines in his notebook. "Talk about feeling lonely and lost. I can't imagine what it would be like to lose an identical twin."

"Why does it say just 'J Davenport,' instead of her full name?" Price asked as she photographed the three-foot-high polished black granite monument.

"Grandma Jessie said she was so grief-stricken that she couldn't bear to see Jill's name spelled out. She always promised she'd get someone to finish it, but she's never done it."

"So the girls lost their parents before they graduated from high school, then Jill died in '42. No wonder your grandma still struggles with her death. There was no one in the family left."

Price stooped to investigate the remnants of withered flowers in a green glass vase. "That was some fancy bouquet. Looks like gladiolus. Funny how they turned dark magenta when they died. I'm used to white and light-colored ones. Did you put them out here?"

"No, they must be left from June. Grandma Jessie always has some sent out on June 2. But she never comes to the grave."

"They look fresher than that to me. Isn't that a card attached to one of the stems?"

Melody stooped to retrieve the faded card, then jumped as if stung by a bee. "Oh! . . . Wow!"

Tony reached over and took her arm. "Are you all right?"

"It's him. . . ." she shouted.

"Who?"

Price glanced around. "Where?"

"No, look, the name on the card. It's that Bennington guy!"

Price took the card from Melody's hand and read it out loud, *"To Jill . . . I'm sorry. Lloyd Bennington."*

"He didn't happen to leave his address or phone number, did he?" Tony put in.

"Hey!" Melody seized the card back. "This florist is in Gig Harbor. They go to our church. Really. I used to baby-sit for them. Do you suppose they have this guy's address or something?"

Price leaned close to the wilted mass of spikes, as though to draw some telling scent from them. "It's certainly worth a try."

"Oh, man, I'm going to add this to my novel. Mystery guy flies in from Maryland, visits the grave, leaves flowers . . . then he flies home to die. Am I talking best seller or what?"

Price led the trio back to the car.

An hour later, the Shadowbrooks scampered around the house changing from damp denims to black Wranglers for Tony and washed aquamarine silk for Price.

She sorted through her earring box searching for something turquoise and silver. "Do you think Melody will find a lead on Bennington?"

Tony pulled on a black-and-white sunburst western shirt. "I don't know, but she's right about one thing. I think there's a story to be told."

"Like, what's the real reason he's so sorry

that it would nag him to the grave? Should I wear the sedate round ones or the Melody-sized ones?" She held both samples to her ears.

"Definitely the long ones. I was thinking the same thing about Bennington. He wasn't just sorry she died. He was sorry when he thought she might still be alive."

"And it can't merely be a conscience stirred over a jilted girlfriend, could it? Why, if I had to go back and apologize to every guy I ever dumped . . ."

"There you go bragging again."

"But I probably did them all a great favor." She paused and turned back to him. "Are you wearing your black boots?"

"No, the python belly." Tony dug through the closet. "I thought you told me they were all creeps."

"Mostly creeps. Do you think I ought to wear boots?"

"So, only some were creeps? I don't care, but your white boots with the turquoise chain would be dynamite with that dress."

She sat on the bed and tugged on one boot, then lay back on the comforter. "Well, there was this *one* creep. Sort of."

Tony noticed the dimples were shining. "What I can't figure, Professor, is how did such a selective and discriminating beautiful young woman fall for a plain, older man like me?"

Price stood up, folded her hands under her chin, and batted her eyes. "Oh, Mr. Shadowbrook, you remind me so much of my father."

"If I hear that one time today, I'll quit signing autographs forever."

"I think it's a nice compliment, actually. But that usually only happens when you're pushing your westerns. Today will be the travel home and AARP crowd, remember? Speaking of which, we'd better get going if we're going to make it to Bellevue on time."

"Bellevue? I thought we were signing in Seattle."

Price dabbed a mixture of Skin Musk and Baby perfume. "Bellevue's a suburb. I hear it's an upscale, yuppie sort of place. Liz says the store's in a great location. She's sure we'll like it."

"Yeah? And she's the one who said I'd love midtown Manhattan."

"Most people do. Try to be nice and smile at the little old ladies."

"I'll be my typical charming, witty, debonair yet slightly rugged and rustic self."

"That would be a delightful change from 'We've been here five minutes already, when can we leave?' "

"Did I ever tell you this self-promotion stuff is one thing about writing that is very difficult for me?"

"About once a day for the past twenty years."

"I thought maybe I mentioned it." He kissed her on top of her head. "Nice perfume . . . clean, not too strong, perfect for the occasion. What's it called?"

"Chapter five."

Tony broke out in a laugh. "Hey, it didn't smell that good."

He had just jammed on his cowboy hat and held the front door for Price, then answered the ringing phone.

"Tony? This is Peter Frankal."

"Hi, Pete. How's the world-famous art director?"

"Let me pick your brain on the cover for the next River Breaks western. We're trying to design the spring catalog. You're going to set *Standoff at Rifle Ridge* on the Yellowstone River, right?"

"Pete, I've got to call you later. I'm heading out the door for a book signing in Seattle, and we're running late. Liz will skin us if we keep them waiting."

"But . . . well . . . when can you call me back?"

"Tomorrow morning. What time do you get into the office?"

"Can't do it tomorrow. Got to meet with an artist in Philadelphia. Then there's the weekend and I need some ideas for Monday's meeting. Are you sure you don't have a minute? Give me twenty minutes and we'll get what we need. You've got that much time for old Pete, don't you?"

"Nope. Petey, call me back when you get a chance. I've got to run. Bye!"

He locked the front door and joined Price in the old white Oldsmobile. "Business?"

"Why does that always happen? They never call me when I have time to talk. Then they slap on some historically inaccurate cover that doesn't even resemble the story, and I have to live with it the rest of my life."

"It's a good thing it doesn't bother you." Price scooted over to the middle of the seat. He slipped his arm around her shoulder.

"Did I ever tell you I like bench seats better than bucket seats?"

"About once a day for the past thirty years. Now, come on, famous author, let's go meet our adoring public . . . both of them."

Tony fiddled to find a country and western radio station, while Price surveyed the Island as they approached the bridge to the mainland.

Lord, if I could give him a special present, it would be that one best-seller. He works so hard at it. He never compromises his standards . . . of excellence or ethics.

Maybe that's why he'll always be my favorite writer.

Lights were still on in the house when they returned around midnight. Melody Mason met them at the door.

"Oh, wow, here you are. I was getting pretty worried. I thought you'd be home in time for supper. I didn't know a book signing would last so long."

"The publisher's rep lined us up with some bookstore folks and a long dinner at the Space Needle," Price reported.

"Isn't it totally awesome up there? The view always takes my breath away."

"It took my appetite away, that's for sure."

"Are you afraid of heights, Dr. S.?"

"No, heights don't bother me. It's fear of falling off heights that's troubling. You didn't have supper waiting for us, did you?"

Melody managed a weary smile. "Oh no. But don't worry about me. I scraped up some leftovers out of the fridge. You didn't mind, did you?"

"Nope," Tony responded. "Why, just the other day, Price and I were commenting how you have become like part of the family."

"Boy, that's really neat. You know what, Mr. S.? I never knew my father very well. But if I could pick out my own father, I'd want him to be just like you."

Tony seemed at a loss for words, so Price said, "You didn't need to stay up for us, Melody."

"It's no big deal. I wanted to talk to you."

Price used the bootjack by the door and slipped off her boots. "Why don't you go boil some water? We'll kick off these dressy things and meet you in the kitchen for a cup of something hot to drink."

"Oh, sure. You want *me* to boil the water?"

"Go for it," Tony urged.

When Tony and Price returned in jeans and sweatshirts, chocolate, tea and packaged espresso mix were lined up behind three mugs, and the chrome teapot whistled with a jarring note.

"It's just like a tea party, isn't it?" Melody beamed as she fussed with the mugs and pot. "How was your autograph signing?"

Price tugged her green sweatshirt sleeves up over her elbows and dipped the Earl Grey five times. "Oh, it wasn't too bad. They had a nice crowd, don't you think, Tony?"

"People came for the grand opening, the drawing for free books, the lattes and biscotti, and as long as they were there, why not buy a Shadowbrook book and get an autograph?"

"How many books did you sell?"

Tony sipped on his coffee. "About 195 for a two-hour signing."

"Is that good?"

"We've done worse," Price added.

"A lot worse," Tony laughed. "I once did a signing in Chicago when only two little old ladies came by during the hour I was there. They wanted to see what I looked like, if I was really wearing a cowboy hat, and to garner another autograph for their collection. But they didn't buy a book."

"Wow, that would be a bummer."

"It keeps me humble."

Price pulled off her earrings and rubbed her earlobes. "But it was a good evening. We visited with a couple book distributors and several store owners . . . important contacts. And they're all looking forward to *Fox Island* coming out next May. It should do well up here."

"Hey, I almost forgot. You had a FedEx package left at the door and a phone call."

"Where's the package?" Tony asked.

"It's over behind Grandma's umbrella stand."

"Who called?" Price quizzed.

"Your daughter."

"Which one?"

Melody waved her hands in front of her, as if trying to generate a word. "Oh . . . the one whose name starts with K. Who is it?"

"They both start with a K. Was it Kit or Kathy?"

"Let's see . . . someone was pouting in her room with the door locked, and the other one called."

Price took a deep breath. "It must have been Kit."

"How old did you say your daughters were?"

"Eighteen, but sometimes going on twelve." Price took a long sip of tea. "When did she call?"

"About seven."

"Well, maybe they'll have it all solved by morning."

Tony entered, examining the contents of a cardboard envelope.

"What about the girls?"

"Oh, probably just a sisterly spat," said Price. "Why don't you fly home tonight and take care of it, dear?"

Tony looked up with a puzzled expression.

"I'll call them in the morning. What did you get?"

"It's the agreement with Davidian. The legal boys at Atlantic-Hampton have worked it over."

"How's it look?"

"I'll have to give it a long read."

"What does Liz think?"

"She said it was up to me." Tony scanned the pages and took a swig of coffee.

Melody slapped the table. "Hey, I haven't told you the big news . . . what I found out about Bennington."

Tony and Price both turned to her.

"I completely forgot," Price said. "Did you talk to the florist?"

"Yes. Lynne Anne, that's my friend, let me check the records. The bouquet was purchased by an older, gray-haired man who paid for it with a credit card in the account of CMI."

"The only CMI I know is Chesapeake Mutual Investments," Tony remarked.

"Bingo! That's exactly what I thought, Mr. S."

"You know about mutual funds?" Price asked.

"Oh, sure. I manage my grandmother's portfolio. Didn't I tell you that?"

Tony and Price looked at each other. "I guess it slipped your mind."

"I've been doing that ever since I graduated from ASU. It gives me some income until the book royalties start rolling in, like you guys. In fact, that's where I met Kenny."

"Where?"

"At the brokers'."

"He really owns early Microsoft stock?"

"Yeah, isn't that wild?"

"It's totally awesome," Price admitted.

"Anyway, just on a lark, I called Chestertown, Maryland, and sure enough they had a number for CMI."

"So you called them?"

"Yeah, but it was already closing time back there. I'll have to call in the morning."

"Well, that is a lead. Maybe Bennington is a stockbroker."

"That's what I was thinking. And maybe he has an unlisted number. I'm hoping I can get a home phone or something."

Tony groaned, slapped the papers and got up to pace the kitchen.

"What's the matter?" Price asked.

"This isn't right."

"What isn't?"

"This contract. They propose to give Davidian 10%, the publishing house 45%, and I receive 45%, less Liz's 10% of my 45%."

"How's that again?"

"Davidian gets 10% off the top, Atlantic-Hampton 45%, Liz 4.5% and that leaves me with 40.5% of royalties earned off the movie rights."

"Is that the way they assign movie royalties?" Melody asked.

"Not for my books," Tony huffed.

"Actually, we have no idea what is usually done," Price corrected, "since this is our first contact with a Hollywood agent."

"Well, I'm not agreeing to this. Why does it always seem like the writer is the least important person in the royalty chain?"

"Davidian hasn't sold the story, either. It might be a big worry over nothing," Price reminded him.

Melody carried her cup and saucer to the sink. "You think Tom Clancy gets that kind of deal?"

Price tucked a stray brunette strand behind her ear. "I think Clancy can get just about whatever he wants."

"Well, I'm glad you're both home safe and sound. I'm going to bed." After a few steps, she turned around. "Hey, did I tell you Kim finally kicked Amigo out?"

"Does that mean you'll be moving in with her?" Price walked with Melody to the front door. "The summer's half over."

"Hey, that's what I was thinking. I might as well just stick it out in the garage. That is, if it's all right with you and Mr. S. Besides, Kim's in one of her dark moods."

"Dark moods?"

"All her paintings are in black and blue."

"What is she painting these days?"

"Kind of a modernistic, surreal, still-life oceanscape thing with angels looking on, you know what I mean?"

"Yes, well, I can see why you'd rather be in the loft."

"Then you two don't mind?"

Price glanced back at Tony in the kitchen, engrossed again in the contract. "We wouldn't know what to do if you weren't around."

"Boy, I can't ever thank you guys enough. You know, I wouldn't have been able to write this new book without your help. I've decided I'm going to dedicate this book to *My good friends Price and Tony Shadow-brook, who taught me all I know about writing.'* No matter how famous I get, I'll always remember how you weren't too busy to help me in the early days. And maybe, someday, I'll be able to help someone else get a start."

"Good night, Melody."

"Good night, Dr. S."

A faint, persistent buzz needled Price out of bed at 6:29 A.M. She fumbled for the alarm. Then she grabbed for the princess phone on the nightstand.

Where's Tony? What time is it? Why does he have to run so early?

"Priscilla Shadowbrook," she mumbled.

"Well, good morning!" the cheery voice chirped. "Hope I didn't pull you out of the garden."

"Who is this?"

"Tulip."

"Who?"

"Tulip. You're on the committee with me to ensure the humane treatment of Fox Island animals held in temporary confinement."

"I'm what?"

"Last week at the community meeting, remember?"

"Oh, yes . . . sorry. I'm a little sleepy."

"Well, we're having a committee meeting

at the Community Center at 10:00 this morning."

"Why?"

"To go over a site selection procedure for finding the proper location for the petting zoo."

"Proper place? Does it matter?"

"I'll pretend you didn't say that. See you at ten. Say, tell Tony he's certainly welcome to come with you."

"I think he'll be busy writing."

"Oh, that's too bad. . . ." Price felt that the woman held on to the word "bad" much too long. "Anyway, Kenny Mallard isn't over there, is he?"

At 6:30 in the morning?

"Eh, no."

"Well, I can't reach him. If you see him, tell him about the meeting."

"Sure."

Then the dial tone.

No "goodbye."

No "thanks."

No "sorry to bother you so early."

Price pulled back the covers and collapsed back into bed.

Why do I get the idea she doesn't give two cents about me? Her agenda drives her right over the top of people. Even if your goals are correct, you've got to care about people along the way. She reminds me of Mrs. Lindsay in the sixth grade. 'You girls are going to learn this material if I have to beat it into you.' Well, we learned.

Whatever it was.

But this morning, I don't have an early class to teach. I don't have to drive to cheerleading practice . . . or hang gliding lessons . . . nor do I have a 4-H animal to feed. I do not have to get up. There is no reason in the world for me not to go back to sleep.

She lay back on a stack of three pillows to study the room and wondered for the hundredth time if it were Melody's design or Jessica Reynolds'. Ribbons of roses and floral lattice covered the comforter, the cases, ruffled round tablecloths and pouf curtains. Tiny floral sprigs scattered broken antique gold stripes on the shams and wallpaper. Even the milk glass lamps were hand painted in shades of pink wood roses. *Like sleeping in a garden,* Price mused.

The pillowcase felt soft and cool as she sank into it with a sigh. Her mind floated off into wonderful, peaceful blackness.

The telephone rang.

On the third ring Price propped herself up on an elbow and yanked up the receiver.

"What is it?" she managed to mumble.

"Price, this is Liz. Is Tony around, or is he out fishing?"

"Fishing? Do you have any idea what time it is here?"

"Oh, I forgot, you're in Pacific time zone now, aren't you?"

"It's 6:47 . . . in the morning!"

"Sorry, just remind Tony he has a radio interview at 3:15. Let's see, I guess that's 12:15 Pacific. Al Germain at WINC in Lafayette, Louisiana. Thirty minutes on comparing the myth of the cowboy as portrayed in western novels of the early and mid-twentieth century to the actual cowboys of history. It's a live show."

"Does Tony know about this?"

"I sent him a fax."

"A fax? Where did you send it?"

"That's your home fax, isn't it? Tell him not to worry; he can wing it. I think it's a call-in show. How did the book signing go?"

"Fine."

"And how's *Fox Island* coming?"

"Except for chapter five, it's moving right along."

"Sorry to wake you, girl. Well, bye-bye. Go back to sleep."

Price could feel the ache and twitch of every bone and muscle in her body as she slipped back between the cotton sheets. She could tell by the grayness that it must be foggy outside. Still, she fumbled in the nightstand drawer to find a black silk sleep mask. She slipped the strap over her hair and settled it against her eyes.

I should have gotten up and taken some Advil. I don't think I used to be this tired when I was young. Getting up in the night with the twins . . . getting all four of them ready for Sunday school . . . hauling the whole gang to the supermarket. Price, darling, how in the world did you do that? Maybe I'm still trying to get over it.

Maybe I should unplug the phone until after breakfast. Maybe I should unplug the phone until after lunch.

She felt like someone had jabbed pencils into each ear at exactly the same time. The nagging telephone harangued her once more. For a moment, she thought very seriously about screaming and throwing the telephone through the window.

This isn't happening. This is a bad dream. Lord, just make it all go away. Put a hedge of protection around this house and cast this demonic phone far from me.

The ringing didn't stop.

She pulled off the sleepshade, hunched on the side of the bed, and squeezed the molded plastic.

"Yeah, what is it?" she growled.

"Mom? Is that you?"

"Kristina? What do you want?"

"Whoa, is it *that* time of the month?"

Price silently counted to ten. "Sorry, Kit, I'm tired this morning. What can I do for you, honey?"

"Oh, it's not me. It's Kath. Did that Melody person tell you I called?"

"Yes, she said Kath is locked in her room or something. We got in too late to call back. What's up?"

"I don't know why she does this. We're just friends."

"Who's just friends?"

"Me and Linc."

"Linc?"

"He's a new guy that works in the admissions office with Kath. You know, the one with the new Camaro convertible?"

"And an awesome smile?"

"Yeah, he's a hunk all right. Anyway, I fixed his car last week, and he wanted to thank me, so he took me out to the Rustler's Roost last night. He's a real nice guy, Mom. You and Pop would like him. He's transferring in from some college in Idaho. His dad's a teacher up there. He said he thought he signed up for one of your classes. Here's the thing, Mom. He likes me just like I am.

He doesn't seem insecure or threatened like the others. But we're just friends, that's all."

"And when you got home, Kath was in her room, pouting?"

"Yeah. What am I supposed to do?"

"Go on to work. Kath will be Okay. You've been a little bit jealous before like that yourself, haven't you?"

"Of Kath? Not really. Usually the guys she goes with are dorks."

"Leave a note for Katherine to call me when she gets up."

"Mom, what should I say if Linc calls and wants to take me out again?"

"What do you usually say when a boy invites you for a second date?"

"None of them ever has."

"Do you want to see him again?"

"Yeah, I think so. I know it's kind of weird, Mom. But I really like talking to him. And I had a real fun time. We laughed a lot, and he made me feel important."

"Well, then, you'd better let him know that."

"How do I do that? Should I call him up?"

"My advice is, don't call him. Let him initiate another conversation. That will be easier to explain to Kathy."

"Thanks, Mom. I'll leave a note for her. This is kind of weird, isn't it?"

"I don't know, Kristina. It seems real normal to me."

"I love you, Mom!"

"I love you too, honey. Bye."

I love you? My tomboy daughter saying "I love you, Mom"? Oh, Lord, help her to avoid temptation and stay within your will.

I'm not sure why we expect our children to exhibit qualities that so eluded us. It was a long time ago. But I was eighteen. That's what worries me.

She heard the front door open and close softly.

Good, he can answer the phone.

"Hi, guys, it's just me," Melody called out. "I know it's early, but it's after 10:00 A.M. in Maryland, and I figured I better try calling CMI. Don't mind me, I'll just use the phone in the hall."

Maybe I could go get a hotel room . . . in Seattle. I could fly to Cabo San Lucas and sleep in the sun on an isolated beach. I could even go back home and stay with the twins. Kit's at work and Kath is pouting in her room. Even that would be more peaceful than this.

Price pulled on her robe and slippers and padded her way out to the kitchen. She stuffed a couple of pain pills into her mouth and swished them down with the dregs of orange juice left in the bottom of the pitcher. Then she just stood and stared into the soupy fog.

Melody bounded into the room, wearing only a Seattle Seahawks shirt that hung to her knees. "CMI does have a Lloyd Bennington. His secretary took my name, message and phone number . . . well, your phone number, really . . . and said she would see that it personally gets to him. He is out of the office this week, but he'll be calling in. I wonder if he's still out here. Wouldn't that be so cool? Oh, wow! I just had a great idea of how to open my book. I can't believe it. Boy, when inspiration hits, a person's got to write. But then, you know all about that. I love it, don't you? Don't you just love being a writer? Boy, you look awful, Dr. S." Melody trotted out of the kitchen, her bare feet slapping the linoleum tile floor.

Shuffling around the small kitchen, Price got a pot of coffee brewing, then slid the glass door open to step out onto the misty deck. The Sound was shrouded in mono-chromatic gloom. A fishy stench ruled the air. She could see no distinguishing feature, but she heard the lapping of the waves and the squawking of the sea gulls. She wished they would both shut up.

Price only faintly heard Tony run up to

the side of the deck, but his voice cut through like a foghorn, a loud, piercing, screeching, wailing, mind-numbing fog-horn.

He pulled an orange beach towel out from under a tarp. "Morning, babe. Boy, it's great to see you up. Isn't this a perfect time of the morning? I love it. Gets the heart pumping and the creative juices flowing, doesn't it? This is one of those mornings I wish I could've carried my laptop with me as I ran. I kept having one idea after another."

He wiped his hair, face and neck. "I was down by the Navy Acoustic Lab, and this great illustration for a concluding paragraph to chapter six came to me. It's just what we need. Remember how you said last night on our way home that it ended weak, and I said it was fine the way it was? Well, I was thinking Price just might be right this time. So I developed an alternative. I'll punch it in and see what you think."

As he rubbed his chest and legs and arms, orange fuzz from the towel left a trail. "And I figured out what to do about that contract with Davidian. I'm going to propose that Davidian get 10%, Liz 5%, and Atlantic-Hampton 25%. That leaves us with 60%. That sounds better, don't you think? Of course, that's only the first book. If they want to do a sequel, everything is up for renegotiation. I read somewhere that the writer should ask for a percentage of gross revenue of the movie, not net profit. Of course, that's assuming they'll pick up an option and actually make a movie. I think I'm getting jazzed about the possibility. I just wish Davidian wasn't such a flaky acting guy."

Price mentally told him to peel away the fuzz, but the words didn't come out.

"Say, you'll never guess what else I thought of. I got direction on my next western series. I'm going to call it the End of the Line series. Each book will be located at a different cattle town that was the end of the railroad line at that time. I can weave in the Mastersons, Earps, Bill Hickok and all those guys. What do you think?"

Half-open eyes peered at him through a face full of wrinkles, but no dimples. "What I think is, I'm at the end of my line. I'm going back to bed."

"To bed? You're kidding. The day's just starting."

"Not for me, it isn't."

Tony was hard at work at his computer and Price was dozing at hers around 2:00 P.M. when Melody burst into the house toting a large blue Icee and a big bag of Cheetos.

"Lunch," she explained. "Hey, you two. I had a great idea. Get your notebooks and let's go interview Grandma right now."

"I thought you said she didn't want to talk to us."

"That was yesterday. She always forgets, so I thought we'd just show up and I'll say, 'Grandma, here are those people who want to talk to you about the old days.' You jump in with a quick question, and maybe she'll forget all about her tirade. What do you think?"

Tony hesitated. "We can try, but if she puts up any major resistance, we're out of there. Our purpose isn't to harass the local citizens."

"Tony, maybe we shouldn't take any notes while we're there. We'll jot down as much as we can back in the car. Maybe she'll feel more at ease."

"Sure, but I don't want her to think we're trying to deceive her."

"Grandma will either talk your leg off or scream you out of the room. But we won't be any worse off than we are now, I think."

Tony and Price shut down their laptops and headed for the bedroom.

"Hey, you guys look just fine as you are.

You always look great. I hope I can still look that sharp when I'm your age. Want some Cheetos?"

"No, thanks," Tony replied. "I'll get my keys."

"How about you, Dr. S.? I've got an extra large Icee. I'd be happy to share. You look like you could use a lift."

"Thanks, I already had lunch."

A delightful repast of four Midol tablets and eight ounces of low-fat plain yogurt.

Jessica Davenport Reynolds perched on a plastic-covered stuffed chair, watching a soap opera. Her gray-streaked hair looked freshly styled, or perhaps carefully hairnetted each night to keep its shape. She wore round pearl earrings, clip style, and a pearl choker, just right for the navy-blue dress with red-and-white pinstripes. Her eyebrows curved down with the bridge of her nose; it would have given her a stern, even menacing look, if it weren't for the very decided smile with which she now graced them. She pushed the mute button on the remote control.

"Grandma Jessie, you had your hair done," Melody crooned as she leaned down to kiss the powdered cheek.

"Melody, honey, are you married yet?"

Turning to Price and Tony, she whispered, *"She always asks me that. . . ."* No, Grandma, not yet."

She shook a thin, white finger. "Don't wait too long. It's a big mistake to wait too long. I ought to know."

"Grandma Jessie, you married Grandpa when you were twenty."

"I waited too long. Who are they?"

"These are the people who want to talk to you about the old days on Fox Island."

Melody, Price and Tony held their breaths, hearing nothing but the ticking of the large wall clock. Jessica glared at them both, then her features softened ever so slightly. "I've seen it all."

Melody started breathing again. Price moved closer and held out her hand. "Mrs. Reynolds, I'm Price Shadowbrook, and this is my husband, Tony. We're so delighted to get to talk to you."

"What kind of name is Price?"

"It's a nickname for Priscilla," Melody bubbled.

"It sounds like the blue light special at K-Mart."

"Grandma!"

"Let's go for a walk. This program stinks. Heather just walked out on Alex, who has spent the last six weeks sending suggestive notes to Stephanie, who thought they were coming from Peter, who secretly lusts after Heather ever since she got out of jail. I can't stand television. But it gives me something to do while I wait for the next meal. Not that the meals are worth waiting for, mind you." She pointed the remote at the screen and flipped it off. "It's the same godless mishmash every day."

Price steadied Jessica's arm as she struggled to her feet. She clutched back with a firm grip. Her skin felt smoother than Price expected.

Melody shoved open the sliding glass door that led out of the small three-room apartment. Shade from umbrella trees splattered the patio cement and the carefully manicured box shrub. Triple-tiered treelike shrubs marked the boundary lines of the long line of apartment patios, all empty. TV scenes shone from all the open-curtained windows.

"Maybe that's why I watch it. God's given up on me, that's for sure," Jessica asserted, stomping her cane for emphasis.

"Grandma Jessie, don't start that again. We didn't come here for you to talk like that," Melody scolded.

Price tried to shush Melody.

"It's true. I wrecked everything. Everything."

"The Lord's mighty good at forgiving," Tony tried to console.

"Grandma, we didn't come here to talk about that old car wreck. Mr. and Mrs. Shadowbrook want to visit with you about what it was like riding the ferryboats in the old days. Come on, let's sit over in the shade, by the azaleas."

"Those are rhododendrons. They're evergreen and odorless as paper bells. I'd prefer azaleas myself, a little pleasant scent to brighten an old woman's day, but I wasn't asked."

The sun beat down through the hazy blue sky, but the shade helped calm them as they tried to sit comfortably on a cement bench next to the raised redwood planter full of scarlet blooms. Melody ran back to get a cushion for her grandmother.

"Mrs. Reynolds," Tony began.

"Call me Jessica. I like everyone to call me Jessica, don't I?" She patted her cane on Melody's knee.

"Jessica, tell us some of your earliest memories of riding the ferry."

She leaned both hands on the top of her cane, which was carved to look like the head of a fox. "There were steam paddleboats in the real old days. Just like those riverboats on the Mississippi. I think one was the *Tyconda*, a stern wheeler. That's when the paddles are in the back."

"What was it like going to school in Tacoma?" Price asked. "How early did you have to get up to catch the ferry?"

"We got up at 4:42 every morning."

"Why 4:42?"

"Papa was very organized. That would allow each of us time to help with the chores, clean up, have breakfast, do our Bible reading and make it to the trading post by 6:15. It used to be down on 9th and Fox Drive, across from the dock, you know."

"How was the ride over? Was it often stormy?"

"Oh no. Most of the time it was just like riding a bus. We got most of our homework done while riding that ferry."

"How about once you got to Tacoma? How did you get to your school?"

"Either by riding the bus, or one of the adults who ferried his car over would give us a ride. Did I tell you that I had a twin sister?"

"Yes, we knew that."

"Her name was Jill. I'm Jessica, and her name was Jill. Yes, that's the way. . . . Papa named us after two singers he once heard in the Yukon. He went north to the gold rush and came back fairly wealthy."

"Mrs. Reynolds, Jessica, were there ever any boat wrecks . . . a storm out on the Narrows, or an accident docking the boat?"

"When the water was too rough, they didn't run the ferry. Sometimes we would miss several days of school. But that didn't happen very often. After dark, or during a rainy or foggy day, they followed a compass course. If you didn't know the tides, you could miss your destination by as much as a half mile. When it was really foggy or snowing, they'd bounce echoes to find their way. Some of those captains could bounce echoes off a clam shell."

"Grandma Jessie, did Auntie Jill ever get hurt in a ferry accident?"

The smile decidedly dropped off as the gray hair seemed to tinge bluer in the filtered light. "Who told you that?"

"I read an old newspaper."

"It was nothing." She rubbed the palms of her hands together as if trying to wash something off.

"But the paper said that Auntie Jill broke both her legs."

"Oh, that." She rubbed her legs as though feeling her sister's pain. "Some cars shifted when we rammed into the dock during a squall. The bumper from a black '27 Ford pushed her into the railing. It caught her right leg about here." She pointed about four inches below her right knee. "And the left leg above the knee about here. She was wearing her favorite green dress. Well, it was both of our favorites. We always dressed alike. The one got ruined, so we had to toss both of them away. She had to stay at home in splints for six weeks."

"That must have been strange for you, going to school without your twin sister," Price commented.

"I just said I couldn't go to school. I had to stay home."

"You mean you both stayed home?"

Mrs. Reynolds gazed off across the patio. "Yes, we both stayed home. We did everything together, you know. Say, do you have a twin sister?" she asked Price.

"No, but we do have twin daughters. I'm afraid they aren't identical. In fact, there is nothing similar about them."

"That's good. That's the way it should be. The other way is too confusing. How would you like to grow up always looking at a mirror image of yourself and always being called by the wrong name?" She tucked her left fist under her chin, the elbow balanced on the cane and right hand, her face drawn tight with concentration. "The car wreck was my fault, you know. I was getting sleepy and she told me to stop and rest, but I wanted to go on. I don't know why I . . ."

"Grandma," Melody interrupted. "Why didn't you ever tell me about the ferryboat accident?"

"You never asked."

Tony paused to study the woman's face. "I have to tell you, Mrs. Reynolds, that I really enjoy your paintings."

"Yes," Price chimed in, "the Two Girl pictures are just delightful. You must tell us what made you think up such a creative idea, especially for that day . . . ?"

"It was tedious to have to sit there for such a long time."

"Sit there?"

"Sit there and sit there. We both sat there."

"Which are you, Mrs. Reynolds? Are you the girl . . . or the reflection?"

Jessica Reynolds twisted her pearl necklace until a welt developed on her neck. She rubbed one black pump against the other, back and forth, back and forth. Melody sent them a warning signal.

"Mrs. Reynolds, I was delighted to discover some of your later works," Tony injected in the long silence. "We stumbled across the collection downstairs . . . the mother-daughter scenes. You were trying a different style. What a very talented and versatile lady you are."

"Trash! That's a pile of trash." The woman's features turned harsh, bitter. Her voice became agitated and angry. "Melody, I told you to throw those away. Why didn't you discard them like I said?"

"Grandma, Mother gave those to me. I like them, and I want to keep them."

"They're a disgrace and you know it. I'm missing my program. Melody, help me to my room."

"Grandma, you said you didn't like it."

She struggled to her feet, almost toppling over. "What I said was, I am not going to give any interviews and that's final. I know what you're up to. I don't want to talk about it anymore."

Melody jumped to her feet and held her grandmother's arm. She turned and shrugged at Tony and Price as Mrs. Reynolds shuffled back into the apartment.

"Can we help?" Price offered.

"It's Okay. I'll be right back."

Price and Tony waited in the white Oldsmobile. Finally, Melody Mason's long dark hair bounced into view. She swung her leather bag and herself into the backseat.

"Well, I tried," she grimaced. "Sorry about that scene. You never know what's going to touch her off. The other day it was Bennington. Today it was my mother's paintings."

Tony and Price gaped at each other. "Your mother's? You mean, it was your mother who painted those pictures down in the family room, not your grandmother?"

"Yeah. It was in the '60s, right before she got married. I think they're great. But Grandma says, 'They lack artistic merit and authentic social observation.' So, Mom won't let me hang them up."

"But they look so professional," Price began.

Melody dismissed the subject with her hands. "Wild, isn't it? But who can argue with a recognized artist? Certainly not my mother."

7 When the Tacoma Narrows Bridge opened up the Kitsap Peninsula to increased motor traffic, the next natural step was building a bridge to Fox Island. The opening of the almost two-thousand-foot Fox Island Bridge on August 28, 1954, by Governor Arthur Langle, was a turning point in the history of this arboreous community. The initial tolls, however, were about the same rate as the ferry passage, with the added burden to the commuter to pay for a car, gasoline and parking. Instead of a gateway for growth, the bridge actually reduced the residency, from 150 families to 115 families. While the bridge is taken for granted by most of the Island's residents today . . . in the short range, its impact was negative rather than positive.

It's never easy to judge both immediate and long-range consequences.

"Hi, Mom! What are you doing here?"

Barbara Mason charged into the house, clinking with glass beads on her chest, half a dozen copper bracelets on each arm and a face mask of powdered makeup obviously layered in a dimly lit room.

"Well," she replied to their stares, "it's my mother's house, and you're my daughter. Do I need any other excuse for stopping by?"

"No, it's just . . . well, you never come to . . . I mean, it's been a long time since you got this far from home," Melody hemmed and hawed as her mother marched down the hall toward Price.

"Nice to see you again, Barbara. Would you like a cup of hot tea?"

Dark brown eyes like Melody's shot her a quick, hard glance. "Do I look like the kind of woman who drinks tea?"

"Coffee, then?"

"Thanks. Is your husband around?"

"Tony? No, he's down the street getting a tour of the Navy Acoustics Lab. Could I help you?"

"Maybe." Her hands trembled as she cradled the hot drink Price handed her. "Don't you have something to do somewhere else?" she said as she glared at Melody.

"Oh, sure," Melody stammered. "I . . . eh, I thought you came to see me."

"Now why would I do that? You're over at my house two or three times a week as it is."

The ever-present smile vanished as Melody winced. "I'll go work on my book." She shuffled out the front door.

Price led Barbara to the living room. A brief wave of alcohol fumes drifted by. "What can I do for you, Barbara?"

Jessica Reynolds' daughter stopped to gaze at the painting titled, "Two Girls on the Train." A pensive passenger about eighteen stared out the window as a small town passed by. Her exact image looked back from the glass of the window. The only difference was a sense of wonder in the girl's eyes and a look of fear in the reflection's.

"I'll never know how she did that so well. She's never bothered to pass on her trade secrets, as far as I know." She turned back to Price. "I hear you and your husband went to interview my mother against her wishes."

Price braced herself against the back of the navy chair. "We did go to visit. As soon as she became agitated, we left."

"Well, I want it to stop right now. All this digging up of old things. It hasn't been good for her. At her age, and in her condition, she doesn't need to be bothered with the past. Her life hasn't been pleasant, and you two pumping her doesn't help."

Price looked straight at Barbara Mason. "We visited with your mother just like we did dozens of other Fox Island residents. I'm sorry if that stirred old hurts. That wasn't our intent."

"But all this talk about a friend of Auntie Jill's coming by. She hasn't been well since she found out about this Bennington fellow."

"The man did stop by asking questions, and we, quite naturally, thought that the family would like to be informed. That's why we told Melody, and I'm sure that's why she told her grandmother."

Barbara Mason's hair, parted crooked in the middle, hung as lifeless as her dark circled eyes. "There is no way my mother needs to put up with that kind of thing. She should be left alone. The painful past is gone."

"How about you?" Price challenged. "Are you still living in a world of past hurts?"

"I can cope," Barbara Mason insisted.

"We saw your beautiful paintings downstairs. I know why your mother stopped painting, but why did you?"

Barbara tromped to the window and looked out, refusing to glance back at Price. "There are many disappointments in life."

Like never pleasing your mother? Or your-

self. My heart breaks for you, Barbara Mason.

"So it doesn't bother you to bury your talent in a basement?"

"I can cope," Mason insisted.

"Do you like how you're coping?"

"What are you talking about?"

"Do you like the way you're living?"

I can't believe I'm saying this. Lord, help me.

"How dare you talk to me like that," Mason huffed.

"Did you ever wonder why an attractive and vivacious young woman like your Melody is not the least interested in getting married?"

"She's still young."

"Yes, she is. And I imagine she's watched the misery of her mother and grandmother who seem content to sit around moping about the past and have no use for the present. You've both passed your bitterness right on to your daughter. No wonder Melody is mistrustful of all men."

Mason shoved her cup and saucer on the end table, banging it against the seashell lamp, and headed to the door. "I don't know why you're saying these things."

Lord, I'm not sure either.

"Because you seem like one of the most unhappy women I've ever met. But you have such a delightful daughter. And you have such marvelous artistic talent. And you have a splendid family history on the Island. And you seem to have a bit of financial independence. It doesn't add up. I think God has something better in life for you than what you've settled for. I guess I really want you to experience his best."

Barbara Mason paused, her hand on the doorknob. "Well, I've been right there at the house all these years. Anytime God wants to deliver something better . . . I'll be more than willing to accept."

"Perhaps you have a few things in the way."

"What do you mean?"

"Everything from lack of confidence to . . . perhaps the drinking."

"I don't have to stay here and listen to this. You don't even know me. You have no right in the world to criticize my life. You've never been through what I had to go through. So don't you look down your prissy, pious professor's nose at me and tell me not to drink. I want you and your husband to stay away from Mother. Is that clear?" She flung open the door for emphasis.

Price's hands and shoulders began to quake. She tried to keep her voice calm. "I'll be praying for you, Barbara. I'm really asking God to help you find joy and peace in him."

The only response was an icy glare. Price watched in dismay as Mrs. Mason hiked out to her car and churned up the driveway.

Oh, Lord, what have I done? I don't know why I'm shaking all over. I don't know why I said those things. Tony should have been here. I can't believe I did this. I took a perfectly unhappy woman and made her life even more miserable. I messed everything up. Maybe I should stay home and teach summer school next year. I'm better with a whole class. I'm not good one on one.

A half hour later Melody crept back into the house.

Clad in white bermuda shorts and a yellow embroidered blouse, Price sat at the kitchen table thumbing through *Roget's Thesaurus* and several dictionaries.

"What are you doing, Dr. S.?"

"Looking for a word."

"What word?"

"I'll know it when I find it. Tony gets on a kick of using the same word over and over in a book, and he expects me to find a creative, dynamic synonym."

"What's the word this time?"

"Sylvan. Every other page talks of the

sylvan island this and the sylvan island that. But I've already used up shady, wild, woodsy, pastoral and provincial. I need another expression that gets the point across."

Melody pried open the refrigerator and dug through the vegetable drawer. She pulled out a bag of peeled baby carrots. "Well, now you've seen my mother on one of her cranky days. Did she get mad at you for criticizing my writing?"

"No, she was upset that we've been agitating your grandmother."

"She said that?"

"I think she blames us for this latest bout your grandmother's going through."

"But this is mainly over that guy, Bennington. It has nothing to do with you. I was the one who told her about him."

"Well, your mom certainly thinks it's our fault. She said she doesn't want us visiting your grandmother."

"Oh, she's just ticked. I'll settle this down. This is what she's like when she's tired of drinking and has had no male companionship for a few days."

"Here it is." Price pointed to a thick book bound in green imitation leather. "Arboreous: having many trees." She punched the word into the laptop, saved the document, then shoved her chair back from the table. "I'm really sorry your mom lives such a miserable life, Melody. When's the last time she had some fun? Other than alcohol and men?"

"She's always been kind of a negative person."

"Well, I don't think I helped things much."

"What did you tell her?"

"Basically, I told her to snap out of it because God had a better plan for her life."

"You did? Really? Oh, wow! You told her that? What did she say?"

"She said no one ever talked to her like that and stomped out the door."

"Don't worry. Mom's that way sometimes. You've just got to leave her alone for a few days. She'll think about what you said, really. Mom's a very thoughtful person. She relives every word of every conversation. Besides, following up with Bennington was my idea, not yours. I didn't get a phone call from Maryland, did I?" She crunched into the carrots.

"No."

"It's been a week since I talked to his secretary. Do you think I ought to call back?"

"Maybe he just doesn't want to talk to anyone out here."

"I know. I've been trying not to think about that. I finally told Grandma about him leaving the flowers. That's probably what put her in a tizzy."

"What did she say?"

"She looked at the picture of the flowers you took, then glanced at the card and said, 'Hah!' and walked away."

"Hah?"

"Yeah, and when I pursued it, she went into a tirade about how it wasn't her fault the car crashed, that there was nothing she could have done."

"Maybe that's what your mom was talking about. Melody, I'm really sorry your mom was so upset. It leaves a horrible knot in my stomach. I don't know why I said those things!"

"Hey, I'm going to Tacoma to clip some coupons and shuffle some stocks, so I'll stop by Mom's on the way home. Don't worry. She'll be all right. I'll let you know how she is."

"Tell her I'm really sorry to have disturbed both her and your grandmother."

"Mom's a good person, really. Life's been such a disappointment. First her father's gone, then her husband. It's pretty hard not to blame yourself. She's just been lonely for so long."

"How about you, Melody?"

"Lonely? . . . not me. Well, actually, I get along just fine because I've never known anything else. This summer with you and Mr. S. has been one of the most fun times in my whole life. Thanks for letting me stay in the loft and bug you all the time. Did I tell you I applied for a teaching job?"

"You did? Where?"

"At a school up in Bremerton. I think maybe I've been too isolated the last few years to be a good writer."

"What grade?"

"Junior high English. Isn't that a kick?"

"That would be a great experience for you."

"I knew you would say that. Anyway, they have to let me know by August 15."

"I'll be praying for you."

Melody bit her lip. "Thanks, Dr. S. I'm beginning to count on your prayers."

"Will you be home for supper?"

"Oh, I'll nab a burger somewhere. You don't have to feed me, you know."

Melody grabbed a handful of carrots, a big bag of corn chips, a Diet Dr. Pepper and scooted out the door.

Price had completed a rewrite of the first six pages of chapter seven and was rummaging in the kitchen for something to fix for lunch when the telephone rang.

"Shadowbrooks."

"I need to speak with a woman named Melody Mason," a weak-voiced man replied.

"She's not here. Can I take a message?"

"This is Lloyd Bennington. I was returning her call."

"Mr. Bennington? My husband met you when you came out to Fox Island. Melody's been waiting for your call. She really needs to talk with you."

"I'm afraid I've been a little under the weather. This is the first day I've felt like calling."

"Have you been ill?"

"Perhaps your husband mentioned the fact that I'm fighting cancer. I just underwent some experimental treatments that supposedly gave me a few more weeks to live. But the ordeal left me so weak that quite frankly I don't know if it was worth it. I don't want to sound brash, but do you happen to know why she was so insistent on calling me?"

"I'll try to fill you in. Jessica Davenport Reynolds, that's Melody's grandmother, is having a difficult time with your showing up after all these years. Especially the visit to the house . . . and the flowers left at the grave? A psychologist at the place where she stays suggested that if you were in the area still, it would be good to have you meet with Jessica one on one. Melody's worried about her grandmother, and was just tracking you down."

"Oh . . . yes . . . well, I suppose it could help her some. At least she could visualize who it is she should hate."

"Why do you think she hates you? You didn't even know her, did you?"

"No, we've never met. But it was, well, a long, long time ago. I'm afraid it was just on a lark that I flew west. Very uncharacteristic of me. I don't expect to feel well enough to travel again. To tell the truth, Mrs. Shadowbrook, just making it to the restroom is quite a chore."

"I understand. I wonder if she might call you when she gets home late this afternoon? I think that might help Melody some."

"It's not that easy. By necessity, I keep my number unlisted. I just couldn't give it out. I don't mean to sound secretive or snobbish, but I receive a lot of calls from people thinking I should lend or give them money."

"Could we set up a time tonight for you to call back?"

"As long as she understands I just might

feel too ill to do so. What time do you suggest?"

"How about 9:00 P.M. your time? That leaves it 6:00 P.M. our time."

"Yes, I'll call her back. Good day, Mrs. Shadowbrook."

Tony came home for lunch, then drove up the Kitsap Peninsula to Bangor for his scheduled submarine ride. Price spent the afternoon at the keyboard trying to punch in a second edit of chapter seven. The confrontation with Barbara Mason kept going through her head.

After a walk along the shoreline, she called Melody's mother. She attempted an apology to a groggy-sounding Barbara Mason and found out, in the process, that Melody had left her mother's headed back to Fox Island at 3:00 P.M. Price walked up the steep driveway to the road to watch for her car turning off Island Boulevard onto 3rd.

Lord, this would be a delightful time for Melody to show up. Bennington's going to call soon.

The warm summer breeze made her think about relaxing in the chaise lounge and sunbathing.

I don't feel good about that apology. Every-

thing I do seems to make the situation worse. Couldn't I just delete today and start all over again?

Price soaked boneless chicken strips in marinade, then lightly fried them in canola oil and diced some vegetables. She heard a rap at the front door and hollered, "Come in, Melody, I'm in the kitchen."

A woman appeared, wearing cutoff blue jeans, olive drab t-shirt and hiking boots. Her earthy brown hair hung in a long, tapered braid down her back. A few wisps garnered her bronzed forehead. Oversized dark glasses covered her eyes.

"Hello, Tulip! Forgive me for not coming to the door. I thought you were Melody."

"Here's the deal." Her thin lips shut tight between each phrase, as though to conserve energy. "There is absolutely no suitable location for the larger animals. According to government studies, it would be psychologically damaging to house any animal over seventy-four pounds in weight in any field less than five acres. I called Cascade Kids-Can Pet, Inc. and instructed them that they might have to leave the larger animals at their wholly inadequate and life-endangering compound."

"I don't suppose they were thrilled with that idea?"

"They protested vigorously and demanded a special community meeting. So, I've prepared this report to take."

"What's in the report?"

"If Cascade KidsCan Pet, Inc. does not intend to abide by the site committee's recommendations, then their contract will be terminated. They threatened to sue, of course, but think of the media attention we can get with a trial. I'm sure the networks would pick it up."

Price tried to guess how old the petite lady was. She had a leathery tan face, with a few deep wrinkles around her eyes. Just a tad of gray in her hair. Yet there was a vitality in her actions and a pixie cuteness in her face. She settled on fortyish.

"The committee hasn't made any recommendation, as far as I know," Price pointed out.

"That's the thing. I need you and Kenny Mallard to sign on to this document. There's a lot of legal jargon in it, but you get the gist of things."

"Has Harvey Peterson seen it?"

"Yes, he has."

"And what did he say?"

Tulip yanked the sunglasses off and

rubbed her nose on the back of her arm. "You're one of those born-again Christians, aren't you?"

Price crossed her arms in front of her and dropped her smile. "Well, yes I am. What in the world does that have to do with this?"

Ms. Tulip's lips flashed in a brief sign of amusement. "Well, then, you don't want me to repeat word for word what Harvey said."

"And you haven't talked to Kenny?"

"Nobody's seen Kenny. What about it? Are you going to sign on or not?"

"No, I'm not."

Tulip groaned, a short croak of disgust. "Yeah, I sort of figured that. You're just one of those do-nothing Christians who sit around in expensive churches isolating yourself from the real world. It's people like you that . . ."

Price's right hand shot forward with the determination of a junior high teacher scolding a hyperactive boy in the back row. "You just wait a minute. Don't give me any of that Christians-lack-compassion garbage! I donate every Tuesday evening during the school year to teach English as a second language, free, in southwest Phoenix. I serve as an emergency counselor for a pregnancy counseling center. My family has, for eight years now, spent every spring break building orphanages and hospitals in Mexico. Not to mention ten years as a Girl Scout leader, volunteer work at the Union Gospel Mission, or summers teaching reading at the Navajo, Hopi, Apache and Tohono O'Odham reservations."

Tulip rubbed the edge of her mouth with her fist, as though trying to erase it. "I was only trying to say . . ."

"What you were trying to do is enforce your own political persuasion on someone else by guilt and inference. Lady, it just doesn't work. If you want me to get excited about your cause, why not work with street kids in Seattle, or run a home for people living with AIDS, or do volunteer work for an adoptions agency so that unwanted babies end up in a loving home? But don't you dare question my faith just because I don't give a squat if a seventy-six pound pig has a five-acre play yard or not."

Tulip spun on her hiking boot heels and stomped toward the door. Tony Shadowbrook stood there, eyes wide and mouth open.

"Goodbye, Tulip," he muttered, holding open the door.

"I don't need some chauvinist middle-aged hunk to open doors for me," she fumed.

Tulip was driving up the driveway before Tony turned back to Price. "Was that an insult or a compliment she gave me?"

Tears swelled in Price's eyes.

"Wow, what was all that about?"

"It's been a lousy day!" she sniffled.

"I heard most of the speech. I thought it was great."

"But," she began, breathing deep to try to hold back the sobs, "I spoke it in anger. I don't know why some days are that way. I didn't want to be this way. And it's not the first time today."

"You had a run-in with Tulip earlier?"

"No, with Barbara Mason, Melody's mother."

"Whoa, stress city. Tell me about it."

"I don't want to talk about it."

"What do you want to do?"

"I think I'll go into the bedroom and cry."

"What do you want me to do?"

"Cook dinner."

"Are you kidding?"

Without looking up, Price plowed through the living room toward the bedroom.

I guess she wasn't kidding. Lord, the woman's almost fifty. Doesn't this every month moody thing ever come to an end?

Maybe I should have stayed up there and had chow with the Navy.

Tony had just finished cooking supper when the telephone rang. He left the receiver on the counter, scouted outside, then tiptoed into the master bedroom.

"Hey, babe?"

"I'm in the bathroom washing my face."

"Mr. Bennington's on the phone. He said he was supposed to call Melody at this time, but Melody's not in her loft. Do you know what's going on?"

"Oh no!" she wailed.

He could hear her cry again. "What's the matter?"

"I don't know where Melody is," she sobbed.

"Is she lost?"

"I don't know."

"What do you want me to tell Bennington?"

"I don't know!"

"Don't worry. I'll take care of it."

Tony had just hung up when Price emerged, eyes red and puffy, hair damp, no dimples.

"Did you fix things with Bennington?"

"It's all set. I persuaded Bennington to

236

give me his number at the hospital. Melody can call him tonight or tomorrow. How are you doing?"

"Better. A good cry and a face wash can help almost anything."

"Do you want to tell me about your day?"

"Not really."

"Are you hungry?"

"What did you cook?" she asked.

"I slaved all afternoon over your favorite stir-fry."

They sat at the counter and ate as Tony related his experiences at the Acoustic Lab and aboard the U.S. Navy submarine. "So they really are developing cloaking devices to throw off the sonar?" Price asked.

Tony waved his hands enthusiastically as he talked. "Yeah, and then working on machines to pick up sound when the cloaking devices are on. It's incredible. Sort of like *Hunt for Red October*."

"How much of that can you use?"

"Oh, all of that is public knowledge. But it makes you wonder what they're keeping secret, doesn't it?"

"You think it will fit into the flow of the book?" Price asked.

"I don't know. Most of it sounds too technical. But listen, I was able to pick up declassified Navy info from the 1940s. It includes the proposed defense plans for the possible invasion of Puget Sound. The data has been cleared by the Freedom of Information Act. It's all cataloged and computerized. I was able to pull out everything that mentioned Fox Island."

"You mean stuff like checking out Harvey Peterson's Japanese invasion claims?"

"Exactly. I haven't had a chance to look through it yet, but isn't that great? There's got to be something in there that will make the book really zing with authenticity. I don't even think old Harvey has seen some of this yet."

"I'm glad one of us is having a good day."

He was on his second cup of coffee when he noticed Price's drooping face. "How you doin', babe? Really?"

"Oh, I'm all right. It's just that I spend my entire life trying to keep my world, my words, my actions under control. Then every once in a while all this stuff spews all over. It's extremely humbling."

"Which reminds me, I had another idea about how to handle chapter five. But maybe now isn't a good time to talk about it."

"No, I'm fine, really. What's your idea?"

"How about you editing it down to twenty-five pages?"

"You'd let me edit it, my way?"

"You work on it, then I thought we'd take a look together."

"Are you doing this because I'm on a crying jag?"

"Probably."

"Then I'm glad it has at least some minor, redeeming value. I'll start on it tomorrow."

"Now, what should we do about Melody?"

"Her mother said she left her house about 3:00, and she thought she was headed back to the Island."

"She might have had car trouble. Should we go out looking for her? She's a grown woman. She could call if she had car trouble or something."

"What would you do if it were one of your daughters?" Price asked.

"We'll go look for her."

"Maybe I should stay here, in case you miss her. That way I could tell her to call Bennington."

"I'll drive over toward her mother's at Gig Harbor. That VW should be easy to spot."

Price let out a deep sigh. "Thanks, Tony. Sorry I'm having such a bad day."

"Babe, you on a bad day are still better than any other woman I know on a good day. And, lady, when you are having a good day . . . wow! You can make my whole life worth living."

"You always were the absolutely craziest guy I ever dated," she smiled, unable to hide the dimples.

"And you're the prettiest one I ever dated."

"I'm the only one you ever dated."

"That, too."

Tony drove clear to Barbara Mason's house, but didn't go in. He headed back to Fox Island and had reached the bridge when he remembered Price's suggestion to check at Kim's and Jessica Reynolds' convalescent home.

It was nearly dark outside when Tony hiked up the overgrown walk to the white-caulked log cabin on Gibson Point. A four-totem pole peered out from behind overgrown shrubs like an ancient grotesque sentinel. To reach the front porch, he rolled aside a four-foot wagon wheel, which slid into a groove in the dirt that seemed to be its permanent position. Only a screen door separated him from the cluttered front room. The walls were crammed with darkly painted unframed artist's canvases. On the floor lay tubes of paint scattered around three separate easels.

He knocked.

There was no answer.

"Excuse me? Anyone home?"

She wouldn't just wander off and leave everything turned on and opened up. Would she?

"Kim? Are you home?"

Finally, he heard a rumble from the back of the cabin. "She ain't here!"

"Kim's not here?"

The voice continued to bounce out. "That's what I said. Go away."

"You haven't seen Melody Mason, have you?"

"No."

"Who are you?"

"Amigo."

"Hey, Amigo, if you could step out to the living room, I'd like to talk to you a minute."

A tall man with shaved head emerged into the dim light wearing only a pair of jeans. The left side of his body was painted black and the right side painted blue. The color scheme included his neck, face, head, arms, chest, stomach and feet.

"Yeah? What are you staring at?"

"Your suntan."

"What about it?"

"I just need to find Melody. When Kim

comes in, could you please ask her to phone the Shadowbrooks down at Melody's grandmother's?"

"Maybe I will. Maybe I won't. Are you Melody's old man?"

"No. I'm her . . . I'm sort of like her father."

"No foolin'?"

"And no foolin' around. You understand?"

"Si, yo comprendo."

"Bueno. Adios, Amigo."

Shadowbrook, you're beginning to sound like the novels you write.

Tony didn't spot the VW bus at the convalescent home, and didn't bother asking if Melody had been there, not wanting to disturb Jessica Reynolds. Finally, he returned home to find a brand-new black Dodge pickup blocking the driveway. He parked on the lawn.

"Great. We've got company."

Fast, high-pitched female voices caught his attention as he hung his cowboy hat on a hallway peg.

"Price?" he called.

She stepped to the hall. Her face, once again, reflected tanned Arizona charm and professorial dignity.

"Tony, Melody's here. Come on, we've

got lots of news for you."

Melody wasn't the only one in the kitchen. Another girl, about Melody's age, wearing jeans and a blue-and-black plaid long-sleeved shirt, auburn braids twisted on top of her head, was inhaling a Diet Coke and potato chips. Melody was dressed similarly, but her dark hair was pulled back in a wavy roll on the sides, hanging down long with ringlets in the back.

"Hi, Mr. S. Sorry I caused you to worry. Actually, it feels sort of nice to have someone worry about me. It's been a long time, if you know what I mean. Hey, this is Kim."

The olive-skinned Kim hopped down from the counter stool and held out her hand. She was a little shorter than Melody, and had a small rose tattoo on the back of her right hand.

"Mr. Shadowbrook, Mel has told me so much about you, I feel like I know you already."

"Well, I did meet a friend of yours just now. I was just down at your place, looking for Melody."

"A friend of mine? Who?"

"Amigo."

"Not at my place?"

Tony nodded.

"Is he in the cabin? Or just in front?"

"Oh, he's inside."

"What color was he?"

Price handed Tony a Coke. "Color? Amigo changes color?" she asked.

"Last time I saw him, he was black and blue."

"Oh yeah, right, sure. Today he decides to be black and blue. But he spent the last two weeks orange and purple. Well, it's too late. He already ruined it for us." Kim swung around and pointed at Melody. One of her braids dropped out of its nest. "I'm staying with you tonight. I'm not about to go home if he's black and blue."

Tony turned to Price. She raised her eyebrows and shrugged.

"Is that your new pickup, Kim?" he finally asked.

"It's mine," Melody piped in.

"Yours?"

"See, here's the thing. I did a pretty good job with the stock trading this past quarter, so I treated myself to a new vehicle. Sure I'll have payments, but what with the teaching job, I figured I could do it. So, after I visited Mom, I picked up Kim and we drove to Tacoma and I bought that sucker."

"That's great," Tony replied, "but why a truck?"

"You said my VW looked like the ultra

radical tree huggers', so I wanted something that expressed my personality better."

"What expression does a woman driving a new black Dodge pickup make, anyway?" Price asked.

"That she's looking for a cowboy," Kim suggested.

Melody grinned from earring to earring and giggled. "He doesn't have to be a cowboy. He just has to look like one."

Kim crunched an empty bag of chips between her hands. "Mel, let's go cruising."

"On Fox Island?" several voices echoed.

"Nah, let's drive up to Bremerton and Silverdale."

"Yeah, let's do it. Dr. S., you'll have to fill him in on the call to Mr. Bennington. Don't stay up for me. Say, Mr. S., can I borrow one of your cowboy hats?"

"Are you serious?"

"Yep."

Tony handed her his old gray one with a slight rip in the brim. "Take good care of it." He laughed and shook his head.

Melody and Kim roared up the driveway.

"Well, Mother," Tony drawled, "our little girl is growing up."

"Sometimes it seems like we're raising her, doesn't it?"

"As long as she doesn't move back to Scottsdale with us," Tony grimaced. "And to think, we've only known her for seven weeks. Come on, kid. You're looking a lot better. Tell me about the conversation with Bennington."

Tony and Price settled comfortably onto the sofa. The light from the kitchen reflected out into the darkened room. The curtains of the front sliding windows were open, and a few stars flickered through the nighttime reflections. Price cuddled close to Tony in the shadows.

"You feeling better, darlin'?"

"Yes, thank you. Oh, I guess I'm a little envious."

"Of whom?"

She laughed. "Of Melody's new pickup."

"Women and pickup trucks. It's a western tradition, isn't it?"

"Or a statement of independence. Anyway, was this Amigo guy really painted black and blue?"

"Yep."

"No wonder Kim doesn't want to go home."

"I was just wondering what we'd do if one of our girls brought home a guy with body paint."

"He'd probably get to see the barrel end

of her daddy's gun collection."

"Tell me about Bennington."

"You were right about his health. He doesn't think he has many weeks left. There's no way he can come back to the West Coast."

"Did you find out why he came out?"

"Yes. He explained it all to Melody, so I only got it secondhand. He met her mother's Auntie Jill in Boston in May of 1942. Jessica had just eloped with Mr. Reynolds. Jill went to a War Bond rally to hear Benny Goodman. The war was raging in Europe and the Pacific, and Bennington knew he would be called up any day. So a bunch of them, guys and gals, went to New York for one last fling. And . . . he and Jill . . . well."

"Had a good time?"

"That's one way to put it. Anyway, she called him a few weeks later to tell him she thought she was pregnant and she wanted to talk to him about it. They were supposed to meet at a certain cafe. But he panicked and didn't show."

"So he stood her up? He ran out on her?"

"That's about it, except he told Melody he wrote a note to her at Radcliffe later on, but it was returned marked undeliverable. After the war he went back to college on the

GI bill, then got into trading stocks and bonds."

"And now he's with CMI?"

"Yes, he's chairman of the board."

"You're kidding."

"That's what he claims. Anyway, when he found out he was dying of cancer, he suddenly became acutely aware of the failures in his life. His wife died a few years ago, and his only child, a daughter, lives in Rio."

"Brazil?"

"Yes. He said she hasn't spoken to him in years."

"So he's a lonely old rich man, dying with memories of personal failure?" Tony mused.

"That's about it. He said he wrote down twelve things he wanted to do before he died, and apologizing to Jill was one of them."

"He's about fifty-some years too late for that."

"He was pretty stunned to learn that Jill had died in 1942. All this time he's lived with the idea that on Fox Island there was a lady and grown child that hated him."

"And Jessica?"

"He figures that Jill must have told her sister about the pregnancy and how he ran out on her. He figures that's the reason she's still so mad at him."

"And if Jill was pregnant, then a baby died, too, in that wreck. Another reason the thought of it haunts Jessica."

"He said he didn't think it would be of any help for him to speak to Jessica. If she knows all about it, he could tell her nothing new. And if she didn't know, say, that Jill was expecting? . . . He thinks maybe it's best not to bring it up."

"He's probably right."

"He's a very humbled, hurting old man."

"Living with the consequences of his actions."

"Look at the misery that action has caused generations to suffer. Tony, he needs to find God's forgiveness before he dies."

" 'What does it profit a man to gain the whole world and lose his soul?' "

"That's the same verse I thought of. He officially apologized to Melody as a representative of the whole Davenport family."

"How'd Melody take all that?"

"Well, she was a little stunned at first, then a little upset, and then a little proud, I think."

"Proud?"

"She sees herself as one to carry on the Davenport tradition on the Island. This is sort of her cross to bear, the family secret that Davenports will be called upon to endure forever."

"And the new pickup helps to ease her burden?"

"That's for sure. Did you ever see a woman giggle so when she got a new rig?"

"Yep."

"Oh, when?"

"When you first drove home that Mustang convertible."

"I didn't giggle."

"You did too."

"I might have been moderately happy, maybe a refined chuckle or two, but I certainly didn't . . ."

She could see that sparkle in his blue eyes. "You giggled like a junior high girl after her first kiss."

"And how does Mr. I-never-dated-anyone-but-you-babe know that junior high girls giggle after their first kiss?"

"You told me."

"Oh."

8 Almost a year before the bridge opened, the U.S.S. Bashaw became the first submarine to "run" the Navy Acoustic Range at the recently constructed facilities on Fox Island. Most submarine testing is done these days in Southeast Alaska, but research and development continues at "The Naval Surface Warfare Center, Fox Island Acoustic Laboratory." Located at the end of a tree-lined lane, the inconspicuous unit is dedicated to generating procedures and equipment for measuring underwater acoustics for ship silencers. While the urgency for development of such devices seems to have lessened with the demise of the Cold War, being prepared for the unknown future drives researchers to continue experimenting.

Unknown futures tend to motivate us all. Sometime after midnight, Price, Tony and Melody returned to the house exhausted.

"You didn't warn us that a day at your Fox Island Fair would be so wearing," Price said as she kicked off her teal and purple tennis shoes and claimed the whole couch for herself.

Melody collapsed on the navy chair, feet stretched out on a tapestry footstool. "Well, we don't usually have some wacko run into the middle of it, painted in tiger stripes, yelling 'set my people free!' and chasing the entire petting zoo into the woods. Mr. S., I still can't believe you roped that Angora rabbit!"

"I roped the donkey, the Shetland and the llama, but you can't toss a loop on a rabbit. My nylon rope must have slapped up against him hard enough to stun him until he was caught." Tony pulled off his boots with a wooden bootjack, then sat on the brick hearth and tugged down his socks.

"I don't suppose as much money was raised as they had hoped," Price added, "what with everyone tramping over the Island looking for Fluffy, Pierre, Nigel . . . and the rest of the animals."

"That's one fair no one will forget." Tony got up and stretched. "Are you sure it was Amigo who set them loose?"

"Yeah, I'd recognize that body paint anywhere," Melody insisted.

"Tulip said she had nothing to do with it, and I believe her," Price injected. "We don't agree on much, but I don't think she wanted those animals running out into the night to get hurt."

"She was a big help out in the woods rounding them up," Tony added.

"You two were in the woods a long time. . . ." Price thought about giving him a suspicious look but was just too tired.

"I figured it was my civic duty."

"What? Chasing animals? Or frolicking with a professional wood nymph?"

Tony shuffled off to the kitchen.

"Mr. S.," Melody called, "can you bring me a Diet Coke? Thanks." Then she turned to Price. "Amigo used to work for them, you know."

"He worked as an environmental activist?"

"Yeah, when he was still in college. Lots of students do it in the summer. It can be pretty good pay, especially if you're still mooching room and board at home."

"They hire protesters?"

"Sure. It pays up to $8.00 an hour, and all you have to do is hold a sign and scream an occasional obscenity. Every spring and summer the want ads are crammed with job offers. But I think Amigo was too weird even for them. I never thought I'd see Tulip and Harvey Peterson working side by side on anything."

"Most issues aren't as black and white as folks make them out to be. Very few people want to see animals needlessly harmed." Tony balanced cold drinks on a tray. "There's points to be made on all sides. We couldn't have found half the animals without Harvey's infrared night vision scope."

"Why would anyone own such a device?" Price asked. "What legal reason does anyone have for wanting to see in the dark?"

"I don't want to know," Melody yawned. "I wonder if they'll ever find the two turkeys or the armadillo?" She took a deep swig of her soda. "It was sort of fun, like a big, all-Island scavenger hunt."

Tony laughed. "Maybe it will become an annual affair — The Fox Island Diversified Animal Night Roundup."

"We haven't been this united since the county tried to change our street names to numbers corresponding to Tacoma. Can you imagine having a 132nd Street on Fox Island? I can't remember ever working together quite like we did tonight."

Tony pulled a dining chair into the living

room and sank down on it. "Here." Price yawned and pointed to the end of the couch, but he stayed put.

"I spent all day responding to thirty-two letters, and all night chasing animals. And all I want to do is write books."

"Do you get much fan mail?" Melody asked.

"He keeps pretty busy with correspondence, for a minor celebrity," Price responded.

"A minor celebrity?"

"That's what our son Josh calls his dad. A few years ago Tony appeared on a television show where the host spent several minutes clarifying who he was and what he had written. Josh decided that true celebrities need only their name for an introduction, but minor celebrities need a whole explanation. So we call him a minor celebrity."

"You're the most famous author I've ever met," Melody assured him.

Tony jumped to his feet at the sound of the telephone. "It's never good news after midnight," he mumbled.

"Shadowbrooks."

"Daddy, it's me, Kath."

"What is it? What's wrong, babe?"

"Nothing. I've just tried to call you all night and you just got home."

"What's up? Is Kit all right?"

"How would I know? I haven't seen her since this morning. When I got home from work, I found a note saying that she and Linc were going to a movie, then out to fix someone's car."

"I'm sure she'll be home soon. Why did you call?"

"Josh was trying to get ahold of you. When he couldn't reach you, he asked me to be sure and call."

"Is he all right?"

"Is who all right?" Price called from the couch.

"Josh," Tony said.

"What emergency ward is he in?"

"What happened, Kath?"

"Nothing, Daddy, relax. Josh got a call this afternoon that they needed him and Paul to fly up to Seattle tonight to do some sort of stunt on a water tower for a TV show. I guess the regular guys got hurt or something. Anyway, Josh hopped on a plane and flew up there. He was thinking maybe it would work out to visit you and Mom."

Tony turned to Price. "Josh is in Seattle. Right now."

"Anyway, Daddy, he said he'd call you when he could. They're supposed to only be there one day, and he doesn't think he'll have a rental car."

"Does he need to stay here tonight?"

"No. They're shooting the scene at some little town near Mount Rainier in the morning, so they're driving straight to the set. I just thought one of you might want to hang around your place tomorrow, in case he called."

"Thanks, Kath. How's Kit's new job going?"

"I wouldn't know. We don't talk much. She spends most of her time on the phone with good old Linc."

"Now, that's a switch. She usually doesn't talk more than three minutes on the phone to anyone, including your mother."

"She was on the telephone for two hours and forty-three minutes last night," Kathy reported. "Not that it makes any difference to me."

"Look after her, Kath. You've had more experience with this sort of thing. Good night, kid."

When he finished explaining the conversation, Melody scooted out the door and the Shadowbrooks got ready for bed.

Tony dreamed of stumbling through a brushy, overgrown forest at night, trying to rope wild turkeys while being chased by a large, vicious Angora rabbit.

Price dreamed of young men jumping off water towers, each one higher than the next. The last one overshadowed Mount Rainier.

Price was up and in the kitchen when Tony returned from his early morning run. He noticed that she had dressed, combed her hair, put on earrings and was wearing a sweet perfume that radiated above the kitchen scents.

"I can't believe this . . . sausage sizzling in the frying pan and a breakfast aroma lapping outside on the deck, Dr. Shadowbrook all dolled up like she was on her way to a faculty meeting. What's the occasion? We were all up late last night."

"Guess who's in the shower?"

"What do you mean?"

"Our middle child is in there."

"Josh?"

"Oh, you do remember his name!"

"You're kidding me. What do you mean he's here? How'd he get here?"

"Their plane was a little late getting in, and they missed some connections, so Josh and Paul hitched a ride out to Fox Island. Paul crashed on the downstairs bed."

"But he didn't know our address, did he?"

"The people that gave him a ride know us."

"Who?"

"A couple of young ladies in a new black Dodge pickup."

"Melody?"

"She called Kim, and they drove to the airport about 2:00 A.M., waited around, then ran back and forth between Alaska Airlines and United until they spotted a couple of Arizona looking guys."

"What do 'Arizona guys' look like, anyway?"

"Suntanned and cute, according to the girls."

"Four of them in the front seat of the pickup? That was a little crowded, wasn't it?"

"Melody whistled in here with a big smile on her face."

"And Josh?"

"He was smiling too."

"I don't believe this. When did he get in?"

"Right after you left to go running."

"How's he look?"

"As handsome as his father, of course. Only younger."

"No, I mean his hand. Is it healed?"

"He said he wears an elastic bandage and it's fine. Looks like it fractured real close to where he hurt himself the first time he jumped off the roof of the house. Remember?"

"When he was ten?"

"No, the first time. He was only seven. You were off in New Mexico on some research trip. I had to rush him to the emergency ward by myself."

"Fortunately we never had a two-story house."

"Melody and Kim are going to drive the fellas over to the shooting. They think they can get the girls passes to watch today's taping, so the whole gang will be heading out after breakfast."

"When do they sleep?"

"They're young, Tony. You do remember being young, don't you?"

"Only vaguely."

Within thirty minutes Josh, Paul, Kim and Melody joined Tony and Price for breakfast on the patio. Price caught herself staring at her son.

Give him twenty-five pounds and twenty-five years and he'll look just like Tony. I see a young man, Lord. But, with my heart, I still think of him as an adventurous little boy. It's tough to give them up.

"You all right, babe?" Tony nudged.

"Oh, sure." She wiped her eyes with her

little finger. "I think I got too close to the onions that I chopped up for the omelettes."

The summer morning fog quickly burned off as they talked of work, movies, a new apartment and Kathy and Kit. Paul's sandy blond hair was cropped shorter than Price remembered. He had lost that surfer look. When they had finished eating, Josh led the procession out to Melody's new pickup.

"Melody's going to take you back to the airport tonight?" Price asked.

"If we wrap up this shooting today. I think it's not much more than falling off the water tower."

"Oh, great. Then it's nothing for a mom to worry about."

Suddenly, Josh swished his mother off her feet and hugged her close. "I love ya, Mom! I'll be careful."

Her eyes welled up, and she turned quickly to Paul and grabbed his hand. "You take care of each other."

"Yes, ma'am," Paul grinned. "Mr. Shadowbrook, I sure like that River Breaks series of yours. I can hardly wait until they're made into movies."

"Thanks, Paul. Take it easy, Josh. We'll be home in about three weeks. Tell Mark and Amanda when you see them that we need to have a big family barbeque when we get back." Then he turned toward Melody. "If it's too cramped in your rig, you guys can take the Oldsmobile."

"Get real, Dad," Josh scoffed as he climbed in next to Melody.

"Yeah, Dad . . ." Melody echoed.

The foursome roared up the drive.

Tony and Price hiked, hand in hand, to the side of the house and up the stairs to the deck. "Josh and Melody?" was all he could mumble.

Price stacked dishes and swatted some flies. "Why not?"

"But it seems, so . . . well, she's almost like family."

"Go take your shower, Shadowbrook."

"But think of it, what if they got serious? We'd have to read all her book proposals for sure."

About midmorning the telephone rang, and Price rushed into the house. Tony had hardly looked up from the pile of notes scattered around his laptop, but when she came back out with her hands on her hips, he knew it was time to stop and pay attention.

"What's up?"

"I just talked to Barbara Mason. Her mother fell and broke her hip. They're rushing her to a hospital in Tacoma. She's desperate to find Melody. I don't think Barbara does well under stress, and Melody usually handles this kind of thing. We don't have any way of reaching her, do we?"

"I don't have any idea where that scene is being taped."

"That's what I told Barbara. After the way I scolded her last week I thought she'd never talk to me again, but she practically begged me to come over and drive her into Tacoma. She doesn't like driving over the Narrows Bridge. I think I should go help her."

"Sure, babe, that's fine with me. But do you feel comfortable doing that?"

"It might give me a chance to follow up on last week's abrupt dialogue. Besides, it was her idea. She did ask if one of us could drive her."

"Then go on. You're about caught up with me anyway, aren't you?"

"Yes, but I still need to re-edit chapter five. I've only got it down to twenty-seven pages."

"Chopping that much isn't easy, is it?"

"No, it's not. But, then, this is not shaping up to be an easy morning, either."

"Apprehensive about being with Melody's mother? You'll do fine."

"Oh no, I meant it won't be easy for you."

"Me?"

"Remember? This is the morning the ladies from the church stop by to get our advice on how to begin a writer's critique group."

"What? Coming here? Today?"

"Remember my asking you about that? You said today would be a good day for them to come over."

"Yes, but I supposed you'd be the one to talk to them. You'll have to call and cancel."

"I can't do that, Tony. I already turned down their first two suggested dates. Besides, they'll be on their way by now."

"I'll tell them you had an emergency. Maybe they can all go out to lunch or something."

"Tony, that's not right. You agreed."

"Well, I certainly didn't agree to sit around and have tea with a dozen old ladies for a couple of hours."

"They're bringing their own homemade doughnuts and an espresso maker. There's only six of them and the oldest doesn't look a day over thirty-nine. But you can have your choice. Do you want to drive Barbara to the hospital? Or stay with the homemade doughnuts?"

"I'll take the doughnuts."

"Behave yourself. Just be fatherly. I'll grab some lipstick and run. I want to get there before Barbara completely falls to pieces. From the sounds of our conversation, that won't be long."

In what seemed to Tony record time, Price was out the door and on her way to Gig Harbor. He stepped out to the deck and watched seagulls near the water's edge fight over a scrap until it dropped into the Sound, buried somewhere below their frantic dives. The sky was hazy, but the sun beat through with a steady summer warmth.

Lord . . . I just want to write. I love to write. I like to dig around dusty roads and ghost towns for research . . . craft characters that jump off the page . . . and live out every one of my scenes . . . Lord, I even like the fun of telling the story of these little Hidden West places.

But all this other stuff. Interviews . . . contracts . . . self-promotion . . . writers' conferences . . . and critique groups. I just don't do them well. They all seem like such distractions. Are you sure I'm supposed to do all these other things, too?

The doorbell rang several times before he shook himself free from his thoughts and sauntered back into the house. He was introduced to eight women. Two had brought their mothers. Within ten minutes he'd been served homemade doughnuts four times and a mug of steaming mocha coffee with a huge dollop of floating whipped cream and chocolate curls.

Cherry somebody was in charge. "Mr. Shadowbrook, I can't tell you what an honor it is to get to meet with you," she said when they circled him in the living room. Tony dragged in extra dining chairs and opened the drapes full length, hoping to distract them with the beach and bird scene.

"Please call me Tony. My wife, Price, is the expert in critique and editing. I'm happy to share what I know, but I'm afraid you got stuck with the lesser of the Shadowbrooks when it comes to this sort of thing."

For the next forty-five minutes Tony sat holding the same cup of espresso, unable to take a sip due to the continuous questions.

"Where do you get your ideas?"

"What's a book proposal look like?"

"Who publishes poetry?"

"What's the best computer program to use?"

"Where do you get writers' guidelines?"

"How many different publishers have you worked with?"

"How much money can you make on writing? Will it pay the bills?"

"Do you copyright your own work?"

They all listened intently to his every word. Several explained their works in progress. Each woman seemed sincerely interested in writing.

A plump woman with kind eyes talked the most. "I'm Cherry's mother, Patsy Mitchell. Well, I'm from out of town, and not a part of this writers' group, but I must say it is one of the highlights of my life to get to meet you today, Mr. Shadowbrook. My husband, Donald, passed away several years ago, and it's been very lonely without him. I've taken to reading books a lot more, and you have become one of my very favorite authors."

"Thank you, Patsy."

She gently touched his arm. "The characters in your books have become my friends. I feel like I know them well. I sometimes find myself worrying about them. Why, I feel I should have a picture of them in my wallet. When your newest book in a series comes out, it's like a letter from home. I get caught up on how everyone's doing."

"That's just about the nicest compliment I've ever received."

"But there's something I have to ask you." She cleared her throat. "You aren't going to let Houston marry Beth Marie, are you? She's no good for him!"

The room roared with laughter as the phone rang. "Excuse me, ladies," Tony said.

"Tony Shadowbrook."

"Is this Anthony Shadowbrook, the famous writer of western novels?"

"This is Tony Shadowbrook. What are you selling?"

"Selling? Tony, this is KSAB in Denver. You're on the air, partner."

"What?"

"This is 103.5 FM live talk radio, and we're calling a dozen of the country's top western writers to ask them if they can remember what the first line of their last novel was."

"Are you kidding?"

"No, but that's exactly what Elmer Kelton just said. Don't grab a copy. Just give us an extemporaneous rendition of the first lines of *Standoff Creek*."

"Eh . . ." Tony scratched his head and paused. " 'The bullet that struck Brownie seemed to fall straight out of the sky. When the horse went down, Houston didn't know whether to dive to the right or to the left. But either way, he knew he had to come up firing.' "

"Right on! I can't believe it. Joaquin Esta-ban couldn't even remember the title of his latest book. Tell us the truth, did you read that?"

"No. I've got eight lovely women here in the room to verify it."

"That's amazing. How are you able to remember that exact sentence?"

"Because I was riding the horse when it happened."

"Would you explain that to our radio audience? Are you saying this really happened to you?"

"I'm saying that I walk through and ride out every one of my scenes, and it becomes a personal memory, just like any real experience."

"Weird, man . . . you writers are wild. So, do you always pack the room with chicks when you write?"

"Actually, it's a group of ladies from the church."

"Like I said, you writers are eccentric. We're going to take a break right now, and when we come back . . . western week continues. Thanks, Tony!"

"Adios, trail partners."

He turned toward eight pairs of astonished eyes.

"That was a radio show?" Cherry asked.

"Yeah, but usually they book things ahead of time. It's not often a spur of the moment thing like that. Sorry for the interruption, gals."

"Do you do lots of radio interviews?"

"I suppose one a week is average. Now that we have a break, you girls will have to tell me about yourselves. Are any of you native Fox Islanders?"

"Oh, yes," Patsy Mitchell began, "I grew up on the Island. After the war I got a job in Olympia, and I've lived there ever since. I used to be a very good friend of Jill's and Jessica's. But after the wreck . . . we lost Jill, you know . . . and Jessica, well, she seemed so lost without her sister."

"I hear she changed quite a bit after the wreck."

"Yes, that's very true," Mrs. Mitchell continued. "The only way we could really tell them apart was that Jessica seemed a little more dominant. She would make decisions for them. It was totally her idea to go off to Radcliffe. Jill was always more quiet and introverted, waiting for Jessie to make their next move. But after the accident, the spark just went out of Jessica. We often wondered what it would have been like, had Jessica died instead. She always seemed so dependent on her sister."

"Then Jessica's sudden marriage to Reynolds must have been a shock to Jill."

"I suppose. It was a complete surprise to all of us, although we all figured Jessica would marry first. But, of course, Jill never made it home to tell us how she felt."

"Did you go to high school with the twins?"

"Yes, we rode the ferry to school all through high school. Did you know Jill broke her legs in an accident?"

"Yes, we read about that."

"All those weeks that Jill was laid up, I rode the ferry with Jessica and we'd bring Jill's schoolwork home to her."

"Jessica went to school during that time? I understood from her that she stayed home to help care for Jill."

"Poor dear. We're all getting a little forgetful, aren't we? But, I can assure you, she attended school."

Once again the telephone interrupted.

Tony wiped his doughnut-covered fingers on a red-and-yellow striped paper napkin.

"Shadowbrooks."

"Tony . . . look . . . Terry Davidian here. Last night I was at this big ranch party in Ojai, and Ted said that TBS might want to look at an option on *Stampede Creek*. But here's the problem. I don't have that signed agreement yet. My hands are tied, pal. Can you FedEx that contract down to me tomorrow?"

"You talked to Ted Turner about making my book into a movie?"

"Did I say Turner? I meant Ted Roberts. He's a VP or something in charge of movie production."

"Davidian, I'm not real happy with that agreement yet."

"Tony, don't you see you're missing the big ones? I can make you a rich man if you'd let me."

"Yeah, that's what Ed McMahon tells me every month. Look, if you don't hear from me in a couple weeks . . . well, then the answer is no."

"No? Anthony. Anthony. What about all the work I've done on this project already?"

"It's a risky business, isn't it?"

"Hey, I believe in this book. I'll give you until el primero de Septiembre. Comprende?"

"Si."

"You drive a tough deal, Tony."

"Good-bye, Terry."

Several of the ladies were picking up cups and plates. The others were gathering purses and notebooks. "We won't bother you anymore, Mr. Shadowbrook. We really couldn't believe we were sitting right here when you were making a movie deal."

"It's just a preliminary agreement . . . with an agent who might be able to sell an option on my book . . . which means they have first rights to make a movie, but even if they pick up an option, it doesn't mean they'll ever make anything out of it."

"But still, talking to someone in Hollywood. This is incredible."

After a few minutes in the kitchen, the ladies traipsed toward the front door. Tony trailed after them. Once again the phone rang.

Patsy Mitchell shooed him away. "We'll let ourselves out. It's probably Harrison Ford asking to play the part of Houston."

"Harrison Ford's too old for the part, Mother."

"Old? Really? But he looks like such a young man."

Tony grabbed the phone.

"Shadowbrooks."

"Daddy?"

Kit's calling me "Daddy"?

"Kit, is that you? What's up, darlin'? I can hardly hear you."

"Eh . . . D-Daddy?"

"Kristina, are you crying? What's wrong, babe? What happened? Where are you?"

"Daddy . . . I'm Okay . . . really. I'm near

273

Oak Creek Canyon."

"What are you doing up there?"

"It's a long story. I'm using Mom's cellular phone 'cause Linc's a jerk," Kit sobbed.

"What did he do?" Tony felt anger and fear leaping right out of his heart and throbbing in his throat.

"Linc drove me up here last night to look at a friend's car, but the friend just happened to be gone. So he suggested we spend the rest of the night at this friend's one bedroom cabin."

"He did, eh? Did you? You didn't?" He could hear her crying. "Do you need to talk to your mother?"

"I told him to take me home, but he wouldn't. He said I was acting immature. That I should grow up and have some fun. Said he brought some whiskey, and we should have ourselves a little party. Then he started hanging all over me."

"What did you do?"

"I shoved him off and told him if he tried to touch me again, he'd get a half-inch ratchet alongside the ear. Then he laughed at me and said I was just fantasizing. Said he couldn't believe that I actually thought he wanted to make love to someone with grease under her fingernails."

"What did you do then?"

"I grabbed my toolbox and hiked over the mountain to I-17. But I didn't have the nerve to hitchhike, so I stayed at a rest stop until daylight. Then I figured I'd call Josh to come pick me up, but I've tried and tried and I can't reach him! What am I going to do?"

Tony could tell she was trying to stop crying, to control herself.

"Josh is up here in the Seattle area doing a stunt."

"He is?"

"Did you call Mark?"

"No, this is the week they were driving over to San Diego to see Amanda's folks, remember? I was too embarrassed to call anyone else."

"How about Kathy?"

"I can't, Pop! I can't call her. She's mad at me dating Linc . . . and now she'll say . . . she'll say I'm stupid and should have never gotten myself into this fix and I'm acting real immature. This is really something that an eighteen-year-old should know how to avoid. I really thought he wanted me to look at this guy's car. Is that naive?"

"Probably. I'll call Kathy. I'll get you a ride. Try to find a shady spot to relax. You done good, kid. I'm proud of you."

"I'm sorry I called up bawling like some junior high girl. I never cried one bit all night. But it was so great to hear your voice. As soon as you started talking, Daddy, I knew everything was going to be all right." Kit began to cry again.

After hanging up, Tony stared into the hall mirror. The man in the reflection reminded him a lot of his father.

Lord, I need to be there. There are times when a girl, even one going to college, still needs her daddy. I want to be there right now. What in the world am I doing twelve hundred miles from home all summer long?

By noon Tony had the crisis solved. Kathy and a girlfriend were driving north on Black Canyon Freeway to pick up Kit.

Tony grabbed a Coke out of the refrigerator and stepped out on the deck.

Lord, here's another morning when I didn't get any work done. Well, at least not much writing. Come to think of it, maybe I did get something accomplished.

He opened his notebook and flipped on the computer. Chapter eight came onto the screen. He glanced down at the partially completed first line. "Almost a year before the bridge opened . . ."

Maybe I should have driven Barbara Mason to the hospital. It surely would have been more peaceful than here.

Price found Barbara Mason decked out in a too-tight red linen suit, red heels, red lipstick and shell-shaped gold wire earrings. Price was still wearing black bermuda shorts, white sandals and a white short-sleeve blouse. She had tied a black-and-white cardigan sweater across her shoulders.

She couldn't tell if she, or Barbara Mason, felt more out of place.

"I zipped over as fast as I could," she explained. "Hope it will be all right to dress like this?"

"I don't know what to do . . . I just don't know what to do. Melody should be here," Barbara stewed. "Why isn't she here when I need her? That girl hangs around in the way most of the time, then just when I really need the help, I don't know what to do!"

"Do you know where the hospital is?"

"Yes, yes."

"Come on, we'll talk on the way." Price ushered Barbara out the door and into the white Oldsmobile.

The conversation was awkward, and they visited about trivial topics all the way to the hospital. Price helped her get all the papers signed, briefly had a word with a muddled and shaky Jessica Davenport Reynolds, then retired to the hospital cafeteria.

Sitting across an antiseptic smelling gray formica tabletop, both women stared at the steam rising from their heavy porcelain cups.

"I'm not real good with this," Barbara Mason began, "but I really appreciate your bringing me to the hospital. I was about to have an anxiety attack. Sometimes I can't believe how much I depend on Melody. She's a rock, the only rock in this family."

"Did you ever tell her that?"

"She knows. She knows how I feel."

"It must have been tough when she went to Tempe to college."

"Those were four of the worst years of my life. But none of them have been too great."

"Do you want to talk about them?"

"No." Barbara Mason stared with sad, tired eyes at Price until she felt uncomfortable. "How old are you?" she finally asked.

Price sat up and sipped her tea. "I'm forty-nine," she admitted.

"Yeah, that's about what I figured. Well, I'm fifty-three. And without this gaudy makeup, I look old enough to be your mother."

"Don't be silly," Price protested.

"No, it's true. Maybe that's why I hated

you when I first met you."

Price swallowed hard. "You hated me?"

"Look at you. Sitting there all cute, thin and tan. My legs haven't seen the light of the sun in thirty years. Nor will they. You look thirty-five, forty tops. You're a successful professor. Married to a man who Melody thinks can walk on water. Leading an exciting life of travel, fame and success. You are exactly everything I ever wanted out of life and never got one ounce of. Every time I see you, I'm reminded of what an absolute failure I've made of my life."

"I'm afraid you've romanticized mine a bit. It's not really all that exciting."

"Nope, I sized it up pretty good, and you know it. But I guess the thing about you that made me the maddest was when, last week, you evaluated my whole life in three minutes."

"I truly am sorry I blurted out those things."

Mason laughed, a deep hoarse laugh. "You sized me up to a tee, and I was mad as . . . well, do you know I haven't had a drink since that day?"

"Really?"

"I guess I decided to prove you wrong."

Tears began to plow through the heavy makeup on Mason's cheeks. "I had no right to say those things to you."

"You were honest. I don't have one friend that is honest with me. I won't even allow poor little Melody to be honest with me. Look at me. I can't even control these tears when I'm sober."

Price reached into her bag, tugged out a small pack of tissues and slipped them across the table. Barbara roughly wiped her eyes and cheeks and sipped her coffee.

"Mine's cold. Can I get you a refill of hot water?" she offered to Price.

"That would be great. Thanks."

Barbara Mason returned and poured four teaspoons of sugar into her coffee.

"Should I call you Dr. Shadowbrook?"

"Oh, please, everyone calls me Price."

"Melody said that was short for Priscilla."

"When I was a little girl my daddy called me his Priceless Priscilla. That led to Price, and it just stuck."

"Is your father still living?"

"Oh yes. He and Mother live in Yuma."

"That must be nice."

"Having older parents is both a joy and a challenge, isn't it?"

"Mother's a chore sometimes," Barbara admitted. "Of course, Father left when I was very young. I wish I'd known him."

"Barbara, I know I'm really blessed to

have a loving husband and caring parents still alive. But the most important relationship in my life is with Jesus Christ."

"This might come as a surprise to you," Barbara said in a slow, quiet tone, "but when I was young I was very religious. I prayed every night that my father would come back."

"I thought he was lost at sea."

"Mother always said that. But I never really believed it. I don't think she believed it either. The two of them argued a lot when I was small. Father would go on long fishing trips to Alaska. He'd be gone for weeks. When he was at home, Mother made him sleep on the divan most of the time. I was too small to know what it was all about. So, after he left, I prayed and prayed. In my dreams I would get a letter or a call from my father, that he needed me to come and help him. Well, after years and years of getting no answer, a person gets tired of praying."

"Mrs. Mason?" The tag on his green hospital gown read "Dr. Alan Crayn."

"Yes?"

"I just did the x-rays on your mother, Mrs. Reynolds." He looked over at Price. "Is this your daughter?"

Price was relieved to notice a slight smile hiding behind the thick red lipstick. "No, just a young friend," Barbara reported.

"Here are the x-rays." He held them up to the fluorescent lighting of the cafeteria. "You can see where the fracture is. We feel there's only a minimum amount of surgery needed, but we want to go in and take care of it right away. Your mother isn't all that old a lady, and we want her to be able to get around on her own for years to come."

"Yes . . . well . . ." Barbara searched for Price's nodding approval. "By all means, go right ahead. Do what would be best for Mother in the long run."

"Good. It's certainly what I would do if she were my grandmother. If you ladies need to do any shopping or anything, it will be at least two hours before we're through."

"Thank you," Barbara replied. "We'll probably just wait here."

As Dr. Crayn began to leave, Price said, "Doctor? Would it be possible to have a copy of that x-ray? I think Mrs. Reynolds' granddaughter would like to see it."

"Certainly. Just stop by the lab. I'll leave word." Green face mask dangling around his neck, Dr. Crayn shoved open the swinging double doors and disappeared into the hall.

Price looked at Barbara. "You did just fine."

"Thank you, daughter."

"It's this Arizona tan. It fools them every time. I'm old enough to be his mother. Hope you didn't mind, but I just thought Melody would like to know about the injury."

"Oh, I'm glad you mentioned that. I didn't even know we could get an x-ray."

"You never had a son who grew up wanting to be a stuntman? A mom learns a lot about x-rays that way."

"It must be nerve-wracking. But sometimes I'm sorry I didn't have more children. I'm an only child, and I swore I'd never put any kid of mine through the same thing. Strange how that happens, isn't it?"

"Barbara, if you had your life to live all over again, what else would you do different?"

Barbara took a deep breath and gazed around the sparsely filled hospital cafeteria. They could hear the clank of trays and muffled voices. The aroma of homemade soup bubbled into the room and mixed with the smell of disinfectant. "Well, my first thought was to say I should have never married Frank. But then there would be no Melody. And she's the most precious thing I've got in my life. So I guess if I had to do it all over, I'd have pulled myself together earlier, gone on to graduate from college, gained some maturity before I married Frank. Maybe I could have done a better job at being his wife. And, if I could do it all over? I would never have started drinking."

"What if I were to tell you that God is anxious to give you a fresh start? Oh, you can't go back to all the ways things were, but you can be forgiven, encouraged, loved and set free from the past. You might have to live with the repercussions of some decisions, but you'll meet those repercussions head on, without being limited by your past."

"I think I'm ready to have a fresh start. I've been on a dead-end street so long, it's hard to imagine there's anything else. To tell you the truth, I don't even know where to begin."

"The doctor said that it would be a couple hours before he could tell us anything. Why don't we go sit out on the patio at one of those tables? I'll tell you what I know."

"I'd like that."

Lord . . . I'm not sure what to say next. I sure wish Tony were here. I'm not good at this. Help me not to sound like a schoolteacher waving a yardstick in my hand.

Maybe I should have stayed at home with the church ladies and let Tony bring Barbara to the hospital.

Tony sat at the table dozing off as he tried to sort through the towering stack of government papers he had procured from the navy. Detailed, meaningless reports followed detailed, meaningless reports.

I need to throw this whole pile away and get back to writing. There's nothing of value in this, and even if there was I wouldn't know how to decipher it.

He pulled his eyelids open with his fingers and stretched, then shuffled down through the stack to a paper labeled "Restricted." Handwritten beneath that were the words "Restriction lifted: 7-1-1990." Under that he found a document entitled "Pearl Harbor retaliation plan #11: the assassination of Emperor Hirohito."

Assassination? We had a plan to assassinate the Japanese emperor?

For the next two hours Tony never looked up from the stack of papers in front of him. It was only the touch of Price's hands rubbing his neck and shoulders that caused him to acknowledge her return.

"You finding something good?" she asked.

"It's incredible! You won't believe this."

"And you won't believe what happened at the hospital."

"Oh yeah, Mrs. Reynolds. How is she?"

"She came through surgery just fine. But it was what happened to Barbara Mason that is really remarkable. Come in the kitchen while I make some coffee, then we'll go outside and sit on the deck."

"What happened to Barbara?"

"The angels are rejoicing. It's a long story. Now, come on, Shadowbrook. What did you find in that horrible stack of government reports?"

"I found out about Harvey Peterson's Japanese invasion."

"You mean it really happened?"

"Something happened. Late in 1942 someone in the navy devised a plan of how specially trained U.S. forces would infiltrate Japan and assassinate Emperor Hirohito."

"The navy made plans to go kill him?"

"Well, someone in the navy did. Anyway, a captured Japanese submarine was brought into Puget Sound, and a crew of a couple dozen men was trained how to operate it. They learned to speak Japanese fluently, and they prowled up and down the Sound, practicing mock invasions."

"So, what Harvey saw was some U.S. troops pretending to be Japanese?"

"Exactly."

"What do you think Harvey will say about these documents?"

"I'm not sure. It seems to shoot down his theory. But you never know about conspiracy fanatics."

"What happened after that? Did they actually try to carry out the assassination? I don't remember anything in the history books about that."

"No, someone from the Pentagon got wind of the plan and scuttled the whole thing. This was called Plan #11 for the retaliation of Pearl Harbor."

"Makes you wonder what the other plans were." Price scooted a mug of coffee in front of Tony. "This is just the kind of new material we need in our book."

"It gets better."

"There's more?"

"I found a second restricted report . . . on the cover-up of Plan 11."

"Then Harvey was right? They did try to cover it up?"

"I guess until the mid-fifties the navy didn't want anyone to know they had actually plotted political assassinations. So they tried to keep everything quiet."

"Tried? Someone figured out what they did?"

"Yeah, one fisherman from Fox Island stumbled onto the cover-up."

"From Fox Island? Who?"

"Hubert Reynolds."

Price set her cup down on the counter with a bang. "Melody's grandfather!"

"Yes."

"How do you know? What does it say about him?"

Tony retreated to the dining room table and returned with a photocopied piece of paper in his hand. "Listen to this: 'June 15, 1948, Hubert Reynolds, of Fox Island and Alaska, was paid $8,000 for his cooperation in keeping confidential the contents of this report.' "

"It's that plain? They really say it like that?"

"Here it is."

"June 15? Then he disappeared right after he got the money."

"Yeah, maybe Barbara was right. Maybe he just took off."

"This is remarkable, Tony. Do you think we ought to tell Melody?"

"Sooner or later. I'm not ready to disturb Jessica, but maybe we ought to tell Barbara Mason, too. What do you think? Will this just bum her out even more?"

"It will be tough, but I think she can handle it now."

"Now? What happened at that hospital?"

"Come on out to the deck and sit down, Mr. Shadowbrook. Let me tell you about God's amazing grace."

"What did you do, anyway?"

"I didn't do anything," she beamed. " 'It's man's part to trust . . . and God's part to work.' Remember?"

9

In the early 1880s, Alexander Graham Bell's amazing talking telegraph had made its way into the businesses and homes of the cattle barons in the frontier town of Cheyenne, Wyoming Territory. It would take considerably longer to reach some of the residents of south Puget Sound.

If the building of the bridge was the golden ring that forever united Fox Island to the mainland, the coming of telephone service in October of 1956 was the wedding present that allowed the residents something they had never had before . . . instant contact with the rest of the world.

The value of that contact is still debated by Island old-timers.

"Liz called while you were at the store," Price announced the minute Tony walked into the house.

"Did she want me to call back?"

"She was headed to New Hampshire for the weekend and said to call her Monday."

"Weekend? It's only Wednesday."

Price closed the sliding glass door behind him. "That's what she said. Have you noticed the rolling fog is getting chillier every day? I wonder if summer is about done?"

"We've got a book about done, Dr. Shadowbrook. I figure on finishing chapter nine tomorrow."

"Did you look at my version of chapter five?"

"Yeah, I've been meaning for us to sit down and talk about it."

"We need to sit down?"

"Listen, babe, we can't leave out that whole section about the dogfish packing industry and the early connection between the Fox Island economy and Puget Sound fishing."

"As I recall, I didn't leave it out at all."

"But you condensed it to a mere paragraph."

"That's what editing is all about."

"That isn't editing, it's amputation!"

"I would rather read about little Sheila McComber's harrowing ride on a raft of timber logs across the Narrows than a detailed description of what the fish packing plant smelled like."

"Well, I wouldn't. How do we know that story about McComber is true, anyway?

One of the old-timers thought the Mc-Combers ran the store on McNeil Island, not Fox Island. So how can we be sure that one letter is authentic?"

Price brushed her light brown hair back with her hand and felt a tightness in her neck. "How do we know any of this research is authentic? Maybe every book we've ever read has been a lie."

"Priscilla, hyperbolic statements to the contrary, we can't make a big deal out of one undated letter."

"Hi, guys!" Melody bounced into the room, then stopped. Her teal green sweatshirt was inlaid with a liquid gold material; her brown eyes danced. "Priscilla? Whoops, another chapter five day, huh? I'll come back. I just wanted you to see this picture."

"What picture?" Price snapped.

"Hey, if you guys want me to, I'll be happy to write chapter five for you."

Tony waved his arm in a wide, sweeping movement. "We can work this out just fine by ourselves!"

"Yeah . . . well . . . sure. Anyway, I thought you might be interested in this picture I found in *People* magazine at the dentist's office. It's dated last spring. There was this big celebrity golf tournament at the

Riviera Country Club in L.A. It has some photos of different groups of golfers. Look at this one."

Tony took the magazine and glanced at the black-and-white photo. "Davidian?"

"Let me see that." Price scooted over by Tony and peeked over his shoulder.

"Yeah," Melody continued. "Terrance Davidian, Michael Ovitz . . . the guy with the Dodgers cap is a VP at Warner Brothers, and you know who that guy is!"

Price snatched the magazine from Tony's hands to examine it more closely. "Clint Eastwood?"

"You mean, Davidian really does know some of the movers and shakers in the movie business?" Tony gasped.

"Apparently." Melody clutched her hands behind her back and swayed on her sandals.

"Well, what do you think?" Price ventured. "You going to let him represent you?"

"This seems to improve his credulity. So, I guess I probably will. But I still have this feeling I'll live to regret it."

Price rubbed the back of her neck with both hands. "You can't be any further away from a movie deal than you are now."

Tony stepped behind her and rubbed her

neck and shoulders. "I guess I'll send the papers on down. I'm not expecting much to come from it, anyway."

"Maybe Josh can be in *Stampede Creek* when they make it a movie. Wouldn't that be cool? I was talking to him on the phone yesterday and he said . . ."

Price turned around and mouthed "Yesterday?" to Tony as he continued to stroke her back.

". . . he said since he's now a member of the Screen Actors' Guild, there's no reason he couldn't be in movies and things." Melody twisted her fingers as though wadding a piece of sticky gum.

"Movies?" Price blurted out. "What he needs is to get married and settle down."

Why on earth did I mention marriage? In front of Melody? No, I just meant he needs to find a real job . . . not a reel job.

Ignoring the sparkle in Melody's big brown eyes, Price quickly changed the subject. "Tony, maybe we ought to send both samples of chapter five to Liz and let her figure it out."

He stopped rubbing and stepped around in front of the two women. "I'm not about to let someone else decide how the flow of my book should go!"

"*My* book? That, my handsome husband,

is the root of the problem, isn't it?"

Tony quickly raised his finger and pointed it at Price. Then he glanced at Melody and lowered his arm.

"Hey, I'll leave if you want me to," Melody offered.

"No," Tony sighed. "Look, there's a good solution to all this. We just haven't found it yet. So, forget chapter five. Let's get to work on other things."

The renewed tightness around Price's eyes relaxed, and she nodded agreement. "Some people say that it's impossible for two writers to exist under the same roof, Melody. But that's not true. It's just mostly impossible. That's different than completely impossible."

"Melody, I really appreciate your finding that picture of Davidian." Tony picked up a notepad near the telephone and turned back to Price. "Are these the things Liz called about?"

She came over and glanced at the notes. "Right. She's rushing you a sample cover for the next book in the River Breaks series."

"I haven't even written *Standoff at Rifle Ridge* yet."

"Well, that should give you some inspiration. Then she wants to know if you can make the regional booksellers convention in Denver next month."

"And she's just now asking me?"

Price hesitated.

"Someone else canceled, right?"

"Sort of."

"Time to send in the subs."

"Anthony, you aren't a sub and you know it. She's got some more interviews and a television deal in El Paso. She'll tell you all about it."

"This is so cool. I can't wait until I get a novel published," Melody purred. "I'll need a whole new wardrobe, won't I?"

"Not for radio interviews," Price noted.

"But television . . . bookstores . . . public appearances. Wow! Do you remember the first time someone asked you for an autograph?"

"Nope," Tony shrugged. "But writing is a lot like any other job. There are times when it's just hard work. But there are always some perks. Kind of like teaching, isn't it, babe?"

"That's for sure. And there are plenty of days when you wonder if it's all worth it. But it is. I think you're really going to enjoy teaching, Melody. Did you take that contract back to the school yet?"

"Oh, well, I've been rethinking that, Dr. S."

"They decided you were the one they wanted, right?"

"Yes, it's exciting to actually have a real job lined up. But lately I've been thinking about other plans."

"What kind of plans?"

Melody reached down and adjusted the straps on her sandals. When she came back up, her smile stretched from one gold dangling earring to the other. "I've been thinking about going down to Arizona and visiting some old friends . . . you know, from college days?"

"A certain daredevil stuntman with a sensational smile didn't have anything to do with this, did he?" Price questioned.

Melody blushed and flung her long dark hair back over her shoulders. "Weelll. . . . actually, Josh did invite me down for a visit. He said there was a big special show at Rawhide over the Labor Day weekend and that he could get me backstage. Then he teased me about going hang gliding with him in the Grand Canyon and stuff like that."

"He wasn't teasing," Tony cautioned.

"He wasn't? Maybe we won't do that. Anyway, he figured I could stay at your house. He said his and Paul's new apartment wasn't very far from there and . . ."

"Stay with us?" Tony repeated, his eyes almost frozen in place.

"Yeah, it would be all right, wouldn't it?"

Price quickly regained her composure. "Of course, but that would mean giving up that teaching job. I'm not sure the program at Rawhide is worth that."

"It's not just the show at Rawhide that interests me." Melody flipped her long dark brown hair behind her shoulders. "Dr. S., does Josh ever get serious with a girl?"

"You mean, does he date them more than two or three times?"

"Yeah."

"I think he dated Terri Carter more than that. She was Miss Arizona. She even finished in the top ten for the Miss America contest."

"Josh dated someone like that?" Melody's face sunk into a scolded puppy position. "I must look like a dork to him."

"Melody," Price continued, "you're cute, fun and smart. Frankly, that's exactly Josh's type."

"Really? Well, what about Miss Arizona?"

"I think Terri holds the record. He dated her five, maybe six times."

"That's all?"

"He wears them out."

"He does?"

"When you go on a date with Josh, it's six to ten hours of nonstop physical adventure. He'll backpack you across the Mazaztals, swim across Roosevelt Lake, raft the Gila and ride horseback from Florence to Casa Grande . . . and that's just the first afternoon."

Tony nodded agreement. "For Josh a day's wasted if he doesn't do something he's never done before and wind up totally fatigued."

"It sounds like a real learning experience," Melody pondered.

"So's teaching junior highers. We'll pray that the Lord gives you wisdom in this."

"Thanks, Dr. S." Melody bounded for the back door. "I'll go get chapter one of my new novel. I think it's ready for your critique."

"Well," Tony offered, "you bring it over, and we'll get to it as soon as we have enough time to give it a proper look."

"No sweat. Take your time. But I did figure we could talk about it tonight when Mom comes over for supper. Did I tell you the new title?"

"I don't think so." Price slightly scrunched one side of her face.

"I'm going to call it *Out Fox Island Way*. Isn't that cool? It sort of looks like outfoxed, but isn't. Wait until you read it. It's awesome, if I do say so myself."

Melody disappeared out the front door.

"She's going to come stay with us in Scottsdale?" Tony sat down.

Price intertwined her fingers and put her hands on top of her head. "How do you think she'll get along with Kit and Kathy? Here we go again, Mr. Shadowbrook. Every summer we collect a passel of new relationships."

"Yes, but we don't always bring them home with us."

"Do you think Melody will ever learn to write?"

"Perhaps, if she slows down, takes her time, pays her dues, finds her niche . . . gets a life. Maybe she will. What she needs is the right project. And what I need is food. What's for lunch? I'm starved."

Price followed him into the well-lit kitchen. "Take it easy with lunch. Remember, you promised to barbeque steaks tonight."

"I did?"

"Yes." She slipped her arms around his waist and hugged tight. "Thanks for the back rub."

Tony and Price both made a point to read Melody's chapter before she or her mother arrived. After he started the charcoal, Tony popped back into the kitchen.

"What are we going to tell her?"

"Tell her the truth."

"You mean, that there's no way in the world it will be published as it is?"

"Well, not that bluntly, of course. Tony, there must have been something you liked."

"She did a pretty good job of describing the girl's feelings when the car sped out of control and was about to hit that tree," he suggested.

"Right." Price jotted a few words down on a pink notepad. "That's what I thought too. Now, what else?"

Tony scratched the back of his head and pushed his Henley shirt sleeves above his elbows. "That's about all I can say. How about you? You've had more experience critiquing."

Price sliced tomato wedges into the green salad. "How about the title? You're good at titles. Do you have some suggestions for her?"

"Naming a book is like naming a baby. I figure it belongs to the author to name it whatever they please. I don't think I should give advice on the title."

"Would you say it was more promising than the other attempt?"

"Definitely more promising."

Price scribbled down a few more ideas.

Tony wandered into the bedroom and pulled on a blue-and-black Brooks & Dunn shirt with lightning flashes across the chest, and changed into his full quill ostrich boots. His big silver belt buckle read, "NFR - '94." When he returned to the kitchen, Price was just hanging up the phone.

"You look mighty sharp, Shadowbrook. Who are you trying to impress tonight? Melody or her mother?"

"Neither. I'm going after that foxy, golden brunette cook." He kissed her on the back of the neck.

"I take it you're not mad about chapter five anymore."

"I'm waiting for a divine miracle about chapter five. Who was on the phone?"

"Sandra Lytoski."

"Your department head at ASU?"

"She wants me to take another freshman English class."

"What did you tell her?"

"I told her to shuffle the independent study around so I wouldn't have to come in on Fridays, and I'd do it."

"Sounds like you struck a deal."

"Sounds like summer is over. It's time to think about classes, faculty meetings, grading papers and fighting early morning traffic. By this time next week, we'll be packing up."

"What time is our company expected?"

"That must be them now. Why don't you go answer the doorbell?"

"The doorbell? I didn't hear anything."

"Your hearing's not too good. You aren't a young man anymore, Mr. Shadowbrook."

"I can still catch you," he boasted.

She raised her eyebrows. "That's only because I've never tried to run away."

Since it was too cool to eat on the deck, they set the oak dining table that occupied one end of the large front room. The sky outside labored under the weight of heavy water saturation. In the far distance, a wall of water splayed McNeil Island. Price and Tony sat across from Melody and her mother.

"Barbara, that new haircut is really attractive," Price mentioned.

"Thanks, but it's all your fault." She first answered in a gruff tone, then lightened up. "You convinced me the Lord would let me have a new start, so I went out and got my hair done and bought new clothes. Being a new person is expensive."

"You didn't need to do all that."

"Yes, she did," Melody piped in. "She looks ten years younger, don't you think?"

Her mother sat up straight. "This way I only look sixty."

"I agree with Melody," Tony added. "That style is youthful, but fits you perfectly. I'd say it definitely makes you look like you're in your forties."

Price noticed a sparkle in Barbara's eyes that she had never seen before. The rest of the evening she exhibited that same relaxed contentment.

As Price served dessert, Melody blurted out, "Well? What about it, guys? Didn't chapter one surprise you?"

Tony sipped his Branding Iron Brew Cowboy Coffee and waited for Price to join them at the table. As they sliced into a blackberry cheesecake, Tony replied, "Well, kid, there's no question, you're getting better."

"See, Mom, I told you it was good. What did you like best, Mr. S.?"

"I'll tell you what I liked best," Price broke in. "You did a very good job of describing the girl's feelings when the car sped out of control and was about to hit that tree. It made me glad my car has an airbag. I really felt it came alive."

"You liked that part? I just added that yesterday. How about you, Mr. S.? What was your favorite part? How about that opening line? I told you it was a grabber, didn't I?"

"What was the opening line, dear?" Barbara Mason asked as she sat twisting the shiny rhinestone rings that circled each of her fingers.

Tony looked Melody in the eyes. "I believe it goes this way," he recited. " 'Ashley figured even if sea gulls could talk they wouldn't have anything worthwhile to say.' "

"Wow, you memorized it!" Melody exclaimed. "But you promised not to use it yourself."

"It's a promise."

"What do you think?"

"It's a very good line," Tony continued, "but one suggestion might be to consider the name of your protagonist. The name Ashley at this time in history carries a whole bag of stuffy yuppiedom. Unless she has a dog named Buffy, and a boyfriend called Lance, I'd pick another name."

"Really? I never thought of that. What do you suggest?"

Tony rolled his eyes at Price as if

searching for help. "If it were me . . . I would use . . . with those freckles and all . . . Julee, J-u-l-e-e."

"Julee? Sure, maybe so. What about the scene with Ashley . . . I mean, Julee . . . and the biker? Where the bridge rips apart in the storm and his bike tumbles into the Narrows and she drags him out of the water with a crab net and nurses him back to health. Doesn't that grab you?"

"Speaking of bikers," Price interrupted, "did I see Kenny Mallard in town again?"

"Yeah. I guess he's been out to Sturgis."

"South Dakota?" Price questioned.

"It must be the time of year for the big Harley Davidson rally," Tony noted.

"I think that was it. Listen, I need your honest opinion, and I know you haven't seen the whole story, but on the strength of this chapter, do you think I can get this book published?"

"Go ahead, honey," Tony motioned to Price, "what do you think?"

She kicked Tony under the table, then turned to Melody with a cheesy grin. "You know I have never written any fiction in my life. I think Tony is a much better judge of that. What do you think, *dear?*"

He looked away from the other two. *You'll pay for this!* he mouthed.

"I think you should definitely go ahead and complete the novel."

"But I thought you said you never wrote the whole works until you had a contract?"

"Oh, that's the way I do it now. But back when I began I had to write the whole thing. Besides, when you get to the end, I'm sure you'll want to come back and change things a bit. You'll be surprised how you see things differently."

"Wow, thanks for the advice, Mr. S."

Barbara Mason wiped her napkin across what remained of her soft pink lipstick. "I don't think you've answered Melody's question. Do you think she will be able to make a career out of writing, or has she been wasting her time?"

"Mother!"

Tony took up the challenge. "Melody has the drive and enthusiasm . . . and she's learning the skills. But it usually takes a subjective quality, call it divine providence if you want, to write for a living. There's no way I'm going to try to second-guess what God is doing in her life."

Melody's mother saluted him with her coffee cup and took a sip. "Spoken like a true politician. Now that we're through this discussion on writing, I have two announcements. First, I was at the hospital today, and they said they are going to transfer Mother back to the apartments tomorrow. Her recovery is going very well."

"You went to Tacoma by yourself?" Melody asked.

"I take it you're astonished?"

"Well . . . it's just been . . . you've never . . ."

"And if you think that's amazing, hold on to your hat. I stopped by and registered to take two art classes at the college this fall. It's time I finished that degree after all these years."

"You did what? Mom! Really? You haven't been . . ."

"I haven't had a drink in three weeks and you know it. I had sixty more units to take, and I think after thirty-four years, it's time to finish."

"What a wonderful idea," Price encouraged. "What made you decide that?"

"I heard a voice tell me to do it."

"A voice?" Melody gawked at her mother. "You mean like an angelic announcement in the night?"

"No, I mean like some middle-aged professor from Arizona saying, 'Get off your duff, Mason, and make something out of your life before it's too late.' "

"I think I must have been having one of

those wonderful menopause days."

"Well, then, thank God for menopause. Even with this episode with Mother, I believe this is turning out to be a very good summer."

Price stood and cleared away some dishes. "Is your mother in a lot of pain?"

"I think the medication keeps the pain in check, but Mother's never very happy. Breaking her hip didn't help much."

"I do wish we could have visited with her more, without disturbing her," Tony added. "She's such a fascinating, complex person."

"I would never think of her in such terms," Barbara said.

"I create characters all the time for my fiction books, so I'm always scouting for interesting personalities. Think about it. She's an identical twin. Grew up on a remote island. Painted some of the most creative and haunting pictures of the 1930s. Went to school in Boston. Lost her sister in a car wreck. Discarded art. Became reclusive. Lived her life on her home island with one daughter and one granddaughter. Always seems preoccupied with the past. It's like she refused to go beyond 1942. That reluctance has greatly affected all three of you, hasn't it?"

"I suppose that's all true," Mason mused. "And you didn't even mention a husband lost at sea . . . or whatever."

Tony looked over at Price, who gently nodded her head.

"Barbara, one of the reasons we wanted you both over here for supper is that I discovered some information about Hubert Reynolds that might be of interest to you."

"Grandpa?" Melody's mouth dangled open between her earrings.

"He didn't die in a boating accident, did he?" Barbara quizzed.

"I don't know about that. Let me tell you all that I found."

And he did.

For almost thirty minutes they pored over the declassified documents.

The rest of the evening the conversation bounced from men who run away . . . to how a war changes people . . . to broken hips . . . to writing novels . . . to stuntman sons . . . to midlife college students . . . to cheesecake recipes. It was after 11:00 when Barbara Mason walked to the door.

Picking up her purse, she handed a large oversized manila envelope to Price. "Here is that x-ray copy of my mother's. If you'd stick it in that black file drawer downstairs, I'd appreciate it. That's where we keep most of Mom's important papers. Thanks again for all you've done for my Melody . . . and me."

"We don't mean to usurp your place," Tony replied, "but Melody has sort of become like a daughter to us this summer."

"Mr. Shadowbrook, I also appreciate your giving us that information about my father. You know the strange thing is, it's a relief. All these years I felt in my heart something like that happened, so it came as no shock. But now it's settled, although I'll always wonder how he could so easily leave my mother and me." Then she turned to Price. "You will stop by before you leave next week, won't you?"

"We'll plan on it. Good night, Barbara. We'll be praying about those college classes."

Melody gave Price and Tony a big hug. Then she walked her mother to her car and retired to her loft above the garage.

Tony dried the dishes as Price swept the floor. "I'm looking forward to getting back into my own kitchen."

"How many more books do we have in this series?"

"Five. But I bet you'll be anxious to leave Scottsdale by next June."

"I suppose so. But I have two novels to write before then."

"Are you bragging or complaining, Anthony Shadowbrook?"

"Neither. But I do think for once it will be more peaceful at home than here."

"Especially when the girls and I are busy at school." Price hung the "I Hate to Housekeep" tea towel on the rack and tugged off her apron. "I'm beat. Could you put that stack of dishes away and take Jessica's x-ray to the downstairs files? I'm going to bed before I fall asleep standing up."

"So the middle-aged college professor is weary?"

"Ugh. I still can't get used to being called middle-aged. But tonight I feel every minute of forty-nine."

"Save me a warm, snuggy place," Tony called out. "I'll be there in a minute or two."

The sheet and blanket covered her like cool cotton heaven, and Price was only vaguely aware that Tony hadn't come to bed yet.

The softly glowing red digital numbers of the clock radio on the nightstand read 3:23. Price blinked twice and reached out and felt an empty pillow beside her.

"Tony?"

She fumbled to find the light switch. The sixty-five-watt bulb seemed like a police interrogation as she tried to shield her eyes. She dug through the closet for her old white terrycloth robe and mauve slippers. She padded out to the living room and found nothing but darkness.

A dim stream of light glowed from the stairs to the lower level of the hillside home. She inched her way across the room, clutched the rail, and eased down the stairs one at a time, peering into the large main room on the downstairs level. Tony was on his knees in the back corner of the basement room. He was digging through the bottom drawer of a four-drawer black file cabinet. File folders and assorted papers were stacked and piled all around him.

He glanced up, stood to his feet, stretched his back and rubbed his eyes.

"What in the world are you still doing down here? Don't you know what time it is?"

"I'm on the trail of solving a great mystery."

"What are you talking about? It's 3:30 in the morning!"

"I'm looking for something."

"Obviously. But that's Mrs. Reynolds' personal files. I don't remember us getting permission to rifle through them."

"I know. But I thought about the options, and this seemed to be the right thing to do."

"I'm still sound asleep. What are you talking about?"

"How about you going upstairs and fixing me a cup of coffee?"

"All I want to do is go back to bed. Come on, whatever it is can certainly wait until morning."

"Wrong. Fix us something to drink. In Melody's words, I've got something to show you that will absolutely knock your socks off."

"I'm not wearing any socks."

"Well, it will knock your . . . I've got a shocker for you."

"What's it about?"

"Jessica Reynolds. I'll be right up."

Price had gotten accustomed to the kitchen light about the time the water boiled. She plopped down at the counter and was basking in the steam that rolled up from the white porcelain cup when Tony bounded into the room.

"I need to keep looking down there a little longer, but I'm into the last drawer."

"What's this so-called news that can't

wait?" she prodded.

"Like you asked me, I carried that x-ray down to the files to store when you went to bed. But I decided to take a glance at it myself."

"The break in her hip didn't look too bad, did it?"

"No, but here's the thing. . . ." Tony held the x-ray up to the kitchen light. "Look on down her leg bones and what do you see?"

"Tony, this seems like an invasion of privacy."

"Yeah, maybe. But look. The one on the left? That would be her right leg. It was broken at some time about four inches below the knee. It must have been a severe break to still show up like that." Tony's voice rose in pitch and intensity. "Then look over here at the left leg. Another break just above the knee an inch or two."

"So, Jessica broke her legs, too, sometime?"

"That's what I surmise. Thought I'd call the hospital tomorrow and see if I could get someone to confirm that analysis."

"Wait." Price blinked her eyes a little wider. "Aren't those the same locations where Jessica said Jill broke her legs during that ferry accident?"

"Exactly."

"So what does it mean?" Price sipped her Lemon Zinger tea as she deliberated over the x-ray in front of her.

"That's one of the reasons I'm still up. I've been trying to figure this out. Here's my list."

"What list?"

"Of the different possibilities."

"Tony Shadowbrook making lists? You're beginning to sound like me."

"You taught me some things."

"Well, maybe this would be a good time to discuss chapter five," she teased.

"Don't change the subject. Here's what I figure . . . either one, these are not breaks, and the x-ray can be interpreted some other way. Or two, Jessica broke her legs in the very same place that Jill broke hers. Or three, it was Jessica, not Jill, who broke her legs."

"Well, Mr. Holmes, which theory do you support?"

"At this point, I'm convinced that those lines represent old breaks in the bones. But that can't be proven until I call the hospital. Second, I don't believe it's probable for Jessica to have broken both legs in the exact same place, even for identical twins."

"And not tell anyone."

"Right."

316

"So you think it was Jessica who actually broke her legs, not Jill?"

"Perhaps," he nodded.

"Maybe the newspaper got the account wrong. I imagine identical twins could have all sorts of mix-ups like that."

"That's what I was thinking. She never told Barbara about breaking her legs, and just let us believe the mistaken article."

"It wouldn't be the first one this summer, would it?"

"Right. But here's what's keeping me up. Patsy Mitchell, who came over with that writers' critique group, said distinctly that she rode to school with Jessica while Jill stayed at home with broken legs."

"I thought Jessica said she stayed home too."

"Mrs. Mitchell insists that wasn't so."

"So Jessica broke her legs. But why does everyone, including Jessica, say it was Jill? What if, for some schoolgirl reason, after the ferry accident the girls decided to switch names for a while?"

"Yeah, maybe. But remember, Mom and Dad Davenport were still alive then. Parents can always tell twins apart. And Mrs. Mitchell said their personalities set them apart."

"If Jessica broke her legs, instead of Jill, what does that tell us, besides she's been covering it up all these years?"

"Hang on to your hat, kid. . . ."

"I'm not wearing a hat."

"Well, then hang on to your . . . get ready for this. What if it really was Jill who broke her legs?"

"Wait a minute, you just said the x-ray proved it was Jessica."

"No, my dear Dr. Shadowbrook, I said the x-ray may prove it was Melody's grandmother whose legs were broken."

"Why is it I feel like I'm in the middle of an Abbott and Costello skit? Melody's grandmother is Jessica."

"What if Melody's grandmother is really Jill, not Jessica Davenport?"

"Are you saying that the twins switched their identities sometime after their folks died? When did they do that? And why?" Price shuffled over to the stove and poured herself another cup of hot water.

"That's what I'm trying to solve."

"What are you looking for in the files? A diary or something?"

"Perhaps. Or maybe a death certificate."

"From the accident? Good heavens, Tony, are you inferring it was Jessica who died in that Iowa car wreck, not Jill?"

"That thought has been haunting me all night."

"But that means . . ." Price's mouth dropped open.

"It might mean that Bennington is Barbara Mason's father, and Melody's grandfather."

"Tony! Do you think so?"

"It's all speculation. But what if a pregnant, unwed Jill Davenport were to come home in shame to this closed little community of 1942, and suddenly find her newly married identical twin sister dead? The sister's husband was off fighting in Europe, and might never have made it through the war."

"So she switches identities on the way home to explain her pregnancy. None of the family is left to identify her, and she fools her friends."

"But what about Reynolds?"

"They had only known each other for a couple months before they got married, and then he goes off to war for almost three years. When he gets back she's different. He's different . . . and they have a daughter."

"I suppose. But if she fooled him, why did he blackmail the navy and leave?"

"But perhaps she didn't love him . . . and

he didn't really love her. He loved the real Jessica. Remember, Mrs. Mitchell said their personalities were different."

"So you think he could have deserted her and the baby because he decided he wasn't in love with her after all, not knowing there had been a switch?"

"That could be. But divorce or desertion wasn't real popular in the forties. I would have thought having little Barbara around would keep him close to hand."

"Unless . . ."

"Unless he discovered something that proved that Jill had deceived him?"

"And therefore, Barbara wasn't his daughter. What would he have found to prove that?"

"Let's say, some sort of document. For instance, what if there was a death certificate from the Iowa coroner stating that it was Jessica, not Jill, who died?"

"She surely would have destroyed such a document, wouldn't she?"

"Not necessarily. She might not have known if she could pull off the ruse. If it came out in the open, or if she changed her mind when she got here, she'd have the evidence of what really happened."

"Maybe she was just going to play the charade until Reynolds returned. But by then it was too late."

"That could be." Tony retreated to the stove for another cup of instant coffee.

"If that's true, it helps explain why Melody's grandmother lost knowledge of art. She wasn't the painter."

"She was just the reflection."

"And the change in personalities? She didn't change all that much if she's Jill."

"And she became reclusive so she could continue to hide her actions."

"And," Price continued talking rapidly, "it might explain why she was so stunned and upset to hear the name of Bennington after all these years. It would certainly justify her 'hah!' "

"Hah?"

"When Melody told her about the flowers at the grave, she just said 'hah!' "

"The grave!" Tony slapped the palm of his hand on the table. "J Davenport! Melody said her Grandma Jessie only put J Davenport on the stone because she didn't want to see her sister's name up there. She didn't want to see her own name up there."

"And if she ever got discovered, she could have the stone completed with Jessica's name, instead of her own."

Price and Tony gaped at each other for a long minute.

She finally broke the silence. "Mr. Shadowbrook?"

"Yes?"

"Is it true that it's extremely late at night and you haven't had any sleep?"

"True."

"Is it true that you spend most of your life writing fiction?"

"True."

"Could it be we're way off course here and are just plotting a new novel series or something? Maybe we're missing a perfectly logical and obvious explanation."

"That could be."

"Why don't you come on to bed, and we'll see what it looks like when we're both awake?"

"I can't. I have to finish looking in those files. Then I want to put all the stuff back before Melody comes in to use the downstairs bath."

"Should we tell her any of this?"

"Not a thing until we have more proof. This would be a horrible emotional ride to take her and her mother on if I turned out to be wrong, especially after dumping on them the other news tonight. If I can't find that death certificate, I'll call the coroner's office in Iowa and see if I can get a copy of the original."

"Let's suppose you gather all the evidence, what do you do then? Tell Melody? Tell Barbara? Do you confront Jessica? She's liable to have a stroke or something if it's true."

"You're right," he mumbled, "you're very right!"

"About chapter five?" she grinned.

"No, about looking at it more clearly after we've had some sleep. I'll go down and shove those papers back. I can continue the search tomorrow night."

"You promise you'll come to bed this time?"

"Yeah, but I won't promise I'll be able to get to sleep."

10 Lila Acheson taught at Fox Island's Benbow School in 1910. Later, she moved to New York and married Dewitt Wallace. They pioneered a new type of magazine, which became fairly successful as the journal known as "Reader's Digest."

Fox Island has housed the famous (Spencer Tracy vacationed there) and the infamous, such as Tacoma's girls of the night, who R & R'd at the Longhouse at the west end of Kamus Drive. Dixie Lee Ray, Washington's first and only woman governor, spent her childhood years exploring Fox Island from the family campsite. The Island became her permanent home when she retired from politics in 1981.

Fox Island still offers its charms to the renowned and the nefarious.

"And I say we can't tell her yet," Price insisted. "We've got to have an objective piece of concrete evidence. This is life-shattering news if it's true, and a cruel joke if it isn't."

Tony flopped the large, hardsided Samsonite onto the unmade bed and unfastened it. "So, you think we should just hop on the plane and fly away from it all? I think Melody's tough enough to handle this. And how about Barbara?"

"I don't know . . . I don't know," Price muttered.

"I think we should tell Melody first. What do you think?"

"I think we should wash the linens and towels and replace them before we make the bed." She stared at the closet. "Are you sure we can fit all this into those four suitcases?"

Tony pulled on his chocolate brown cowboy boots and tossed his wooden bootjack into the open suitcase. "There, I'm packed."

"Funny . . . very funny."

"Honey, I've stewed over this all week. We just have to tell Melody. We've got to be honest with what we think we know. It's eating away at me. At least we can show her what we found. Maybe we should let her trace it down further if she wants."

"We've gotten so close to her. Maybe we could just write it all out in a letter and have her decide."

"You know I couldn't do that. I've got to look 'em in the eye when I talk to them. And if we try to ignore it, the summer will seem incomplete. I know it will be tough on her at first. It would be devastating to anyone."

Price, clothed in slip and hose, stood straight in front of her husband, almost a full foot shorter. "We do have one thing complete."

"What's that?"

She hugged him tight. "We have just finished a very fine book."

He held her close and kissed her hair. It smelled squeaky clean and fresh, like she washed it with baby shampoo. "Yep. 'Course it did take us until midnight last night."

"And," she backed away and pulled on her denim skirt and fringed white blouse, "we still have to deal with the celebrated chapter five."

"I told you. We'll settle that on the plane ride home."

"I pity those who sit around us."

"Babe, now don't say that. It's really not that complicated. I know it's going to work out."

"I don't know how you can be so confident. Are you planning a sneak attack, an ambush when my guard's down?"

"Anthony Shadowbrook is a straight shooter, ma'am," he drawled.

"Yeah, so far, but you haven't made it to the end of the trail yet, buckaroo."

The telephone ring was simultaneous with a shout from the kitchen: "I'll get it!"

"Melody's here?" Price gasped.

"Did she hear what we said?"

After a minute Melody shouted again, "It's Kathy . . . and I've just about got breakfast fixed for you."

"Melody's cooking?" Tony whispered.

Price picked up the tan Princess phone near the bed. "Hi, Kath, what's up, honey?"

"It's going to be so great having you home. And don't worry. Everything's real clean."

"Except for the backyard behind the tool shed."

"Kit?"

"I'm on the other phone."

"What's this about the tool shed?"

"That's where I'm keeping Pugie."

"Pugie?"

"The calf Pop and I rescued. I named him after Puget Sound. The animal shelter didn't have room, so they let me keep it until they locate the owner. Don't worry, it hasn't been a problem."

"Except once," Kathy corrected.

"What do you mean, once?"

"I'll tell you what happened at the Greenwells' when you get home."

"Our neighbors, the Greenwells?"

"Mom, it's no big deal. Trust me."

Price let out a deep sigh. *Trust me? Did they learn that from their dad?*

"Mom, we wanted to tell you," Kathy continued, "that Josh is going to pick you guys up at the airport instead of me and Kit."

"That's fine. Is something wrong? Are you two getting along?"

"Hey, it's cool, Mom. Really. Kath has been a big help with the Linc thing. She is so smart when it comes to men, you know?"

"Oh?"

"Good old Linc had the nerve to call the other day and try to apologize. Kathy answered the phone. Man, she tore him apart up one side and down the other. Practically had him begging for his life. It was so excellent. He wouldn't dare ever call me again. She's a bulldog, Mom."

"I'm glad you two are working things out."

"Kit and I wanted you to know about the welcome home party for you guys tonight. Mark and Amanda are coming up. They can spend the night, can't they?"

"Sure. It'll be great to see you all."

"And Mark says he has something important to talk to you both about."

"What?"

"How would we know? Big brother doesn't tell little sisters anything, you know, but I have my guesses."

"Well, don't work too hard on a party. It will be a delight for all of us just to be together."

"That's why Josh insisted on picking you up. He wanted to make sure we had time to get things ready."

Josh insisted on giving us a ride from the airport? The son who doesn't like waiting three seconds for anything? Something's going on here.

"Tell Josh that Paul is welcome tonight, too."

"Yeah, well," Kit added, "we sort of wanted just family, you know?"

"That's great, girls. I'll tell your father. We'll see you tonight."

"Bye, Mom! Could you put Mel back on?"

"Mel? You mean Melody?"

"Just for a minute."

Price was sorely tempted to listen.

But she didn't.

She dabbed on makeup, slipped on her liquid silver jewelry and began packing toiletries. "We might as well get done early and maybe have time for a walk along the shoreline."

"Sounds great, darlin'."

"What do you think about these feathered earrings?"

"Ravishing."

"I don't know why I even ask you."

"Because I give you one man's honest opinion," he winked. Price rolled her eyes.

"I'll go see if Melody is really cooking breakfast."

"Are we going to tell her about the x-ray?"

"Can we do it without trying to jump to conclusions? Let's don't beat her over the head with it all at once."

"Me?" Tony protested.

"Yes, you. The Wyatt Earp of subtlety."

Don't say it . . . don't say it!

"Trust me, darlin'."

He said it.

The kitchen smelled of burnt eggs and weak orange juice, but the counter housed a bouquet of fresh yellow dahlias and bakery-made cinnamon rolls.

"I'm not a very good cook yet," Melody apologized. "I've never had anyone to cook for. But I had to do it. I'd regret not fixing you at least one meal."

"Thanks, kid. It seems strange to be packing up."

"Did I hear you say you got the book all finished by midnight?"

Tony looked her in the eyes. "What else did you hear?"

"Oh, just a little. I didn't mean to be listening, really." Melody turned back toward the stove. There was a long silence as he poured a cup of coffee.

"You were talking about my book, weren't you? It's bad and you just don't know how to tell me. Is that it? Really, Mr. S., I can take it now. I know I might sound kind of, you know, flighty sometimes, but I do understand. I'm not a total ditz. Looking at you and Dr. S. this summer, I can tell I'm a long way away from being a real writer. Please level with me. Don't lead me on. It's very important to me that you treat me like an adult and you give it to me straight."

Tears rolled down her brown cheeks. "My grandmother and my mother have spent most of their lives in make-believe worlds. I'm determined not to do that. I'm twenty-five years old. I want to face facts." She tried to wipe her eyes with the back of her hand and smeared grease instead.

"Come here, young lady," he commanded. "You need a daddy hug."

Instantly she threw her arms around his waist, and he put his arms around her shoulders. He held her close and rocked her back and forth as she alternated between sighing and sobbing.

"Well, I hope I'm not interrupting something," Price said in a low tone as she entered the kitchen. "On the other hand, maybe I do want to interrupt. Did you tell her . . . ?"

Tony shook his head.

"You know," Melody replied as she dried her eyes on a tea towel. "I can't remember the last time I got a hug from a man who wasn't trying to take advantage of me. I really needed that, Mr. S. Thanks for that daddy hug. Now I'm ready. Go ahead and tell me about my book."

"Her book?" Price asked.

"Melody heard us blabbing away and thought we were discussing *Out Fox Island Way.*"

"You weren't talking about my book? Then what is it you're afraid to tell me?"

Tony looked over at Price as she nodded her head in approval.

"Let's step out on the deck and get some fresh air," he suggested. "We ran across some information about your grandma. So we'll tell you what we know . . . and what we don't know."

For thirty minutes Tony, Price and Melody paced the deck under a pale, late August morning sky that hovered over the blue-green waters of Carr Inlet. They told her all about the x-ray and their suspicions of the Davenport sisters.

There were tears.

Prayers.

Daddy hugs.

Mommy hugs.

Laughter.

Lots of questions.

And more tears.

When they finally returned to the kitchen, Melody didn't bother serving the cold eggs, but they drank the juice and ate all the rolls.

"I can't believe you guys knew this for a week and didn't tell me."

"Melody, we wanted to make sure. We hoped to find something that proved our suspicions."

"It sounds convincing to me."

"Dr. Crayn in Tacoma said your grandmother definitely broke both legs years ago. And Patsy Mitchell reaffirmed that it was Jill, not Jessica, who had the ferryboat accident. But the coroner's office in Pottawattamie County, Iowa, said they lost their records in a 1964 tornado. So unless we had a death certificate or your grandmother's confession . . ."

"Or both," Price added.

". . . we can't prove it for certain. But for the life of me," Tony paused as though going through his list again, "I can't explain it any other way. I know better than to jump to too many conclusions. Maybe there's a piece of the puzzle that we haven't thought of."

"Perhaps there'll be a way you can talk to your grandmother about it someday. Maybe you could start with the x-ray and make it sound like you were checking up on her health," Price suggested.

"Do you think Grandma Jessie . . . I mean . . . oh, man, if this is true, it's going to be hard . . . Grandma Jill would keep a thing like a death certificate around?"

"Maybe at one time. There's a slight possibility that if she wasn't sure she could pull it off, she would want the records. But after all these years of getting away with it, I'm not sure she'd keep such a document. Like I said, I dug around in her files and found nothing."

"But you didn't look in her safe, did you?" Melody asked.

"Her safe?"

"Yeah, the one behind the 'Two Girls at the Theatre' painting downstairs."

"No, of course not."

"Let's go look. I know the combination. It's my grandma's birth date." Melody led them toward the stairs.

"This is totally up to you, kid," Tony continued. "From here on we're stepping out of it. You only have to press this as far as you want."

"Do you know what this means if this is true? Oh, man . . . Bennington might be my grandfather. And my mom? She'd have a father . . . still alive!"

"For a little while," Tony added.

Price spun around at the dong of the doorbell. "I'll get the door. You two go on. But no more hugging until I get there."

"Is Dr. S. the jealous type?" Melody whispered.

"Like a wounded mama bear," Tony whispered back. "She's dangerous to be around if she gets jealous."

"Wow, she is so sophisticated. She doesn't look that sort at all."

Melody was still spinning the dial on the safe when Price joined them, carrying something wrapped in green tissue.

"Who was at the door?" Tony inquired.

"Kenny Mallard."

"What's that?"

"A long-stemmed red rose."

Melody stopped spinning the dial. "Isn't it just like a jerk? He thinks he can make up for everything by bringing me a red rose. Some people are so naive."

"Actually, it isn't for you. I think it's sort of a going away present for me," Price sheepishly replied.

"You're kidding?" Melody gasped. "For you? Kenny Mallard gave you a flower?"

Tony stood arrow straight and jammed his hands on his hips. "What did he say?"

"Something to the effect of . . . 'If you ever get tired of the old man and need me to unlock your computer or anything else, just call and I'll charter a plane. I can be in Arizona in four hours.' "

Tony flung both hands in the air. "He said that?"

"Yes, wasn't that sweet of him?" Price flashed a plasterlike smile and batted her eyes.

"If that leather jacketed gigolo shows up in Arizona, he'll face forty grains of powder and two hundred grains of lead," Tony snarled.

Melody drew her hands across her face in mock horror. "Whoa, he's like a wounded mama bear when he gets jealous, isn't he?"

Price cocked her head sideways. "Where have I heard that before?"

Tony's tension relaxed into a smile. "Well, come to think of it, old Kenny is pretty smart."

"How do you figure that?"

He looked at Price and then at Melody. "He's got good taste in women." Tony patted the safe. "Come on, kiddo, open that sucker up."

The iron-gray safe was about eighteen inches square and showed no sign of much use. Inside were stacks of papers and policies and several cigar boxes. Melody dug around in the boxes, filled mainly with assorted pieces of Victorian jewelry. The last box was sealed with thick, yellowed cellophane tape. The only item in the box was a small locked journal.

"Did you find anything in those papers?" she asked Tony as he spread the contents across the couch.

"Nothing yet. Maybe these old insurance policies have a clue. You should read them over carefully."

"It could be in here." Melody held up the brown leather book.

"Is that a diary?"

"I think so."

"Is there a key?"

"No, but we could just cut the strap, couldn't we?" Melody suggested.

Tony examined the book and handed it back to Melody. "Well, that's got to be your decision. It's your family. Your grandmother. We can't tell you what to do. There may not be anything in here. Then your grandmother Reynolds might want this, and it would be tough to explain."

"Wait a minute," Melody shouted. "This might not be Grandma's diary."

"Well, it does say Jessica Davenport on the cover," Price pointed out.

"Exactly! If Grandma Jessie is really Jill, then this isn't her diary but her *sister's!*"

"Melody, if that is Jessica Davenport's diary from her years as an artist, it could be really exciting in itself," Price suggested.

"Talk about a writing project," Tony continued. "*The Davenport Diary* . . . there's your writing project. That, young lady, would be highly publishable."

"Oh, man, this is turning out to be an incredible day! Do you think there could be some of Jessica's personal papers inside?"

"Seems like a mighty good place to stick Jessica's legal papers," Tony suggested.

Melody tried to pull the strap loose. "Do you have something sharp?"

Tony reached into his pocket for his buckhorn cattleman's knife.

Melody shoved the book toward Tony. "Cut it open for me."

"Nope." He opened the knife and handed it to her. "You've got to do it all yourself, kid. It's got to be totally your choice. Because once it's cut, it can never be locked again."

She nodded her head and sliced through the leather. Melody began to flip through the yellowed pages. Most of the entries were written in pencil and very faded. But two neatly folded papers fluttered to the ground as she turned the pages. Tony stooped over and picked them up.

"What are they?" Melody's voice was tight and high. "Read them to me!"

Tony handed them over. "You'll have to tell us, darlin'. This is your family."

She slowly opened the one with gold embossing. "It's Jessica Davenport's baptism certificate from 1932."

"And the other?" Price urged.

Melody held the sheet away from her as though it would catch fire any moment. She unfolded it carefully. The room was dead silent, except for the crinkling of the page. Tony could tell it was some type of legal document. She stared at it for a minute, then her lips quivered. Her eyes puddled. She began sucking air in big deep gulps.

"Oh, dear Lord . . ." she moaned.

"It's the death certificate for Jessica Davenport, isn't it?" Tony asked.

Nodding her head, she flung her arms around Price for a second round of tears.

Twenty minutes later they walked Melody to her truck.

"Don't worry about us," Price assured her. "We'll arrange for someone else to take us to the airport. You've got a lot of things to take care of."

"No, I want to do it, really. I'll try to be back before 2:30. But if I'm not here, Kim is on standby. She said she would be happy to drive you to the airport. I want to show all this to Mom. The x-ray, the doctor's evaluation and the death certificate. I just couldn't tell her on the phone."

"What will you do after that?"

"I don't know. Mom and I will have to decide."

"Do you think she'll be able to handle it?" Price asked.

"She'll be in total shock, just like me. But Mom was serious about that commitment she made to the Lord. She'll do a lot better than she would have before."

"Do you want us to come with you?" Tony offered.

"I know you've got a lot of last-minute details, toting those documents back to the museum and all that. Besides, Mom and I might blubber all afternoon. I'm not about to make you late for your plane."

"Listen, kid, if you need us, we'll cancel the flight and help you work this through," Tony offered. Price nodded agreement as she stepped up and slipped her right arm in his, using her left hand to shade her eyes.

Melody stared at them for a minute. "You mean it, don't you?"

"Yes, we do," Price affirmed.

"Sometimes I don't believe you two. You haven't seen your family all summer, and you'd stay here with me?"

"Just say the word."

Melody bit her lip. "Well, here's the word: Go home! I just can't figure out why you two treat me so good. Go home before I start crying like a kid being left at camp."

"If your mother needs to talk, have her call me," Price said. "I'd love to talk with her before we leave."

"I'm sure she'll appreciate that."

They were still standing in the driveway when a small green sedan zipped down toward them. Barefoot and wearing camouflage shorts and an olive drab tank top, Tulip jumped out of her car carrying a 20' x 3' artist's canvas. Her braid flew out in a long tail behind her.

"Hey, you aren't gone yet. That's good."

"Tulip! We've hardly seen you since the night of the Island Fair. How have you been?"

Her narrow green eyes peered right at Price.

"I . . . I've been fine. Thanks for asking." Then she turned to Tony. "Here, this is for you." She shoved the canvas into his hands.

"Did you paint this?" he asked.

"Yeah, I had to rush it when I found out you were leaving today. It's my way of saying thanks for helping round up the animals. I could tell you really cared about them. It's a quality in a man I find very appealing."

Tony showed the artwork to Price.

"That big rock represents Tony, and the little flower is the Angora rabbit," Tulip explained.

"Oh?"

". . . and the beam of light is the rope . . . see how it surrounds the flower? Just like when you roped that rabbit."

"Actually, I didn't rope it. I think I

stunned it when the rope . . ."

"Why does this cloud seem to have lipstick and a smile?" Price asked.

"That's me. Well, not me, really. I have no need to paint my lips with caustic, polluting chemicals. It's more like Mother Nature giving her approving kiss on the whole evening."

"I see."

"I believe the whole piece is ecologically balanced and correct, of course."

"Of course."

"But it's still kind of wet. You might not want to stick it in an overhead bin. It could get smeared. If I were you, I'd just carry it on my lap."

"Oh?"

"Listen." She looked up at Tony. He noticed a light sprinkling of freckles on her all-natural face. "If you ever need someone to review your books? To make sure they're politically correct? I'd be happy to check them out. You could call me anytime. Here's my home number." She handed him a card shaped like a whale. One phone number was crossed out and another written in pencil.

"Thanks, Tulip. I appreciate your stopping by," Tony murmured, still gazing at the dark background with splotches of abstract color. "But I have one question I've really been wanting to ask you."

Tulip laid her right hand on Tony's arm. "What's that?"

"Just out of a writer's curiosity, is your real name Tulip?"

She first glanced over at Price, then, on tiptoe, whispered in Tony's ear, "It's Ashley."

"Ashley? I like that," he nodded. "It fits."

Without warning, she threw her thin arms around Tony's neck and hugged tight, then kissed his cheek and pulled back. "Thanks for saving those animals." She tossed a perfunctory wave at Price, flung herself into the sedan and ripped up the driveway to the road.

Price shook her head. "Oh my, I'm afraid Tulip has a bad crush on that famous author, Anthony Shadowbrook."

"Don't be silly, it's not . . ."

"She's stuck on you, Tony. That's obvious."

"That's ridiculous. Look at this painting! It's . . ."

"It's a love gift."

"You're not serious?"

"Shadowbrook, I know when a woman is making a serious move for my husband. If that lady shows up in Scottsdale banging at our door, I'll seriously rip her lips off."

"This is getting bizarre." Tony tugged Price back toward the house. "I think it's time to go home."

Tony was running the vacuum across the living room floor when he noticed Price race across the room to the telephone. He shut down the machine and waited.

"No, she's not here, Josh. Can I give her a message? She's over at her mom's. Maybe she called from there. Josh, give her some time. She's got something important to tell her mother. Josh?" Price found herself talking to the dial tone.

"What's our middle child up to?" Tony asked.

"I haven't known what that kid is up to since he was six and took his bicycle to the top of the church bell tower. He said he wanted to talk to Melody."

"With what she's going through today, he's in for a long conversation." Tony started winding up the vacuum cleaner cord. "I'm through in here. You want me to leave this vacuum out?"

"Yes, I'll get the bedroom next."

"I'm going to sweep the deck."

"Well then, I'll get the front door."

Tony went to the kitchen and retrieved

the broom as a familiar voice boomed from the front screen door.

"Shadowbrook? You going to scoot off the Island without saying good-bye to old Peterson?"

Tony held out his hand. "Thanks for stopping by, Harvey. Say, did you get a chance to look over those declassified Navy papers? I figured you'd be interested."

"I can't begin to thank you enough. These papers are absolutely amazing."

"I was wondering how you thought they'd affect your book."

"I think sales will really boom. Especially when I bring out my new book, based on these documents."

"Your new book?"

"Yep. I'm going to call it *The Conspiracy Continues*. Amazing how they concocted that entire assassination story just to cover up the invasion, wasn't it? This is the smoking gun, Shadowbrook. I've got proof in my hand."

"Well, I wish you luck in your new writing venture."

"I figure this will take a little more time to develop than the first book. It'll probably take me a month to write this one."

"A whole month?" Price quizzed.

"Hey, that's the sacrifice we writers have

to make, right? It's a shame you folks don't settle down on the Island. We could use a few more straight-thinking folks. You know the type that's movin' in. Makes a man want to pack up for Alaska. Hey, partner, I got you and the missus a little memento of this summer."

Harvey stepped to the back of his old Jeep CJ5 and pulled out a three-foot piece of driftwood. A two-foot-high seagull perched on top.

"Is it a carving?" Price asked.

"Carving? Shoot, it's the real thing. I trapped him and stuffed him myself. A little souvenir taxidermied right here on the Island."

"But I thought . . . isn't it illegal to . . . ?"

"Hey, don't mention it. Happy to do it. You two brought a little excitement to all of us. Why, everyone I know is wondering who will be mentioned in your book."

"Actually," Price began, "we don't usually put the names of . . ."

Ignoring her, Harvey sidled up to Tony. "Listen, it's all right with me if you tone down my language at the community meeting. I get a little spicy, and I wouldn't want the parents upset when their children read that account."

"I guarantee none of those colorful

phrases will be included."

"I knew I could count on you. Well, I'll see you folks. If I ever get to Scottsbluff, I'll look you up."

"No, we live in . . ." Price elbowed Tony midsentence. "Yes, well, thanks for the present, Harvey."

Peterson retreated toward his Jeep, then yelled back. "Take it easy with that bird. Those legs aren't all that strong, and you could snap them off if you banged it good. You'd best carry it in your lap. Adios, amigos! Hey, I almost forgot to tell you," he shouted from the driveway. "Anthony Shadowbrook is now an honorary member of the Chainsaw Militia!"

They waved as he departed.

"We are not taking that home!" Price insisted.

Over the next two hours they finished packing, scrubbed the house and entertained six more visitors.

"Do you think we've got everything in the four suitcases and two briefcases?" Price asked as she dusted the picture frame of *Two Girls at the Beach*.

"Everything's packed except for one red rose, a confusing acrylic painting, a sea gull, a dozen brownies, a basket of fried chicken and homemade biscuits, a bag of miniature daffodil bulbs, a Clay Baby in the shape of a rotund hula dancer and a jar of wild cherry preserves."

"And chapter five," Price added.

"Two copies of chapter five," he corrected.

"We'll take them with us on the plane."

Tony studied the recently acquired treasures. "But what about the rest?"

"Let's eat the food for lunch. I'll cram the bulbs and the rock in my briefcase and . . ."

"Yes, go on."

"The rest should go in the basement. But I'll feel real guilty."

Tony pointed at the sea gull. "Guilty enough to carry those lovely items on your lap all the way back to Scottsdale?"

"Not that guilty. Come on, let's eat. Then we can have that last walk."

They had just settled down on the redwood table on the deck when Melody and her mother banged through the front door and out to where they were seated.

"Well, the Shadowbrooks turned my world upside down . . . again!" Barbara Mason boomed.

Price searched the woman's eyes for a hint of her condition.

Lord, I surely hope we did the right thing.

349

This woman doesn't need any more disappointments in life.

"What am I going to do now?"

"Mom and I had a really good talk. We both believe Grandma changed her name to Jessica after the wreck."

"It would certainly seem that way," Price replied. "Are you going to talk to her about it?"

"Frankly . . ." Barbara Mason confided with her characteristic loud voice, "I don't have the slightest idea how to bring the subject up without falling to pieces or causing Mother a heart attack. How would you suggest we tell her we think she has been pretending to be her dead twin sister for over fifty years?"

Price shook her head. "I'm not sure. Would you like us to go with you?"

Tony felt his heart sink.

No . . . no . . . no! We have no idea how to do that, either. And I don't think I want to learn.

"That would be great, Dr. S.," Melody brightened. "We were hoping you would say that. But maybe we ought to get a bite to eat first."

"Why don't you join us?" Price offered.

Barbara Mason pulled up a chair and sat down next to Price. "Don't just stand there. Get us some plates."

It was after 2:00 P.M. when the four of them left Mrs. Reynolds' apartment and trudged back to the car. Tony chauffeured them in the white Oldsmobile back to the house.

"It's going to take a while for Mother to get used to us knowing about this," Barbara observed.

"At least she wasn't hostile or bitter," Price added.

"I think both of you being loving and understanding of her helped a lot," Tony encouraged. "It could have been real easy for you and Melody to be angry."

"A few weeks ago, I would probably have cussed her out, then gone home for a drunken jag."

"You were real calm, Mom. I was proud of you," Melody sighed. "I was a nervous wreck."

"That's a switch. Well, I'm glad she admitted the whole thing."

"Do you think she'll recant? Tomorrow she might claim to be Jessica again."

Barbara Mason pulled off her heavy dark sunglasses and wiped her eyes. "She's got to work it through her own way. But so do Melody and I."

Price turned around to look at Melody and her mother in the backseat. "I did hear her admit that Bennington was your father."

"Yes," Melody added, "but she said he was a jerk whom she hoped would rot in Hades."

"She's been bitter, angry and living in deception for a long time," Tony reminded them. "It will be difficult to change."

"What are you two going to do now?" Price asked.

Melody twirled a lock of her hair. "I'm going to get you guys to the airport. Then . . ." She sat straight up and slapped the palms of both hands on her knees. "I'm going to be a schoolteacher."

Price smiled her full approval. "I'm sure you'll be a great one!"

"The first thing I've got to do . . . is call up this Mr. Bennington," Barbara began, and then choked up. Melody slid closer to her mother and slipped her arm around her.

"Go ahead and say it, Mom."

Barbara sniffled a little, then wiped the corner of her eyes with her fingers.

"I'm going to call my father and introduce myself before he dies," she managed to say with a shaky voice. "I hope I can keep from yelling and screaming about him showing up fifty years too late."

"Do you want to call him from our house?" Tony prompted.

"Oh no, I'll just wait. No, you're right. It would be better to call when everybody's around. I'm afraid I'll chicken out if I wait. You go ahead and load the bags in the car."

When they reached the house, Melody and her mother marched off to the kitchen phone. After the car was packed, Price and Tony hiked down to the beach for one last look at Puget Sound.

The penitentiary island across Carr Inlet spread with one great expanse of wooded mystery, full of stories yet to be heard. To the northwest a hazy outline of the Olympic Mountains shimmered like a mirage on the horizon. A seagull flopped in the air above them, as though expecting a free tidbit to be thrown. Tony skipped a rock across the water and the gull swooped down for inspection. Price picked up some litter . . . a flyer for a luau sponsored by the Yacht Club and some scratched-out lottery tickets.

Tony bent at the waist and swept his arm above the gravelly shore. "And now we bid a fond farewell to Fox Island . . . a memorable respite in a sea of turbulence."

"Phoenix was 106 yesterday," Price

intruded. She hugged Tony's arm close to her chest.

"Good, we'll be going home during a cool spell."

"What do you think's happening up there?" She nodded toward the house.

"About fifty years of suppressed emotions, I suppose."

"Do you think the shock will be bad for his health?"

Tony squeezed Price, then pulled away to peer at a car coming down the driveway. "I don't figure his health can get any worse. We better go see who that is."

Kim and Amigo bounded out of the flaking gray '58 Mercedes and ambled toward them. It was the first time that Tony had seen Amigo without body paint. "Hey, Melody must have made it back in time. We just came down to make sure you had a ride to the airport."

"Thanks for the offer, Kim. We'll make it fine," Tony answered.

"If we leave in the next five minutes," Price murmured. She pushed her sunglasses up on her head. "We really appreciate your coming by, don't we, Tony?"

"Yes, we do. In fact, we have something for you. Don't go away."

"You do?"

"We do?" Price echoed.

Tony ducked inside the front door and returned with the acrylic painting. "Kim, you are so into art, I thought you could appreciate this original piece." He turned it around slowly.

"Wow, for me? It's great!"

"What is it?" Amigo asked.

"He doesn't know squat about art. See that big rock, it's symbolic of the forces of the universe . . . and the sunlight represents the centuries of time. And this flower is you and me, Amigo."

"It is? What about the cloud thing with the red lipstick?" he prompted.

"That's the breath of life about to be kissed into us!"

"I knew you'd like it," Tony crowed.

"Boy, someday, I'd sure like to paint like that."

"Did you paint it, Mr. S.?"

"Oh no, I assure you, I couldn't paint anything like that. But it is an original piece from a local artist. You won't find another like it anywhere."

"Wow!"

"What about me?" Amigo pouted. "Do you have something for me?"

"As a matter of fact . . ." Tony ignored Price's frantic motions. He ducked back in the house. Out came the stuffed sea gull. "I want you to have this."

"A sea gull?"

"Not just any sea gull. Guess what this gull's name is?"

"Arapaho?"

"No, its name is Adios! Is that awesome, or what?"

"I don't get it."

Kim shook her head. "You don't get it? Come on, its name is Adios and your name is Amigo. Adios, Amigo . . . see?"

"Oh, wow, that's cool. It's like the dawning of Aquarius. It's a sign, a cosmic omen. Do-do-do-do-do-do-do . . . a *Twilight Zone* thing. I can hardly wait until I show the guys at work."

"Where do you work?" Price asked.

"Dos Amigos restaurant."

"What do you do?" Tony pressed.

"Dos Amigos? That's me and my dad. We own the place."

"Your real name is Amigo?"

"Amigo, Jr."

"Well, Amigo, Jr., thanks for stopping by to check on us."

They blew diesel smoke all the way up the driveway.

Price glanced at her watch. "We've got to go."

"You want me to check with the ladies?"

"Here they come."

Melody grabbed a box of tissue as they scooted out the door.

"Well, what did he say?" Price quizzed.

"We'd better get you to the airport." Melody motioned toward the car. "Mom said she'd ride with us. That way we can tell you everything on the way. Mr. S., would you drive to Sea-Tac? I think my eyes might get a little blurred."

The trip whizzed by as Melody and Barbara Mason retold, word for word, Bennington's reaction.

"So," Tony finally broke in. "He didn't croak right on the phone?"

"After the shock, he truly sounded relieved."

"Settling the score on another of his list of twelve?"

"Yes, but he really seemed sad that he didn't meet us when he was out here," Melody continued. "The doctors are saying he's got two to four weeks at best."

"Isn't this ironic?" Barbara Mason wheezed. "All my life there's been an emptiness about my father. Now I've found out the truth, and he's dying three thousand miles away."

"I think the Lord had something to do

with the timing. Maybe you weren't able to handle this until after you got some priorities straight in your own life."

"Yeah," Barbara mused. "Yeah, you sure might be right about that."

"What time is it?" Tony asked.

"It's ten after three."

"That's cutting it close. I'll check us in at the curb and let you ladies out. You grab our boarding passes. Then I'll park the car and meet you at the gate."

"No," Melody blurted out. "Let me park the car. You want to wait here, Mom, or do you want to go with me?"

"I think," Barbara Mason replied, "I'll go straight to the ticket counter and book a flight for Maryland."

"What?" Melody gasped.

"Go for it," Price encouraged.

"Mother, do you want me to go with you?"

"Nope. There are some things a daughter has to do for herself. And this time, I'm the daughter. You've got a teaching job waiting. It's important to me to do this on my own."

Price gave Melody a hug. "Just in case you can't find a parking place, you know that we love you, don't you?"

Melody scrunched her nose. "Oh, bother, I'm going to start bawling all over again."

Tony wrapped his arms around her.

"You've got the best daddy hugs in the world," Melody sniffled. "I'll see you at the gate . . . really."

Tony and Price said goodbye to Barbara Mason inside the terminal. They left her in line at the ticket counter, then rushed toward Concourse D.

"It takes a lot of nerve to do what she's doing," Price remarked as she tried to keep up with Tony's long stride. "I don't think I could do it."

"Gate D12?" he asked.

"Yes, it's down at the end." She pointed up ahead, then glanced at a mirrored glass window. She tugged Tony back and directed him toward her reflected image.

"Do you think I need a little more color in my hair to cover the gray?"

Tony skimmed over their images. "Babe, you aren't very gray at all. It's just this glass. It has sort of a silver tint to it. Look," he pushed his cowboy hat to the back of his head, "see how gray it makes my hair look?"

"Your hair is that gray, Mr. Anthony Shadowbrook."

"No way. Why, it hardly has any. . . ."

"Excuse me?"

The woman wore a wide v-neck sequined blouse and trim white leather miniskirt. Her platinum blond hair billowed down her back, pulled to one side by jewelled barrettes. Price detected a strong scent of violets.

"I couldn't help but overhearing. Are you by any chance Anthony Shadowbrook, the one that writes those westerns?"

Price slid her arm into Tony's. "Yes, he is. And I'm his wife."

"I can't believe it. You start out thinking it's just an ordinary day. Just going through the motions and then, all of a sudden, I meet someone famous. Can I have your autograph? Look . . . look . . ." She dug into a plastic sack she was carrying. "I just bought your book, *Shotgun Creek*! It would be tremendous if you'd sign it for me."

"We're in a real hurry." Price tugged at his arm.

"Oh, well, I always have time for an autograph," Tony replied and took the book. "What name shall I put in it?"

"Sarah."

"Are you S-a-r-a or S-a-r-a-h?"

"With an *h*, thanks. But I'm not Sarah."

"You aren't?"

"Oh no! This isn't for me. I don't read westerns."

"You don't."

"No, this is for my grandmother, bless her

heart. She can't get out anymore. So she reads everything she can get her hands on. You're one of her favorite authors."

"Oh, how nice," Price gushed.

"Well, we have to be running," Tony said.

"Yes," the blonde continued, "she says Mr. Shadowbrook never stoops to 'smutty' language or compromising situations. Now, personally, that sounds too wimpy for me. But thanks so much, Mr. Shadowbrook. This will be a perfect present for Grannie Sarah!"

The young lady strutted toward Gate 11.

"Wasn't she a sweet girl?" Price commented. "Come on, Gramps. Get your walker and let's shuffle onto our flight. I think they let old geezers board first, don't they?"

The plane had not yet begun to board. They searched the crowd for Melody's shining dark head and infectious smile. Finally, they sat down in black padded chairs. Tony leaned over to pick up a newspaper from the floor. He pulled out the sports section and read about the upcoming Ellensburg Rodeo.

"Tony, are they calling our name?"

"What? I didn't hear anything."

"Listen, there it is again. Maybe there's

something wrong with the tickets."

Tony waded through the crowded boarding area and waited at the check-in counter until it was his turn.

"Did you call for Shadowbrooks?"

A short-haired, uniformed woman put down her microphone and pointed toward a courtesy phone.

He made his way to the white phone, then spent several minutes in animated conversation. By the time he returned to Price, they were preboarding the Phoenix flight.

"It was Kathy."

"Our Kathy?"

"Who else would call us at the airport?"

"What's wrong now?"

"If I got this right, Kit borrowed Kathy's pink shorts and matching lace-trimmed blouse without asking her. I guess Kathy wanted to wear them tonight when we get home."

"Kit never wears shorts like that!"

"Apparently she does now."

"So why did Kathy call?"

"For me or you to tell Kit to give the clothes back."

"Oh, brother. Well, father of the twins, what did you tell them?"

"I told Kit not to rifle through Kathy's clothes. If she wanted some shorts, she should go out and buy herself a pair. And I told Kathy to let Kit wear them tonight because I was hoping she'd wear that purple western dress with the white fringe yoke."

"And she fell for that switch?"

"Yep. Kath would probably wear a gunny sack if old Dad asked her."

"No way," Price laughed. "Oh, that's our row. We can board now. Kit would wear the gunny sack for you. Kath would wear it only if it were fashionably correct, and flattering to blond hair and a great tan."

"Come on, Mama, our babies need us at home."

"It feels good to be going home, doesn't it?"

They crowded down the jetway and into the plane. At Row 17, Tony pushed his briefcase into the overhead bin. "Do you need anything from yours?"

"No, I've got my copy of chapter five. How about you?"

"Yep." He shoved her briefcase beside his.

"Have we got the aisle and the window?"

"Yeah, they said it wasn't full, so we could probably have the seat between us. Do you want the window?"

Price slid in first. "Sure."

Tony sat down and fastened his seatbelt. He rolled up chapter five in his hands as he watched passengers of all shapes and sizes file by.

"I'm glad we had a chance to say goodbye to Melody earlier. She must have had trouble finding a parking place. You know, I wouldn't be surprised to see that girl standing at our door someday," Price remarked.

"Not until spring break, I presume." Tony gave Price a close look. "You're looking beautiful today, Mrs. Shadowbrook. Do you feel beautiful?"

"Well, I feel a lot better since that thing in the slinky white leather told us about her grandmother reading your books. And I'm so glad Melody agreed to take the teaching job. It just seems like the right thing for her."

"Both Barbara and Mrs. Reynolds will need her around, I would imagine. I don't think I've seen another family where the youngest member is the most stable. Melody will hold that family together. She's a lot more stable than I sized her up at the beginning of summer."

"Hi, guys!"

Tony and Price looked up in unison. The impish smile, the flowing black hair, the jangle of earrings struck them as very familiar.

"Melody, you didn't have to come on board to see us off!" Price began.

"Excuse me, Mr. S. Don't get up. I'll scoot by." Melody shoved herself in between Tony's knees and the seat in front of him.

"Wh . . . what?" Tony stammered.

"I'm sitting in seat B."

"You're going to Phoenix?"

"Yeah, to Scottsdale, actually. Just for the Labor Day weekend. That way I can keep my teaching job. Is this cool, or what? You always said I've got to do those things I'd regret not doing. Well, I said to myself when I met Mom at the ticket counter, 'Mel, why don't you fly down to Arizona and take up the Shadowbrooks on their offer of hospitality?' So here I am. Isn't this wild?"

"Yes, but what about clothes?"

"Just what I'm wearing. Mom's driving the car home. She'll fly out on Sunday and leave the car for me to pick up Monday. It's working out so smooth. It just must be the Lord's will . . . know what I mean?"

"But," Price persisted, "what will you wear?"

"Oh, I just called Josh, and he said . . ."

"You talked to *our* Josh?"

"Yes, did you know he's picking us up at Sky Harbor?"

Price just shook her head in amazement. *It's all beginning to sound like a conspiracy to me.*

"Actually, I guess Josh and I talked several times today. He's so . . . so . . ."

"Cool?" Tony prompted.

"Just like you, Mr. S. Anyway, Josh said clothes were no problem, that I could borrow some from Kit and Kathy when I get to your place."

Kit and Kathy? Price closed her drooping mouth. *You actually think you're going to be allowed to wear their clothes?*

"Boy, am I hyped for this," Melody continued. "In the same day I find out I have a grandfather, send my mother off to Maryland and impetuously hop in a plane to spend the weekend in Arizona with my favorite people in the whole world."

Price patted her arm. "Who just happen to have a single son with an awesome smile?"

"Yeah, it just doesn't get any better than this, does it?" Melody clutched both of their hands, head whirling from one to the other. "This might go down as Melody Davenport Mason's finest hour."

Tony sank down into the seat and

scrunched against the headrest.

Price took a deep breath and reached for the inflight magazine.

"Well, now," Melody urged, "what are we going to do about chapter five?"

The employees of Thorndike Press hope you have enjoyed this Large Print book. All our Large Print titles are designed for easy reading, and all our books are made to last. Other Thorndike Press Large Print books are available at your library, through selected bookstores, or directly from us.

For information about titles, please call:

(800) 257-5157

To share your comments, please write:

Publisher
Thorndike Press
P.O. Box 159
Thorndike, Maine 04986